W9-CCS-587

Colloquial
German

The Colloquial Series

The following languages are available in the Colloquial series:

Albanian
Amharic
Arabic (Levantine)
Arabic of Egypt
Arabic of the Gulf and Saudi Arabia
Bulgarian
Cambodian
Cantonese
Chinese
Czech
Danish
Dutch
English
Estonian
French
German
* Greek
Gujarati
Hungarian
Indonesian
Italian
Japanese
Malay
Norwegian
Panjabi
Persian
Polish
Portuguese
Romanian
* Russian
Serbo-Croat
Somali
Slovene
* Spanish
Spanish of Latin America
Swedish
Thai
Turkish
Ukranian
Vietnamese
Welsh

Accompanying cassette(s) are available for the above titles.
* Accompanying CDs are also available.

Colloquial German

A Complete Language Course

Glyn Hatherall and
Dietlinde Hatherall

London and New York

First published 1995
by Routledge
11 New Fetter Lane, London EC4P 4EE

Simultaneously published in the USA and Canada
by Routledge
29 West 35th Street, New York, NY 10001

Typeset in Times Ten by Florencetype Ltd, Stoodleigh, Devon

Illustrations by Bethan Hatherall; cartography by John Williamson

Printed and bound in England by Clay Ltd, St Ives PLC

British Library Cataloguing in Publication Data
A catalogue record for this book is available from the British Library

Library of Congress Cataloguing in Publication Data
A catalogue record for this book has been requested

ISBN 0–415–02799–3 (book)
ISBN 0–415–02800–0 (cassettes)
ISBN 0–415–04938–5 (book and cassettes course)

To
BG and BJ

plus

those whose skills, advice, and even names,
were borrowed for these pages

Contents

Maps

Map 1 Bundesrepublik Deutschland

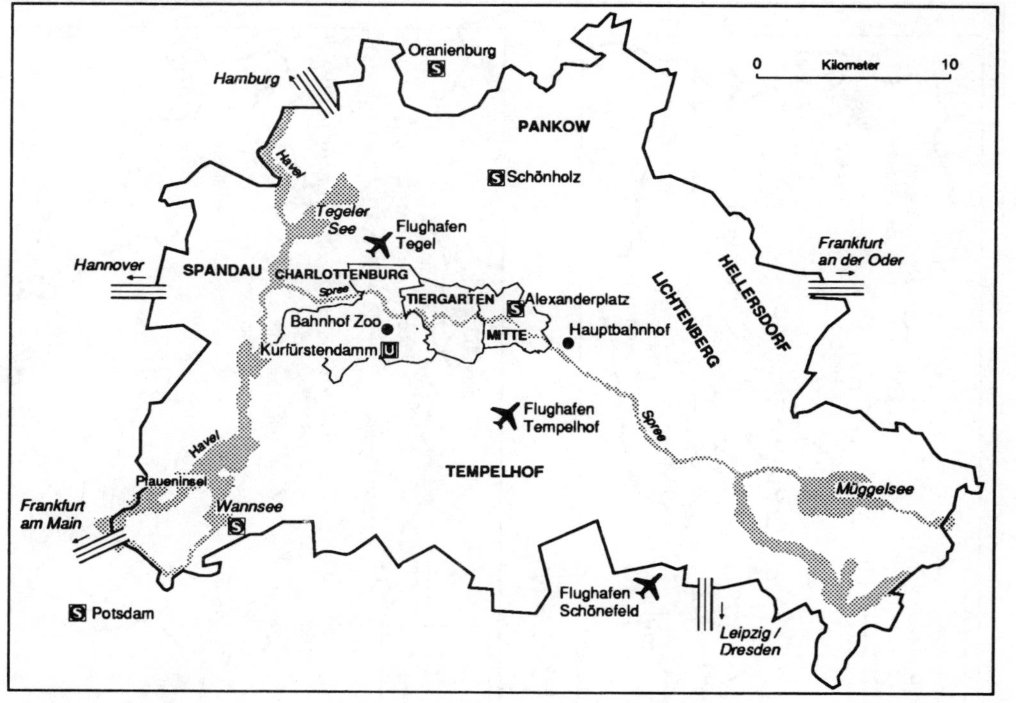

***Map 2* Berlin**

Names in capitals indicate districts mentioned in the text. The **Bundesland** surrounding Berlin, of which Potsdam is the capital, is Brandenburg.

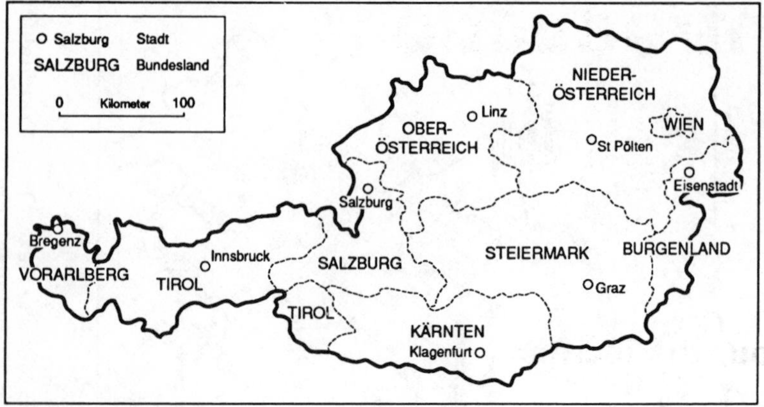

Map 3 Österreich

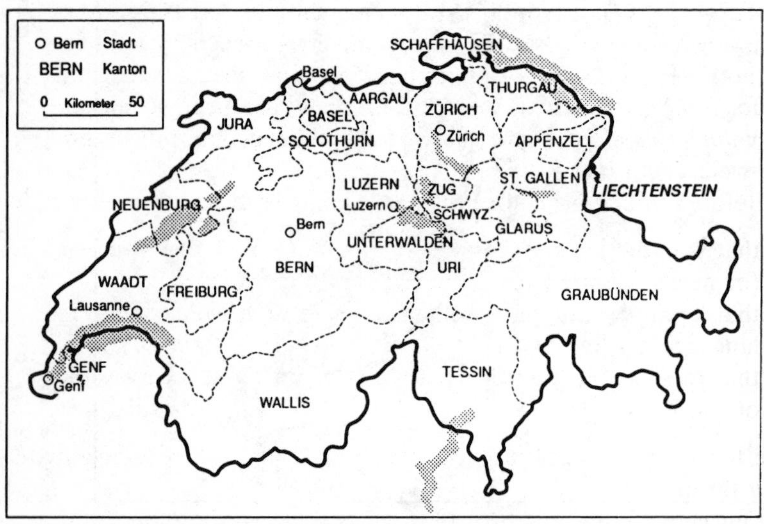

Map 4 Die Schweiz und Liechtenstein

Introduction

You, the learner

Arguably the language learner's greatest strength is hope, and hope is unfortunately sometimes dashed when it becomes clear that language learning inevitably involves regular long-term application (see advice below!). But it is also sometimes dashed by textbook authors' over-ambition. Authors need to know their language, of course, but on behalf of their readers they also need to *imagine they don't*. We are not sure that we have succeeded, but this is how we went about it . . .

Before putting this course together we made these assumptions:

- that you, the learner, know no German at all *or* that you want (or need) to start again from the very beginning;
- that you may not have had experience of learning a foreign language before;
- that you may be seeking to learn German without the assistance of a teacher.

We felt we had an obligation to try to make the course *usable by you* throughout.

Our general objectives for *Colloquial German*, therefore, were:

- to put together a (genuinely) self-contained package;
- to set a steady, manageable pace throughout;
- to keep you interested and thinking.

We hope to have achieved this by, for example,

- presenting tightly graded learning materials;
- carefully controlling the number of different words used;
- restricting grammar coverage to essentials;
- frequently ringing the changes on the language covered;

- being explicit even at the risk of stating the obvious;
- offering ideas, particularly in the early units, on *how* as well as *what* to learn.

In other words, we have tried to take into account the real needs of new learners, particularly independent learners, of German.

Making progress

Because things need to be remembered, language learning requires not so much aptitude as time and determination. Given that we have all acquired a native language, we obviously all have the *ability* to learn. But the *conditions* for learning are different later in life: we can never get as much practice in the new language as we did with our first one when we were children.

As adults we may become impatient and fall into the trap of thinking we *ought* to be learning our new language more quickly than is actually possible. After all, did not some advert or other imply that fluency was achievable in a fortnight or so? Don't be intimidated: you will, of course, need much more than a fortnight to assimilate fully what *Colloquial German* has to offer – assuming that your aim is to *use* spoken German rather than just browse through the book.

Let learning come slowly, but – this is the key – keep it coming. If at all possible, spread your study of German. The *more often* you sit down to learn, the *more knowledge* you will retain. Six days a week at fifteen minutes a day will be more productive than three hours of study in just one weekly sitting.

Don't tackle *new* material immediately every time you open the book. Spend at least a short time going over some of the *old* before moving forward. And before you close the book, go back briefly over the *new* material that you have just tackled. It will take *less* time in the long run to hold on to the German you have learnt if you stick to 'double stitching' i.e.

go back to go forward

Sounds

If you like imitating different accents of English, you will probably already have the confidence to produce the unfamiliar sounds that German requires of you. If not, you may need a while to convince yourself that your personality remains intact when you switch languages! Tackle this head-on: speak German to yourself – out loud and often. If possible, record and listen to yourself reading German. You'll quickly get over the initial shock and start to feel at ease.

Especially if you are learning German for the first time, do buy and *use constantly* the RECORDINGS that accompany this book. These provide a clear and invaluable model for pronunciation practice; but also – the more you listen to German *and* look at German on the page, the more German you will retain for future use.

Seeing a language in action in its social context also aids memory, so watch German FILMS with sub-titles when you have the opportunity. Not only do films make a language come alive, they also have an immediate linguistic benefit: your ear becomes attuned to different accents and 'tones of voice', you soon start hearing words or phrases you have met in *Colloquial German*, and before long you're picking up new ones. If you have any recorded German films on video, watch at least one – one with a particularly clear soundtrack – several times. As far as language learning is concerned, whatever the medium,

repetition works wonders

With this in mind, get some CDs/cassettes of SONGS in German, ones you can personally live with: pop, folk, classical. Buy recordings with printed texts and go for clear solo voices rather than choirs. Listen regularly and sing along! Songs generate hours of effortless pronunciation practice: they teach individual sounds, sentence rhythms, new vocabulary, and grammar patterns – subliminally, and all in one go.

Words

To use any language we need to know *all* its sounds but, fortunately, only *some* of its words.

It might be imagined that the more words one knows the better, but when speaking we restrict the number of words we use to a manageable number. In fact, we usually fight shy of using uncommon words for fear of giving listeners the wrong impression, and become adept at ringing the changes on a surprisingly small number of ordinary, everyday ones. It is these sorts of words that *Colloquial German* concentrates on.

A particularly good method of keeping a record of what you are learning is to use a CARD INDEX – one card for each new word. That way it's easy to keep words in alphabetical (or indeed any other) order, and if you write translations of each word on the back of its card, you can also use the cards to test yourself.

On the front of the card, note down phrases or short sentences you have met containing the word in question. These will help you to remember the contexts in which you are likely to want to use the word. The act of writing vocabulary down systematically, having to check meanings, contexts, spellings, etc. – every little helps!

If you add to each card the number of the page of *Colloquial German* where you met your new word, you will have a complete reference system which gets more and more useful as it grows. A card based on one of the words from the first unit of the book might look like this:

die Zitrone	[p. 21]
Tee mit Zitrone, bitte! *mit Milch oder Zitrone?* *eine Zitrone, zwei Zitronen*	

and on the back:

lemon . . .
etc.

Incidentally, you will also want to remember whether a noun (such as **Zitrone** above) is masculine, feminine or neuter. Try engaging your visual memory with the help of three different coloured highlighters, one for each 'gender' – it really does work!

Patterns

In addition to sounds and words, languages have what are usually called GRAMMATICAL RULES. These can sometimes seem daunting but are, of course, really no more than agreed ways of changing the forms and the sequence of words to convey the meanings speakers of a language require. Rules are therefore useful.

To be understood (which is what matters) when using German, you need to apply the really useful rules consistently and the others less so. Try to get *most* things right, but don't get hung-up on 100 per cent grammatical accuracy, which is probably unnecessary in order to get a given point across: it's *communication* that counts. Most native German speakers are not used to hearing native English speakers speak German and are generally delighted when an English speaker has a go, however obviously non-native the language is that comes out.

As a learner try to *think functionally*. What matters is not whether you got the 'endings' wrong but whether you got the message right, that you managed, somehow or other, to say what you wanted to (broadly), and that you were able to understand (more or less). But don't cut corners: set out to achieve *realistic* aims and move forward *steadily*.

English and German

Some learners come to German with preconceptions about its being 'remote' or even 'exotic', which often means that they are expecting German to be like French or Spanish, for example. However, for native English speakers German is far from remote: English and German are historically very closely related. Where these historical links still shine through today they will help you remember many German words, their forms and/or their meanings.

Everyday German words such as those listed below are more closely related to English and therefore more easily remembered than are their French equivalents, given here for comparison:

GERMAN	**zu**	**machen**	**danken**	**Haus**	**Mutter**	**Tochter**	**Vater**	**Sohn**
ENGLISH	to	make	thank	house	mother	daughter	father	son
FRENCH	*à*	*faire*	*remercier*	*maison*	*mère*	*fille*	*père*	*fils*

The reason for the strong similarities between English and German is that, unlike Romance (Latin-based) languages (such as French, Italian, Spanish), English, German, Dutch and the Scandinavian languages have their origins in what has been called 'Common Germanic'.

Different dialects of 'Common Germanic' developed as Germanic tribes on the European continent migrated. One distinct group of dialects emerged in Scandinavia, and another, a 'West Germanic' group, in central/western Europe.

West Germanic eventually sub-divided into 'high' and 'low' varieties. 'Low' describes those that developed in the continental lowlands towards the North Sea, such as Dutch and Anglo-Saxon (the forerunner of modern English); 'high' describes those varieties that were and are spoken at higher altitudes, i.e. further inland towards the Alps. 'Standard' German belongs to this 'high' group and is indeed often called **Hochdeutsch** ('high' German).

After the Norman invasion of England in 1066, a large number of French words were absorbed into English, which nevertheless still remained essentially a Germanic language. Many longer English words such as 'characteristic', 'particular', 'invasion', 'influence' and even 'language' tend to be of French/Latin origin, whereas most shorter, more everyday words – e.g. 'speak' **sprechen**, 'over' **über**, 'and' **und**, 'word' **Wort**, 'as' **als**, 'were' **war**, 'in' **in**, 'often' **oft** – are Germanic in origin and therefore frequently have, as indicated, look-alikes in modern German.

Much more recently, German has imported a large number of words from English, which of course is also helpful to the English-speaking learner.

How *Colloquial German* is structured

Immediately following this introduction you will find a section entitled

Pronunciation reference

You will probably want to work through this section – preferably with the assistance of the recordings on which the key words are recorded – before starting Lesson one (**Lektion eins**). However, don't try to remember too much pronunciation information before going further! Just keep coming back to it as necessary during the course.

The course itself is divided into twenty **Lektionen**, i.e. chapters, lessons or units, each with the German title **Lektion**.

Lektionen

Each **Lektion** begins with a set of broad *objectives*. In order to stand a reasonable chance of achieving them, you need of course to complete the tasks in the unit. The objectives can be of several kinds:

- functional: learning to use and understand language characteristics of real-life situations involving speakers of German;
- linguistic: getting to grips gently but systematically with the rules of the language;
- strategic: developing language learning techniques which will stand you in good stead throughout the course.

Units (**Lektionen**) contain texts (**Texte**) in German (usually dialogues). A text will encapsulate a situation or situations in which you, as a learner, *could* find yourself in the not-too-distant future – not in *every* detail, perhaps, but broadly. Each text is preceded by a *summary* in English of its content or story-line, and is also accompanied by explanatory Notes, to be found at the end of the text. We think these two features are particularly important for independent learners who are without a teacher ready and waiting to 'bail them out' when they encounter difficulties.

In each **Lektion** expect to meet notes which attempt to 'broaden the context', to provide useful and/or interesting additional information, linguistic and/or cultural. For example, in the first dialogue you will meet the greeting **Guten Tag!** which leads us on to suggest a few more ways of saying 'Hello!' in German, plus a comment on tea- and coffee-drinking customs in German-speaking countries.

Expect also systematic information on grammar and vocabulary, backed up by lots of **Übungen** ('exercises') that are designed to help you 'internalise' rules and relevant German words, phrases and sentences. These **Übungen** are vital to your progress in the language. Make your learning as *active* as possible by doing *all* the exercises, even inventing your own exercises as a top-up if you feel the need. Clearly, the more often you *say and write down* German words and particularly phrases, the more likely you are to remember them. So always do the exercises orally *and* on paper *before* using the KEY at the back of the book to check whether you have got them right.

It is worth bearing in mind that language-learning, like learning to play the piano, is a cumulative process. Words and patterns – or, in the case of the piano-player, notes and patterns – that you learn at the beginning will still be needed at the end. So even if, say, German numerals first appear in **Lektion eins** of *Colloquial German*, expect your knowledge of them to be 'reinforced' in subsequent units throughout the book. Go back whenever necessary to revise anything you only half remember.

At the back of *Colloquial German* you will find a

Key to exercises

giving the solutions to most of the **Übungen**, i.e. the 'homework', set in the **Lektionen**. **Übung** also means 'practice' by the way. Here's your first whole German sentence, and it's one well worth remembering:

Übung macht den Meister

In other words, practice makes perfect!

Glossary

The German–English glossary at the back of the book lists virtually all the German words you will meet in *Colloquial German*. It's a comprehensive checklist which could also be used for vocabulary learning or revision.

We expect, however, that you will want to explore a German–English/English–German dictionary as well during your studies, because as you progress you will inevitably have occasional linguistic queries which go well beyond the scope of our introductory course. At the time of writing, dictionaries published by Collins or by Oxford University Press can be strongly recommended.

Also at the back of *Colloquial German* is a section entitled

Grammar index

which gives a quick checklist of grammatical points discussed in the units.

We wish you every success in your learning, but above all **Viel Spaß!** The glossary will tell you what these two words mean and the next section will tell you how to pronounce them.

Enjoy your German!

Pronunciation reference

In the tables below we describe German speech sounds and how to make them. Any description of speech on paper can only be very approximate of course and is best combined with *listening* to German sounds. The sounds and sample German words given in the tables can therefore be found on the first recording that accompanies *Colloquial German*.

The relationship between the way the language is written and the way it is pronounced is fortunately much more predictable with German than it is for English. And compared with French there are few 'silent letters' in German, which is also a bonus. Nevertheless, in German too there can be several ways of representing most speech sounds in the written language. These ways are covered in column one below.

For readers familiar with the International Phonetic Alphabet (IPA), we have listed in the second column German sounds as represented by the IPA. These symbols are frequently used in dictionaries to indicate pronunciation, and differ in principle from most ordinary 'letters' in that each IPA symbol represents only one sound. In spoken English, for instance, the first and last *sounds* of 'zoos' are the same in spite of the fact that they are written with different *letters*. The sound of these two different letters in this word is unambiguously represented in the IPA with the single symbol [z].

You don't of course need to know the IPA in order to learn to pronounce German – just *listen long and often* (see Introduction: 'Sounds') and *repeat, repeat, repeat*! Treat the comprehensive description of sounds below as back-up to the early **Lektionen** and then as a convenient check-list for future reference.

German letters used as vowels are A E I O U Ä Ö Ü Y. The rest are consonants.

Written	IPA	Key Word	pronounced approximately as:
a, ah, aa	[a:]	**ja**	'yaah' **A Abend Sahne Staat** This is a long, open 'aaa . . .'
a	[a]	**Stadt**	'shtat' **Man Kanada Hamm** (town) This 'a' is a short, 'flat', open [a] and occurs in e.g. northern UK English, Spanish and French. Try *starting* a long 'aaa . . .' as in **ja** but then, without changing your tongue position, cut the sound off short.
ai, ay	[ai]	**Mai**	'my' **Main** (river) **Kaiser Bayern** (Bavaria) Same sound as **ei**, **ey** in **mein**, **Meyer** below.
au	[au]	**Haus**	'house' (with mouth more open than for English) **Auto Frau Passau** (town)
ä	[ɛ]	**Länder**	'lender' (with no clear 'r' sound) **Männer Ärger** Same short, open sound as **e** in **Text** below.
ä, äh	[ɛ:]	**spät**	'shp + air (with no 'r' sound)+ t' **Ä wählen Mädchen** The long version of the open [ɛ] in **Mäntel**. In **spät**, the vowel is either long, and open (as above), or long and close (as below).
	[e:]	**spät**	'shp + [e:] + t' This long, close **ä** sound is the same sound as **ee** in **Tee** (see description below).
äu	[ɔʏ]	**Häuser**	'hoyzer' (with no 'r' sound) **Fräulein** Same sound as **eu** in **neun** below.
b, bb	[b]	**Bonn**	'bonn' **B Berlin bitte Ebbe**

b	[p]	**ab**	'ap' **lieb halb** At the ends of words and syllables **-b** is always pronounced [p].
c	[k]	**clever**	'clever' **Café Cottbus** (German town)
ce, ci	[ts]	**cis**	'tsiss' **C Mercedes CD** Same sound as **z** in **zu** below.
ch	[ç]	**ich**	'i (as in 'it') + [ç]' **Milch Kännchen sechzig durch** To pronounce [ç] try putting your tongue in position for 'y' as in 'yes' or 'h' for 'huge' and breathing out hard over the top to produce *audible friction in the front* of the mouth. Or say 'ish' but with the tip of the tongue forward against the *bottom* teeth. IPA [ç] is not the French 'ç' sound, which is IPA [s].
	[x]	**Loch**	'Loch' (as in 'Loch Ness') **auch acht Buch** Put the tongue in position for [k] in 'lock' but instead of stopping off and then suddenly releasing the air at the end of the word, release the air continuously to produce *audible friction* in the back of the mouth.
chs	[ks]	**sechs**	'zecks' **Sachsen** (Saxony) **Wechsel**
d, dd	[d]	**denn**	'denn' **D deutsch paddeln**
d, dt	[t]	**Kind**	'kint' **Wald Land Bad und Stadt** At the ends of words and syllables **-d** is always pronounced [t].
e, eh, ee, é	[e:]	**Tee**	*thé* (as in French for 'tea') **E den zehn gehen Beethoven Café** Long, 'straight' close vowel as in French *bébé*, with no hint of a second vowel after the [e:]. Not the same sound as that in southern UK

			English 'bay' which contains two vowel sounds, more like 'ay-ee' than [e:]. Same sound as long, close **ä** in **spät** above.
e	[ɛ]	**Text**	'text' **eng essen** Same sound as short, open **ä** in **Mäntel** above.
-e	[ə]	**kennen**	'ken + -en' (as in 'slacken') **Basel bekommen danke bitte**
-er	[ɐ]	**bitter**	'bitter' (with no 'r' sound) **Kellner Schubert Bier Bayern** The last sound in German **bitter** needs to be distinguished clearly from the final sound in **bitte** which is spoken higher in the mouth. The higher **-e** in **bitte** is close to the 'e' in 'slacken'. For some English speakers the low **-er** in **bitter** is close to the 'a' in 'Linda'.
ei, ey	[ai]	**mein**	'mine' **Ei klein Meyer** ***Die Zeit*** Same sound as **ai**, **ay** in **Mai**, **Bayern** above.
eu	[ɔʏ]	**neun**	'noyn' **deutsch teuer** Same sound as **äu** in **Häuser** above.
f, ff	[f]	**Steffi**	'shteff-ee' **F Koffer Flughafen**
g, gg	[g]	**gut**	'gooot' **G Tage Roggen**
-g, -gt	[k]	**Tag**	'taahk' **sagt Berg Burg**
-ig	[ç]	**neunzig**	'noyn + tsi + [ç]' **billig Honig Leipzig** The sound of **-ig** is the same as that of **-ch** as in **ich** above. In the south, however, **-ig** is usually pronounced [k] rather than [ç].
h	[h]	**Haus**	'house' **H haben Hotel**
i, ie, ih	[i:]	**ihn**	'eeen'

			I nie Wien Berlin A somewhat tenser sound than the lax English 'ee', German 'ee' is made with the tongue higher and further forward in the mouth (like French *i* in *ici*).
i	[ɪ]	**in**	'in' **Schilling**
j	[j]	**ja**	'yaah' **J Jochen Jamaika Jacke**
k, kk, ck	[k]	**Kind**	'kint' **K Knochen Mokka Zucker**
l, ll	[l]	**elf**	'elf' **L Elbe Wilhelm toll kalt Fall** German **l** is always soft, like 'l' in 'leaf', and never hard like the very different final sound which many English speakers use in 'call'. Try to keep the blade of the tongue close to the roof of the mouth for *all* German **l** sounds.
m, mm	[m]	**mit**	'mit' **M Name kommen**
n, nn	[n]	**nein**	'nine' **N ohne**
-ng	[ŋ]	**Finger**	'finger' (but with '-ng' as in 'singer') **lang England**
-nk	[k]	**Bank**	'bangk' **danke denken trinken**
o, oh, oo **ow**	[o:]	**Boot**	'b + [o:] + t' **O schon Mohn also Pankow** (district of Berlin) German [o:] is a long, 'straight' vowel like French *eau* with no hint of a second vowel after the [o:]. It is not the same sound as that in southern UK English 'boat' which contains two vowel sounds, more like 'oh-oo' than [o:]. For [o:] try saying 'bought' but rounding your lips strongly.

o	[ɔ]	**oft**	‘offt’ **Bonn London Rostock**
ö, öh, oe	[ø:]	**schön**	‘shurn’ (lips very rounded, with no ‘r’ sound) **Ö König Söhne Goethe** (German poet) In English ‘ur’ is said with lips in a lax ‘neutral’ position. For [ø:] in **schön**, round (protrude) the lips strongly for ‘sh’ and keep them rounded while saying the whole word.
ö	[œ]	**können**	‘k + [œ] + n + -en’ (as in ‘slacken’) **Knöchel zwölf Köln** (Cologne) This **ö** is the open, short equivalent of the first **ö** above. For [œ] first say the **e** of **kenn-** with lips spread, then, keeping the tongue in that position, with lips rounded.
p, pp	[p]	**Pik**	‘peeek’ **P Appetit**
pf	[pf]	**Pfennig**	‘pfenn + i [ç]’ (as in ‘ich’) **Apfel Pferd** In rapid speech, **p** before **f** at the beginning of words is often inaudible.
ph	[f]	**Photo**	‘f + [o:] + t + [o:]’ **phantastisch** **ph/f** are often interchangeable, as in **Photo/Foto**. For [o:] see **o** in **Boot**.
qu	[kv]	**Qual**	‘kvaahl’ **Quelle**
r, rh, rr **-r** > -er	[ʀ]	**Rhein**	‘RRRine’ **R Rathaus Rostock Franken Werra** (German river) The majority of German speakers use a trill in the *back of the throat* for **r** in exposed positions such as at the beginning of a word or in front of a vowel. This **r** is essentially a gargle – try **Rhein** with a good sip of water! Another way of approaching

			[ʀ] is via [x], the **ch** in **Loch**. Try gargling this **ch** sound in front of English '-ine'. If you can't gargle – or produce a French *r*, which is quite close to German **r** (though more breathy and less trilled) – but can trill with the *tip of your tongue*, as in Spanish, Italian, Scottish, Welsh, etc., then use that 'r', since it is used by most southern German speakers.
	('r' coloured)		**Berg** 'bare + k' **Burg Birgit Mozart der für vor** An **r** after a vowel is sometimes heard as a 'gargled' **r** but in rapid speech may only 'colour' the vowel sound; so **Berg** may sound like 'bare-k' though never like 'beck'.
s	[s]	**bis**	'biss' **S eins Pils Hans Brahms** At the ends of German words, **-s** is always pronounced [s]. English uses two sounds for 's' in this position, e.g. 'dock[s]' but 'dog[z]'. At the beginnings of words before vowels, however, English pronounces 's' as [s], as in 'send', whereas German pronounces 's' as [z] (see **Senf** below).
	[z]	**Senf**	'zenf' **Sachsen** (Saxony) **Sahne sagen**
ss, ß	[s]	**Neuß**	'noyss' (German town) **ß** ('ess-tset') **wissen weiß gewußt** **ß** is not used in Switzerland, only **ss**. In Austria and Germany, **ss** is only used between vowels, and even then the front vowel has to be short: compare **Masse** with its short 'a' as in **Stadt**, and **Maße** with a long 'a' as in **ja**.
sch	[ʃ]	**Schiff**	'shiff' **Schnaps schmeckt Schweiz**

sp	[ʃp]	**Spaß**	'shpaahss'
			Speisekarte sprechen
st	[ʃt]	**Stop**	'shtop'
			Straße bestellen Stock (but: **Rostock** has [st] not [ʃt])
t, th, tt, dt	[t]	**Tag**	'taahk'
			T Theater nett Stadt
-ti-	[tsi:]	**Lektion**	'leck + tsee + [o:] + n'
			Station
tsch	[tʃ]	**deutsch**	'doy + ch' ('ch' as in 'chip')
			Kitsch
u, uh	[u:]	**gut**	'gooot'
			U USA Kuchen Uhr
			Pronounced with lips more tightly rounded than in standard English 'coo'. Try lengthening the 'ooo' of 'coo' to get the right German lip position.
u	[ʊ]	**und**	'[ʊ] (as in 'put') + nt'
u > qu			**Bus Kolumbus**
			This **u** is shorter than for [u:] in **gut** and the lips are less firmly rounded.
ü, üh	[y:]	**Übung**	'[y:] + b + [ʊ] (as in 'put') + ng'
			Ü über süß früh für
			Pronounce a long 'ee' and then, without changing your tongue position, round your lips tightly. French has this **ü** sound in e.g. *tu*.
ü	[ʏ]	**Glück**	'gl + [ʏ] + k'
			Stück müssen fünf Tschüs
			Pronounce a short **i** with lips spread, as in 'glick'. Then, without changing your tongue position, round your lips and repeat.
v	[f]	**viel**	'feeel'
			V Volkswagen aktiv vor Hannover
rarely	[v]	**Vasen**	'vaahz + en' (as in 'slacken')
w	[v]	**Wien**	'veeen'
			W VW Wein wollen zwanzig
x	[ks]	**Fax**	'fax'
			X Praxis
y	[ʏ]	**Sylt**	'z+ [ʏ] +lt' (German island)

			Ypsilon (German name for letter 'y') Same short, loosely rounded sound as **ü** in **Glück** above.
	[y:]	**Typ**	't + [y:] + p' Same long, tightly rounded sound as **ü** in **über** above.
z, zz	[ts]	**zu**	'ts + ooo' **Z Zoo Heinz Pizza** Note that German **z** is always [ts] and never [z] as in English 'zoo'.

glottal stop

Iß auch ein Ei! ('You, too, eat an egg!' – an advertising slogan)
Each of the above German words begins with a vowel and it is standard to close the glottis (vocal chords) before each, rather than run the words together as in **'I–ßau–chei–nei'** which would be virtually incomprehensible to a native German speaker. The glottal stop, as this closing of the vocal chords is called, occurs in many varieties of English (notably in London) when words such as 'What?' and 'butter' are spoken without the audible 't' sound. Not only German words but also German syllables beginning with a vowel are preceded by a glottal stop, so that e.g. **gearbeitet** ('worked') is always 'ge-arbeitet' and never sounds quite like 'garbeitet', however quickly it is spoken.

1 Tee oder Kaffee?

A first taste of German

Language activities

- 'hello' and 'please'
- choosing and paying
- 'goodbye' and 'thank you'

Language focus

- patterns and phrases
- nouns and verbs
- 'I' and 'you'
- numbers 1 to 10, 20 to 90, and prices

Learning strategies

- spotting patterns
- guessing meanings
- listening efficiently
- using a glossary

If you have the recordings that accompany *Colloquial German*, please read the following advice on how best to use them. If not, go straight to Text 1A.

To learn German efficiently you need to develop and stick to a sequence of 'learning activities' – for *every* Text, not just the first! The sequence below has much to recommend it, but whatever sequence you choose, remember that listening, looking and speaking need to be learned systematically and to some extent separately. The crucial test is invariably: can you *remember* what you have just done, i.e. have you really learnt anything?

STAGE 1 **Listening**
Listen to the recording of the conversation more than once before proceeding. Become reasonably familiar with the sounds you are hearing before you see how they are spelt.

STAGE 2 **Listening *and* looking**
Now look at the text *and* listen to the conversation – without stopping the recording, playing it as many times as you feel the need to.

STAGE 3 **Listening *and* speaking**
Stop the tape after each phrase or sentence and try to repeat what you have heard. If you do this without looking at the text, your pronunciation will not be deflected by the spelling.

STAGE 4 **Listening, looking *and* speaking**
On the other hand, you do need to know how the spelling relates to the way words are pronounced: this is best achieved after you *know* how to pronounce them. So repeat STAGE 3 but look as well this time.

STAGE 5 **Looking *and* speaking**
Now try to read the conversation aloud without listening.

For any residual problems, try going back over one or more of the above stages.

Text 1A Tee...

Montag vormittag[1]

The setting You decide on impulse to take a five-day, non-package, do-it-yourself break in Berlin, leaving home on a Sunday and arriving on Monday morning by train at the Zoo Station in the city's 'West End'. Just around the corner is your first objective, the Kurfürstendamm, Berlin's best-known boulevard, with its irresistible cafés. You enter the most spacious and comfortable café you have ever encountered and take a seat. The waitress approaches . . .

The dialogue The waitress greets you with the words 'Good day' and you simply repeat. She asks you what you want. You choose tea – and you don't want it with lemon but with milk. The waitress then asks you something which you surmise might imply 'Can I get you a thick slice of gateau covered in cream?', so to be on the safe side you politely say 'no'. The tea you hope you have ordered actually does arrive! You now even feel confident enough to ask for the bill and, like a native, to round up the price stated (= 2,60) to the nearest whole Mark. You give the waitress a ten-Mark note and get seven Marks change. You finish your tea, saying goodbye as you leave

KELLNERIN:[2] Guten Tag!
SIE:[3] Guten Tag!
KELLNERIN: Bitte schön?
SIE: Tee, bitte.[4]
KELLNERIN: Mit[5] Zitrone?
SIE: Nein, mit Milch, bitte.
KELLNERIN: Ja. Möchten Sie sonst noch etwas?[6]
SIE: Nein, danke.

KELLNERIN: Bitte[7] schön! Tee mit Milch.
SIE: Danke schön! Ich möchte bitte zahlen.[8]
KELLNERIN: Zwei Mark sechzig,[9] bitte.
SIE: Drei Mark. [*you hand over a ten Mark note*]
KELLNERIN: Danke sehr! Und sieben Mark zurück.[10]
SIE: Danke schön![11]

SIE: Auf Wiedersehen!
KELLNERIN Auf Wiedersehen!

Notes

1 'Monday morning', literally: 'pre-midday'
2 the **-in** ending of this word is the equivalent of '-ess' in 'waitress'. 'Waiter' = **Kellner**
3 'You'
4 here **Bitte!** means 'please'. Immediately above, **Bitte?** is essentially an invitation for you to speak
5 'with'
6 'would you like anything else?'
7 yet another use of **Bitte!** It is also used, as here, when giving something to someone
8 'I would like to pay'
9 *DM 2,60*
10 literally: 'back', i.e. 'charge, in return'
11 **schön** and **sehr** are completely interchangeable (and optional) with **Danke** and **Bitte**

Übung 1A

Once you feel fairly familiar with Text 1A, try writing down – from memory – the German equivalents from the Text of the following English phrases. In many cases, the equivalents are *not* word-for-word translations. When you have finished, check back with the Text before proceeding to the Key to exercises (see box below).

1 Hello!
2 Can I take your order?
3 Tea, please.
4 With lemon?
5 With milk, please.
6 Would you like anything else?
7 No thank you.
8 I would like to pay, please.
9 Two Marks sixty.
10 Three Marks.
11 And seven Marks change.
12 Goodbye!

The symbol ✎ is a TASK symbol. Whenever you reach it, *do something!* Sometimes the paragraph immediately following the exercise gives answers to the questions; more often the answers are given in the Key to exercises in the back of the book. Wherever the answers are, to gain full benefit from the course, you need to *stop* at every task symbol, *do* the exercise following it, and only then move on.

The symbol ⚷ is the KEY symbol. Whenever it follows the task symbol it means that our answers to the exercise are printed in the Key to exercises section at the back of the book.

Numbers and prices

A firm grasp of numbers in German is one of the most useful things to take with you on a first visit to a German-speaking country. It's helpful to be able to *say* numbers, but particularly to *understand* them – and to understand them when spoken quickly under adverse acoustic conditions: in banks, shops, restaurants, theatres, cinemas, museums, art galleries, swimming pools, railway-, bus- and petrol-stations, at airports, on the phone, etc.

The normal way to write a sum of money in Marks, using figures, is **DM 1,60** or **1,60 DM**. The way to *say* this is **eine Mark sechzig**, or, less frequently, **eine Mark sechzig Pfennig**.

Übung 1B

Practise *reading* the numbers below from left to right in random combinations, following the pattern **eine Mark sechzig**, **sechs Mark achtzig**, etc.

1	**eine**			
2	**zwei**		***zwan*zig**	**20**
3	**drei**		**drei*ßig***	**30**
4	**vier**		**vierzig**	**40**
5	**fünf**	—— **Mark** ——▶	**fünfzig**	**50**
6	**sechs**		***sech*zig**	**60**
7	**sieben**		***sieb*zig**	**70**
8	**acht**		**achtzig**	**80**
9	**neun**		**neunzig**	**90**
10	**zehn**			

Übung 1C

Again using the table above, *write out* in figures the prices given in the list below, as e.g. **DM 3,40** – with a *comma* between the Mark and Pfennig figures.

1 **fünf Mark fünfzig**
2 **sieben Mark achtzig**
3 **drei Mark dreißig**
4 **eine Mark neunzig**
5 **sechs Mark siebzig**
6 **acht Mark vierzig**
7 **zwei Mark sechzig**
8 **neun Mark zwanzig**
9 **vier Mark dreißig**
10 **eine Mark sechzig.**

Übung 1D

Now, without looking at **Übung 1C**, read out loud and write in German *words* the prices indicated by the figures in Key 1C. Afterwards check the spelling again, particularly for the multiples of ten, some of which (those italicised in **Übung 1B**) are less predictable in their spelling than others.

Übung 1E

Write in German the words for the following prices:

1 DM 6,70
2 DM 1,20
3 DM 5,50
4 DM 4,30
5 DM 3,90
6 DM 7,60
7 DM 3,60
8 DM 4,40
9 DM 2,90
10 DM 6,20
11 DM 9,80
12 DM 1,50
13 DM 2,30
14 DM 9,20
15 DM 7,40

- In German there is no ending on **Mark** in the plural: in English we would of course add an '-s'.
- The number 1 used in counting is **ein*s*** (e.g. **Lektion eins**), but **1 Mark** is always **ein*e Mark***.
- **DM** in German stands for (**die**) **Deutsche Mark**, *not* Deutsch(e)mark, which is an Anglo-American expression!
- When talking about their currency, Germans normally *say* just **Mark** or **D-Mark**.
- The unit of currency in Austria is (**der**) **Schilling** (= 100 **Groschen**).
- The unit of currency in Switzerland is (**der**) **Franken** (= 100 **Rappen**).

Text 1B ... oder[12] Kaffee?

An alternative scenario Having practised thoroughly your German prices you are now equipped to spend up to ten Marks ninety, so this time it's a pot (= two cups) of coffee and a piece of chocolate cake. This time a waiter rather than a waitress serves you. You give him exactly the amount you wish to pay (rounded up) and tell the waiter to keep the change.

KELLNER:[13] Guten Tag!
SIE: Guten Tag!
KELLNER: Bitte schön? Was bekommen Sie?[14]
SIE: Kaffee, bitte.
KELLNER: Eine Tasse oder ein Kännchen?
SIE: Ein Kännchen.
KELLNER; Das wär's?[15]
SIE: Und ein Stück Sachertorte.[16]

KELLNER: Bitte sehr.[17] Ein Stück Sachertorte, ein Kännchen Kaffee.
SIE: Vielen Dank![18] Ich möchte gleich[19] zahlen.
KELLNER: Das macht[20] neun Mark fünfzig, bitte.
SIE: Zehn Mark. Bitte schön. Stimmt so.[21]
KELLNER: Ich danke Ihnen.[22]

SIE: Auf Wiederschauen![23]
KELLNER: Auf Wiederschauen!

Notes

12 'or'
13 'waiter' = **Kellner**, 'waitress' = **Kellnerin**
14 literally: 'What get you' ('What do you get')? i.e. 'What can I get you?' There are, of course, numerous ways in German of asking what a customer wants – the waiter may even say nothing at all at this point. Whatever is said or not said, you are bound to get the message: you reply by placing your order
15 this is an alternative to **Sonst noch etwas?** Literally: 'That would be it?' i.e. 'Will that be all?'
16 a variety of chocolate gateau, invented in 1832 by Metternich's Viennese cook, Franz Sacher
17 the waiter places your order on the table in front of you
18 literally: 'Many thank' (always singular in German), an alternative to **Danke**, **Danke schön**, **Danke sehr ...**

19 'immediately'
20 literally: 'That makes', i.e. 'comes to'
21 literally: '(That)'s correct like that' i.e. 'please keep the change!'
22 literally: 'I thank you' – an alternative to **Danke**, **Danke schön**, **Vielen Dank ...**
23 an alternative to **Auf Wiedersehen!** You are more likely to hear it in Austria and Bavaria than Berlin

Übung 1F

Once you feel familiar enough with Text 1B, try writing down – from memory – equivalents of the following phrases. Check your answers against the Text before proceeding to the Key.

> If you are using the recordings, did you approach Text 1B in listening/reading/speaking stages just as systematically as you did Text 1A at the start of this **Lektion**? If not, please do: it's worth it!

1 What can I get you?
2 Coffee, please?
3 A cup or a pot?
4 Will that be all?
5 And a piece of Sacher cake.
6 I'd like to pay immediately.
7 That comes to DM 9,50.
8 Keep the change.
9 (I) thank you.
10 Goodbye.

Patterns of language

If you had enough time and enough exposure to German, you *could* learn it the way you learnt your native language: by slowly teasing out the patterns by trial and error. In *Colloquial German* these patterns – the essential rules of German – are of course pre-packaged for you, but some alertness on your part about *possible* patterns *before* we spell them out will help you in your learning. So (a) keep smiling, (b) keep guessing!

Übung 1G

You can test your ability to spot possible patterns, i.e. grammatical rules, by looking hard at Text 1A and Text 1B. Can you detect any similarities between any of the words on the basis of the way they are written?

You may have noticed, for instance, that:

- many words in the middle of sentences, e.g. **Kännchen** and **Stück**, are written with a capital letter;
- ***ein*** **Kännchen** and ***ein*** **Stück** also have ***ein*** in common;
- ***eine*** **Tasse** is close to, but clearly different from, ***ein*** **Stück**;
- the two-word phrases **Gut*en* Tag**! and **Viel*en* Dank**! have ***-en*** in common;
- before and after **Sie** there are words in ***-en***: **möcht*en* Sie**, **Sie bekomm*en***;
- whereas **möcht*en*** and **Sie** seem to belong together, **möcht*e*** goes with **ich**;
- there are two words ending in ***-t***: **mach*t*** and **stimm*t***.

We will be picking up these patterns of language and explaining them in stages. To do this it's helpful to introduce a few labels so that we can refer succinctly to the patterns as we go along. The important thing is not to learn the labels but to be able to *see the patterns* they denote and so ultimately apply the appropriate rules. Let's look at our first handy label: NOUN.

Nouns

Nouns are much easier to spot in German than in English because German nouns, *regardless of where they come in a sentence*, are written with a *capital letter*. At the beginning of a sentence, a word written with a capital might, of course, be a noun but more often than not it isn't.

Übung 1H

The English words listed below in three columns are *nouns* which have their German counterparts in Texts 1A and 1B. Draw up a similar table listing their German equivalents. If you find the right words, your German nouns will (a) all have capital letters, and (b) be in alphabetical order in each column.

thank(s)	pot [of coffee]	waitress
coffee	piece	Mark [German currency]
waiter	goodbye [2 versions]	milk
day		chocolate gateau
tea		cup
		lemon

Nouns and gender

Übung 1J

Look up in the Glossary at the back of the book the German nouns you have written in answer to **Übung 1H**, check the spelling if necessary, but now add to each German word in your lists the three-letter word – **der**, **das** or **die** – that precedes it in the Glossary.

Der, **das**, **die** – and 'the' in English – are called DEFINITE ARTICLES. Articles belong to nouns, and they differ in German because *all* German nouns have GENDER. German has three genders:

- *masculine* (the **der** nouns in column one in the answer to **Übung 1J**)
- *neuter* (the **das** nouns in column two)
- *feminine* (the **die** nouns in column three)

Verbs

Verbs are often words which indicate some kind of action. In English they can immediately follow, for example, a noun, or 'I, you, we, they', etc.

The *form* of an individual verb will vary depending on meaning and context (e.g. 'pay, pays, paying, paid'), but the convenient starting point for learning such changes is the *base* form as listed in dictionaries and in the Glossary to this book.

Übung 1K

The following words from Texts 1A and 1B are all verbs, but some (not all) of them are not in their base (i.e. their Glossary) form.

Find the base forms of the verbs as given in the Glossary, plus their meanings.

1 möchte	5 möchten
2 zahlen	6 macht
3 bekommen	7 stimmt
4 wär'(wäre)	8 (ich) danke.

Although you had eight words to look up, you should have found only five different base forms in the Glossary. In their base form all German verbs end in ***-n***. In fact, most end not only in ***-n*** but in ***-en***. The very common verb **sein** 'to be' is an exception in most things.

You may have noticed that verbs in the Glossary are accompanied by abbreviations such as *v.reg.* or *v.irreg. V.* means verb. *Irreg.* indicates that the verb in some of its forms is irregular, i.e. does not follow the 'standard' regular pattern. Verb patterns – both regular and irregular – will be looked at in stages throughout this book.

Verbs and pronouns

Ich ('I') and **Sie** ('you') are PERSONAL PRONOUNS.

The **ich** form of the verb generally ends in ***-e***. The **Sie** form generally ends in ***-en***. If we list verbs we have had so far, and give them their **ich** and **Sie** forms, we get:

	ich zahle	**Sie zahlen**	I/you pay
	ich möchte	**Sie möchten**	I/you would like
	ich bekomme	**Sie bekommen**	I/you get
	ich mache	**Sie machen**	I/you do, make
exception:	**ich bin**	**Sie sind**	I am/you are

All the above forms are in the PRESENT TENSE. English has two present tense forms, as in e.g. 'I pay', and 'I'm paying', for both of which there is only one German version to learn, i.e. **ich zahle**.

Words versus phrases

If you look up the three words **Sonst noch etwas** (Text 1A) one by one in a German–English dictionary you will find the following English equivalents: 'otherwise – yet, still – something'. We will later in the book meet and use these three German words separately with these meanings. However, in certain contexts, such as the waitress's question in Text 1A, the three words *together* constitute a 'set phrase' meaning 'Anything else?'

The lesson to be drawn from this is that words are frequently best learnt in groups because the meaning of the group is not easily deduced from the meanings of the individual parts – think of some English examples: 'come up with', 'over the top', 'down and out'. . . .

Always learn set phrases *as units* in order to be able to recall them complete when needed. In fact, it's better to learn most words *in groups*. After all, apart from 'yes' **ja** and 'no' **nein** there are few words we commonly meet or use in isolation. To be able to string words together easily and quickly, it is best to remember words in context rather than learn them from lists. Which is not to say that lists don't have their uses: after all, a glossary is a list.

'Hello' and 'goodbye'

The phrase **Guten Tag!** is used not as 'Good day!' is in English to take one's leave but when meeting people you don't know particularly well. **Guten Tag!** is also used in formal introductions when we might say 'How do you do?' in English. When you expect or are hoping for service, it could be interpreted as impolite *not* to say **Guten Tag!** as an opener. **Guten Tag!** can be used at any time of day. **Grüß Gott!** ('May God greet (you)') is often used in the south rather than **Guten Tag!**

Guten Morgen! can be used before noon, **Guten Abend!** in the evening and **Gute Nacht!** before going to bed. There is no 'Good afternoon!' in German.

For leave-taking you will hear **Auf Wiedersehen!** and **Auf Wiederschauen!** The former is more common in the north, whereas the latter is often heard in the south. They both literally mean 'to again-seeing' – cf. French *au revoir!* – which means they can't be used on the phone: the equivalent over the phone is **Auf Wiederhören!** (literally 'to again-hearing').

The expression **Tschüs!** (which may ultimately be related to Spanish *adios*) is informal – comparable to English expressions such as 'Bye!', 'See you!', 'Take care!' – and is becoming increasingly common. **Servus!** is often used informally for leave-taking in the south.

'Please' and 'thank you'

Bitte has a very large number of uses. **Bitte** or **Bitte schön** or **Bitte sehr** can be used to

- mean 'please' or 'thank you';
- attract attention ('Can I help you?' 'Can you help me?');
- confirm a transaction ('There you are');
- acknowledge thanks ('You're welcome', 'Don't mention it').

The context makes clear which of these is meant.

Danke is the commonest equivalent of 'thanks', 'thank you' and, like **Bitte**, is often followed by **schön** or **sehr**: **Danke schön** or **Danke sehr** followed by **Bitte schön** or **Bitte sehr** are frequently heard exchanges. It can be impolite *not* to follow a **Danke (schön/sehr)** with a **Bitte (schön/sehr)** since to a German speaker the exchange is then incomplete.

Vielen Dank ('Many thanks') or **Ich danke Ihnen** ('I thank you') also require a **Bitte (schön/sehr)** response.

Tea and coffee

The commonest way of drinking tea in German-speaking countries is from a glass with lemon. If you want milk rather than lemon you will need to say **Tee mit Milch** rather than just **Tee**.

Coffee is served strong and black with separate cream or condensed milk. In some cafés and restaurants you might have to have **ein Kännchen** rather than **eine Tasse**. Decaffeinated coffee – **koffeinfrei, bitte** – is usually available. In Austria, in particular, coffee is often served with a glass of water – to clear the palate and enhance the coffee taste.

Übung 1L

Let's return to the café. How much do you remember in *German*? Do you remember:

1 how much you paid for your tea in Text 1A;
2 how much you paid for your coffee and gateau in Text 1B;
3 what sort of gateau it was and how much you ordered?

If your memory of the above is hazy, read through the texts again (and listen to the recordings if possible) before moving on.

Übung 1M

Match up the following phrases.

1	Anything else?	A	**Und sieben Mark zurück.**
2	Can I take your order?	B	**Vielen Dank!**
3	That's 2 Marks 60.	C	**Mit Zitrone?**
4	And 7 Marks change!	D	**Das macht zwei Mark sechzig.**
5	Is that all?	E	**Sonst noch etwas?**
6	With lemon?	F	**Tee mit Milch, bitte.**
7	Many thanks.	G	**Das wär's?**
8	Tea – with milk, please!	H	**Was bekommen Sie?**

Übung 1N

Now prove to yourself that you can get service in a German café:

1 You enter the café. What do you say as a polite opener?
2 You are asked for your order. Say you would like coffee.
3 You are asked whether you want a cup or a pot. Say you would like a pot.
4 You are asked whether you would like anything else. Say no, thank you.
5 Ask for the bill.
6 Tell the waiter to keep the change.
7 Say thank you and goodbye.

Extra: Torten, Kuchen, Gebäck

The text below is about some delicious **(köstlich)** 'cakes/pastries' (which is very broadly what all three words above mean) and where such culinary delights come from.

Übung 1P

Try to get as much as you can of the *general gist* of the text by listening and looking simultaneously. Even if you don't understand anything *fully*, there is still much benefit to be gained by listening repeatedly in order to get a 'feel' for the language. When you feel you might have understood *some* of the text, try the questions in **Übung 1Q**.

Torten, Kuchen, Gebäck in Deutschland, in Österreich und in der Schweiz – köstlich aber auch teuer! Zum Beispiel:

Ein Stück Sachertorte kostet im Wiener Hotel Sacher circa achtzig Schilling – das macht zehn deutsche Mark! Sachertorte ist eine feine Schokoladentorte. Original-Sachertorte ist mit Aprikosenmarmelade bestrichen. Natürlich ist Wien auch für Apfelstrudel bekannt.

Die deutsche Hauptstadt Berlin bietet Berliner Pfannkuchen. Ein frischer, warmer Berliner Pfannkuchen schmeckt immer gut.

Auch Schwarzwälder Kirschtorte – am besten gekühlt – aus Baden-Württemberg in Südwestdeutschland schmeckt wunderbar.

In Basel in der Schweiz bekommen Sie Basler Leckerli, ein Gebäck aus Honig, Mandeln, Zucker und Mehl, und natürlich *sehr* süß.

Oder wie wär's mit Thüringer Mohnkuchen aus Thüringen in Ostdeutschland? Oder Dresdner Stollen aus Dresden in Sachsen – mit und ohne Schlagsahne? Wer die Wahl hat, hat die Qual.

Mit Tee oder Kaffee? Und vielleicht auch noch einen kleinen Schnaps dazu? Tja, was bekommen Sie nun? Auf alle Fälle Appetit. Na also! Bitte schön. Guten Appetit!

Übung 1Q

This exercise is to help you pinpoint some of the things you may have understood in the above text. Read the questions below, check through the text above twice for possible answers and then, if still in doubt about the answers to some of the questions, guess!

1 How many different kinds of cakes are mentioned? List their German names.
2 What are the German names for the three German-speaking countries?
3 How many different place-names (towns and regions, not countries) are mentioned? What are they?
4 What – in English – does **Sachertorte** always contain?
5 What does it sometimes contain?
6 Before you look them up in the Glossary, try guessing the four ingredients given for **Basler Leckerli**.
7 What might you order to drink with tea or coffee?
8 Can you find the German word for 'capital city' in the text?

9 **Wer die Wahl hat, hat die Qual!** is a common German saying. Find its meaning in the Glossary.

Übung 1R

To say 'in', as with most languages, German like English simply puts **in** immediately before the name.

The text contains two examples of this general rule, plus one exception. What are they?

Übung 1S

As with **Übung 1K**, the aims of this exercise are (a) to encourage you to use the Glossary at the back of the book, and (b) to underline the fact that no dictionary or glossary can invariably list a word in exactly the form in which you are looking for it. None of the words in the list below is in its base form, i.e. the form in which it occurs in the Glossary in the back of this book. Find the base forms in the Glossary and list them with the meaning of each.

1 **Torten**	5 **deutsche**	9 **schmeckt**
2 **kostet**	6 **bietet**	10 **Mandeln**
3 **eine/einen**	7 **frischer**	11 **kleinen**
4 **feine**	8 **warmer**	12 **Fälle**

Übung 1T

Which of the words in **Übung 1S** above are (a) nouns (b) verbs?

- The meanings of German words you meet in *Colloquial German* can be found in the Glossary.
- Of the words you have met so far, it's not the long but the short ones like **sehr**, **auch**, **also**, **und**, **oder**, **aber**, **auf**, **in**, **aus**, **mit**, **ohne**, **noch**, **ist**, **hat**, **was**, **wie**, **wer** that you will be meeting most frequently and which you will therefore find easiest to remember in the long run.
- Don't try to remember *everything* in each **Lektion** but, before moving on, always go back over a **Lektion** if you really know you need to. . . .

2 Stadtpläne

A little shopping

Language activities

- buying goods
- specifying (small) quantitites and unit costs
- stating destinations

Language focus

- pattern changes: questions
- form changes: verbs, articles, adjectives
- three prepositions
- numbers 21 to 99 and more prices

Learning strategies

- distinguishing between subjects and objects
- interpreting endings

Text 2

Montag mittag[1]

After your **Tee, Kaffee und Kuchen** you decide to venture into a stationer's – literally, a 'writing wares shop': **ein Schreibwarengeschäft** – in order to buy a map (**Stadtplan**) of Berlin. The shopkeeper/sales assistant – **der Verkäufer** – has a choice of two maps (**Stadtpläne**) and asks you if you want a small or a big map. You settle for the smaller one. You have already selected some black-and-white postcards from a stand outside the shop. You pay for these, too, and buy the stamps you need on the spot.

VERKÄUFER: Guten Tag! Bitte schön?
SIE: Guten Tag! Haben[2] Sie einen Stadtplan von Berlin?
VERKÄUFER: Ja. Möchten Sie einen großen[3] oder einen kleinen Stadtplan?
SIE: Einen kleinen Stadtplan, bitte.
VERKÄUFER: Möchten Sie sonst noch etwas?[4]
SIE: Ja, die[5] vier schwarzweißen[6] Ansichtskarten. Haben Sie vielleicht[7] auch[8] Briefmarken?
VERKÄUFER: Ja, wir haben auch Briefmarken.
SIE: Was kostet eine Postkarte[9] nach[10] Großbritannien?
VERKÄUFER: Achtzig Pfennig.
SIE: Und nach Amerika?
VERKÄUFER: Zwei Mark zwanzig.
SIE: Ich möchte zwei Briefmarken zu[11] achtzig Pfennig und zwei Briefmarken zu zwei Mark zwanzig. Was macht das?[12]
VERKÄUFER: Der Stadtplan kostet[13] zwei Mark fünfzig, vier Ansichtskarten kosten[14] zwei Mark, vier Briefmarken eins sechzig[15] plus vier vierzig – das macht zusammen[16] zehn Mark fünfzig.
SIE: Bitte schön.
VERKÄUFER: Danke schön, zwanzig Mark.[17] Und neun Mark fünfzig zurück.[18]
SIE: Vielen Dank. Auf Wiedersehen!
VERKÄUFER: Auf Wiedersehen!

Notes

1 'Monday midday'
2 'have'
3 **groß** ≠ **klein**: 'large' ≠ 'small'
4 'would you like anything else?' cf. **Lektion eins**
5 i.e. the ones you are showing to the shopkeeper/sales assistant: in English = 'these' rather than 'the' here
6 literally: 'blackwhite'
7 'perhaps'
8 'also, too'
9 **eine Postkarte** is strictly a postcard with space for writing on both sides but is also used loosely for **eine Ansichtskarte**, a 'view card', i.e. one with a photograph on the front
10 'to' (a country)
11 @, i.e. costing 80 Pfennig each
12 'How much is that?'
13 here the verb 'cost' is in the singular
14 here the verb is in the plural
15 a shorter way of saying **eine Mark sechzig**
16 'altogether'
17 the shopkeeper has been given a twenty Mark note and is acknowledging this before giving the change
18 literally: 'back, in return', i.e. 'change'

Übung 2A 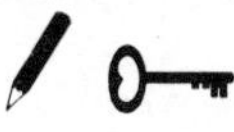

Listed below are English equivalents of NOUNS that occur in Text 2 above. Find their German equivalents in the Text and write them down in two columns, preceded by **der** or **die**. Where the text contains a plural form, you need to *check the Glossary for the singular*. German nouns must always be written with a capital letter. When you have finished, your German equivalents should appear in alphabetical order in each column.

masculine	*feminine*
Pfennig (currency)	picture postcards
plan of the city	postage stamps
day	Mark (currency)
sales assistant	postcard

Übung 2B

Find German equivalents in Text 2 for the following sentences/ phrases.

1 That's DM 10,50 altogether.
2 How much is a postcard to Britain?
3 Would you like a big map or a small map?
4 I'd like two 80 Pfennig stamps.
5 Would you like anything else?
6 Yes, these four black-and-white postcards.
7 Yes, we have stamps, too.
8 DM 9,50 change.

Questions

As in English, there is more than one way of asking questions in German. For example:

(a) You can use a *question word* at the beginning of a sentence. Most German question words begin with **W-** (pronounced like English 'v'):

***Was* bekommen Sie? (Lektion eins)**
Literally: 'What get you?' (i.e. 'What can I get you?')

***Was* kostet eine Ansichtskarte nach Amerika?**
Literally: 'What costs a picture postcard to America?'

***Was* macht das?**
Literally: 'What makes that?' (i.e. 'How much do I owe you?')

***Was* machen Sie?**
Literally: 'What do/make you?' (i.e. 'What are you doing?')

(b) Or you can put the *verb* at the beginning of a sentence – in first rather than second position (sometimes called *inversion*), e.g.

1	2	3	2	1	3
Ich	**habe**	**Briefmarken.**	**Haben**	**Sie**	**Briefmarken?**
			Literally:	Have you	stamps?
Ich	**trinke**	**Kaffee.**	**Trinken**	**Sie auch**	**Kaffee?**
			Literally:	Drink you too	coffee?
Ich	**möchte**	**Ansichtskarten.**	**Möchten**	**Sie**	**sonst noch etwas?**
			Would you like		anything else?

Note that German questions are grammatically simpler than their English equivalents because, unlike English, the German verb does not change when it is inverted, cf.

> ***Trinken* Sie Kaffee?**
> vs. *Do* you *drink* coffee? / *Are* you *drinking* coffee?
> **Was *machen* Sie?**
> vs. What *are* you *doing?* / What *do* you *do*?

Endings etc.

In general, individual words in English tend to have fewer different forms than their German counterparts: many more German words change their 'endings' in sentences than is the case with English words – and there is also a greater variety of endings in German.

English does have some add-on endings, e.g. '-s' (as in 'takes') or '-n' (as in 'taken') or '-ed' (as in 'asked') but 'the' (the definite article), for example, never changes, whereas in German the definite article can appear in one of six different forms, viz. **der**, **das**, **die**, **den**, **dem**, **des**.

Indefinite articles

In English, the indefinite article has two forms, 'a' and 'an'. In German the indefinite article in its dictionary form is **ein**, but it frequently acquires endings which tell us about its relationship to other words in a sentence. The fact that it does or does not have a particular ending can indicate, for example,

- whether the noun which follows it is masculine, neuter or feminine;
- whether the noun is the subject or object of the sentence.

In **Lektion eins** we met ***eine* Mark** and ***eine* Tasse** – ***eine*** indicating that **Mark** and **Tasse** are feminine. And there was also ***ein* Kännchen** – indicating that **Kännchen** is *not* feminine: it is neuter. Here are some indefinite articles in German sentences:

Masculine	**Ich möchte**	***einen***	**Stadtplan.**
Neuter	**Ich möchte**	***ein***	**Kännchen Kaffee.**
Feminine	**Ich möchte**	***eine***	**Briefmarke zu achtzig Pfennig.**

Relationships within sentences

Subject and object (nominative and accusative cases)

The nouns on the right in the three German sentences above are all the direct OBJECT of the verb and are therefore in what in German grammar books is called the ACCUSATIVE case. If they were not the object but the SUBJECT of the verb, ***einen*** **Stadtplan** would appear as ***ein*** **Stadtplan** – ***ein*** **Kännchen** and ***eine*** **Briefmarke** would be the same in either case. In German grammars the subject of a sentence is described as being in the NOMINATIVE case. For most learners, 'shorthand' tables such as the one below for the indefinite article (English 'a' or 'an') can be a useful visual aid towards retaining such information:

	masculine article	*neuter* article	*feminine* article
subject nominative	**ein**	**ein**	**eine**
object accusative	***einen***	**ein**	**eine**

Übung 2C

Provide the missing German words. They are all in the accusative case so will need to be preceded by **einen** or **ein** or **eine** depending on whether the noun is masculine, neuter or feminine.

1 **Ich möchte** [a map of the town/city].
2 **Haben Sie** [a Mark]?
3 **Ich habe** [a Pfennig].
4 **Ich möchte bitte** [a postage stamp].
5 **Möchten Sie** [a piece (of) Sachertorte].
6 **Nein, danke, ich möchte** [a schnapps: Glossary has spelling and gender].
7 **Sie bekommen** [a cup of tea].
8 **Ich möchte** [a postcard] **von Berlin**.

Understanding case relationships can be something of a challenge to English-speaking learners of German since although English sentences, too, need subjects and objects, changes to the *forms* of words – *case changes* – associated with this are rare in modern English: we normally pick up who or what is the subject and who or what is the object not from the form of words but exclusively from the *sequence* in which they are used in a sentence, as in

subject (nominative)	*verb*	*object (accusative)*
The customer	paid	the waiter
The waiter	paid	the customer (!)

However, there are times when standard modern English does in fact make changes to the form of words in order to make a subject/object relationship quite clear, as in

subject (nominative case)	*verb*	*object (accusative)*
She (not 'her')	paid	him (not 'he')
He (not 'him')	paid	her (not 'she')
I (not 'me')	paid	them (not 'they')

It is worth noting that if case relationships are clear from the forms of words, word order is potentially less important. An English sentence such as 'Him paid she' may be very odd stylistically but it's still reasonably clear who pays who(m)! Because German *frequently* changes the forms of words to indicate case relationships, unlike English it can quite naturally often put the object before the subject (e.g. for emphasis) without changing the basic meaning of a sentence. For example, there is nothing odd about either of the following replies to the question

Was möchten Sie?
—Ich möchte einen Stadtplan von Berlin.
—Einen Stadtplan von Berlin möchte ich.

Adjectives

Adjectives describe nouns, e.g. 'a *big* map, *good* day, *black*-and-*white* postcards'. The following sentence from Text 2

Möchten Sie einen *großen* oder *kleinen* Stadtplan?

contains two adjectives, ***groß*** ('large') and ***klein*** ('small'). Immediately in front of the noun they describe, adjectives must have appropriate endings; away from their noun they do not, e.g.

Ein Stadtplan ist *groß*.

Ein Stadtplan ist *klein*.
Ich möchte ein*en* groß*en* Stadtplan.

	masculine article	adjective	*neuter* article	adjective	*feminine* article	adjective
subject nominative	**ein**	*kleiner**	**ein**	*kleines**	**eine**	*kleine**
object accusative	**einen**	**kleinen**	**ein**	*kleines**	**eine**	*kleine**

* These forms are given here for interest only: they have not yet occurred in context in the book and will therefore not be practised in this **Lektion**.

Übung 2D

In all the sentences below the *masculine* noun is the item (object) you want, so 'a' is **einen**. When you slot in an adjective as well, the adjective also has to end in **-en** (see **einen kleinen** in the table above). Choose a plausible adjective from the following list to slot into each sentence, using up all four adjectives

guten 'good'; **starken** 'strong'; **großen** 'large'; **neuen** 'new'

1 **Ich möchte ein*en* ______ Stadtplan.**
2 **Haben Sie ein*en* ______ Schnaps?**
3 **Ich möchte ein*en* ______ Kaffee.**
4 **Ich möchte ein*en* ______ Volkswagen.**

Some very common expressions contain masculine words in the accusative case, e.g.

Guten Tag! Guten Abend! Guten Morgen!
Guten Appetit! Vielen Dank!

These are in effect the object of 'I wish (you)' with the subject and verb omitted.

Verbs

In **Lektion eins** we identified the dictionary form of verbs, i.e.

the 'base' form*, as e.g.		***machen*** (to do, make)	***zahlen*** (to pay)
the 'I' form as:	**ich**	**mache**	**zahle**
and the 'you' form as:	**Sie**	**machen**	**zahlen**

In **Lektion zwei** we also now have

			kosten (to cost)
the 'he/she/it' form	**das**	**macht**	**kostet**
and the 'they' form	**sie**	**machen**	**kosten**

* The 'base' form is also called the INFINITIVE.

The following table gives the *sequence* in which the various verb forms to date are generally presented:

	regular	***machen*** (to do)	*irregular*	***haben*** (to have)
I	**ich**	**mache**	**ich**	**habe**
he/she/it	**er/sie/es**	**macht**	**er/sie/es**	**hat**
we	**wir**	**machen**	**wir**	**haben**
they/you	**sie/Sie**	**machen**	**sie/Sie**	**haben**

Because most verbs undergo changes following the pattern indicated by **machen**, they are called 'regular' verbs. We will concentrate on using regular rather than irregular verbs for the time being.

Übung 2E

Translate the following, using the correct verb form. The 'base' or 'infinitive' form – which in some sentences needs to be changed along the lines indicated for **machen** above – is given in italics.

1 **bestellen** I'll order (literally: 'I order') coffee.
2 **zahlen** He's paying (literally: 'He pays').
3 **kosten** Four stamps cost two Marks.
4 **kosten** A cup of tea costs ninety Pfennigs.
5 **machen** That makes ten Marks fifty.
6 **bestellen** Are you ordering (literally: 'Order you') tea with milk?

7 **bestellen** Yes, I'm ordering ('I order') tea with milk.
8 **bestellen** She's ordering ('she orders') tea with lemon.

Übung 2F

Provide the missing words (write out the numbers in words).

1 **Eine Ansichtskarte von Berlin kostet neunzig Pfennig.**
Drei ______ von Berlin ______.
2 **Zwei Postkarten nach England kosten eine Mark sechzig.**
Eine ______ nach England ______.
3 **Ein Brief* nach Australien kostet drei Mark.**
* For this word you will need to look up the meaning and plural form in the Glossary.
Drei ______ nach Australien ______.
4 **Zwei Stadtpläne von Frankfurt kosten neun Mark sechzig.**
Ein ______ von Frankfurt ______.

Übung 2G

Fill in the verb endings.

1 **Was kost ______ die Postkarte?**
2 **Was kost ______ eine Ansichtskarte?**
3 **Was kost ______ die Briefmarken?**
4 **Was kost ______ der Stadtplan?**
5 **Was kost ______ die Postkarten?**
6 **Was kost ______ Ansichtskarten?**
7 **Was kost ______ ein Brief nach Amerika?**
8 **Was kost ______ die Stadtpläne?**

Prepositions

Prepositions are generally found in front of nouns and pronouns, and are mostly used to indicate when, how or where. English examples:

in London; *to* Berlin; *on* Tuesday; *with* great difficulty; *before* breakfast; *after* you . . .

Von, **nach**, **zu** are very common prepositions in German, and, as is the case with most common words, have a wide range of uses and therefore of meanings. So far we have met three of these uses:

nach Where the destination is a country, town or village, 'to' is usually expressed as ***nach***, e.g.
Was kostet eine Ansichtskarte *nach* Amerika?
What does a postcard to America cost (i.e. what does it cost to send it?)

von ***Von*** can be used to mean 'of/from' in contexts such as
Haben Sie einen Stadtplan *von* Berlin?
Do you have a map of Berlin?
***Von* Berlin *nach* London**
From Berlin to London

zu If there is a choice of items at different prices, **zu** is used before the price(s) of the one(s) you want, e.g.
Ich möchte sechs Briefmarken *zu* neunzig Pfennig.
I would like six stamps @ 90 Pfennig (each).

Numbers 21–99 and prices

Übung 2H

Practise *reading* the numbers in the table below from left to right in random combinations, following the pattern **ein*und*fünfzig**, **drei*und*zwanzig**, etc. German numbers under a million are written as one word!

1	**ein***			
2	**zwei**		***zwan*zig**	**20**
3	**drei**		**drei*ßig***	**30**
4	**vier**		**vierzig**	**40**
5	**fünf**	→ **und** →	**fünfzig**	**50**
6	**sechs**		***sech*zig**	**60**
7	**sieben**		***sieb*zig**	**70**
8	**acht**		**achtzig**	**80**
9	**neun**		**neunzig**	**90**

* The number 1 used in isolation, e.g. when counting 'one–two–three', is **eins**.

Note that DM 1,20 = ***eine* Mark zwanzig** (**Mark** is a feminine noun)
but DM 21,00 = ***ein*undzwanzig Mark**
and DM 21,21 = ***ein*undzwanzig Mark *ein*undzwanzig (Pfennig)**.

Übung 2J

Write in figures (following the example indicated) the prices spelt out below.

e.g. ***eine Mark einundzwanzig*** = *DM 1,21*

1 **eine Mark vierundsechzig**
2 **fünf Mark zweiundzwanzig**
3 **drei Mark achtunddreißig**
4 **zehn Mark siebenundneunzig**
5 **sechs Mark sechsunddreißig**
6 **acht Mark neunundvierzig**
7 **zwei Mark fünfundsechzig**
8 **neun Mark vierunddreißig**
9 **vier Mark zweiundzwanzig**
10 **sieben Mark neunundneunzig**

Übung 2K

Use the answers to **Übung 2J** in the Key to write out numbers in words. Refer back to the original list in 2J above to check your spellings.

Übung 2L

Write out the following prices in words.

1 DM 6,77	2 DM 1,25	3 DM 5,55
4 DM 4,31	5 DM 3,99	6 DM 2,43
7 DM 7,66	8 DM 9,38	9 DM 10,82
10 DM 8,21		

Übung 2M

If there is a choice of items at different prices, **zu** is used before the price(s) of the item(s) you want. Write out in figures *and* words the cost of each transaction.

1 SIE: Ich möchte sechs Briefmarken *zu* neunzig Pfennig.
VERKÄUFER: Bitte schön, das macht ______ .
2 SIE: Ich möchte fünf Briefmarken *zu* zwei Mark.
VERKÄUFER: Bitte schön, das macht ______ .

3 SIE: Ich möchte einen Stadtplan *zu* vier Mark zwanzig und zwei Ansichtskarten *zu* achtzig Pfennig.
VERKÄUFER: Bitte schön, das macht ______ .
4 SIE: Ich möchte eine Telefonkarte *zu* fünfzig Mark und zwei Ansichtskarten *zu* zwei Mark zwanzig.
VERKÄUFER: Bitte schön, das macht ______ .

Übung 2N

Try matching the following English and German sentences.

1 Would you like anything else?
2 Do you have a street plan (map of the city/town)?
3 Do you have stamps, too?
4 What does a postcard to Australia cost?
5 I would like two stamps @ 80 Pfennig and three @ two Marks twenty.

A **Haben Sie einen Stadtplan?**
B **Ich möchte bitte zwei Briefmarken zu achtzig Pfennig und drei zu zwei Mark zwanzig.**
C **Möchten Sie sonst noch etwas?**
D **Was kostet eine Postkarte nach Australien?**
E **Haben Sie auch Briefmarken?**

Übung 2P

If you succeeded in matching the above sentences correctly, cover up sentences A to E above and try translating 1 to 5 into German – either orally or (better still) in writing, too.

Übung 2Q

Read through Text 2 again at the beginning of this **Lektion**. Then try to write out the conversation below in the original order without referring back. Finally, check your written version with the original.

VERKÄUFER: Möchten Sie sonst noch etwas?
SIE: Guten Tag! Haben Sie einen Stadtplan von Berlin?
VERKÄUFER: Ja, wir haben auch Briefmarken.
SIE: Einen kleinen Stadtplan, bitte.
VERKÄUFER: Achtzig Pfennig.

Sie:	Ich möchte zwei Briefmarken zu achtzig Pfennig und zwei Briefmarken zu zwei Mark zwanzig. Was macht das?
Verkäufer:	Danke schön, zwanzig Mark! Und neun Mark fünfzig zurück.
Sie:	Ja, die vier schwarzweißen Ansichtskarten. Haben Sie vielleicht auch Briefmarken?
Verkäufer:	Der Stadtplan kostet zwei Mark fünfzig, vier Ansichtskarten kosten zwei Mark, vier Briefmarken eins sechzig plus vier vierzig – das macht zusammen zehn Mark fünfzig.
Sie:	Vielen Dank. Auf Wiedersehen!
Verkäufer:	Ja. Möchten Sie einen großen oder einen kleinen Stadtplan?
Sie:	Was kostet eine Postkarte nach Großbritannien?
Verkäufer:	Guten Tag! Bitte schön?
Sie:	Und nach Amerika?
Verkäufer:	Auf Wiedersehen!
Sie:	Bitte schön.
Verkäufer:	Zwei Mark zwanzig.

3 Rechts oder links?

Asking the way

Language activities

- stopping someone politely
- asking the way
- giving a telephone number

Language focus

- how and where
- **zu, zum, zur**
- useful destinations
- numbers 10 to 19, 1st to 10th

Learning strategies

- spotting questions and commands
- confirming you have understood

Text 3

Montag nachmittag (1)[1]

After your successful purchase of a map, postcard and stamps, you feel confident enough to stop a passer-by and ask the way to your preferred hotel – a typical, family-run hotel, named after the owner, Müller. You politely stop the first friendly young face you meet – **einen freundlichen jungen Berliner** – and ask the way to the hotel. He first tells you to go straight ahead. To confirm what he says and to make sure you remember, you repeat the vital information: 'Straight ahead?' He confirms that you've got it right and proceeds with his instructions. After a little hesitation, he suggests you now take the third road on the right and that you will then find the hotel on the left hand side of the street. You thank him and he wishes you a good time in Berlin.

Das Hotel Müller ist auf der linken Seite

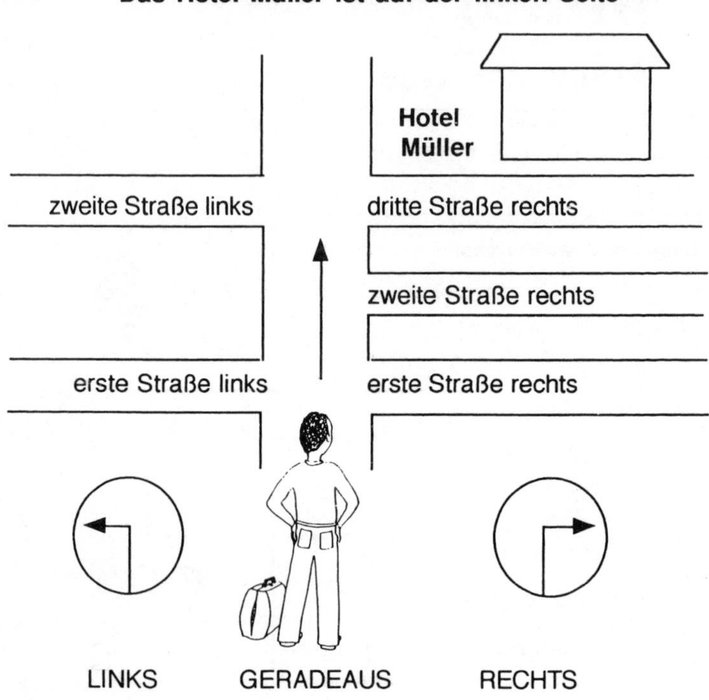

SIE:	Entschuldigen Sie,[2] bitte!
BERLINER:	Ja?
SIE:	Wie[3] komme ich zum[4] Hotel Müller?
BERLINER:	Gehen Sie geradeaus![5]
SIE:	Geradeaus?
BERLINER:	Richtig.[6] Nehmen[7] Sie dann die zweite[8] – nein, Moment mal[9] – die dritte Straße rechts!
SIE:	Die zweite Straße rechts?[10]
BERLINER:	Nein, nicht die erste[11] und auch nicht die zweite sondern[12] die dritte Straße rechts!
SIE:	Die dritte Straße rechts?
BERLINER:	Ja, ganz richtig.[13] Und das Hotel Müller ist auf der linken Seite.[14]
SIE:	Also:[15] dritte Straße rechts auf der linken Seite?
BERLINER:	Ja, genau.[16]

SIE:	Vielen Dank.[17]
BERLINER:	Bitte schön. Viel Spaß[18] in Berlin!
SIE:	Danke schön. Auf Wiedersehen!
BERLINER:	Auf Wiedersehen!

Notes

1 'Monday afternoon'
2 to stop someone politely you can either use a verb – as here (literally 'excuse!') – or a noun – **Entschuldigung!**
3 literally: 'How come I . . .?', i.e. 'How do I get to . . .?'
4 **zum** or **zur** literally means 'to the'
5 **gerade** means 'straight', **geradeaus** means 'straight ahead'
6 'right, correct'
7 'take'
8 **zwei** = '2', **zweite** = '2nd'; **drei** = '3', **dritte** = '3rd'
9 'just a moment!'
10 **rechts** ≠ **links** 'right' ≠ 'left'
11 **eins** = '1', **erste** = '1st'
12 **nicht** . . . **sondern**: 'not . . . but'
13 'quite right'
14 **auf der linken Seite** ≠ **auf der rechten Seite**: 'on the left (side) ≠ on the right'
15 'so, therefore' (NB English 'also' = German **auch**)
16 'exactly'
17 see **Lektion eins**
18 literally: 'Much fun! = Have a good time, enjoy yourself'

Übung 3A

Listed below are English equivalents of the nouns that occur in Text 3A above. Find their German equivalents in the Text and write them down, each with a capital letter and preceded by **der**, **das** or **die**.

masculine	*neuter*	*feminine*
thanks [singular in German]	hotel	side
moment		street
fun		

Übung 3B

Using Text 3 write German equivalents for the following sentences/phrases:

1 Go straight ahead.
2 Have a good time in Berlin.
3 Take the second street on the right.
4 Excuse me, please.
5 Yes, exactly.
6 Hotel Müller is on the left(-hand) side.
7 Not the second but the third street.
8 How do I get to Hotel Müller?
9 (That's) right.
10 Many thanks.

Übung 3C

There are many places you might wish to find the way to. If you have the recordings, listen to the words in addition to reading them and then do the exercise that follows.

masculine	*neuter*	*feminine*
a) **der Bahnhof**	b) **das Kino**	c) **die Post**
d) **der Parkplatz**	e) **das Theater**	f) **die Apotheke**
g) **der Flughafen**	h) **das Parkhaus**	i) **die Jugendherberge**
j) **der Konzertsaal**	k) **das Rathaus**	l) **die U-Bahn**
m) **der Dom**	n) **das Krankenhaus**	o) **die Bushaltestelle**
p) **der Hafen**	q) **das Reisebüro**	r) **die Oper**
s) **der Flohmarkt**	t) **das Kaufhaus**	u) **die Tankstelle**
v) **der Campingplatz**	w) **das Freibad/ Hallenbad**	x) **die Telefonzelle**
y) **der Zoo/Tiergarten**	z) **das Schloß**	ß) **die Bank**

Try *guessing* the meanings of some of the above words. Find German words above to match some or all of the English words below, entering the appropriate letters in the boxes.

1 bus-stop	☐	15 petrol/gas station	☐
2 town hall	☐	16 department store	☐
3 train station	☐	17 underground/subway	☐
4 camping site	☐	18 post office	☐
5 cinema	☐	19 car park/parking lot	☐

6 youth hostel ☐
7 hospital ☐
8 port/harbour ☐
9 airport ☐
10 cathedral ☐
11 castle ☐
12 concert hall ☐
13 travel agent ☐
14 fleamarket ☐
20 theatre ☐
21 multi-storey car park ☐
22 swimming bath ☐
23 chemist/drugstore ☐
24 phone/call box ☐
25 bank ☐
26 opera ☐
27 zoo ☐

Übung 3D

Here are some real addresses in Berlin. What do they refer to? Read through the English descriptions and try to match them with the German addresses (enter the appropriate letter after each of the numbers).

masculine

1____ der Kurfürstendamm
2____ der Reichstag
3____ Alexanderplatz
4____ Wannsee

neuter

5____ das Brandenburger Tor
6____ Schloß Charlottenburg
7____ das Pergamonmuseum
8____ das Operncafé

feminine

9____ die Philharmonie
10____ die Humboldt-Universität
11____ die Pfaueninsel
12____ die Nikolaikirche

(a) Berlin's best-known monument, seen on publicity material for the city.
(b) Berlin's oldest building, a 13th century church.
(c) Completed in 1894, this 'house of parliament' was set alight in 1933.
(d) A large lake in south west Berlin.
(e) An idyllic island, named after its peacocks.
(f) A modern concert hall, home of the Berliner Philharmonisches Orchester.
(g) The oldest of Berlin's universities but given this new name in 1949.
(h) A 17th century palace/castle in west Berlin.
(i) West Berlin's most distinguished boulevard.
(j) A square: gave its name to a novel, got its name from a Russian tsar.

(k) Contains a magnificent collection of antiquities.
(l) A rebuilt version of the Princesses' Palace, near an opera house and open for refreshments.

Preposition: zu

When we last met **zu**, it meant '@', as in

Fünf Briefmarken *zu* zwanzig Pfennig kosten eine Mark.

Zu also means 'to' in many contexts. **Zum** and **zur** are shortened forms of **zu dem** and **zu der**.

	'How do I get to the ...?' can therefore be		
either	**Wie komme ich *zum* ...?**	or	***zu dem***
or	**Wie komme ich *zur* ...?**	or	***zu der***

Whether you use **zum** or **zur** depends on the gender of the noun you wish to refer to:

masculine and neuter			*feminine*
***der* Bahnhof**	→	***zum* Bahnhof**	***die* Post** → ***zur* Post**
***das* Hotel**	→	***zum* Hotel**	

Here are two alternative ways of asking the way:

Wie komme ich zur Post?	or	**Zur Post, bitte?**
Wie komme ich zum Bahnhof?	or	**Zum Bahnhof, bitte?**
Wie komme ich zum Hotel?	or	**Zum Hotel, bitte?**

Übung 3E

Write out all the enquiries in full in German.

1 **Entschuldigung! Zum** [Brandenburg Gate], **bitte?**
2 **Zum** [theatre], **bitte?**
3 **Zur** [youth hostel], **bitte?**
4 **Entschuldigen Sie! Wie komme ich zur** [underground/subway]**?**
5 **Wie komme ich zum** [travel agent]**?**
6 **Wie komme ich zum** [airport]**?**
7 **Wie komme ich zur** [bus stop]**?**
8 **Zur** [opera], **bitte?**

Übung 3F

Do the same with these: **Entschuldigen Sie . . .**

1 **Wie komme ich** [to the museum]?
2 **Wie komme ich** [to the post office]?
3 **Wie komme ich** [to the airport]?
4 **Wie komme ich** [to the chemist/drugstore]?
5 **Wie komme ich** [to the Brandenburg Gate]?
6 **Wie komme ich** [to the telephone kiosk]?
7 **Wie komme ich** [to the underground/subway]?
8 **Wie komme ich** [to the Pergamonmuseum]?
9 **Wie komme ich** [to the department store]?
10 **Wie komme ich** [to the youth hostel]?

Questions and commands

Although in spoken German questions and commands sound very different, in written German they often look the same. Whether **Gehen Sie zum Bahnhof** ('Go you to the station') is a question ('Are you going to . . .?') or command ('Go to . . .!') is made clear only by the punctuation, so watch out for the question-mark or, for commands, an exclamation-mark or full-stop.

Übung 3G

In spoken German a clear distinction is made through intonation (tone of voice): rising intonation for questions, falling for commands. For the following exercise you need the recording. Listen to the sentences below, repeat them and decide whether the sentence is a question (?) or command (!). Write ! or ? as appropriate at the end of each sentence.

1 **Nehmen Sie die dritte Straße rechts . . .**
2 **Die dritte Straße rechts . . .**
3 **Die dritte Straße rechts . . .**
4 **Nehmen Sie Milch oder Zitrone . . .**
5 **Nehmen Sie Milch . . .**
6 **Gehen Sie zum Alexanderplatz . . .**
7 **Gehen Sie zum Kurfürstendamm . . .**
8 **Kaufen Sie einen Stadtplan . . .**
9 **Kaufen Sie zwei Stadtpläne . . .**

10 **Nehme ich die erste Straße rechts . . .**
11 **Nehmen Sie die dritte Straße rechts . . .**
12 **Entschuldigen Sie bitte . . .**
13 **Oh, entschuldigen Sie . . .**
14 **Gehen Sie zum Bahnhof . . .**
15 **Gehen Sie zum Bahnhof . . .**
16 **Gehen Sie geradeaus . . .**
17 **Gehen Sie geradeaus . . .**

Wo . . .?

Instead of saying	(a) How do I get to . . .?
you could of course say	(b) Where is . . .?
or	(c) Where is the (nearest) . . .? e.g.

			masculine		*neuter*
(a)	**Wie komme ich**	***zum***	**Parkplatz?**	***zum***	**Parkhaus?**
(b)	**Wo ist**	***der***	**Parkplatz?**	***das***	**Parkhaus?**
(c)	**Wo ist**	***der nächste***	**Parkplatz?**	***das nächste***	**Parkhaus?**

			feminine
(a)	**Wie komme ich**	***zur***	**Apotheke?**
(b)	**Wo ist**	***die***	**Apotheke?**
(c)	**Wo ist**	***die nächste***	**Apotheke?**

Übung 3H

Say and write out the following sentences in German:

1 **Wo ist** [the Kurfürstendamm]**?**
2 **Wo ist** [the airport]**?**
3 **Wo ist** [the youth hostel]**?**
4 **Wo ist** [the Pergamon Museum]**?**
5 **Wo ist** [the flea market]**?**
6 **Wo ist** [the harbour]**?**

More tentatively, you might ask:

	masculine	*neuter*	*feminine*
Wo ist (hier)	***ein*** **Parkplatz?**	***ein*** **Parkhaus?**	***eine*** **Apotheke?**

Übung 3J

Say and write the following sentences in German:

1 **Wo ist hier** [a phone/call box]**?**
2 **Wo ist hier** [a petrol/gas station]**?**
3 **Wo ist hier** [a cinema]**?**
4 **Wo ist hier** [a camping site]**?**
5 **Wo ist hier** [the nearest hotel]**?**
6 **Wo ist hier** [the nearest post office]**?**
7 **Wo ist hier** [the nearest station]**?**
8 **Wo ist hier** [the nearest swimming bath]**?**

Ordinal numbers 1st–10th

First, second, third, etc. in German generally function like adjectives in front of nouns and therefore need appropriate endings. The general rule for forming an ordinal number is:

cardinal + **t** + ending   e.g. **die zweite (zwei+t+e) Tasse.**
the second cup

The basic form, to which endings have to be added, of the ordinal numbers 1st–10th is listed below. Exceptions to the general rule are indicated in italic.

cardinal	*ordinal*
ein(s)	***erst-*** [+ ending]
zwei	**zweit-**
drei	***dritt-***
vier	**viert-**
fünf	**fünft-**
sechs	**sechst-**
sieben	***siebt-*** (less often: **siebent-**)
acht	***acht-***
neun	**neunt-**
zehn	**zehnt-**

Übung 3K

Read through the above list several times, then cover up the ordinals. Write down the ordinal form of each. Then uncover and check.

A dot after a cardinal number in German indicates that it is to be read as an ordinal

e.g.	**die 6. Straße**	=	**die sechst*e* Straße**
	der 3. Mann	=	**der dritt*e* Mann**
	Henry VIII.	=	**Heinrich der Acht*e***
	Elizabeth II.	=	**Elisabeth die Zweit*e***
	die 2. Tasse Tee	=	**die zweit*e* Tasse Tee**

Übung 3L

Re-write the following phrases, using words for the ordinals. All your ordinals should *here* have the ending ***-e*** (although this is not always the case).

1 das 1. Hotel
2 der 5. Zoo
3 der 3. Parkplatz
4 die 7. Jugendherberge
5 das 4. Kaufhaus
6 der 9. Bahnhof
7 die 10. Apotheke
8 die 8. Tankstelle
9 das 6. Reisebüro
10 der 2. Konzertsaal

Cardinal numbers 0–19

0 null
1 ein(s)
2 zwei
3 drei
4 vier
5 fünf
6 sechs
7 sieben
8 acht
9 neun
10 *zehn*
11 *elf*
12 *zwölf*
13 dreizehn
14 vierzehn
15 fünfzehn
16 *sech*zehn
17 *sieb*zehn
18 achtzehn
19 neunzehn

Übung 3M

Add up the numbers in each of the three columns below, and write the answers in full in German.

(a)	(b)	(c)
siebzehn	**dreizehn**	**elf**
sechzehn	**achtzehn**	**fünfzehn**
zwölf	**vierzehn**	**neunzehn**
________	________	________
________	________	________

Übung 3N

When German telephone numbers – **Telefonnummern** – are spoken, the digits are often given in pairs, as indicated below. Write the appropriate phone numbers in digits.

(a) **null–siebenundsiebzig–zwanzig–sechzehn** _ __ __ __
(b) **fünf–elf–achtzehn–achtundreißig** _ __ __ __
(c) **sieben–zweiundsiebzig–siebzehn–siebenundvierzig** _ __ __ __
(d) **eins–sechsundvierzig–fünfunddreißig–null neun** _ __ __ __
(e) **drei–vierundsechzig–neunzig–zwölf** _ __ __ __

Übung 3P

Write down your home and office telephone numbers or two other phone numbers important – **wichtig!** – for you, and practise them out loud in German until you can say them quickly without having to think!

Meine erste wichtige Telefonnummer ist:
Meine zweite wichtige Telefonnummer ist:

Übung 3Q

In the dialogue below you are asking a friendly young woman – **eine freundliche junge Berlinerin** – the way to the nearest bus stop. Construct and read out aloud your own dialogues using the same basic text but changing the words in bold as necessary so that each of your dialogues gets you to where you need to go, i.e.

die nächste Bushaltestelle [sign: Bus]
die nächste U-Bahn-Station [sign: U]
der Flohmarkt [sign: Flohmarkt]
der Bahnhof [sign: DB = Deutsche Bahn, German Rail]
die nächste Bank [Eurocheque sign]
die nächste Sparkasse [sign: dotted S = municipal savings bank]
die nächste Post [sign: posthorn]
die nächste Apotheke [sign: A]

das Rathaus [sign: Berlin bear = the city's coat of arms]
die nächste S-Bahn-Station [sign: S]
die nächste Taxi-Stand [sign: taxi]
eine Toilette [sign: WC]

The locations are all indicated on the following plan.

SIE: Entschuldigen Sie, bitte!
BERLINERIN: Ja?
SIE: Wo ist **die nächste Bushaltestelle?**
BERLINERIN: Gehen Sie hier geradeaus!
SIE: Hier geradeaus?
BERLINERIN: Richtig. Nehmen Sie dann die **erste** Straße **rechts**!
SIE: Die **erste** Straße rechts?

BERLINERIN: Ganz richtig. **Die Bushaltestelle** ist auf der **linken** Seite.

SIE: Also: die **erste** Straße rechts auf der **linken** Seite?

BERLINERIN: Ja, genau.

SIE: Vielen Dank.

BERLINERIN: Bitte schön. Viel Spaß in Berlin!

SIE: Danke schön. Auf Wiedersehen!

BERLINERIN: Auf Wiedersehen!

4 Zimmer mit Dusche

A place to stay

Language activities

- booking accommodation
- specifying dates and months
- giving personal information

Language focus

- 'How's' your name (etc.)?
- adjectives + nouns
- *my* and *your*
- numbers 11th to 99th

Learning strategies

- finding genders in longer nouns
- scrambling a text

Text 4

Montag nachmittag (2)

You have found your way to Hotel Müller and ask the receptionist for a quiet room. She asks you whether you want a single or double room and if you want it with bath or with shower. You plump for the cheaper. You say how long you want to stay and give the dates. The receptionist fills in a registration form with your name, nationality, passport number and place of residence, and asks you how you wish to pay. You sign the form, are given your room number and key and are told how to get to your room on the first (US: second) floor: either up the stairs or via the lift (US: elevator). You have a very heavy suitcase, so you take the lift.

SIE:	Guten Tag!
EMPFANGSDAME:	Guten Tag!
SIE:	Haben Sie ein ruhiges[1] Zimmer frei?[2]
EMPFANGSDAME:	Möchten Sie ein Einzelzimmer oder ein Doppelzimmer?
SIE:	Ein Einzelzimmer, bitte.
EMPFANGSDAME:	Möchten Sie mit Bad oder mit Dusche?
SIE:	Was kostet ein Zimmer mit Bad?
EMPFANGSDAME:	Mit Bad DM 80,- und mit Dusche DM 72, -.
SIE:	Ich nehme das Zimmer mit Dusche.
EMPFANGSDAME:	Für wie lange,[3] bitte?
SIE:	Für fünf Nächte[4] – bis zum[5] 11. Mai.
EMPFANGSDAME:	Ja, das geht.[6]
SIE:	Schön.
EMPFANGSDAME:	Also von heute[7] – vom 6. Mai – bis zum 11. Mai.
SIE:	Ganz richtig.
EMPFANGSDAME:	Wie[8] ist Ihr[9] Name, bitte?
SIE:	Peter Bennett. Mein[10] Nachname ist Bennett: B-E-NN-E-TT, mein Vorname[11] is Peter: P-E-T-E-R.
EMPFANGSDAME:	Woher kommen Sie?[12]
SIE:	Ich bin[13] Engländer.[14]
EMPFANGSDAME:	Wie ist Ihre Paßnummer,[15] bitte?
SIE:	Meine Paßnummer ist 22 45 12 13 E.
EMPFANGSDAME:	Wo wohnen Sie?[16]
SIE:	Ich wohne in York: Y-O-R-K.
EMPFANGSDAME:	Und wie möchten Sie zahlen?[17]
SIE:	Mit Kreditkarte.
EMPFANGSDAME:	Ihre Unterschrift,[18] bitte.
EMPFANGSDAME:	Vielen Dank. Das ist Ihr Zimmerschlüssel. Ihr Zimmer ist Nummer 18 – im ersten[19] Stock. Die Treppe ist geradeaus. Haben Sie viel[20] Gepäck?
SIE:	Ich habe einen sehr schweren[21] Koffer.
EMPFANGSDAME:	Dann nehmen Sie hier links den Fahrstuhl![22] Zimmer 18 ist das vierte Zimmer auf der rechten Seite.

Notes

1 **ruhig** = 'quiet, peaceful'
2 'free'

3 'for how long?'
4 the singular would be **eine Nacht**
5 '(up) until the'
6 literally: 'That goes = that's OK, we can manage that'
7 'today'
8 literally: 'How (= what) is your name?'
9 'your'
10 'my'
11 **Vorname/Nachname**: as free-standing prepositions, **vor** means 'before' and **nach** 'after'
12 'Where do you come from?' You might also (more formally) be asked **Wie ist ihre Nationalität?**
13 'I am'. Note that German does not normally use **ein/eine** before nouns of nationality
14 literally: 'Englishman'. A woman would say **Engländerin**. For further nationalities, see **Lektion acht**
15 the letter **ß** is not used in Switzerland where **Paß** would be spelt **Pass** [see Pronunciation reference]
16 'Where do you live?' On the actual form, the noun **Wohnort** appears = 'place of residence'
17 'how would you like to pay?' Both **zahlen** and **bezahlen** are used
18 'signature'. A verb could have been used instead here, viz. **Unterschreiben Sie, bitte!** – 'Please sign'
19 Germany uses the same numbering system for floors/storeys as does e.g. the UK: first floor is the floor above ground floor
20 'much, a lot of'
21 'heavy'
22 there are three possibilities here in German: **der Fahrstuhl**, **der Aufzug**, **der Lift**

If you were booking a room over the phone rather than in person, you might be asked for your credit card number and the card's expiry date

EMPFANGSDAME:	Und wie ist Ihre Kreditkartennummer, bitte?
SIE:	4552 9118 5727 6336.
EMPFANGSDAME:	Bis wann ist Ihre Karte gültig? *Until when is your card valid?* [i.e. *What is the expiry date?*]
SIE:	Bis Oktober neunundneunzig.

Übung 4A

Find equivalents in Text 4 for the following nouns. Write them, each with a capital letter, in three columns and preceded by **der**, **das** or **die**. When you have finished, your German nouns should appear in alphabetical order in each column.

masculine	*neuter*	*feminine*
thanks	bath	shower
Englishman	double room	receptionst [female]
lift	single room	credit card
suitcase	luggage	night
May	room	nationality
surname		number
name		passport number
floor, storey		side
first name		stairs [singular in German]
place of residence		signature
room key		

Übung 4B

Find German equivalents in Text 4 for the following sentences/ phrases.

1 Where do you come from?
2 Where do you live?
3 How would you like to pay?
4 Do you have a quiet room free?
5 My surname is . . .
6 Your signature, please.
7 I have a very heavy suitcase.
8 This is your room key.
9 The stairs are straight ahead.
10 Would you like a room with bath or shower?

Compounds

Words are more often written together in German than in English to produce compounds. English is more likely to keep words separate or use hyphens to connect them, e.g.

room key	double room	room number
Zimmerschlüssel	**Doppelzimmer**	**Zimmernummer**

The gender of a compound noun in German is determined by the *last* word in the compound.

masculine	*neuter*	*feminine*
der Schlüssel	***das Zimmer***	***die Nummer***
der* Zimmer*schlüssel	***das* Doppel*zimmer***	***die* Zimmer*nummer***

Question words

We have now met three **W-** words: ***Was? Wie? Wo?***
The contexts have been, e.g.

1	***Was* kostet ein Zimmer mit Bad?**	What does a room with bath cost?
2	***Wo* wohnen Sie?**	Where do you live?
3	***Wie* komme ich zum Hotel?**	How do I get to the hotel?

On the basis of the above examples it is tempting to equate **Was?–Wo?–Wie?** with 'What?–Where?–How?' However, **Wie?** is frequently used in German not only where English uses 'How?' but also where we might say 'What?' e.g.

4	***Wie* ist Ihr Name, bitte?**	What (literally: 'How') is your name, please?

In the following exercise, it is this latter use of **Wie?** that we are targeting.

Übung 4C

Say and write the question in German. Then write down its answer in figures. When you check your answers, pay particular attention to spelling: each of your questions should contain four words only, and three of the four words need to be written with a capital letter!

1Q What is your credit card number?
1A **vier fünf fünf zwei–neun eins eins acht–fünf sieben zwei sieben–sechs drei drei sechs**
2Q What is your telephone number?
2A **null–vierundfünfzig–neunundachtzig–einunddreißig–neunzehn**

3Q What is your passport number?
3A **zweiundzwanzig–fünfundvierzig–zwölf–dreizehn–E**

Adjectives

If we wish to describe any noun by putting an adjective in front of it, we have to give the adjective an ending. What happens to adjectives in front of masculine nouns was described in **Lektion zwei**. If we want to describe neuter nouns e.g. **Bad**, and feminine nouns e.g. **Dusche**, we have to use different endings. After **ein** this neuter ending is **-es**, after **eine** the feminine ending is **-e**:

subject	*verb*	*object*			
Ich	**möchte**	***ein***	**heiß*es***	**Bad**	(I'd like a hot bath)
Ich	**möchte**	***eine***	**kalt*e***	**Dusche**	(I'd like a cold shower)

Unlike the masculine pattern, these endings stay the same whether the noun is the subject (in the nominative case) or the object (accusative) of a sentence:

	masculine article	adjective	*neuter* article	adjective	*feminine* article	adjective
subject nominative	**ein**	*kleiner**	***ein***	***kleines***	***eine***	***kleine***
object accusative	**einen**	**kleinen**	***ein***	***kleines***	***eine***	***kleine***

* The 'missing' nominative (the masculine in the above table) is introduced in **Lektion acht**.

In context, our set of three 'accusatives' therefore looks like this:

masculine	**Ich möchte *einen***	**klein*en***	**Stadtplan**	(a small city map)
neuter	**Ich möchte *ein***	**ruhig*es***	**Zimmer**	(a quiet room)
feminine	**Ich möchte *eine***	**groß*e***	**Ansichtskarte**	(a large postcard)

Note In general, it is not essential to get these endings right to be understood, but it is worth trying to learn them because:

(a) it can actually be done – as not only native German speakers have proved;
(b) you will then be understood with little extra effort on the part of your listeners;
(c) even if you get the endings right only occasionally, you will be admired by native German speakers: they are very flattered by genuine efforts to learn their language!

Übung 4D

Slot the following adjectives, using the correct endings, into the sentences below. Use a different – but plausible – adjective in each slot.

dritt–freundlich–groß–gut–klein–nett–ruhig–schwarzweiß–schwer–stark–zweit
third–friendly–large–good–small–nice–quiet–black & white–heavy–strong–second

1 **Möchten Sie einen _______ oder einen. _______ Stadtplan?**
2 **Ich möchte einen _______ Kaffee.**
3 **Nehmen Sie die _______, nein, die _______ Straße rechts!**
4 **_______ Tag!**
5 **Haben Sie ein _______ Zimmer frei?**
6 **Ich habe einen sehr _______ Koffer.**
7 **Haben Sie eine _______ Ansichtskarte vom Brandenburger Tor?**
8 **Hotel Müller ist ein _______ Hotel.**
9 **Die _______ Empfangsdame wohnt in Charlottenburg.**

Prepositions

			masculine and neuter nouns		
In Text 3 we met	**zu**	in the context of	**zu*m***	(= **zu dem**)	**Hotel**
In Text 4 we met	**von**	→	**vo*m***	(= **von dem**)	**sechsten* Mai**
	in	→	**i*m***	(= **in dem**)	**ersten* Stock**

		feminine nouns		
In Text 3 we met **zu**	in the context of	**zur**	**(= zu der)**	**Post**
auf	→	**auf** ***der***		**rechten* Seite**

* Note that these words have the ending **-en** here. This pattern is put in context in **Lektion sieben.**

Übung 4E

Our complete list of prepositions to date is **von/vom**; **nach**; **zu/zum/zur**; **bis zum**; **mit**; **auf**; **in/im**; **für**. Slot the correct preposition into each of the following sentences. We have provided an equivalent English preposition to 'translate' in each case, but note that a given English preposition is not always translated by one and the same preposition in German.

1 **Was kostet eine Postkarte** [to] ______ **Großbritannien?**
2 **Ich möchte zwei Briefmarken** [@] ______ **achtzig Pfennig.**
3 **Wie komme ich** [to the] ______ **Hotel Müller**?
4 **Das Hotel ist** [on the] ______ **linken Seite.**
5 **Möchten Sie ein Zimmer** [with] ______ **Bad oder** [with] ______ **Dusche**?
6 **Ich möchte ein Einzelzimmer** [for] ______ **fünf Nächte** [until the] ______ **11. Mai.**
7 [From] **heute** [until the] ______ **6. Mai.**
8 **Ihr Zimmer ist** [in/on the] ______ **ersten Stock.**
9 **Wie möchten Sie zahlen?** [With/by] ______ **Kreditkarte.**
10 **Entschuldigen Sie, bitte! Wie komme ich** [to the] ______ **U-Bahn**?

Ordinal numbers 11th–99th

To form the ordinal number:

add **-t-** to the cardinal for nos. 11 to 19 (**elf** ***bis*** **neunzehn**)
add **-st-** to the cardinal for nos. 20 to 99 (**zwanzig** ***bis*** **neunundneunzig**)

	cardinal	+	e.g.	*ordinal*
	elf	**-t-**	**vom**	**elf*t*en**
	zwölf	**-t-**	**vom**	**zwölf*t*en**
	dreizehn	**-t-**	**vom**	**dreizehn*t*en**
bis	**neunzehn**	**-t-**	**vom**	**neunzehn*t*en**
	zwanzig	**-st-**	**vom**	**zwanzig*st*en**
	einundzwanzig	**-st-**	**vom**	**einundzwanzig*st*en**
bis	**neunundneunzig**	**-st-**	**vom**	**neunundneunzig*st*en**

The ordinal almost always needs an ending after the ***-t*** or ***-st***, but what that ending is depends on the context. In the table above, endings after ***vom*** are given as an example.

Months

Plural **die *Monate***
Singular **der *Monat*** – all the months are *masculine*
In context **Ich möchte ein ruhiges Zimmer ... *vom* vierzehn*t*en** (14.) ***bis zum*** **achtundzwanzig*st*en** (28.) ***Mai***.

Januar	**Februar**	**März**	**April**
Mai	**Juni**	**Juli**	**August**
September	**Oktober**	**November**	**Dezember**

Übung 4F

Supply the missing dates (in words, not figures).

Ich möchte ...

1 **ein ruhiges Zimmer für zwei Nächte vom zweiten Januar bis zum ...**
2 **ein Einzelzimmer für vier Nächte vom vierzehnten Februar bis zum ...**
3 **ein Zimmer für sieben Nächte vom sechsundzwanzigsten März bis zum ...**
4 **ein schönes Zimmer für neun Nächte vom neunten Mai bis zum ...**
5 **ein Doppelzimmer für eine Nacht vom neunzehnten Juni bis zum ...**
6 **ein Einzelzimmer für eine Nacht vom einunddreißigsten Juli bis zum ...**

7 **ein ruhiges Zimmer für zwei Monate vom ersten September bis zum . . .**
8 **ein Einzelzimmer für drei Nächte vom achtzehnten Oktober bis zum . . .**
9 **ein Doppelzimmer für einen Monat vom zwanzigsten November bis zum** . . .
10 **ein Zimmer für acht Nächte vom vierundzwanzigsten Dezember bis zum . . .**

Birthdays

If you want to say your birthday is *on the* first of July, you use **an dem**, or, more usually, the shortened form ***am*** – **am ersten Juli**. As in English, both the day and the month in German can also be expressed as an ordinal number, but in German you don't say 'on the first *of the* seventh', just 'on the first seventh' – **am ersten siebten**. Like ***der* Monat**, ***Geburtstag*** 'birthday' is a masculine noun.

Written	*Spoken*
Mein Geburtstag ist *am* 4. Juni.	**Mein Geburtstag ist am vier*ten* Juni.**
Mein Geburtstag ist *am* 4. 6.	**Mein Geburtstag ist am vier*ten* sechs*ten*.**

Übung 4G

Say the following pairs of sentences in German, i.e. giving the same date in two different ways. The second sentence of each pair can be checked in the Key.

1 **Mein Geburtstag ist am 12. August** ______ **ist am 12.8.**
2 **Mein Geburtstag ist am 7. September.** ______ **ist am 7.9.**
3 **Mein Geburtstag ist am 22. Oktober.** ______ **ist am 22.10.**
4 **Mein Geburtstag ist am 31. Dezember.** ______ **ist am 31.12.**
5 **Mein Geburtstag ist am 14. März.** ______ **ist am 14.3.**
6 **Mein Geburtstag ist am 30. April.** ______ **ist am 30.4.**
7 **Mein Geburtstag ist am 15. Juli.** ______ **ist am 15.7.**
8 **Mein Geburtstag ist am 10. Juni.** ______ **ist am 10.6.**
9 **Mein Geburtstag ist am 29. Februar.** ______ **ist am 29.2.**
10 **Mein Geburtstag ist am 19. November.** ______ **ist am 19.11.**
11 **Mein Geburtstag ist am 5. Mai.** ______ **ist am 5.5.**
12 **Mein Geburtstag ist am 1. Januar.** ______ **ist am 1.1.**

Übung 4H

Use the Key to **Übung 4G** to reverse the above exercise, e.g. if the Key reads: . . . **zwölften achten**

you say: ***Mein Geburtstag ist am* zwölften *August*.**

Übung 4J

Now try some 'real' birthdays! Starting with your own birthday, draw up a list of dates of birth you know, or feel you should know, and practise them in German until you no longer need to think about how to say them!

1 **Mein [eigener] Geburtstag ist am** ______
My [own] birthday
2 e.g. **Williams Geburtstag ist am** ______
3 e.g. **Marys Geburtstag ist am** ______

Personal pronouns

The ***possessive*** form of 'I' is 'my', of 'you' is 'your', or in German:

ich → ***mein***
Sie → ***Ihr***

Note that because **Sie** is written with a capital letter, **Ihr** must have one, too.

These possessive forms, like the indefinite article **ein**, are used in front of nouns and so they, too, sometimes need endings. We have met

Wie ist *Ihr* Name? — ***Mein* Nachname ist . . .**
Wie ist *Ihre* Paßnummer? — ***Meine* Paßnummer ist . . .**

Also, any adjectives which follow **mein** and **Ihr** need endings, just as adjectives do after **ein** etc. (see **Übung 2D**). Clearly, the easiest endings to remember in the table below are the FEMININE ones: they are all the same, so try to retain those first!

	masculine pronoun	adjective	*neuter* pronoun	adjective	*feminine* pronoun	adjective
subject nominative	**Ihr** **mein**	**eigen*er***	**Ihr** **mein**	**eigen*es***	**Ihr*e*** **mein*e***	**eigen*e*** (*own*)
object accusative	**Ihr*en*** **mein*en***	**eigen*en***	**Ihr** **mein**	**eigen*es***	**Ihr*e*** **mein*e***	**eigen*e*** (*own*)

Übung 4K

Let's return to the hotel. Try matching the following sentences/phrases.

1 **Für wie lange, bitte?**
2 **Möchten Sie ein Einzel- oder Doppelzimmer?**
3 **Für fünf Nächte.**
4 **Ja, das geht.**
5 **Wie ist Ihre Paßnummer?**
6 **Haben Sie ein ruhiges Zimmer?**
7 **Was kostet ein Zimmer mit Bad?**
8 **Ihr Zimmer ist Nummer achtzehn.**
9 **Ich nehme das Zimmer mit Dusche.**
10 **Im ersten Stock.**

A Do you have a quiet room
B What does a room with a bath cost?
C For how long, please?
D Your room is number eighteen.
E Would you like a single or double room?
F For five nights.
G On the first floor.
H I'll take the room with the shower.
J Yes, that's OK.
K What is your passport number?

Übung 4L

Read through (even better: listen to) Text 4 again before doing this next exercise. Then try to write out the conversation below in the original order without referring back. Finally, check your written version with the original.

SCRAMBLING A TEXT: A particularly convenient way of doing this sort of exercise is to photocopy the text, cut it up into sections, then mix and reassemble them e.g. on the kitchen table! You can, of course, do this usefully with *any* of the German texts in this book.

EMPFANGSDAME: Möchten Sie mit Bad oder mit Dusche?
SIE: Guten Tag!
EMPFANGSDAME: Ja, das geht.
SIE: Peter Bennett. Mein Nachname ist Bennett: B-E-NN-E-TT, mein Vorname ist Peter: P-E-T-E-R.
EMPFANGSDAME: Mit Bad DM 80,- und mit Dusche DM 72,-.
SIE: Haben Sie ein ruhiges Zimmer frei?
EMPFANGSDAME: Also von heute – vom 6. Mai – bis zum 11. Mai.
SIE: Meine Paßnummer ist 22 45 12 13 E.
EMPFANGSDAME: Möchten Sie ein Einzelzimmer oder ein Doppelzimmer?
SIE: Ich bin Engländer.
EMPFANGSDAME: Für wie lange, bitte?
SIE: Für fünf Nächte – bis zum 11. Mai.
EMPFANGSDAME: Wo wohnen Sie?
SIE: Ganz richtig.
EMPFANGSDAME: Guten Tag!
SIE: Was kostet ein Zimmer mit Bad?
EMPFANGSDAME: Und wie möchten Sie zahlen?
SIE: Schön.
EMPFANGSDAME: Wie ist Ihr Name, bitte?
SIE: Ich nehme das Zimmer mit Dusche.
EMPFANGSDAME: Woher kommen Sie?
SIE: Ich wohne in York – Y-O-R-K.
EMPFANGSDAME: Wie ist Ihre Paßnummer, bitte?
SIE: Mit Kreditkarte.
EMPFANGSDAME: Dann nehmen Sie hier links den Fahrstuhl! Zimmer 18 ist das vierte Zimmer auf der rechten Seite.
EMPFANGSDAME: Ihre Unterschrift, bitte.
SIE: Ich habe einen sehr schweren Koffer.
EMPFANGSDAME: Vielen Dank. Das ist Ihr Zimmerschlüssel. Ihr Zimmer ist Nummer 18 – im ersten Stock. Die Treppe ist geradeaus. Haben sie viel Gepäck?
SIE: Ein Einzelzimmer, bitte.

Übung 4M

Prove to yourself that you can now book a room in a German hotel.

1 You enter a hotel and enquire about a quiet, single room.
2 Say you want a room with a shower.
3 Ask about the price of the room.
4 You tell the receptionist you want it from the 29th of May to 1st of June.
5 You are told the room is no. 23 on the first floor on the right hand side: repeat the information given.
6 Say you have a heavy suitcase.
7 Ask whether they have a lift/elevator.

5 Rührei mit Schinken

Eating out

Language activities

- ordering a three-course meal
- expressing dis/satisfaction
- specifying dates with years

Language focus

- the past tense
- modal verbs
- present tense patterns
- numbers from 100

Learning strategies

- using the stem of a verb
- looking for irregular forms

Text 5

Montag abend

After a rest you go downstairs, via the reception desk, to the restaurant. The waiter greets you and asks where you want to sit – in the corner, in the centre of the room, or by the window. You prefer to sit by the window. He offers you a chair with the words **Bitte schön!** and hands you the menu. You decide on a French onion soup followed by scrambled egg and ham/bacon plus a mixed side-salad, one ingredient of which is 'green beans'. You decide you would like to have wine – white rather than red, dry rather than sweet – with the meal, and you order a quarter of a litre rather than a whole bottle. You confirm that you are a resident ('a hotel guest') for the meal to be charged to your hotel bill. After initially thinking you do not have your room number, you give the waiter the number as indicated on your room key. After you have finished the soup and the main course the waiter returns to ask whether you enjoyed the meal and whether you would like a dessert. As is often the case in Germany, the choice of desserts is rather limited: you reject the ice cream and go for the fresh fruit salad with cream, and you order coffee. The waiter lets you know your order will be brought to you immediately.

EMPFANG:[1] Guten Abend!
SIE: Guten Abend! Wo ist das Restaurant,[2] bitte?
EMPFANG: Gehen Sie hier links, dann geradeaus. Es[3] ist auf der rechten Seite.
SIE: Danke schön.
EMPFANG: Bitte schön.

OBER:[4] Guten Abend! Für eine Person?[5] Wo möchten Sie sitzen?[6] In der Ecke, in der Mitte, oder vielleicht[7] am Fenster?
SIE: Ja, lieber[8] am Fenster.
OBER: Hier, bitte schön.[9]
SIE: Danke schön.
OBER: Hier ist die Speisekarte.[10]

OBER: Haben Sie schon[11] gewählt?[12]
SIE: Ja, ich möchte eine französische[13] Zwiebelsuppe, danach[14] Rührei[15] mit Schinken – und einen grünen Bohnensalat dazu.
OBER: Einmal[16] die französische Zwiebelsuppe, dann Rührei mit Schinken und einen grünen Bohnensalat.
SIE: Ja, richtig.
OBER: Möchten Sie etwas[17] dazu[18] trinken?
SIE: Wein, bitte.
OBER: Einen Weißwein oder einen Rotwein?
SIE: Weißwein, bitte.
OBER: Wir haben einen trockenen Sylvaner[19] und einen lieblichen[20] Riesling.
SIE: Ich nehme den[21] trockenen.
OBER: Ein Viertel oder eine Flasche?
SIE: Ein Viertel, bitte.

OBER:	Sind Sie[22] Hotelgast?
SIE:	Ja, ich wohne im Hotel.
OBER:	Wie ist Ihre Zimmernummer?
SIE:	Wie bitte?[23]
OBER:	Ihre Zimmernummer?
SIE:	Oh Entschuldigung! – ich weiß[24] nicht . . .
OBER:	Haben Sie Ihren Zimmerschlüssel? Die Nummer steht[25] auf dem Schlüssel.
SIE:	Ach ja![26] Das stimmt.[27] Zimmer 18.
OBER:	Vielen Dank.

OBER:	Hat es[28] (Ihnen) geschmeckt?[29]
SIE:	Danke, ja, ausgezeichnet![30]
OBER:	Möchten Sie einen Nachtisch?
SIE:	Was haben Sie heute?
OBER:	Wir haben gemischtes[31] Eis oder frischen[32] Obstsalat.
SIE:	Ich nehme den Obstsalat.
OBER:	Mit oder ohne Sahne?
SIE:	Mit Sahne, bitte. Und ein Kännchen Kaffee dazu.
OBER:	Kommt sofort.[33]

Notes

1 literally: 'reception' (masculine gender): implies a person, but the sex of the person is not stated here

2 pronounced more or less in the French manner without sounding the final **-t**

3 **Es** = 'it', referring here to 'restaurant' which in German is a neuter noun

4 **Herr Ober!** is the standard form of address for a waiter (**Kellner** or **Ober**), with **Fräulein!** the equivalent for a waitress (**Kellnerin**). Outside this professional context, **Fräulein** is used for 'Miss' but it is impolite to use it without the person's name attached

5 note the feminine gender: the gender is feminine, whether the person is male or female

6 'sit'

7 'perhaps'

8 'preferably, rather'

9 the phrase in this context roughly means 'Here you are', i.e. you are offered a table/chair

10 menu. The (regular) verb **speisen** can mean 'to dine'

11 literally: 'already'. The very common word **schon** does little more here than lengthen the sentence

12 literally: 'Have you (already) chosen?' i.e. 'Are you ready to order?' The infinitive form of the verb (regular) is **wählen**
13 French: adjectives of nationality are not spelt with capital letters in German
14 'after that, thereafter'
15 literally: 'stir-' or 'mix-', i.e. 'scrambled egg'. 'Egg' = **das Ei**, plural **die Eier**
16 literally: once, i.e. 'for one'. It may seem superfluous for the waiter to say this when there is obviously only one person at the table, but it is nevertheless common
17 'something'
18 'with it, therewith'
19 **Sylvaner** and **Riesling** are varieties of grape
20 **lieblich** suggests not *dry* (**trocken**) without being too *sweet* (**süß**)
21 just as **ein** (nominative masculine) → **einen** (accusative), **der** (masc.) → **den**
22 'are you?'
23 the easiest polite way of asking for a repeat = 'I beg your pardon? Sorry?', etc.
24 'know'. The dictionary form of the verb (irregular) is **wissen**
25 literally: 'stands', i.e. 'is'. The infinitive form of the verb (irregular) is **stehen**
26 a common expression of surprise, confirmation or recognition
27 a set use of the (regular) verb **stimmen**. **Das stimmt** = 'That's right/correct'
28 another common set phrase, meaning 'did you enjoy the meal?' Literally: 'Has it to you tasted?'
30 literally: 'excellent/excellently', i.e. 'very much'
31 **gemischt** is literally: 'mixed', i.e. probably three 'scoops': vanilla, chocolate and strawberry
32 **frisch** = 'fresh'
33 literally: '(it, the order) comes immediately'. This is very much a set phrase amongst German-speaking waiters and can be interpreted in the context as 'Expect me back in the not too distant future'

Übung 5A

Find equivalents in Text 5 for the following nouns. Write them, each with a capital letter, in three columns and preceded by **der**, **das** or **die**. When you have finished, your German nouns should appear in alphabetical order in each column.

masculine	*neuter*	*feminine*
evening	ice cream	corner
bean salad	window	apology (sorry!)
thanks [singular]	pot [coffee]	bottle
hotel resident	restaurant	middle
coffee	scrambled egg	number
dessert	quarter (litre)	person
fruit salad	room	cream
red wine		side
ham/bacon		menu
white wine		room number
room key		onion soup

Übung 5B

Find German equivalents from Text 5 for the following sentences/phrases.

1 It [the restaurant] is on the right.
2 Preferably by the window.
3 Here is the menu.
4 I don't know.
5 Did you enjoy the meal?
6 I'll take the fruit salad.
7 Are you ready to order?
8 That's right.
9 The number's on the key.
10 Would you like a dessert?
11 I beg your pardon?

Verbs: modals etc.

Modal verbs – and their relatives – are extremely common in English and German. The English equivalents of the German modals cover meanings such as

> would, should, could, can, may, might, must, would like/want (to), ought to

These verbs often need another verb in its infinitive form to complete the sense of a sentence, e.g. 'go' or 'to go' in the following sentences:

I would/should/could/can/may/might/must	→	go.
I would like/want/ought	→	to go.

If the infinitive is felt to be 'obvious', it may be omitted, hence e.g. (a) is more usual than (b):

(a) Would you like	a cup of tea?
(b) Would you like to have/drink	a cup of tea?

In general terms, the same applies in German.

Our one German modal to date is **möchten**, which we have met in sentences such as:

Ich möchte eine Tasse Tee.	I'd like a cup of tea.
Möchten Sie sonst noch etwas?	Would you like anything else?
Möchten Sie einen kleinen oder einen großen Stadtplan?	Would you like a small or a large plan of the city?
Wie möchten Sie zahlen?	How would you like to pay?
Wo möchten Sie sitzen?	Where would you like to sit?
Was möchten Sie trinken?	What would you like to drink?

Note that in the **Wie?**, **Was?**, **Wo?** examples above, the infinitives are at the end of the sentences, as indeed they would be in an English equivalent, e.g.

Wo	**möchten Sie**	**sitzen?**
Where	would you like	to sit?

However, when there is no question word, the German word order is often different from English: in German, even in statements the infinitive appears at the end of the sentence:

Ich möchte	**am**	**Fenster**	**sitzen.**
I would like	at the	window	to sit.

A rough and ready rule of German word order is: infinitives 'live' at the ends of sentences!

Übung 5C

How would you say the following in German?

1 I would like a room with (a) bath.
2 Would you like to sit at the window?
3 Would you like a single room or a double room?
4 Would you like to take a big or a small map?
5 I would like two stamps @ 80 Pfennig (each).

6 Would you like to order coffee?
7 I would like to pay by ['with'] credit card.
8 I would like the dry wine.
9 I would like a strong [**stark-**] black [**schwarz-**] coffee.
10 Would you like the fresh fruit salad?

Before looking up the answers in the Key, check that

- you have used **möcht*e*** with **ich** and **möcht*en*** with **Sie**;
- you have written all the nouns with a capital letter;
- the adjective endings match the gender of the noun;
- any infinitives are at the end of their sentences.

Verbs: talking about the past

The most common way of talking about the past in English and German is to use a *past tense* of the verb. In spoken German, the most common past tense by far is called the *perfect* tense. It usually consists of a form of the verb **haben** (as an auxiliary, i.e. 'helping out' verb) + a past participle of the verb that carries the notion you wish to convey, e.g.

				past participle
	Haben Sie	**schon**		**gewählt?**
	Have you	already		chosen?
	Ich habe	**schon**	**Eis**	**gewählt.**
	I have	already	ice cream	chosen
	Hat es	**(Ihnen)**		**geschmeckt?**
Literally:	Has it	to you		tasted?

Note that past participles, like infinitives, usually 'live' at the end of German sentences.

The German equivalent of 'Have you enjoyed/Did you enjoy your meal' literally means 'Has it tasted (to/for you)?' The 'to/for you' = **Ihnen** is optional, as is the 'to/for me' = **mir** in a reply. Here are some possible replies, all in the perfect tense, ranging from wholly positive to the extremely negative:

		Hat es (Ihnen) (gut)		**geschmeckt?**	
++++	**Ja,**	**es hat (mir)**	***ausgezeichnet***	**geschmeckt**	'excellent'
+++	**Ja,**	**es hat (mir)**	***sehr gut***	**geschmeckt**	'very good'
++	**Ja,**	**es hat (mir)**	***gut***	**geschmeckt**	'good'

+	**Ja,**	**es hat (mir)**		**geschmeckt**	
–	**Nein,**	**es hat (mir)**	***nicht gut***	**geschmeckt**	'not good'
– –	**Nein,**	**es hat (mir)**	***nicht***	**geschmeckt**	'not'
– – –	**Nein,**	**es hat (mir)**	***gar nicht gut***	**geschmeckt**	'not at all good'
– – – –	**Nein,**	**es hat (mir)**	***gar nicht***	**geschmeckt**	'not at all'

Übung 5D

Express your likes and dislikes emphatically out loud, using the faces as cues! Follow the sentence pattern given in the answer to the question in 1:

1 **Hat Ihnen das Rührei geschmeckt?**
Ja, das Rührei hat mir *gut* geschmeckt.
2 **Hat Ihnen der Bohnensalat geschmeckt?**
3 **Hat Ihnen das Eis geschmeckt?**
4 **Hat Ihnen der Wein geschmeckt?**
5 **Hat Ihnen die französische Suppe geschmeckt?**
6 **Hat Ihnen die Sachertorte geschmeckt?**
7 **Hat Ihnen der Kaffee geschmeckt?**
8 **Hat Ihnen die Schwarzwälder Kirschtorte geschmeckt?**

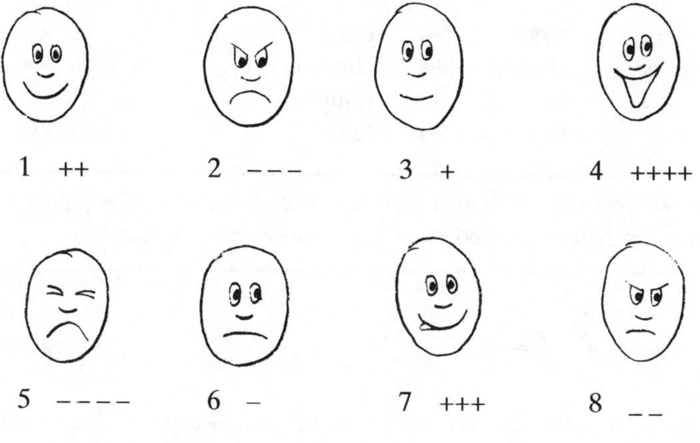

Übung 5E

How would you say in German that you have already chosen the following?

1 a bean salad
2 a bottle (of) white wine
3 the fresh fruit salad
4 scrambled egg with ham
5 a French onion soup
6 a quarter litre (of) red wine
7 a dessert
8 a 'mixed' ice cream

Verbs: past participles

All German *regular* verbs form their past participles like this:

infinitive				*stem*			*past participle*
wählen	→	**ge**	+	***wähl***	+ **t**	→	***gewählt***
schmecken	→	**ge**	+	***schmeck***	+ **t**	→	***geschmeckt***

So if you know the German verb is regular, the above rule can be used to form it.

German irregular verbs form their past participles in many different ways, which shouldn't be too much of a surprise, given that the same happens in English (though not necessarily to 'the same' verbs as in German) e.g.

regular	bake	→	baked
irregular	choose	→	chosen
	buy	→	bought
	feed	→	fed

> How can you tell whether a German verb is REGULAR or IRREGULAR? Initially, the safest method is to look it up in the Glossary!

Übung 5F

Complete the following sentences in the past (perfect) tense. Only **kaufen** is completely regular, so the past participles of the other verbs will need to be found in the Glossary.

1	**Ich habe**	[a single room]	**(bestellen)**
2	**Sie haben**	[a double room]	**(bestellen)**
3	**Ich habe**	[tea]	**(trinken)**

4	**Sie haben**	[coffee]	**(trinken)**
5	**Ich habe**	[scrambled egg]	**(essen)**
6	**Sie haben**	[ham]	**(essen)**
7	**Ich habe**	[a small city map]	**(kaufen)**
8	**Sie haben**	[a large city map]	**(kaufen)**
9	**Ich habe**	[the fresh fruit salad]	**(nehmen)**
10	**Sie haben**	[a 'mixed' ice]	**(nehmen)**

Prepositions

In Text 5, ***in der Mitte*** (in the middle), ***in der Ecke*** (in the corner), ***am Fenster*** (by/at the window) were used and can now be included in our prepositions table:

prep-ositions	*masculine/neuter nouns*		*feminine nouns*	
zu	**+ dem**	→ ***zum*** **Hotel**	**+ der**	→ ***zur*** **Post**
von	**+ dem**	→ ***vom*** **sechsten Mai**	**+ der**	→ ***von der***
in	**+ dem**	→ ***im*** **ersten Stock**	**+ der**	→ ***in der*** **Ecke/Mitte**
an	**+ dem**	→ ***am*** **Fenster**	**+ der**	→ ***an der***
auf	**+ dem**	→ ***auf dem*** **Schlüssel**	**+ der**	→ ***auf der*** **rechten Seite**

Cardinal numbers 100 +

German counts 'hundred-one', 'thousand-one' and *not* 'hundred-*and*-one', 'thousand-*and*-one'.

Übung 5G

Read aloud the numbers printed in italic, following the pattern of those spelt out.

100 **hundert [oder: einhundert]**
101 **hunderteins**
102 103 104 105 106 107 108 109
110 **hundertzehn**
111 **hundertelf**
112 113 114 115 116 117 118 119

120 **hundertzwanzig**
121 **hunderteinundzwanzig**
122 123 124 125 126 127 128 129
130 140 150 160 170 180 190
200 **zweihundert**
300 400 500 600 700 800 900 990
999 **neunhundertneunundneunzig**

1 000 **tausend [oder: eintausend]**
2 000 **zweitausend**
3 000 6 000 9 000 12 000
4 000 7 000 10 000 20 000
5 000 8 000 11 000 50 000
90 000 **neunzigtausend**
100 000 **hunderttausend**

999 999 **neunhundertneunundneunzigtausendneunhundert-neunundneunzig**
1 000 000 **eine Million**
2 000 000 **zwei Millionen**
6 000 000
1 000 000 000 **eine Milliarde**
2 000 000 000 **zwei Milliarden**
7 000 000 000

- Note the space – no commas! – before each 000 in multiples of a thousand. In German, a comma between numbers is a decimal point, as in e.g. DM 6,90.
- When numbers are expressed in words, the words up to 999 999 are all written together! But long numbers, of course, are rarely spelt out, except on cheques.

Übung 5H

Read out the following numbers and write them in figures.

1 **zweihundertvierunddreißig**
2 **siebenhundertneunundsechzig**
3 **dreihundertdreiundsiebzig**
4 **sechshundertsechzehn**
5 **siebentausendfünfhundertdreiundzwanzig**
6 **achttausendneunhundertneunundvierzig**

7 **eine Million dreihundertfünzigtausendsiebenhundert-einundachtzig**
8 **fünf Milliarden fünftausendfünfhundertfünfundfünfzig**
9 **viertausendsiebenhundertelf**
10 **zwölf Millionen eintausendeinunddreißig**

Years

plural	**die *Jahre***
singular	**das *Jahr***

Übung 5J

When calender years are stated in German, as in English, hundreds are generally counted rather than thousands. Write the following years in figures:

1 **achtzehnhunderteinundsiebzig**
2 **neunzehnhundertneunzehn**
3 **fünfzehnhundertvierundsechzig**
4 **vierzehnhundertzweiundneunzig**
5 **achtzehnhundertsiebenundsechzig**
6 **achtzehnhundertvierundneunzig**
7 **sechzehnhundertzweiunddreißig**
8 **siebzehnhundertsechsundsiebzig**
9 **(ein)tausendsechsundsechzig**
10 **zweitausendundeins**

Übung 5K

Use the Key to **Übung 5J** to reverse the above exercise, i.e. read off the numbers printed there in digits.

Birthdays

In **Lektion vier** you met one way of saying when you were born:

***Mein Geburtstag ist* am 5. (fünften) November.**

Here is an alternative:

				past participle
Ich	***bin***	**am**	**5. (fünften) November**	***geboren.***
I	am	on the	5th of November	born.

Note that standard spoken German requires 'I *am* born', not 'I was born', and that the past participle in German is, as usual, at the end of the sentence.

Now we can put in the year of birth as well:

written ***Ich bin*** **am 5. November 1950** ***geboren.***
spoken ***Ich bin*** **am fünften November neunzehnhundertfünfzig** ***geboren.***

Übung 5L

Learn your own answers to these questions by heart:

Wann **sind Sie geboren?**
When were you born?
Ich bin am **(Tag) (Monat) (Jahr)** ***geboren.***

Wo **sind Sie geboren?**
Where were you born?
Ich bin in **(Stadt [*town*])** ***geboren.***

Wann und wo **sind Sie geboren?**
When and *where* were you born?
Ich bin am **(Tag) (Monat) (Jahr)** ***in*** **(Stadt)** ***geboren.***

Übung 5M

Here are some famous native German speakers, now deceased (**gestorben**). Using the information given below, complete this three-column table, indicating in figures when the people named were born and when they died.

	Name	**geboren**	**gestorben**
1	Wolfgang Amadeus Mozart	21. 1. ___	________
2	Karl Marx	________	14. 4. ___
3	Ludwig van Beethoven	________	26. 3. ___
4	Johann Wolfgang Goethe	28. 4. ___	________
5	Willy Brandt	18. 12 ___	________

6	Jacob Grimm	________	20. 9. ___
7	Albert Einstein	________	18. 4. ___
8	Wilhelm Grimm	24. 2 ____	________
9	Marlene Dietrich	________	6. 5. ____
10	Albrecht Dürer	21. 5. ____	________

A Er ist am achtundzwanzigsten vierten siebzehnhundertneunundvierzig in Frankfurt am Main geboren und am zweiundzwanzigsten dritten achtzehnhundertzweiunddreißig in Weimar gestorben.

B Er ist am vierten ersten siebzehnhundertfünfundachtzig in Hanau geboren und am zwanzigsten neunten achtzehnhundertdreiundsechzig in Berlin gestorben.

C Er ist auch in Hanau geboren und in Berlin gestorben. Er ist am vierundzwanzigsten zweiten siebzehnhundertsechsundachtzig geboren und am sechzehnten zwölften achtzehnhundertneunundfünfzig gestorben.

D Er ist am einundzwanzigsten ersten siebzehnhundertsechsundfünfzig in Salzburg geboren und am fünften zwölften siebzehnhunderteinundneunzig in Wien gestorben.

E Er ist am fünften fünften achtzehnhundertachtzehn in Trier geboren und am vierzehnten vierten achtzehnhundertdreiundachtzig in London gestorben.

F Er ist am siebzehnten zwölften siebzehnhundertsiebzig in Bonn geboren und am sechsundzwanzigsten dritten achtzehnhundertsiebenundzwanzig in Wien gestorben.

G Er ist in Nürnberg geboren und gestorben. Er ist am einundzwanzigsten fünften vierzehnhunderteinundsiebzig geboren und am sechsten vierten fünfzehnhundertachtundzwanzig gestorben.

H Sie ist am siebenundzwanzigsten zwölften neunzehnhunderteins in Berlin geboren und am sechsten fünften neunzehnhundertzweiundneunzig in Paris gestorben.

J Er ist am achtzehnten zwölften neunzehnhundertdreizehn in Lübeck geboren und am achten zehnten neunzehnhundertzweiundneunzig in Unkel am Rhein gestorben.

K Er ist am vierzehnten dritten achtzehnhundertneunundsiebzig in Ulm geboren und am achtzehnten vierten neunzehnhundertfünfundfünfzig in Princeton gestorben.

Übung 5N

Cover up 1 to 10 in **Übung 5M** above and, looking only at A to K, find the place names missing from the following lists:

	Name	*geboren*	*gestorben*
1	Einstein	1879 in ______	1955 in ______
2	Marlene Dietrich	1901 in ______	1992 in ______
3	Mozart	1756 in ______	1791 in ______
4	Marx	1818 in ______	1883 in ______
5	Dürer	1471 in ______	1528 in ______
6	Willy Brandt	1913 in ______	1992 in ______
7	Jacob Grimm	1785 in ______	1863 in ______
8	Wilhelm Grimm	1786 in ______	1859 in ______
9	Goethe	1749 in ______	1832 in ______
10	Beethoven	1770 in ______	1827 in ______

Übung 5P

Answer the following questions, following this pattern:

Wo ist Albert Einstein geboren? — **Er ist in Ulm geboren.**
Where was Albert Einstein born? — He was born in Ulm.

1 **Wo ist Albrecht Dürer geboren?**
2 **Wo ist Mozart gestorben?**
3 **Wo ist Karl Marx geboren?**
4 **Wo ist Marlene Dietrich gestorben?**
5 **Wo ist Albert Einstein gestorben?**
6 **Wo ist Willy Brandt geboren?**
7 **Wo ist Jacob Grimm gestorben?**
8 **Und Wilhelm Grimm?**
9 **Wo ist Goethe gestorben?**
10 **Wo ist Beethoven geboren?**

Übung 5Q

Match the following verbs with their meanings.

1	**zahlen**	A	to cost
2	**machen**	B	to have
3	**gehen**	C	to take

4	**kommen**	D	to sit
5	**schmecken**	E	to be
6	**sitzen**	F	to taste
7	**wählen**	G	to go
8	**trinken**	H	to do/make
9	**kosten**	J	to pay
10	**nehmen**	K	to drink
11	**haben**	L	to come
12	**sein**	M	to choose/elect

Verb patterns

In order to illustrate tense patterns we can usefully divide the infinitives of verbs into their

stem + ending, e.g. ***zahl*** + **en**.

In the *present tense* the first eight verbs in **Übung 5Q** all follow the pattern:

'I'	stem + ***e***	**ich**	→	**komm*e***
'he/she/it'	stem + ***t***	**er** **sie** **es**	→	**komm*t***
'we/you/they'	stem + ***en***	**wir** **Sie** **sie**	→	**komm*en***

The next three verbs in **Übung 5Q** follow the above pattern for 'I' and 'we/you/they' but not for 'he/she/it':

stem + ***e***	**ich**	→	**kost*e***	**nehm*e***	**hab*e***
but	**er** **sie** **es**	→	***kostet***	***nimmt***	***hat***
stem + ***en***	**wir** **Sie** **sie**	→	**kost*en***	**nehm*en***	**hab*en***

The last verb, ***sein***, the common verb 'to be', does not follow the above pattern at all. The various forms have to be remembered individually:

ich	→	***bin***	['am']
er **sie** **es**	→	***ist***	['is']
wir **Sie** **sie**	→	***sind***	['are']

Übung 5R

The task here is to supply (a) the right verb and (b) the right form of the verb in the present tense. The verbs in their infinitive form are listed in **Übung 5Q** above. Remember that ***er*** can refer to any masculine word, ***sie*** to any feminine word: they do not refer only to males and females.

1a	buy	**Ich**______	**einen großen Stadtplan.**
1b	buy	**Sie** [you]______	**einen kleinen.**
2a	take	**Er**______	**die dritte Straße rechts.**
2b	take	**Ich**______	**die zweite Straße links.**
3a	sit	**Er**______	**in der Mitte.**
3b	sit	**Sie** [she]______	**am Fenster.**
4a	have	**Ich**______	**Zimmernummer 18.**
4b	have	**Sie** [she]______	**Nummer 19.**
5a	go	________**Sie** [you]	**zum Hotel Müller!**
5b	go	**Ich**________	**zur Post.**
6a	cost	**Das Eis**______	**drei Mark.**
6b	taste	**Es** [it]______	**ausgezeichnet.**
7a	drink	**Sie** [she]______	**ein Viertel Weißwein.**
7b	drink	**Er**______	**eine Flasche Rotwein.**
8a	taste	**Der frische Obstsalat**____	**nicht gut.**
8b	be	**Er** [it]______	**gar nicht frisch.**
9a	be	**Ich**______	**Engländer.**
9b	be	________**Sie** [you]	**Engländerin?**
10a	buy	**Ich möchte die schöne**	**Briefmarke**________.
10b	cost	**Sie** [it]______ **aber**	**fünf Mark.**

Übung 5S

Let's return to the restaurant. How much do you remember? Match the following sentences/phrases.

1	Wie ist Ihre Zimmernummer?	A	Ja, ausgezeichnet.
2	Wo möchten Sie sitzen?	B	Ein Viertel Weißwein.
3	Haben Sie schon gewählt?	C	Ja, frischen Obstsalat mit Sahne.
4	Was möchten Sie trinken?	D	Am Fenster.
5	Möchten Sie einen Nachtisch?	E	Achtzehn.
6	Hat es geschmeckt?	F	Ja, ich möchte eine französische Zwiebelsuppe.

Übung 5T

Read through Text 5 once more, then come back to the following exercise. Prove to yourself that you can cope in a German-speaking restaurant.

1 You enter the restaurant in the evening: what do you say as an opener?
2 Say you want to sit by the window.
3 Ask for the menu.
4 Say you'd like a dry, white wine.
5 Order scrambled egg with ham and a salad to go with it.
6 Tell the waiter you enjoyed the meal.
7 The waiter asks you whether you'd like a dessert: ask him what's on today.
8 Order a pot of coffee.
9 Tell the waiter you would like to pay.
10 Take your leave.

Wilhelm Grimm geboren 24. Februar 1786, gestorben 16. Dezember 1859

Jacob Grimm geboren 4. Januar 1785, gestorben 20. September 1863

The Brothers Grimm, portrayed here on a thousand-Mark note, **Tausend-Mark-Schein**, were not only collectors of folk-tales but also pioneers in the history of the Germanic languages. They began the massive German dictionary, the ***Deutsches Wörterbuch***, one volume of which is illustrated above. It was not completed until 1960. The brothers were born in Hanau near Frankfurt am Main. Jacob (on the right above) was called to a professorship at what is now the **Humboldt-Universität** on **Unter den Linden**. The brothers are buried in Berlin in the **Matthäus-Kirchhof**, **Großgörschenstraße**.

6 Für halb drei

Round the clock

Language activities

- booking a ticket
- getting around
- telling the time of day

Language focus

- plurals of nouns
- verbs of 'going'
- separable verbs
- the dative case

Text 6

Dienstag früh

It's early-ish on Tuesday morning. A sightseeing tour by coach is a good way of gaining a quick overview of Berlin, particularly during a short stay in the city. You ask the receptionist at the hotel to book you a ticket. She wants to know for which day. You have no time to lose: you want to go today if at all possible. It *is* possible and you even have two options: a shorter tour at 10.30 in the morning and a 'grand' tour starting at 2.30 in the afternoon. You want to know how long the tours take. The morning tour takes one-and-a-half to two hours, the afternoon tour three-and-a-half to four hours. You decide to go in the afternoon. You give her your name which she enters on the ticket, and you get five Marks fifty change from a twenty Mark note. The receptionist draws your attention to information on the ticket indicating that the coach leaves from the Europa-Center in the Budapester Straße. You don't know where that is, so the receptionist points you in the right direction: from your hotel to the Europa-Center it's an eight minutes' walk.

EMPFANG: Guten Morgen!
SIE: Guten Morgen! Ich möchte gern[1] eine Fahrkarte für eine Stadtrundfahrt. Können[2] Sie für mich[3] bestellen?
EMPFANG: Ja, selbstverständlich.[4] Für welchen[5] Tag bitte? Mittwoch, Donnerstag . . .?
SIE: Für heute, Dienstag, wenn's geht.[6]
EMPFANG: Das geht.[7]
SIE: Schön.[8] Wie[9] lange dauert eine Fahrt?[10]
EMPFANG: Es gibt[11] zwei Stadtrundfahrten heute – eine kleine[12] Stadtrundfahrt heute morgen[13] um[14] halb elf[15] und eine große Stadtrundfahrt heute nachmittag[16] um halb drei. Die kleine Fahrt dauert eineinhalb[17] bis zwei Stunden, die große Fahrt dreieinhalb bis vier Stunden.
SIE: Ich möchte eine Karte für die große Stadtrundfahrt um halb drei.
EMPFANG: Also für heute, vierzehn Uhr[18] dreißig[19] – kein[20] Problem. Auf welchen Namen,[21] bitte?
SIE: Bennett: B-E-NN-E-TT.[22] Vorname Peter – wie[23] Peter.
EMPFANG: Danke, Herr Bennett. Die Karte kostet neununddreißig Mark fünfzig.
SIE: Bitte schön.
EMPFANG: Danke schön – fünfzig Mark. Sie bekommen[24] zehn Mark fünfzig zurück. Hier ist Ihre Karte. Sie sehen[25], der Bus fährt vom[26] Europa-Center[27] in der Budapester Straße ab. Kennen[28] Sie das Europa-Center?
SIE: Nein, noch nicht.[29]
EMPFANG: Das Europa-Center ist nur acht Minuten zu Fuß[30] vom Hotel entfernt.[31] Hier gleich[32] links und immer geradeaus.
SIE: Vielen Dank.
EMPFANG: Bitte sehr. Gute Fahrt![33]

Notes

1 on its own **gern** = 'yes, willingly'. Here it suggests 'very much' as in 'I would very much like . . .'
2 'can you . . . order/book'
3 'for me' (accusative case after **für**)

4 'of course, it goes without saying'
5 'for which/what' (accusative case after **für**)
6 literally: 'if it goes', i.e. 'if possible'
7 literally: 'that goes', i.e. 'OK, fine'
8 'fine, good!'
9 **Wie** can mean 'how' or 'what' or even 'like/as' (see note 23)
10 here the general word **die Fahrt** ('trip, journey') is used as a shortened version of **Stadtrundfahrt**
11 literally: 'it gives', a common set expression meaning 'there is/there are'
12 **klein** ≠ **groß** ≠ 'little' ≠ 'big' (in this context: 'short' vs. 'long')
13 literally: 'today morning', i.e. 'this morning'
14 **um** is a preposition with many meanings, here = 'at'
15 'at half past ten' (not 'half past eleven', as you might expect. See **Übung 6G**)
16 literally: 'today afternoon', i.e. 'this afternoon'
17 'one-and-a-half' can be **eineinhalb** or **anderthalb**
18 **Uhr** here means 'o'clock', but **die/eine Uhr** is 'the/a clock' or 'watch'
19 to avoid possible confusion, the 24-hour clock is commonly used with reference to travel times
20 'no, (that's) not (a)'
21 literally: 'on which name?' i.e. 'in whose name?' Mostly an indirect way of asking for your, the customer's, name. This is a set phrase in the accusative: in the nominative the singular of 'name' is **Name**, as with **Vorname** in the next line
22 spelling aloud in German is covered fully in **Lektion achtzehn**
23 'like'. He pronounces the first 'Peter' in English, the second in German
24 literally: 'get . . . back', i.e. '(this is your) change'
25 literally: 'you see', i.e. something is being pointed out for you to look at
26 'from the': **vom** is a shortened version of **von dem**
27 a large shopping complex near the eastern end of the Kurfürstendamm
28 'know', in the sense of 'to be acquainted with'
29 literally: 'still not', i.e. 'not yet'
30 'only 8 minutes' walk', literally: 'to foot'
31 literally: 'distanced', i.e. 'from the hotel'
32 literally: 'immediately left', i.e. 'first left'
33 cf. French: *Bon voyage!*

Übung 6A

Find German equivalents in Text 6 for the following nouns. Write them, each with a capital letter, in three columns and preceded by **der**, **das** or **die**. When you have finished, your German nouns should appear in alphabetical order in each column.

masculine	*neuter*	*feminine*
bus/coach	centre	trip/journey
Tuesday	hotel	ticket
Thursday	problem	Mark
foot		minute
Wednesday		city sightseeing tour
morning		street
name		hour
day		clock, watch
first name		

Übung 6B

Write out the phrases/sentences from Text 6 in which masculine words are used. As a clue, the first letter of each of the relevant words is given below with the masculine words indicated in bold print.

1 G– **M**– !
2 F– w– **T**– , b– ?
3 **M**– , **D**– ?
4 F– h– , **D**– , w– '– g– .
5 A– w– **N**– , b– ?
6 **V**– P– , w– P– .
7 D– , **H**– B– .
8 S– s– , d– **B**– f– v– E– C– i– d– B– S– a– .
9 D– E– C– i– n– a– M– z– **F**– v– H– e– .
10 V– **D**– .

Übung 6C

Find and write out equivalents from Text 6 for the following sentences/phrases.

1 How long does a tour take/last?
2 Do you know the Europa-Center?

3 No problem!
4 There are two tours today.
5 Can you book for me?
6 For today, Tuesday, if possible.
7 Here's your ticket.
8 Not yet.
9 1430 hours.
10 At half past ten.

A selection of Berlin theatre tickets. Find the information needed to complete the table overleaf.

Name of theatre	*Time of performance*	*Day of performance*
Komische Oper		
Kabarett-Theater Distel		
Deutsches Theater		
Maxim Gorki Theater		
Schaubühne		
Berliner Ensemble		
Kammerspiele	(time not indicated)	
Volksbühne		
Deutsche Oper		

Nouns: plurals

A very common way of forming the plural of a German noun – especially if the noun ends in **-e** – is to add **-n** (cf. **Übung 2E**):

singular	*plural*
eine Briefmarke	**zwei Briefmarke*n***
(a postage stamp)	

When the noun is feminine, 'the' is the same in the nominative and accusative singular and plural:

subject	*singular*	*plural*
nominative	**die Briefmarke**	**die Briefmarke*n***
object		
accusative	**die Briefmarke**	**die Briefmarke*n***

The following nouns from this **Lektion** and previous **Lektionen** also follow the **Briefmarke** pattern:

Ansichtskarte	**Apotheke**	**Bushaltestelle**
(picture postcard)	(chemist/drugstore)	(bus stop)

(Fahr)karte	**Kirche**	**Minute**
(ticket)	(church)	(minute)
Postkarte	**Straße**	**Stunde**
(postcard)	(street)	(hour)

Übung 6D

Translate the following.

1 I would like ten tickets @ twelve Marks ninety (each).
2 Only fifteen minutes on foot.
3 The tour of the city takes four hours and twenty minutes.
4 I would like four postcards and postage stamps.
5 Berlin has five hundred churches and two hundred chemists.
6 The streets of [**von**] London.
7 Two picture postcards cost only one Mark.

Other plural forms (nominative and accusative cases) so far encountered include:

	singular	*plural*	*change*	
trip/journey	**die Fahrt**	**die Fahrt*en***		+ ***-en***
month	**der Monat**	**die Monat*e***		+ ***-e***
letter	**der Brief**	**die Brief*e***		+ ***-e***
night	**die Nacht**	**die Nächt*e***	a → ***ä***	+ ***-e***
city/town map	**der Stadtplan**	**die Stadtplän*e***	a → ***ä***	+ ***-e***

Days of the week

plural **die *Tage* die *Wochentage***
('days of the week')

singular **der *Tag* der *Wochentag***
[all days are masculine]

in context **Für welchen Tag, bitte? Für Dienstag.**

am	***Montag***	*on*	Monday
	Dienstag		Tuesday
	Mittwoch		Wednesday

Donnerstag	Thursday
Freitag	Friday
Samstag (***Sonnabend****)	Saturday
Sonntag	Sunday

* Over the German-speaking area, both **Samstag** and **Sonnabend** are understood, but **Sonnabend** is less widespread: it is used mainly in northern and eastern Germany.

Übung 6E

First learn the list of days above, then test yourself by reading off the following in German:

		Mo	Di	Mi	Do	Fr	Sa	So
1 Für welchen Tag, bitte?	Für				x			
2 Für welchen Tag, bitte?	Für			x				
3 Für welchen Tag, bitte?	Für		x					
4 Für welchen Tag, bitte?	Für					x		
5 Für welchen Tag, bitte?	Für							x
6 Für welchen Tag, bitte?	Für	x						
7 Für welchen Tag, bitte?	Für						x	

Times of the day

plural	***die Tageszeiten***	(times of the day)
singular	**die Tageszeit**	(time of the day)

heute	**morgen**	*this*	morning	(any time a.m.)
heute	**vormittag**	*this*	morning	(any time a.m.)
heute	**früh**	*this*	morning	(ditto or early a.m.)
heute	**mittag**	*this*	lunchtime	(midday)
heute	**nachmittag**	*this*	afternoon	
heute	**abend**	*this*	evening	
heute	**nacht**	*to-*	night or *last* night*	

* There is potential ambiguity here, where **heute nacht** can mean the night to come or the night just past. Usually, the general context or the tense of the verb used makes it clear what exactly is meant.

If you need to say 'early this morning', then it's safer to say **heute *sehr* früh** rather than **heute früh**, since the expression without **sehr** (= very) doesn't necessarily indicate earliness.

Übung 6F

Replace the English with German.

> **Es gibt zwei** [sight-seeing tours] **heute – eine kleine Stadtrundfahrt** [this morning] **um** [half past eleven] **und eine** [big] **Stadtrundfahrt** [this evening] **um** [half past seven].

Telling the time [part 1]
[see Lektion sieben for part 2]

The only expression of time that is *very* different from English is 'half past the hour', so let's learn the odd one out first. The German way of looking at, say, 10.30 is not in terms of 'half past the last hour' but as 'half way towards the next'. So **halb drei** is not 'half (past) three' but 'half *to* three', i.e. in English terms 'half past *two*'.

Übung 6G

Try writing these German times in figures.

> *e.g.* ***Es ist halb drei. 2.30***

1 **Es ist halb fünf.**
2 **Es ist halb elf.**
3 **Es ist halb zwei.**
4 **Es ist halb vier.**
5 **Es ist halb sechs.**
6 **Es ist halb eins.**

Übung 6H

And the other way round: write down in words the times indicated.

e.g. 7. 30 **Es ist halb acht.**

1 9.30
2 6.30
3 11.30
4 8.30
5 4.30
6 12.30

Hours, minutes and seconds

are all feminine, all end in **-e** and therefore follow the common plural pattern + **-n**:

eine *Stunde*	**eine *Minute***	**eine *Sekunde***
zwei Stunden	**zwei Minuten**	**zwei Sekunden**

Übung 6J

For each pair of sentences below, keep sentence B covered until you have read out sentence A.

1A **1 Stunde hat 60 Minuten.**
1B ***Eine Stunde hat sechzig Minuten.***

2A **1 Stunde hat 3600 Sekunden.**
2B ***Eine Stunde hat dreitausendsechshundert Sekunden.***

3A **1½ Stunden haben 90 Minuten.**
3B ***Eineinhalb Stunden haben neunzig Minuten.***

4A **1½ Stunden haben 4400 Sekunden.**
4B ***Eineinhalb Stunden haben viertausendvierhundert Sekunden.***

5A **2½ Stunden haben 150 Minuten.**
5B ***Zweieinhalb Stunden haben hundertfünfzig Minuten.***

Duration: Wie lange . . .?

How long something takes or lasts can be expressed in terms of, for example,

Sekunden	**Minuten**	**Stunden**	**Tage**	**Wochen**	**Monate**	**Jahre**
seconds	minutes	hours	days	weeks	months	years

Übung 6K

Answer the questions below, using **er** for masculine words, **es** for neuter words and **sie** for feminine words.

e.g. ***Wie lange dauert die kleine Stadtrundfahrt?***	***Sie dauert eineinhalb Stunden.***
1 **Wie lange dauert die große Stadtrundfahrt?**	____ **dauert** (3½ hours).
2 **Wie lange dauert der Film?**	____ **dauert** (95 minutes).
3 **Wie lange dauert das Oktoberfest?**	____ **dauert** (2 weeks).
4 **Wie lange dauert die Busfahrt nach Berlin?**	____ **dauert** (24 hours).
5 **Wie lange dauert die Oper?**	____ **dauert** (5½ hours)!
6 **Wie lange dauert das Theaterstück** [*play*]?	____ **dauert nur** (79 minutes).
7 **Wie lange dauert der Kaffee?**	____ **dauert nur** (3 minutes).

Getting around

You can walk:	**Das Europa-Center ist 20 Minuten *zu Fuß*.**
But by car it's quicker:	**Es ist nur 2 Minuten *mit dem Auto*.**

Note the distinction which has to be made in German between 'I'm going (on foot)' and 'I'm going (by car)'. If you're walking you use the verb **gehen**, if you have transport you use **fahren**:

Ich *gehe* zu Fuß and **Ich *fahre* mit dem Auto.**

Here are various ways of going = travelling:

masculine	*neuter*	*feminine*
mit dem Zug	**mit dem Auto**	**mit der Bahn**
mit dem Wagen	**mit dem Taxi**	**mit der U-Bahn**
mit dem Bus	**mit dem Fahrrad**	**mit der Straßenbahn**
	mit dem Schiff	**mit der S-Bahn**
	mit dem Motorrad	

Übung 6L

Guess–match the English translations below with the German phrases above.

1 by ship
2 by train
3 by taxi
4 by motorbike
5 by 'suburban railway'
6 by tram/streetcar
7 & 8 by car [2 possibilities]
9 by underground/subway
10 by bicycle
11 by rail
12 by bus/coach

Übung 6M

Fill in the blanks below, paying particular attention to **mit *dem*** (for masculine/neuter nouns) vs. **mit *der*** (for feminine nouns). Most of the Berlin addresses you met in **Übung 3D**.

1 **Ich fahre heute früh** [by train] **nach Berlin**.
2 **Ich fahre heute mittag** [by underground] **zum Alexanderplatz.**
3 **Ich gehe** [on foot] **zum Brandenburger Tor**.
4 **Ich fahre heute nachmittag** [by bicycle] **zum Reichstag**.
5 **Ich fahre heute abend** [by boat] **nach Spandau**.
6 **Ich fahre heute nacht** [by bus] **zum Hotel**.
7 **Ich fahre am Dienstag** [by suburban railway] **nach Potsdam**.

Verbs

	to go/walk	*to go/travel*
In the present tense	**gehen** is regular,	**fahren** is slightly irregular:
ich	**gehe**	**fahre**
er/sie/es	**geht**	**fährt**
wir/Sie/sie	**gehen**	**fahren**

We met the form ***fährt*** in Text 6 in the sentence:

Der Bus *fährt* vom Europa-Center in der Budapester Straße *ab*.

Although in the above sentence ***fährt*** and ***ab*** are separated by seven other words, they do in fact 'belong' together and will be listed in a dictionary as a single word, with the **ab** in front of the infinitive:

abfahren = to leave (by transport), to depart.

In English there are many verbs consisting of two parts, such as to 'set off' (e.g. on one's own), to 'sit in' (e.g. on a discussion), to 'run up' (e.g. a bill). This phenomenon is common in German, too – with the difference that in German the parts of two-part verbs are sometimes separate and sometimes not, for example,

Ich	***fahre***	**um halb neun**	***ab***
I	set	at half eight	off!
Ich	**möchte**	**um halb neun**	***abfahren***
I	would like	at half eight	to depart/set off

Such German verbs are called SEPARABLE VERBS because they can and often have to be divided up. The first parts of separable verbs are called prefixes and almost all such prefixes *look* just like prepositions. Separable verbs are marked in the Glossary thus: *v. reg. sep.* or *v. irreg. sep.* Not *all* verbs which look as though they *might be* separable turn out to be so in practice: therefore, it is always worth checking the Glossary or a dictionary if at all in doubt. Here are five examples of separable verbs, each with a different prefix:

ab|fahren	→	**ich fahre ______**	**ab**	(leave/depart)
an|kommen	→	**ich komme ______**	**an**	(arrive)
auf|machen	→	**ich mache ______**	**auf**	(open)
zu|machen	→	**ich mache ______**	**zu**	(shut/close)
aus|gehen	→	**ich gehe ______**	**aus**	(go out)

Model sentences containing separable verbs:

subject (nominative)	*verb*	*'rest of sentence'*	*prefix*
Der Bus	***fährt***	**um halb zehn vom Europa-Center**	***ab.***
Der Zug	***kommt***	**um halb zwei in Berlin**	***an.***
Das Restaurant	***macht***	**heute um halb elf**	***auf.***
Die Post	***macht***	**am Samstag um halb eins**	***zu.***
Peter	***geht***	**heute abend mit der Kellnerin**	***aus.***

Übung 6N

Read through the model sentences above once more, then cover them up and translate the following:

1 The bus leaves at half past nine from the Europa-Center.
2 The train arrives at half past one in Berlin.
3 The restaurant opens today at half past ten.
4 The post office closes on Saturday at half past twelve.
5 Peter is going out this evening with the waitress.

Prepositions

For reference, the prepositions table is updated below to include words occurring in Text 6.

		masculine and neuter nouns		*feminine nouns*
zu	**→zum**	**[zu dem]**	**Hotel**	**zur [zu der] Post**
von	**→*vom***	**[von dem]**	***Europa-Center***	**von der**
in	**→*im***	**[in dem]**	***Operncafé***	***in der Budapester Straße***
an	**→*am***	**[an dem]**	***Dienstag***	**an der**
auf	**→**	**auf dem**		**auf der rechten Seite**

		masculine only nouns	*feminine nouns*
auf	**→**	***auf den*** ***Namen***	**auf die**
für	**→**	***für (den)*** ***Dienstag***	***für die Oper***

You will eventually need to know that one of these prepositions always takes the *accusative* case, others (**zu**, **von**) always take the *dative* case, and the rest (**in**, **an**, **auf**) sometimes take the accusative and sometimes the dative! Clearly, you will need to absorb this sort of information slowly if it is to stick: the bit to try to hang on to for this **Lektion** is that **für** always takes the accusative case, which is why after **für** we get **-en** endings near masculine nouns, and **-e** endings near feminine ones, e.g.

masculine **Für welch*en* Tag?**
feminine **Für *die* Oper/Für *die* groß*e* Stadtrundfahrt**

This pattern is very similar to that which we met in another table (see **Lektion vier**):

	masculine		*neuter*		*feminine*	
	article	adjective	article	adjective	article	adjective
accusative	**ein*en***	**klein*en***	**ein**	**kleines**	**ein*e***	**klein*e***

On the basis of the above, you would be right in guessing that **für** plus a neuter noun would produce, for example, the following pattern:

Für welch*es* Jahr? **Zehn Mark für ein gemischt*es* Eis?!**
For which year? Ten Marks for a mixed (i.e. ordinary) ice-cream?!

Übung 6P

Replace the English words in the sentences with the appropriate German nouns and prepositions taken from the lists given below. Some words will need to be inserted more than once.

Nouns			*Prepositions*	
masculine	*neuter*	*feminine*	**um**	**für**
Bus	**Opernhaus**	**Karten**	**mit**	**am**
Dienstag	**Rathaus**	**Minuten**	**von**	**vom**
Fuß	**Tor**	**Oper**	**zu**	**zum**
		Stunde	**in**	**im**

Ich habe zwei [1] tickets for **die** [2] opera **'Fidelio' von Beethoven** [3] on (the) Tuesday **abend in Berlin. Möchten Sie mitkommen? Der** [4] coach **fährt** [5] at **halb sechs** [6] from the town hall **in Potsdam ab. Wir fahren eine** [7] hour with **dem Bus bis** [8] to the **Alexanderplatz. Der Bus kommt also** [9] at **halb sieben an. Das** [10] opera house **ist zwanzig** [11] minutes **on Fuß** [12] from the **Alexanderplatz entfernt. Die** [13] opera **beginnt** [14] at **halb neun. Wir haben noch eine** [15] hour **und zehn** [16] minutes for **ein Kännchen Kaffee oder eine Flasche Wein** [17] in the **schönen Operncafé** . . .

Pronouns

Now that the dative case has been mentioned, it gives us a handy label to explain why there are two forms of 'me' in German.

'I'	**ich**	is in the nominative case
'me'	**mich**	is in the accusative case
'me'	**mir**	is in the dative case

Here are some examples of contexts in which these three forms have so far occurred in the book:

Ich is in the nominative case as the subject of the sentence in e.g.

***Ich* fahre am Dienstag mit der S-Bahn nach Potsdam.**
On Tuesday I'm taking the S-Bahn to Potsdam.

Für takes the accusative case, the accusative form of **ich** is **mich** so 'for me' = **für mich**, as in:

Können Sie das für *mich* machen?
Can you do/arrange that for me?

In **Lektion fünf** we also met the dative form **mir** in the context:

Ja, es hat *mir* sehr gut geschmeckt!
Literally: Yes, it tasted to me very good (i.e. I enjoyed the meal)

Übung 6Q

Read through Text 6 once more, then come back to the following exercise to prove to yourself that you really could buy a ticket for a sight-seeing tour.

1 Say: Good morning! I'd like a ticket for a tour of the city.
2 You are asked whether you want one for Wednesday or Thursday: say you want one for today, Tuesday.
3 There are two tours: say you want a ticket for this afternoon at 2.30.
4 Ask how long the trip takes.
5 How would *you* reply to: **Auf welchen Namen, bitte?**

6 You are told: **Die Karte kostet neununddreißig Mark fünfzig**. You hand over a 50 Mark note and are given your change, the amount of which is stated by the salesperson in German. What does s/he say?
7 How would you tell an enquirer that the Europa-Center is only a twenty minute walk from their hotel?
8 How might someone wish you a pleasant trip in German?
9 Thank your well-wisher emphatically (i.e. use more than just one word!).

BERLINER
FLOHMARKT

TÄGLICH GEÖFFNET 11.00-19.30 UHR
AUCH SONNABENDS UND SONNTAGS
DIENSTAGS GESCHLOSSEN

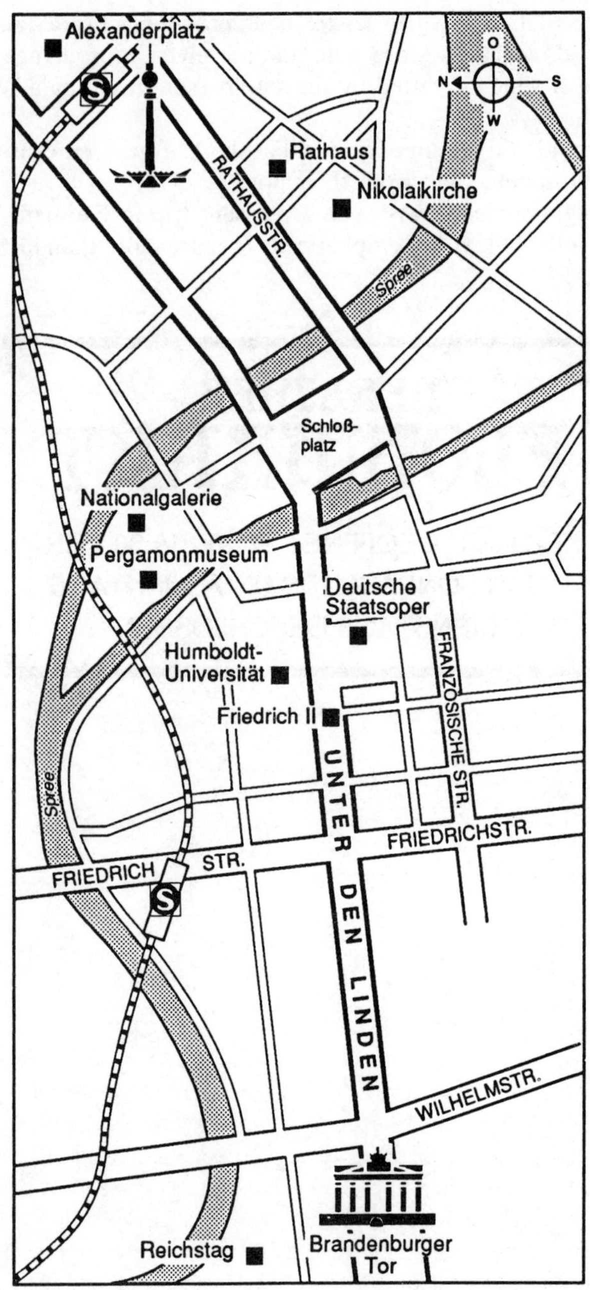

Map 5 Berlin-Mitte

7 Stadtrundfahrt

Seeing the sights

Language activities

- listening/reading and understanding
- telling the time (completed)
- specifying dates with years

Language focus

- vocabulary: verbs, adjectives, nouns
- present tense patterns

Learning strategies

- spotting case/gender patterns
- looking for regular/irregular forms

Text 7

Dienstag nachmittag

You have found your way to the Europa-Center in the Budapester Straße and have boarded the coach. Your twenty-eight year old guide, a student and native of Berlin, welcomes the guests on board. They come from all over the world. Having confirmed that everyone can hear him clearly, he gives some general information about the city before commenting on the sights you are about to see.

Berlin, he says, has become the German capital again. He gives the area of the city, the number of inhabitants, and the age of the city. He indicates the number of administrative districts into which Berlin is divided and mentions the names of four: in the north, south, east and west.

The first of the sights he points out is the **Kurfürstendamm** – often called **Ku'damm** for short. It's a broad, up-market tree-lined boulevard in Berlin's 'West End' which you leave behind as you head due east to the older city centre.

You reach this by driving through the Brandenburg Gate, the official symbol of Berlin, built in a classical style in the late eighteenth century and topped by a quadriga, a chariot drawn by four horses abreast. You continue east along Berlin's most famous boulevard, **Unter den Linden**, till you come to a large monument in the middle of the street of Frederick the Great mounted on his favourite horse, Condé.

At this point, your guide suggests you have had enough culture and it's time for a break. The coach will be stopping next to one of Berlin's three opera houses – not for music but for refreshments in a building restored in 1961–3 on the lines of the eighteenth-century 'Princesses' Palace' that was previously on the site. Your guide asks you to alight and recommends a particularly delicious variety of German gateau. You establish that you have an hour in which to eat it . . .

REISEBEGLEITER:[1] Guten Tag!

SIE: Guten Tag!

REISEBEGLEITER: So, wir sind jetzt[2] alle da. Wir können jetzt fahren. Herzlich[3] willkommen in Berlin, meine Damen und Herren![4] Mein Name ist Jochen Richter, ich bin heute Ihr Reisebegleiter. Ich bin achtundzwanzig Jahre alt. Ich bin Student und Berliner.[5] Ich glaube,[6] wir haben heute im Bus Fahrgäste[7] aus[8] aller Welt[9] – aus Nordamerika, Südamerika, Südafrika, England, Australien, Japan und natürlich[10] Deutschland. Können Sie[11] mich[12] alle gut hören?[13] . . .

Berlin ist wieder[14] die Hauptstadt[15] Deutschlands:[16] eine große Stadt, fast[17] neunhundert Quadratkilometer[18] groß. Berlin hat heute mehr als[19] drei Millionen Einwohner. Berlin ist auch eine alte Stadt – über[20] siebenhundertfünfzig Jahre alt.

Berlin hat dreiundzwanzig Bezirke,[21] zum

Beispiel[22] Spandau in Westberlin, Pankow in Nordberlin, Tempelhof in Südberlin und Hellersdorf in Ostberlin. Wir stehen[23] im Moment[24] am Kurfürstendamm in Westberlin im Stadtbezirk Charlottenburg. Sie wissen schon,[25] der Kurfürstendamm – die Berliner sagen oft Ku'damm – ist eine große, vornehme[26] Einkaufsstraße.[27] Wir fahren heute nach Mitte.[28] Berlin-Mitte ist das historische Zentrum Berlins . . .

Wir fahren jetzt durch[29] das Brandenburger Tor, *das* Wahrzeichen[30] Berlins, zweihundert Jahre alt. Sie sehen, der Baustil[31] ist klassizistisch.[32] Der Architekt: Carl Gotthard Langhans (1732 bis 1808). Aber die schöne Quadriga[33] ist von Johann Gottfried Schadow (1764 bis 1850).

Wir fahren weiter[34] geradeaus, eine breite[35] und berühmte[36] Straße entlang.[37] Diese[38] schöne Straße heißt[39] Unter den Linden.[40] In der Straßenmitte sehen Sie[41] ein großes[42] Standbild, vierzehn Meter hoch[43] – Mann und Pferd. Der Mann: Onkel Fritz[44] – König[45] Friedrich der Große von Preußen, 1786 gestorben. Das Pferd: Friedrichs Lieblingspferd[46] Condé. Das Standbild aus dem Jahr[47] 1851 ist das Meisterwerk[48] von Christian Daniel Rauch.

Meine Damen und Herren, eine Stadtrundfahrt ist anstrengend![49] Es ist halb vier. Es ist Zeit[50] für Kaffee und Kuchen. Der Bus hält[51] gleich auf der rechten Straßenseite. Da sehen Sie die Oper – nein: da[52] sehen Sie *eine* Oper, da sehen Sie die Deutsche Staatsoper,[53] denn[54] Berlin hat *drei* Opernhäuser.[55] Hinter[56] der Staatsoper ist das herrliche[57] Operncafé. Das Operncafé ist übrigens[58] nicht original sondern[59] eine Kopie. Früher[60] war es das Prinzessinnenpalais . . .

Aber wir sind alle müde.[61] Genug[62] Kultur! Jetzt Kaffee und Kuchen! Der Bus hält. Alle aussteigen,[63] bitte! Ich empfehle[64] die köstliche Nußtorte[65] und wünsche Ihnen 'Guten

	Appetit!'[66]
FAHRGAST::	Herr Richter! Um wieviel Uhr fahren wir weiter?
REISEBEGLEITER:	Um halb fünf. Meine Damen und Herren, wir fahren Punkt[67] sechzehn Uhr dreißig wieder weiter!

Notes

1 'guide': **Reise** = 'journey', **Begleiter** (female form: **Begleiterin**) comes from **begleiten** = 'to accompany'
2 'now all there' i.e. 'present'
3 **das Herz** = 'heart', so **herzlich** = literally: 'heartily'
4 this German expression is used much more widely than the English 'Ladies and Gentleman'
5 female form: **Berliner*in***. Note there is no **ein** in this sentence. However, during his Berlin visit in 1963, President Kennedy famously declared **'Ich bin *ein* Berliner!'** – a statement of solidarity which was greatly acclaimed but which a German satirical magazine pointed out can be interpreted as meaning 'I am a doughnut!' More idiomatically, and less ambiguously, he should have said **Ich bin Berliner!**
6 'believe'
7 literally: 'travel guests'. Singular: **der Fahrgast**, **der Gast**
8 the preposition **aus** ('from/out of') always takes the dative case
9 literally: 'out (of) all world'
10 'of course'. He could equally well have said **selbstverständlich**
11 as in English, 'you' = **Sie** is singular or plural: the verb form stays the same. Here **Sie** is clearly plural since the guide says **Sie . . . alle** = 'you all'
12 'me'
13 'hear'
14 'again'
15 literally: 'main town/city', i.e. 'capital'. German does not have separate words for town and city
16 both **Deutschlands Hauptstadt** and **die Hauptstadt Deutschlands** are possible
17 'almost'
18 '900 km^2'
19 'more than'
20 'over': **mehr als** could have been used instead
21 literally: 'districts', i.e. 'boroughs/administrative areas', each with its own town hall etc.

22 often abbreviated **z.B.** = 'e.g.'
23 'stand'
24 note that 'at the moment' is literally in German 'in the moment'
25 'you know already'
26 'distinguished, posh'
27 the verb **einkaufen** = 'to shop, do the/go shopping'
28 literally: 'middle', but **Berlin-Mitte** is also the actual name of Berlin's central district
29 the preposition **durch** ('through') always takes the accusative case
30 a combination of **wahr** ('true') and **das Zeichen** = 'mark/sign'. An alternative for **Wahrzeichen** = **das Symbol**
31 'building' + 'style'
32 i.e. not 'really classical' (which would have been **klassisch**) but 'neoclassical'
33 in 1806 during the Napoleonic Wars the quadriga was removed to Paris. It was returned in 1814
34 'further'
35 'broad'
36 'famous'
37 **entlang** follows the noun. Thus: 'along the street' = **die Straße entlang**
38 'this' (feminine). Masculine = **dieser**, neuter = **dieses**
39 'is called'. An alternative to **Mein Name ist Jochen** would be **Ich heiße Jochen** (see **Lektion acht**)
40 means 'under the lime-trees'
41 note the typically German word order here, i.e. not 'In the middle of the street you see . . .' but 'In the middle of the street see you . . .'
42 the monument is neuter, hence **ein großes** . . .
43 'high/tall'
44 'Uncle Fritz' is the nickname given to Frederick the Great of Prussia
45 'queen' would be **Königin**
46 literally: 'darling horse', i.e. 'favourite horse'
47 literally: 'out of', i.e. 'from'
48 literally: 'master' + 'work'
49 'strenuous, tiring, exhausting'
50 'time'. There is a quality German weekly newspaper called ***Die Zeit***
51 from **halten**, 'to stop'
52 'there'. Again note the word order: 'There see you . . .' rather than 'There you see . . .'
53 literally: 'State Opera'. Note that **Staat** (long 'aah' . . .) is 'state', but **Stadt** (short 'a') is 'town/city'
54 'for, as, since'
55 singular: **das Haus**, **das Opernhaus**

56 preposition: 'behind'
57 'splendid, marvellous'. In origin, shares its stem **herr-** with **Herr** = 'lord and master, gentleman, Mr'
58 'incidentally, by the way'
59 **nicht** . . . **sondern**: 'not . . . but'
60 literally: 'earlier, previously was it', i.e. 'it used to be'
61 'tired'
62 'enough'
63 'get out, alight, disembark'
64 **empfehlen** = 'recommend'
65 **die Nuß** = 'nut'
66 literally: 'I wish to you good appetite!' Before a meal, it is polite to wish **Guten Appetit!**
67 'punctually, on the dot'

Übung 7A

Find equivalents in Text 7 for the following nouns. Write them, each with a capital letter, in three columns and preceded by **der**, **das** or **die**. Where the text contains a plural form you may need to check the Glossary for the singular. When you have finished, your German nouns should appear in alphabetical order in each column.

masculine	*neuter*	*feminine*
appetite	example	lady
architect	Brandenburg Gate	shopping street
building style	year	capital
Berliner	favourite horse	copy
district	masterpiece	culture
bus	Opera Café	lime tree
inhabitant	opera house	million
travel guest	horse	middle
gentleman	Princesses' Palace	nut gateau
coffee	monument	opera
king	symbol	quadriga
cake	centre	town
Ku'damm		city sightseeing tour
man		street
metre		middle of the street
moment		side of the street
square kilometre		clock, o'clock
guide		world
student		time

Übung 7B

Find and write out the German equivalents in Text 7 of the following sentences/phrases.

1 Welcome to Berlin!
2 I'm twenty-eight years old.
3 Can you all hear me (well)?
4 Berlin is again the capital of Germany .
5 Today Berlin has more than three million inhabitants.
6 Berlin is . . . over seven hundred and fifty years old.
7 We are standing at the moment on the Kurfürstendamm.
8 . . . the Brandenburg Gate, the symbol of Berlin.
9 Ladies and Gentleman . . .
10 the German State Opera
11 behind the State Opera
12 Enjoy your meal!

Übung 7C

All the verbs listed here occur in Text 7. The text will give you the forms that are missing below. We have provided all the others for reference, i.e. in each case the 'I' form, the 'he/she/it' form and the 'we/you/they' form.

	infinitive		
sein	be	*ich*	1 _____
		mein Name	2 _____
		wir	3 _____
glauben	believe	*ich*	4 _____
		er/sie	glaubt
		wir/Sie/sie	glauben
haben	have	ich	habe
		Berlin	5 _____
		wir	6 _____
können	be able, can	ich	kann
		er/sie/es	kann
		Sie	7 _____
hören	hear	ich	höre
		er/sie/es	hört
		wir/Sie/sie	hören
stehen	stand	ich	stehe
		er/sie/es	steht

		wir	8 _____
wissen	know	ich	weiß
		er/sie/es	weiß
		Sie	9 _____
sagen	say	ich	sage
		er/sie/es	sagt
		die Berliner	10 _____
fahren	travel/go	ich	fahre
		er/sie/es	fährt
		wir	11 _____
sehen	see	ich	sehe
		er/sie/es	sieht
		Sie	12 _____
heißen	be called	ich	heiße
		diese . . . Straße	13 _____
		wir/Sie/sie	heißen
halten	stop	ich	halte
		der Bus	14 _____
		wir/Sie/sie	halten
aussteigen (separable verb)	get off, alight	ich	steige aus
		er/sie/es	steigt aus
		wir/Sie/sie	steigen aus
empfehlen	recommend	*ich*	15 _____
		er/sie/es	empfiehlt
		wir/Sie/sie	empfehlen
wünschen	wish	*ich*	16_____
		er/sie/es	wünscht
		wir/Sie/sie	wünschen

Übung 7D

This is an exercise in recognizing irregular verb forms. The most common present tense pattern is as for **kommen** ('to come'):

		stem	*ending*
stem + **e**	**ich**	**komm**	**-e**
stem + **t**	**er/sie/es**	**komm**	**-t**
stem + **en**	**wir/Sie**	**komm**	**-en**

Find the ten different verb forms in the completed right-hand column in **Übung 7C** which differ from this pattern.

Telling the time [part 2]

Asking: *What's the time?*

either **Wie spät ist es?** literally: How late is it?
or **Wieviel Uhr ist es?** literally: How much (o')clock is it?

Answering: full hours **Es ist ein Uhr.** It's one o'clock.

Some examples:
Wie spät ist es?
If it's time to get up, you might answer: **Es ist sieben *Uhr*.**
Wieviel Uhr ist es? ... time to go to work ... **Es ist acht *Uhr*.**
Wie spät ist es? ... time for a lunch break ... **Es ist zwölf *Uhr*.**
Wieviel Uhr ist es? ... time to go home ... **Es ist fünf *Uhr*.**
Wie spät ist es? ... time for TV ... **Es ist neun *Uhr*.**
Wieviel Uhr ist es? ... already time for bed ... **Es ist *schon* elf Uhr!**

Answering: 24-hour clock

The 24-hour clock is widely used for travel and appointments in German-speaking countries in order to avoid any ambiguity arising out of forgetting – or forgetting to mention – a.m. or p.m., for which German does not have neat equivalents. When using the German 24-hour clock, use the 'full-hour' pattern and tack any minutes on at the end, e.g.

0.04	**null *Uhr* vier**
1.15	**ein *Uhr* fünfzehn**
1.45	**ein *Uhr* fünfundvierzig**
10.30	**zehn *Uhr* dreißig**
10.31	**zehn *Uhr* einunddreißig**
10.59	**zehn *Uhr* neunundfünfzig**
13.30	**dreizehn *Uhr* dreißig**
21.20	**einundzwanzig *Uhr* zwanzig**
23.55	**dreiundzwanzig *Uhr* fünfundfünfzig**

Übung 7E

Times of trains. Make a note in the table below of departure times from Vienna (**Wien**) and **Leipzig**, plus arrival times in **Berlin**. **Abfahrt** ('departure') is related to **abfahren**, **Ankunft** ('arrival') to **ankommen** – both separable verbs. The first answer is already provided.

1a Der erste Zug fährt um neun Uhr in Wien ab.
The first train leaves Vienna at nine a.m.
1b Er fährt um elf Uhr dreißig in Leipzig ab.
1c Er kommt um vierzehn Uhr eins in Berlin an.
2a Der zweite Zug fährt um zehn Uhr zwanzig in Wien ab.
2b Er fährt um zwölf Uhr siebzehn in Leipzig ab.
2c Er kommt um sechzehn Uhr elf in Berlin an.
3a Der dritte Zug fährt um zwölf Uhr einundzwanzig in Wien ab.
3b Er fährt um vierzehn Uhr einunddreißig in Leipzig ab.
3c Er kommt um sechzehn Uhr fünfzehn in Berlin an.
4a Der vierte Zug fährt um einundzwanzig Uhr neunzehn in Wien ab.
4b Er fährt um dreiundzwanzig Uhr zwei in Leipzig ab.
4c Er kommt um null Uhr fünfundfünfzig in Berlin an.

	Zug 1	**Zug 2**	**Zug 3**	**Zug 4**
Abfahrt ***Wien***	9.00			
Abfahrt ***Leipzig***				
Ankunft ***Berlin***				

Übung 7F

Work through the table below, asking and answering questions, using the sentence patterns, changing the information in brackets:

(At) what time does the train leave Ostende?
Um wieviel Uhr fährt der Zug in [Ostende] **ab? Um** [siebzehn] **Uhr** [sieben].

(At) what time does the train arrive in Frankfurt?
Um wieviel Uhr kommt der Zug in [Frankfurt] **an? Um** [vierundzwanzig] **Uhr.**

Ankunft	*Ostende–Wien–Express*	Abfahrt
	Ostende	17.07
20.30	**Aachen** Hbf*	20.44
21.23	**Köln** Hbf	21.35
21.55	**Bonn** Hbf	21.57
22.32	**Koblenz** Hbf	22.35
23.28	**Mainz** Hbf	23.32
24.00	**Frankfurt (Main)** Hbf	0.18
3.11	**Nürnberg** Hbf	3.28
5.52	**Passau** Hbf	6.14
9.45	**Wien** Westbf†	

* Hauptbahnhof = main/central station † Westbahnhof = west station

Telling the time [part 3]

In the normal course of events, when asking someone the time you do not expect them to reply using the patterns of the 24-hour clock. In general conversation, times do not go beyond 12.59. Also, use is made of expressions relating to halves or quarters of hours, and to time still to pass *before* the hour, not only time lapsed *after* it.

Asking 'What's the time?'
either **Wie spät ist es?** literally: 'How late is it?'
or **Wieviel Uhr ist es?** literally: 'How much (o')clock is it?'

Answering: full hours
Es ist ein Uhr. It's one o'clock.
[Note that **Uhr** is only used with full hours]

Answering: half hours
Es ist halb zwei. It's half (past) one
[see also **Lektion sechs**]

Answering: quarters
Es ist Viertel ***NACH eins.*** It's a quarter *past* one
Es ist Viertel ***VOR eins.*** It's a quarter *to* one

Übung 7G

The key words in connection with telling the time in conversational German are **um–halb–vor–nach**. If you get them mixed up, you could be in deep trouble with appointments, travel arrangements, etc. Slot the appropriate words plus the time (spelt out) into each sentence below.

1 10.00 **Ich fahre** ______ ______ **Uhr mit dem Schiff nach England.**
2 10.30 **Er fährt** ______ ______ ______ **nach Berlin.**
3 12.15 **Der Bus hält** ______ **Viertel** ______ ______ **am Bahnhof.**
4 9.30 **Die erste Stadtrundfahrt ist** ______ ______ ______.
5 2.30 **Die zweite Stadtrundfahrt ist** ______ ______ ______.
6 12.45 **Sie fahren** ______ **Viertel** ______ ______**vom Hotel ab.**
7 7.45 **Ich fliege*** ______ **Viertel** ______ ______ **von Frankfurt nach Dallas.** [*literally: I fly]

Übung 7H

Write down the following times in figures:

1 **Viertel vor zwei**
2 **ein Uhr**
3 **halb fünf**
4 **Viertel nach drei**
5 **Viertel vor sechs**
6 **halb drei**
7 **halb zehn**
8 **Viertel nach neun**

Übung 7J

Now try the reverse: having checked your answers to **Übung 7H**, hide the words and read off the times from the numbers.

Nach and **vor** are used not only with quarters: any of the thirty minutes after the hour can be expressed using **nach**: any of the thirty minutes *before* the hour can be expressed using **vor**. As in English, with *some* multiples of five – see below – you do not have to say 'minutes'. With others, however, you do, so it's safer on the whole to say 'minutes' throughout. Here is an overview, with brackets indicating where **Minuten** can, but need not, be left out:

9.00	***neun Uhr***			
9.01	**eine**	**Minute**	**nach**	**neun**
9.05	**fünf**	**[Minuten]**	**nach**	
9.10	**zehn**	**[Minuten]**	**nach**	
9.15	***Viertel***		**nach**	
	fünfzehn	**Minuten**	**nach**	
9.20	**zwanzig**	**[Minuten]**	**nach**	
9.25	**fünfundzwanzig**	**[Minuten]**	**nach**	
9.29	**neunundzwanzig**	**Minuten**	**nach**	
9.30	***halb zehn***			
9.31	**neunundzwanzig**	**Minuten**	**vor**	**zehn**
9.40	**zwanzig**	**[Minuten]**	**vor**	
9.45	***Viertel***		**vor**	
	fünfzehn	**Minuten**	**vor**	
9.55	**fünf**	**[Minuten]**	**vor**	
9.59	**eine**	**Minute**	**vor**	
10.00	***zehn Uhr***			

The above list does not exhaust the possibilities! You will also hear e.g.

9.29 **eine Minute *vor halb zehn***
9.31 **eine Minute *nach halb zehn***

But it's best not to be unnecessarily ambitious and to get 'the basics' right!

Übung 7K

You are asked the time. Read off the questions and, using the patterns given in the **vor/nach** table above, write the answers in words.

1 **Wie spät ist es?** **Es ist 6 Uhr.**
2 **Wieviel Uhr ist es?** **Es ist 6.02.**
3 **Wie spät ist es?** **Es ist 6.15.**
4 **Wieviel Uhr ist es?** **Es ist 6.23.**
5 **Wie spät ist es?** **Es ist 6.30.**
6 **Entschuldigen Sie, bitte! Wieviel Uhr ist es?** **Es ist 6.44.**
7 **Entschuldigen Sie, bitte! Wie spät ist es?** **Es ist 6.45.**

8	**Wieviel Uhr ist es?**	**Es ist**	**6.50.**
9	**Entschuldigung! Wie spät ist es?**	**Es ist**	**6.56.**
10	**Entschuldigung! Wieviel Uhr ist es?**	**Es ist**	**7 Uhr.**

Übung 7L

Using the same times, ask and answer these questions:

1	**Um wieviel Uhr fahren wir heute?**	**Um**	**6 Uhr.**
2	**Um wieviel Uhr fahren wir heute?**	**Um**	**6.02.**
3	**Um wieviel Uhr fahren wir heute?**	**Um**	**6.15.**
4	**Um wieviel Uhr fahren wir heute?**	**Um**	**6.23.**
5	**Um wieviel Uhr fahren wir heute?**	**Um**	**6.30.**
6	**Um wieviel Uhr fahren wir heute?**	**Um**	**6.44.**
7	**Um wieviel Uhr fahren wir heute?**	**Um**	**6.45.**
8	**Um wieviel Uhr fahren wir heute?**	**Um**	**6.50.**
9	**Um wieviel Uhr fahren wir heute?**	**Um**	**6.56.**
10	**Um wieviel Uhr fahren wir heute?**	**Um**	**7 Uhr.**

Case and gender patterns

It takes time for any learner to come to terms with this apparently complicated feature of the German language. The information we have presented below is essentially for the curious! If you want, passively, to make some sense of the various gender/case endings you see in a Text, the table provides a framework. It contains some combinations of article-and-adjective that you have not yet met in context: such combinations are given here in order to underline the fact that *patterns are repeated.*

Note, for example, that adjective endings are mostly **–e** or (even more often) **–en**. More good news: the endings of **ein** and of adjectives following **ein** are identical for e.g. **mein** and **Ihr**, so the number of different *sets* of endings is essentially two. And the endings of **ein** etc. (set 1) are similar to most of those for the definite article (set 2), when you really come to look at it!

Your aim in the exercise following the table is not to learn to use the various endings but to *raise your awareness* of the patterns they contain. First of all *see* the patterns – in order (not now!) to absorb them.

	masculine article + adj.		neuter article + adj.		feminine article + adj.	
(1) Nominative	**ein**[4]	**-er**	**ein**	**-es**	**eine**[5]	**-e**[5]
Accusative	**einen**	**-en**	**ein**[1]	**-es**[1]	**eine**	**-e**
Dative	**einem**	**-en**	**einem**	**-en**	**einer**	**-en**
(2) Nominative	**der**[10]	**-e**[10]	**das**[2]	**-e**[2]	**die**	**-e**
Accusative	**den**	**-en**	**das**	**-e**	**die**[3]	**-e**[3]
Dative	**dem**[8]	**-en**	**dem**[9]	**-en**	**der**[6,7]	**-en**

Übung 7M

In the tables we have entered superscript numbers against the grammatical patterns to which the numbered phrases listed below correspond *as they are used in Text 7*. Using the tables, find the appropriate genders and cases: 1 has been completed as an example.

		gender	*case*
1	**ein großes Standbild**	neuter	accusative
2	**das historische Zentrum**		
3	**die köstliche Nußtorte**		
4	**mein Name**		
5	**eine große Stadt**		
6	**in der Straßenmitte**		
7	**hinter der Staatsoper**		
8	**im Moment [im = in dem]**		
9	**aus dem Jahr 1851**		
10	**Friedrich der Große**		

Übung 7N

Note that out of context, 1, 2, 3 and 5 above could all be nominative *or* accusative (the endings would be the same either way). We had to check these phrases against Text 7 to establish which case they are in: their function there – as subject (nom.) or object (acc.) of the sentence – told us. Would you have come to the same conclusions? When you investigate, note that the verb ‘to be’ does not take an object (accusative) but **sehen** and **empfehlen** do.

Übung 7P

Memory check! Write out the German version, in the *singular*, of the nouns below, adding their gender as **der**, **das** or **die** (i.e. nominative case) in front of them as you go along. The English translations are listed in the order in which their German equivalents occur in Text 7.

1 lady; 2 gentleman; 3 name; 4 guide; 5 year; 6 student; 7 guest; 8 world; 9 capital; 10 town, city; 11 square kilometre; 12 million; 13 inhabitant; 14 administrative district; 15 example; 16 moment; 17 Kurfürstendamm; 18 shopping street; 19 middle; 20 centre; 21 gate; 22 symbol; 23 style; 24 architect; 25 quadriga; 26 lime tree; 27 middle of the street; 28 monument, statue; 29 metre; 30 man; 31 horse; 32 king; 33 favourite horse; 34 masterpiece; 35 city; 36 tour; 37 time; 38 coffee; 39 cake; 40 bus, coach; 41 side of the street; 42 opera; 43 opera house; 44 café; 45 copy; 46 culture; 47 nut gateau; 48 appetite; 49 Mr. 50 clock, o'clock.

Übung 7Q

The German words missing in the phrases/sentences below are all *adjectives*. Slot them in with their *appropriate endings* where needed – without initially looking at Text 7.

original; fein; klassizistisch; vornehm; groß (x 3); gut; historisch; alt; berühmt; anstrengend; deutsch; schön; recht; herrlich; breit; köstlich

1 **Berlin ist eine** [large] **Stadt.**
2 **Berlin ist auch eine** [old] **Stadt.**
3 **Der Ku'damm ist eine** [distinguished] **Einkaufsstraße.**
4 **Berlin-Mitte ist das** [historical] **Zentrum Berlins.**
5 **Wir fahren durch das Brandenburger Tor. Der Baustil ist** [neo-classical].
6 **Die** [beautiful] **Quadriga ist von Johann Gottfried Schadow.**
7 **Wir fahren eine** [broad], [famous] **Straße entlang.**
8 **Diese** [fine] **Straße heißt Unter den Linden.**
9 **In der Straßenmitte sehen Sie ein** [large] **Standbild, 14 Meter** [high].
10 **Onkel Fritz – Friedrich der** [Great] **von Preußen.**
11 **Eine Stadtrundfahrt ist** [exhausting]!
12 **Der Bus hält gleich auf der** [right] **Straßenseite.**

13 **Da sehen Sie die** [German] **Staatsoper!**
14 **Hinter der Staatsoper ist das** [magnificent/splendid] **Operncafé.**
15 **Das Operncafé ist übrigens nicht** [original] **sondern eine Kopie.**
16 **Ich empfehle die** [delicious] **Nußtorte!**
17 [Good] **Appetit!**

Bettina von Arnim geboren 4. April 1785, gestorben 20. Januar 1859

Bettina von Armin, portrayed here on a German five-Mark note, **Fünf-Mark-Schein**, was a writer and social critic, who was born in Frankfurt am Main but moved to Berlin where she hosted an influential cultural salon in her **Palais** in the **Wilhelmstraße** just south of the **Brandenburger Tor**.

8 Ich . . . . Und Sie?

Getting to know you

Language activities

- describing yourself
- expressing general likes and dislikes
- stating your age
- asking 'what sort of?'

Language focus

- nationalities and professions
- 'dative' prepositions
- **erst**

Text 8

***Dienstag spätnachmittag*[1]**

Towards the end of your sightseeing tour, one of the other passengers on the coach asks you whether you like Berlin. You do and so does she. Your German accent is not perfect (yet), so she suggests you may be a foreigner, which you confirm, and then wants to know exactly where you come from. She turns out to be German and comes from a pretty village called Dorfmark in the Lüneburg Heath area of northern Germany, somewhere between Hanover and Hamburg. You tell her that you come from York: that it's a medium-sized town, beautiful, historic, with an old cathedral, large railway museum and a modern university. You discover that you both arrived in Berlin yesterday. You exchange names and she accepts your invitation to a drink – as long as it's a **Berliner Weiße!** – at the end of the sightseeing tour.

DEUTSCHE:[2] Und wie gefällt[3] Ihnen Berlin?
SIE: Berlin gefällt mir sehr gut. Und Ihnen?
DEUTSCHE: Mir gefällt Berlin auch gut. Sind Sie vielleicht[4] Ausländer?[5]
SIE: Ja, ich bin Engländer.
DEUTSCHE: Woher[6] kommen Sie?
SIE: Ich komme aus[7] York – nicht New York sondern[8] 'old' York.
DEUTSCHE: Sie sind also kein Amerikaner.[9]
SIE: Nein, ich bin Engländer. Und Sie?
DEUTSCHE: Ich bin Deutsche. Ich komme aus Norddeutschland – aus der Lüneburger Heide. Ich wohne[10] in Dorfmark. Dorfmark ist auch *wirklich*[11] ein Dorf – aber[12] ein sehr schönes Dorf. Es liegt[13] zwischen[14] Hamburg und Hannover. Wo liegt York eigentlich?[15]
SIE: Zwischen London und Edinburg.[16] York liegt in Nordengland.
DEUTSCHE: Was für[17] eine Stadt ist York?
SIE: York ist eine mittelgroße[18] Stadt. Es ist auch eine schöne, historische Stadt. York hat eine alte Kathedrale, ein großes Eisenbahnmuseum, aber auch eine moderne Universität.
DEUTSCHE: Seit wann[19] sind Sie hier in Berlin?
SIE: Ich bin erst seit gestern hier.[20] Und Sie?
DEUTSCHE: Ich bin auch erst[21] seit gestern hier. Mein Name ist Dettmann, Heidi Dettmann. Und wie heißen Sie?[22]
SIE: Ich heiße Bennett, Peter Bennett. Eine Stadtrundfahrt ist tatsächlich[23] anstrengend, nicht wahr?[24] Darf[25] ich Sie vielleicht nachher[26] zu einem Glas Bier oder Wein oder Saft[27] einladen?[28] Oder wie wär's mit einer "Berliner Weiße"?[29]
DEUTSCHE: Mit Schuß?
SIE: Natürlich![30]
DEUTSCHE: Ja, dann. . .[31] Aber gern![32] Ich danke Ihnen[33]. . . .

Notes

1 'late afternoon'
2 the first speaker is German and female, hence **Deutsche**. The male form would be **Deutsch*er***
3 literally: how pleases to you Berlin? i.e. 'how do you like . . . ?' The infinitive is **gefallen**
3 'perhaps'
5 (a) 'foreigner'. A female foreigner would be **Ausländerin. Das Ausland** is 'abroad'
6 'where from' (cf. antiquated English: 'whence?')
7 **ich komme aus** = 'I come from: that's where I live'. **Ich komme *von***: 'that's where I have just come from'
8 **nicht . . . sondern**: 'not . . . but' (without **nicht**, or a negative, 'but' is **aber**: see note 12)
9 literally: 'you are therefore not (an) American', i.e. 'So you're not American'
10 'live in' = 'am resident in'. There are two words for 'live' in German: **Ich lebe** is more existential and can mean 'I'm alive'
11 'really'
12 'but'
13 'lies' = 'is (situated)'
14 'between'
15 'actually, in fact'
16 Edinburgh is the only British town spelt differently in German. 'The Thames' = **die Themse**
17 **Was für** = 'what sort of?'
18 'medium-sized'
19 literally: 'since when are you here. . .' i.e. 'how long have you been here . . . ?'
20 literally: 'I am only since yesterday here', i.e. 'I've only been here since yesterday'
21 **nur** is another and more common word for 'only' but would not be used here with reference to a point in time
22 'how are you called?' i.e. 'what is your name?'
23 'really, indeed' (an alternative to **wirklich** above). The speaker is referring back to the comment Jochen Richter made on the coach earlier in the day
24 literally: 'not true?' = 'isn't it? don't you think?' The German expression is often shortened to **nicht?**
25 'may', from the irregular modal verb **dürfen**
26 'afterwards'

27 'fruit juice' (historically related to the English word 'sap')
28 'invite'
29 a light, fizzy beer, usually drunk (through a straw!) outdoors in hot weather, with a **Schuß** ('shot') of *raspberry or woodruff syrup*! – **mit Himbeere oder Waldmeister**
30 'naturally, of course'
31 humorously: 'Well, in *that* case . . .' i.e. 'Yes!'
32 literally: 'but willingly', i.e. 'sure, I'd love to' (accept your offer)
33 **danken** is one of the few German verbs which takes the dative: **Ihnen** is the dative form of **Sie**

Übung 8A

Find equivalents in Text 8 (and in the notes above) for the following nouns. Write them, each with a capital letter, in three columns and preceded by **der**, **das** or **die**. Where the text contains a plural form you may need to check the Glossary for the singular. When you have finished, your German nouns should appear in alphabetical order in each column.

masculine	*neuter*	*feminine*
American	abroad	foreigner [female]
foreigner [male]	beer	Berlin's own 'summer' beer
English(man)	village	German (woman)
name	railway museum	raspberry
fruit juice	glass	cathedral
woodruff	northern Germany	Lüneburg Heath
wine	northern England	town/city
		town/city sightseeing tour
		university

Übung 8B

Find and write out the German equivalents in Text 8 of the following sentences/phrases. Don't try to translate the English sentences word for word, otherwise they won't be German: look for whole-sentence equivalents.

1 I like Berlin a lot.
2 Are you a foreigner maybe?
3 Where do you come from?
4 I come from the north of Germany.
5 York is a medium-sized town.

6 How long have you been here in Berlin?
7 What is your name?
8 A sightseeing tour is really tiring, isn't it?
9 Can I invite you to a glass of beer or wine afterwards?
10 How about a Berliner Weiße?

. . . erst gestern

Erst as used in Text 8 is common in time expressions where in English we might say 'only' or 'not until' or 'not before', e.g.

Ich bin *erst* seit gestern hier.	I have only been (literally: I am only) here since yesterday.
Ich komme *erst* um halb eins.	I won't be coming before/until half past twelve.
Ich fahre *erst* morgen nach Berlin.	I won't be travelling to Berlin until tomorrow.

Erst in this sense meaning 'only' never changes. We first met **erst-** with an ending after the **t-** in **Lektion drei** as meaning 'first', as in e.g. **am ersten Mai** (on the first of May).

Preposition: seit

The preposition **seit** is used to indicate an activity that began in the past and continues to the present, the time you are talking about. Events that start in the past and continue into the present are often described in English using complex forms of the verbs concerned. German is much simpler: when you think **seit**, think *present tense!* Compare the following:

	literally
Ich *wohne seit* 1990 in Berlin.	I *live* since 1990 in Berlin.
I *have been living* in Berlin since 1990.	
***Seit* wann *sind* Sie in Berlin?**	Since when *are* you in Berlin?
Since when *have you been* in Berlin?	
Ich *bin seit* Dienstag in Berlin.	I *am* since Tuesday in Berlin.
I *have been* in Berlin since Tuesday.	
Ich *bin* erst *seit* dem ersten Mai hier.	I *am* only since the first May here.
I *have* only *been* here since 1 May.	

Prepositions: with dative case

Some German prepositions always require that anything which follows them should be in the dative case; others require the accusative case. A third group requires sometimes the one case and sometimes the other.

The commonest prepositions taking the dative case – we can call them 'dative prepositions', for short – are:

aus bei mit nach seit von zu

You have now met all of these except **bei** (for which see **Lektion elf**). In the long run, it is worth being able to recite this short list off by heart.

A grammatical explanation for the phrase **seit dem ersten Mai** is given below. Check the explanation against the information laid out in the table in **Lektion sieben**.

Ich bin seit dem ersten Mai in Berlin.

(a) **Mai** is a *masculine* noun: **[der] Mai** in the nominative
(b) **seit** takes the *dative*
(c) **dem** is the dative form of the masculine definite article
(d) the ending of any adjective or ordinal after a dative article is **-en**

Übung 8C

Here are some English sentences with German translations – but the German sentences have each been divided into two. Match them up with their English equivalents by putting the right parts together again.

1 I won't be coming until half past one.
2 I've been in Germany only since 3 October.
3 I won't be travelling to England until Wednesday.
4 I'm not going shopping until Thursday.
5 I've only been living here for eight weeks.
6 I'm not allowed to come till Friday.

A **Ich bin**	a **erst um halb zwei.**
B **Ich fahre**	b **erst am Donnerstag einkaufen.**
C **Ich gehe**	c **erst am Freitag kommen.**
D **Ich komme**	d **erst seit acht Wochen hier.**
E **Ich wohne**	e **erst seit dem dritten Oktober in Deutschland.**
F **Ich darf**	f **erst am Mittwoch nach England.**

Verb: heißen

Heißen broadly means 'to be called'. It has several uses, some of which are rendered in English by 'is' or by another form of the verb 'to be'. In Text 8 **heißen** provides an alternative way of asking/stating one's name, as in (a) below, but (b) and (c) indicate two other very common uses.

(a) **Wie ist Ihr Name?** — **Mein Name ist. . . .**
Wie heißen Sie? — ***Ich heiße. . . .***
What is your name? — My name is . . .
Wie heißt die Straße? — ***Sie heißt* Unter den Linden.**
What's the street called? — (It's called) Unter den Linden.

(b) ***Wie heißt* 'gestern' auf Englisch?** (**'Gestern' heißt**) 'yesterday'.
What is **gestern** in English? What does **gestern** mean in English?
Wie heißt 'today' **auf Deutsch?** ('Today' **heißt**) **'heute'**.
What is *today* in German? What does *today* mean in German?

(c) ***Das heißt. . . .*** — i.e. . . .

Verbs of 'being able'

Darf in **Übung 8C** above comes from **dürfen** and is our third MODAL verb. The first was **möchten** ('would like': **Lektion eins**), the second **können (Lektion sieben)**. Both **dürfen** and **können** can mean 'to be able'. All three are irregular in some of their forms and often need the infinitive of another verb to complete the sense of the sentence:

Ich	***darf***	***kann***	***möchte***	
Er/sie/es	***darf***	***kann***	***möchte***	+ e.g. **heute *kommen***
Wir/Sie/sie	***dürfen***	***können***	***möchten***	

Strictly, **dürfen** and **können** differ in meaning:

Ich *kann* heute kommen = I can (i.e. *am able to*) come today
Ich *darf* heute kommen = I can (i.e. *may* = *am allowed to*) come today

However, **können** (like English 'can') is often used less precisely to cover both meanings.

In Text 8 the man invites the woman for a drink saying:

Darf ich Sie vielleicht nachher zu einem Glas Wein einladen?

The use of **dürfen** here suggests a politely tentative approach, literally translated by 'Am I permitted to invite you . . .?' but better formulated in English by turning the sentence round, e.g. 'Could you (join me . . .)?' or 'Would you mind (joining me . . .)?'

Verbs of 'liking'

The verb in **Wie *gefällt* Ihnen Berlin?** has **gefallen** as its infinitive. **Gefallen** is one of a small number of German verbs that follow the same pattern as 'like' in the 'Shakespearean' sentence:

It	liketh	me	not
Es	**gefällt**	**mir**	**nicht**

We met another German verb of this type in **Lektion fünf**. Both verbs mean 'like' but one is reserved for eats! They are tabled below side-by-side. Crucially, with these verbs it is *what* you like – and not who likes it – that comes first in the sentence.

For the record, the **mir/Ihnen** forms of **ich/Sie** are indirect objects of the verbs and therefore in the dative case.

(How) *do* you like . . .

(Wie) gefällt Ihnen Berlin?
(Wie) gefällt es Ihnen? — **Es gefällt mir gut.**

(Wie) gefällt Ihnen der Film?
(Wie) gefällt er Ihnen? — **Er gefällt mir gut.**

(Wie) schmeckt Ihnen die Torte?
(Wie) schmeckt sie Ihnen? — **Sie schmeckt mir gut.**

(How) *did* you like . . .

(Wie) hat Ihnen Berlin gefallen?
(Wie) hat es Ihnen gefallen? — **Es hat mir gut gefallen.**

(Wie) hat Ihnen der Film gefallen?
(Wie) hat er Ihnen gefallen? — **Er hat mir gut gefallen.**

(Wie) hat Ihnen die Torte geschmeckt?
(Wie) hat sie Ihnen geschmeckt? — **Sie hat mir gut geschmeckt.**

Here are some possible replies to the question 'How do you like ...?' They range from the very positive to the extremely negative:

Wie gefällt Ihnen Berlin?				
++++	**Berlin [es]**	**gefällt mir**	**ausgezeichnet**	'excellent'
+++		**gefällt mir**	**sehr gut**	'very good'
++		**gefällt mir**	**gut**	'good'
+		**gefällt mir**		
–	**Berlin [es]**	**gefällt mir**	**nicht gut**	'not good'
– –		**gefällt mir**	**nicht**	'not'
– – –		**gefällt mir**	**gar nicht gut**	'not at all good'
– – – –		**gefällt mir**	**gar nicht**	'not at all'

Übung 8D

Make a quick list of towns/cities you are familiar with, write up to four pluses or minuses against them, and then say in German what you think of them, as in the table above. Use the faces in **Übung 5D** again as a visual stimulus!

Nationalities, professions

To state your profession, nationality or any other allegiance, the German structure is simple and consistent:

name or noun or pronoun + form of the verb 'to be' + noun.

For example, we could say about Jochen Richter, the guide in **Lektion sieben**:

Er ist Student	He's a student
Er ist Berliner	He's a Berliner
Er ist Deutscher	He's German

Note that German has nothing where English uses 'a', and that **Deutscher** is a noun, not an adjective. This last point is clearer if we say:

Peter Bennett *ist Ausländer.*	literally: 'Peter Bennett is foreigner'
Peter Bennett *ist Engländer.*	literally: 'Peter Bennett is Englishman'

Übung 8E

Read aloud the questions and each of the answers, slotting in the missing words as appropriate. Assume that *you* are all the people below and that where you live is indeed an indicator of your nationality. You will need to know a little geography, and should always specify your sex by choosing a nationality from *either* the left *or* the right column. The missing words (don't look them up in the Glossary until you have done as much of the exercise by guesswork as you possibly can!) are:

female	*male*
Amerikanerin	**Amerikaner**
Australierin	**Australier**
Deutsche	**Deutscher**
Engländerin	**Engländer**
Inderin	**Inder**
Irin	**Ire**
Kanadierin	**Kanadier**
Neuseeländerin	**Neuseeländer**
Österreicherin	**Österreicher**
Schottin	**Schotte**
Schweizerin	**Schweizer**
Südafrikanerin	**Südafrikaner**
Waliserin	**Waliser**

Woher kommen Sie?

1 **Ich komme aus London.** **Ich bin . . .**
2 **Ich komme aus Kalkutta.** **Ich bin . . .**
3 **Ich komme aus Washington.** **Ich bin . . .**
4 **Ich komme aus Edinburg.** **Ich bin . . .**
5 **Ich komme aus Wien.** **Ich bin . . .**
6 **Ich komme aus Auckland.** **Ich bin . . .**
7 **Ich komme aus Hamburg.** **Ich bin . . .**
8 **Ich komme aus Sydney.** **Ich bin . . .**
9 **Ich komme aus Basel.** **Ich bin . . .**
10. **Ich komme aus Cardiff.** **Ich bin . . .**
11. **Ich komme aus Kapstadt.** **Ich bin . . .**
12. **Ich komme aus Dublin.** **Ich bin . . .**
13. **Ich komme aus Ottawa.** **Ich bin . . .**

Übung 8F

Now read off the information in reverse order, e.g.

Ich bin Engländer(in). Ich komme aus London.

Übung 8G

If your nationality is none of the above, look it up in a large, modern English–German dictionary and write it down for reference. Find the female form, if needed. Dictionaries usually list female forms second or not at all: if the nationality ends in **-er** in the dictionary, add **-in** for the female form.

Übung 8H

Choose a profession and sex, then ask and answer questions randomly, starting with **Ja** or **Nein** and using these exchanges as your model:

Sind Sie Student(in)? ***Ja, ich bin Student(in).***
Sind Sie Pilot(in)? ***Nein, ich bin Politiker(in).***

***arbeitslos**	**arbeitslos**	unemployed [adjective]
Ärztin	**Arzt**	doctor (medical)
***Beamtin**	**Beamter**	civil servant/state employee
***Büroangestellte**	**Büroangestellter**	office worker
Dolmetscherin	**Dolmetscher**	interpreter
***Hausfrau**	**Hausmann**	housewife/'househusband'
Ingenieurin	**Ingenieur**	engineer
Lehrerin	**Lehrer**	teacher
Managerin	**Manager**	manager
Pilotin	**Pilot**	pilot
Politikerin	**Politiker**	politician
Rentnerin	**Rentner**	old-age pensioner
Studentin	**Student**	student
Taxi/Busfahrerin	**Taxi/Busfahrer**	taxi/bus driver
Übersetzerin	**Übersetzer**	translator
Verkäuferin	**Verkäufer**	sales assistant
Vertreterin	**Vertreter**	sales representative

* These do not follow the standard male/female ***-er*** /***-erin*** pattern.

Übung 8J

Learn to say what your own job is. If your profession is not listed above, try looking it up in a large, modern English–German dictionary. If your job is a fairly uncommon one, it may not be listed there either, in which case ask a native speaker of German to help out.

Was für . . .?

Was für doesn't mean 'what for?' but 'what kind of, what sort of?' Although **für** on its own is a preposition taking the accusative (see **Lektion sechs**), **Was für?** is often followed by the nominative, because what follows **Was für** . . . can be the subject of the sentence, as in:

masculine	***Was für ein*** **Tee ist es?**	**Es ist *ein* englisch*er* Tee.**
neuter	***Was für ein*** **Dorf ist Dorfmark?**	**Es ist *ein* schön*es* Dorf.**
feminine	***Was für eine*** **Stadt ist Hamburg?**	**Es ist *eine* groß*e* Stadt.**

Übung 8K

Answer each question below, using an appropriate adjective from this list and not using any adjective more than once:

alt; **deutsch**; **französisch**; **historisch**; **lang**; **modern**; **ruhig**

Each answer needs to follow one of three patterns:

		article	*adjective*	*ending*	*noun*
(a)	**Es ist**	***ein***		**-er**	masculine
(b)	**Es ist**	***ein***		**-es**	neuter
(c)	**Es ist**	***eine***		**-e**	feminine

1. **Was für ein Hotel ist es?** (Say it's a modern hotel)
2. **Was für ein Zimmer ist es?** (Say it's a quiet room)
3. **Was für eine Kathedrale ist es?** (Say it's a very old cathedral)
4. **Was für eine Straße ist es?** (Say it's a long street)
5. **Was für eine Stadt ist es?** (Say it's an historical town)
6. **Was für ein Auto ist es?** (Say it's a German car)
7. **Was für eine Suppe ist es?** (Say it's a French onion soup)

Age: das Alter

Age is expressed in German very much as in English:

Wie alt sind Sie? How old are you?	(***Ich bin***) ***dreißig*** (***Jahre alt***). (I am) thirty (years old).
Wie alt ist der Reisebegleiter? Woher kommt er?	**Er ist achtundzwanzig Jahre alt. Er kommt aus Berlin. Er ist also** [therefore] **Berliner, aber** [but] **er ist auch** [also] **Deutscher.**
Wie alt ist die Kellnerin? Woher kommt sie?	**Sie ist vierzig Jahre alt. Sie kommt auch aus Berlin. Sie ist also Berlinerin, aber sie ist auch Deutsche.**

Übung 8L

Answer these questions about yourself. Remember for future use both the questions and answers!

Wie alt sind Sie?	**Ich bin. . . .**
Woher kommen Sie?	**Ich komme aus** [town/city]. **. . .** **Ich bin** [nationality]. **. . .**

Übung 8M

Number practice: how old were the following when they died?

1 **Johann Wolfgang Goethe**
ist am achtundzwanzigsten vierten siebzehnhundertneunundvierzig geboren und am zweiundzwanzigsten dritten achtzehnhundertzweiunddreißig gestorben.
Er war ___________ Jahre alt.

2 **Jacob Grimm**
ist am vierten ersten siebzehnhundertfünfundachtzig geboren und am zwanzigsten neunten achtzehnhundertdreiundsechzig gestorben.
Er war ___________ Jahre alt.

3 **Wilhelm Grimm**
ist am vierundzwanzigsten zweiten siebzehnhundertsechsundachtzig geboren und am sechzehnten zwölften achtzehnhundertneunundfünfzig gestorben.
Er war ___________ Jahre alt.

4 **Wolfgang Amadeus Mozart**
ist am einundzwanzigsten ersten siebzehnhundertsechsundfünfzig geboren und am fünften zwölften siebzehnhunderteinundneunzig gestorben.
Er war ____________ Jahre alt.

5 **Karl Marx**
ist am fünften fünften achtzehnhundertachtzehn geboren und am vierzehnten vierten achtzehnhundertdreiundachtzig gestorben.
Er war ____________ Jahre alt.

6 **Ludwig van Beethoven**
ist am siebzehnten zwölften siebzehnhundertsiebzig geboren und am sechsundzwanzigsten dritten achtzehnhundertsiebenundzwanzig gestorben.
Er war ____________ Jahre alt.

7 **Albrecht Dürer**
ist am einundzwanzigsten fünften vierzehnhunderteinundsiebzig geboren und am sechsten vierten fünfzehnhundertachtundzwanzig gestorben.
Er war ____________ Jahre alt.

8 **Marlene Dietrich**
ist am siebenundzwanzigsten zwölften neunzehnhunderteins geboren und am sechsten fünften neunzehnhundertzweiundneunzig gestorben.
Sie war ____________ Jahre alt.

9 **Willy Brandt**
ist am achtzehnten zwölften neunzehnhundertdreizehn geboren und am achten zehnten neunzehnhundertzweiundneunzig gestorben.
Er war ____________ Jahre alt.

10 **Albert Einstein**
ist am vierzehnten dritten achtzehnhundertneunundsiebzig geboren und am achtzehnten vierten neunzehnhundertfünfundfünfzig gestorben.
Er war ____________ Jahre alt.

Übung 8N

Return to Text 8 and re-cast it with yourself in either of the two roles. Make any changes (e.g. to the places mentioned) which would be needed in order to 'personalize' the dialogue, but limit the changes to what you can manage linguistically at this early stage!

9 Gestern und vorgestern

The recent past

Language activity

- in this **Lektion** we concentrate on talking about the past

Language focus

- past participles
- auxiliary verbs: **haben** and **sein**
- adverbs

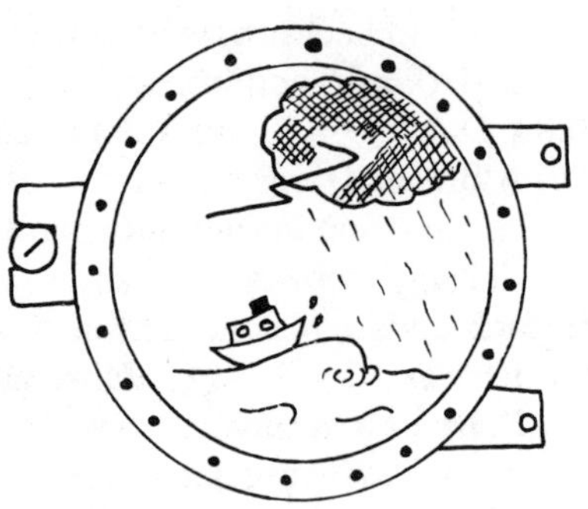

Text 9

Dienstag abend [1]

Our German learner, who until recently we were calling **Sie**, now has a name: Peter Bennett. In all subsequent **Lektionen**, you will need to 'be' him or his acquaintance, Heidi Dettmann! Or at least you will need to imagine yourself at some time in the future wanting to say very broadly similar sorts of things, using identical linguistic devices. Doubtless, you too will not want to enter a German-speaking environment equipped with only one tense of the verb, the present, so in Text 9 and thereafter Peter and Heidi, your *alter egos*, are given the tools to proceed beyond the here and now and discuss the past.

They talk about how they got to Berlin: by coach, train, boat or plane, what route each of them took, what the journey was like, when they arrived and what they did in Berlin before they met on the sight-seeing tour.

Peter experienced a wet and stormy crossing from Hull to Hamburg (he slept on the boat) and was glad that the subsequent train journey was less eventful. Heidi came by coach. Having arrived in Berlin, their actions were more or less identical, though they *are* staying at different hotels. . . .

PETER B: Wie sind[1] Sie nach Berlin gekommen, Frau[2] Dettmann? Mit[3] dem Bus oder mit dem Zug?

HEIDI D: Mit dem Bus. Und Sie, Herr Bennett? Sind Sie geflogen?[4]

PETER B: Nein, ich bin vorgestern[5] mit dem Schiff von Hull nach Hamburg gefahren. Ich habe auf dem Schiff geschlafen,[6] und in Hamburg habe ich den Zug genommen.[7]

HEIDI D: Wie war die Fahrt?[8]

PETER B: Oh, sie war nicht sehr gut. Die lange Überfahrt[9] war leider[10] naß[11] und stürmisch. Aber die Zugfahrt war in Ordnung.[12]

HEIDI D: Um wieviel Uhr sind Sie angekommen?[13]

PETER B: Ich bin gestern vormittag gegen[14] elf Uhr in Berlin angekommen. Ich bin dann[15] in ein Café gegangen.[16] Ich habe ein Stück Torte gegessen[17] und eine Tasse Kaffee getrunken.[18]

HEIDI D: Ach nein![19] Ich bin gestern gegen halb zwölf angekommen und bin auch zuerst[20] in ein Café gegangen. Ich habe auch eine Tasse Kaffee getrunken.

PETER B: Haben Sie dann vielleicht einen Stadtplan gekauft?

HEIDI D: Ja, ich habe einen großen Stadtplan von Berlin gekauft – und Ansichtskarten und Briefmarken.

PETER B: Na so was![21] Sie auch?! Typische Touristen![22] Sind Sie danach[23] zum Hotel gegangen oder was haben Sie gemacht?

HEIDI D: Ich bin zum Hotel gegangen.

PETER B: Nicht etwa[24] zum Hotel Müller!?

HEIDI D: Nein, nicht zum Hotel Müller sondern[25] zum Hotel Schmidt. . . .

Notes

1 literally: 'How *are* you come to Berlin?' = 'How did you come to Berlin?'

2 **Frau** is the most common (and the official) term of address for a woman these days, whether married or not. The use of **Fräulein** for an unmarried woman is felt by many to be antiquated

3 'by' with a mode of transport is always **mit** in German
4 'Did you fly?' The infinitive of the verb is **fliegen**
5 **gestern** is 'yesterday', so **vorgestern** is the 'day before yesterday'
6 the infinitive of **geschlafen** is **schlafen**, 'to sleep'
7 the infinitive of **genommen** is **nehmen**, 'to take'
8 **fahren**, 'to travel', and **Fahrt**, 'journey', are clearly related: they have the same stem **fahr-**
9 literally: 'over-journey' i.e. 'crossing', here 'sea crossing'
10 'unfortunately': a short and very useful word
11 'wet and stormy'. **Der Sturm** = 'storm'
12 **die Ordnung** = 'order'
13 **angekommen** is the past participle of **ankommen**, a separable verb (see **Lektion sechs**)
14 'towards'
15 'then'
16 **gegangen** is the past participle of **gehen**. The use of **gehen** indicates that he is now walking
17 **gegessen** is the past participle of **essen**
18 **getrunken** is the past participle of **trinken**
19 an expression of surprise: e.g. 'Really!? Well, well, well!'
20 'first of all'
21 expression of even greater surprise: e.g. 'You don't say! Well I never!'
22 'typical tourists'
23 both **dann** and **danach** mean 'then, after that'
24 **nicht etwa** suggests 'not, by any chance . . .?'
25 **nicht** . . . **sondern** = 'not . . . but'. 'But' without **nicht** = **aber**

Übung 9A

Find equivalents in Text 9 (and in the Notes above) for the following nouns. Write them, each with a capital letter, in three columns and preceded by **der**, **das** or **die**. Where the text contains a plural form you may need to check the Glossary for the singular. When you have finished, your German nouns should appear in alphabetical order in each column.

masculine	*neuter*	*feminine*
bus/coach	café	picture postcard
coffee	Miss	postage stamp
street map	hotel	journey
storm	ship/boat	Mrs/woman
tourist	piece	order

train	cup
	gateau
	crossing
	clock/o'clock
	train journey

Übung 9B

Find and write out the German equivalents in Text 9 of the following sentences/phrases. Don't try to translate the English sentences word for word: look for 'whole-sentence' equivalents and stick to the original German word order.

1 How did you get to Berlin?
2 The day before yesterday I went by boat from Hull to Hamburg.
3 In Hamburg I took the train.
4 What was the journey like?
5 Unfortunately the long crossing was wet and stormy.
6 At what time did you arrive?
7 I arrived yesterday morning, getting on for eleven o'clock.
8 First I went into a café.
9 Well I never!
10 I went to the hotel.

Verbs: talking about the past

Übung 9C

Before we discuss in detail the formation of the past tense in German, let us look at where it occurs in Text 9. As you know from **Lektion fünf**, it is signalled by the *past participle*, a form of the verb often starting with **ge**- and ending in -**t**, e.g. **gewählt** (chosen) or -**en**. For the list of verbs below, which are given in their infinitive form, find the corresponding past participles in Text 9. Nine of the ten past participles you are seeking begin with **ge**-, and the other one (because the verb in this case is separable) will have -**ge**- not at the beginning but after its prefix.

	infinitive		*past participle*
1	**kaufen**	to buy	
2	**fahren**	to go [by transport]	
3	**fliegen**	to fly	
4	**gehen**	to go [walk]	
5	**kommen**	to come	
6	**ankommen**	to arrive	
7	**machen**	to do	
8	**nehmen**	to take	
9	**schlafen**	to sleep	
10	**trinken**	to drink	

In **Lektion fünf** we learnt that the most common way of talking about the past in English and in German is to use a *past tense* of the verb. In spoken German, the most common past tense is called the *perfect* tense. It usually consists of a form of the verb **haben** (as an auxiliary, i.e. 'helping out' verb) + a past participle of the verb that carries the notion you wish to convey, e.g.

	auxiliary			*past participle*
	***Haben* Sie**	**schon**		***gewählt?***
	Have you	already		chosen?
	Ich *habe*	**schon**	**Eis**	***gewählt.***
Literally:	I have	already	ice cream	chosen
	***Hat* es**	**(Ihnen)**		***geschmeckt?***
Literally:	Has it	to you		tasted?
	[= Did you like (the taste of) it?]			
	Berlin *hat*	**mir gut**		***gefallen!***
Literally:	Berlin has	me well		pleased
	[= I liked Berlin a lot]			

In **Lektion neun** there are five more examples of verbs following the pattern above:

	infinitive	*auxiliary* (*in italic*)	*past participle*
buy	**kaufen**	***Haben* Sie einen Stadtplan**	***gekauft?***
do	**machen**	**Was *haben* Sie**	***gemacht?***
take	**nehmen**	**In Hamburg *habe* ich den Zug**	***genommen.***
sleep	**schlafen**	**Ich *habe* auf dem Schiff**	***geschlafen.***
drink	**trinken**	**Ich *habe* auch eine Tasse Tee**	***getrunken.***

Note that the German perfect tense has two possible meanings in English, depending on context, e.g.

er hat Eis gewählt (a) he *chose* ice-cream.
(b) he *has chosen* ice-cream.

Happily, German does not usually make this distinction in meaning (see box below).

The missing verbs in **Übung 9D** below follow this pattern:

kaufen	I	**ich**	***habe***		***gekauft***
trinken	he/it	**er**			***getrunken***
essen	she/it	**sie**	***hat***	+ 'rest of sentence'	***gegessen***
schlafen	it	**es**			***geschlafen***
nehmen	we	**wir**			***genommen***
	you	**Sie**	***haben***		
	they	**sie**			

Übung 9D

Supply the missing verb in the perfect tense:

buy 1 **Herr Bennett _____ Briefmarken _________.**
drink 2 **Ich _____ eine Tasse Kaffee _________.**
eat 3 **Er _____ ein Stück Torte _________.**
buy 4 **Frau Dettmann _____ einen großen Stadtplan ______.**
sleep 5 **Ich ______ nicht im Bus __________.**
take 6 **Sie** [*she*] **_____ den Bus nach Berlin _________.**

> NB There is another German past tense, rarely used by speakers of southern varieties of German, called the preterite, simple past or (misleadingly) the imperfect, cf. English 'I have chosen' (perfect) vs. 'I chose' (preterite). In general – and unlike English – there is *no difference in meaning in German between the two past tenses.* In Text 9 we have used a preterite form of the verb 'to be', viz. **war** (meaning 'was' *or* 'has been'), rather than the perfect form (which would be **ist** . , . **gewesen**), simply because **war** is more commonly used in most parts of Germany than **ist** . . . **gewesen**.

Verbs: past (perfect) tense with haben *or* sein?

The other five of the ten verbs in **Übung 9C** follow a different pattern from that described above, in that they use as their auxiliary not the verb **haben** but the verb **sein**.

Übung 9E

Provide the missing auxiliary verb forms for the following sentences taken from Text 9:

1 **Wie _____ Sie nach Berlin gekommen?**
2 **_____ Sie geflogen?**
3 **Nein, ich _____ mit dem Schiff von Hull nach Hamburg gefahren.**
4 **Um wieviel Uhr _____ Sie angekommen?**
5 **Ich _____ gestern vormittag gegen elf Uhr angekommen.**
6 **Ich _____ zuerst in ein Café gegangen.**
7 **_____ Sie danach zum Hotel gegangen?**
8 **Ich _____ zum Hotel gegangen.**

The verbs in **Übung 9E** therefore follow the following pattern:

fahren	I	**ich**	*bin*		***gefahren***
gehen	he/it	**er**			***gegangen***
kommen	she/it	**sie**	*ist*	+ 'rest of sentence' +	***gekommen***
ankommen	it	**es**			***angekommen***
fliegen	we	**wir**			***geflogen***
	you	**Sie**	*sind*		
	they	**sie**			

> This division of German verbs into '**haben**-verbs' and '**sein**-verbs' often seems odd to speakers of modern English. It may be of interest (if not of direct practical use!) to note that speakers of older forms of English would have found such a division quite normal, cf. Shakespeare's *Hamlet*, where Polonius says to the Prince:
> 'The ambassadors from Norway, my good lord, *are* joyfully return'd.'

On the whole, verbs that can have direct objects need **haben** as auxiliary; verbs that can't need **sein**. Also, verbs of motion, because they can't have direct objects, tend to use **sein**. The following two sentences illustrate the point:

(a) **Sie *ist* nach Potsdam *gefahren.***	She went/she's gone to Potsdam
(b) **Sie *hat* in Potsdam einen Berliner *gekauft.***	She (has) bought a doughnut in Potsdam

In (b) the doughnut is the direct object of the verb **kaufen**, i.e. the doughnut is 'what' she bought. The verb can take a direct object (accusative case), so uses ***haben*** as auxiliary.

In (a) there is *no* direct object of the verb **fahren**, i.e. in relation to the action indicated by the verb, Potsdam is not '*what* she travelled' but '*to where* she travelled'. **Fahren** cannot here take a direct object (accusative case), so uses ***sein***.

nominative subject	auxiliary	where?	*accusative* object: what?	past participle
Sie	***ist***	**nach Potsdam**		***gefahren***
Sie	***hat***	**in Potsdam**	**einen Berliner**	***gekauft***

Verbs: past participles

The most common 'regular' patterns for German past participles are:

infinitive						*past participle*
stem|ending		**ge-**	*[stem]*	**-t**		
mach|en	→	**ge-**	**mach**	**-t**	→	***gemacht***
kauf|en	→	**ge-**	**kauf**	**-t**	→	***gekauft***
dauer|n	→	**ge-**	**dauer**	**-t**	→	***gedauert***
kost|en	→	**ge-**	**kost**	**-et**	→	***gekostet***

As in English (see **Lektion fünf** for English examples), the 'irregular' past participle patterns vary widely. But many verbs with irregular past participles are common verbs and are learnt quickly through being seen and heard frequently. These are the verbs with irregular past participles in **Lektion neun**:

infinitive		*past participle*
trinken	**ich habe (ein) Bier**	***getrunken***
essen	**ich habe ein Stück Torte**	***gegesssen***
nehmen	**ich habe den Bus**	***genommen***
fahren	**ich bin nach Berlin**	***gefahren***
ankommen	**ich bin am Montag**	***angekommen***
gehen	**ich bin zu Fuß zum Hotel**	***gegangen***

All irregular past participles of verbs used in this book are listed alphabetically in the Glossary on their own and cross-referenced to their infinitive form.

Word order

Perhaps the most striking difference between word order in English and in German sentences is that the German verb (or part of it) often seems to 'get left' to the end, a phenomenon which inspired the witticism: 'In the best academic works in German, the verbs appear in the second volume.' German past participles, certainly, mostly bring up the rear of German sentences:

Ich *fahre* am Mittwoch mit dem Zug nach Berlin
Idiomatically: 'On Wednesday I'm taking the train to Berlin.'

Ich *bin* am Mittwoch mit dem Zug nach Berlin *gefahren.*
Idiomatically: 'On Wednesday I took the train to Berlin.'

Übung 9F

Imagine you are having a conversation with a partner. Write out the questions in German: in each case we have given a possible answer.

1 [Did you fly from Dallas to Berlin?]
Nein, ich bin nicht von Dallas sondern von Denver geflogen.
2 [Did you go yesterday to the hotel?]
Nein, ich bin nicht gestern sondern vorgestern zum Hotel gegangen.
3 [Did you go by bus from Dorfmark to Berlin?]
Nein, ich bin nicht mit dem Bus sondern mit dem Zug gefahren.
4 [Did you, too, arrive on Monday at around 11 a.m.?]
Nein, ich bin heute nachmittag gegen zwei Uhr angekommen.
5 [Did you take the first train?]
Nein, ich habe den zweiten genommen.
6 [Did you like Berlin?]
Berlin hat mir gar nicht gut gefallen!
7 [How did you like the Berliner Weiße?]
Sie hat mir leider nicht sehr gut geschmeckt.
8 [Did you buy the big streetmap?]
Nein, ich habe den kleinen gekauft.

Übung 9G

Now answer your German questions (check that you got them right) in the affirmative, first by looking and then without looking at **Übung 9F**.

Adverbs

In the same way that adjectives describe nouns, an adverb will say something extra about the action of the verb, e.g.

when it happened	→	adverbs of *time*	e.g. **heute**
how it happened	→	adverbs of *manner*	e.g. **gut**
where it happened	→	adverbs of *place*	e.g. **hier**

> Conveniently, many German adjectives/adverbs have only one form; e.g. **gut** can mean 'good/well', **natürlich** 'natural/naturally', depending on context.

When an adverb consists of more than one word, it is often called an *adverbial phrase*, e.g. **am Mittwoch** (time), **mit dem Bus** (manner), **in Berlin** (place).

Times of (yester)day

A table such as that below could also be drawn up for **vorgestern** = the day before yesterday.

gestern **morgen**	yesterday	morning	(any time a.m.)
gestern **vormittag**	yesterday	morning	(any time a.m.)
gestern **früh**	yesterday	morning	(ditto or early a.m.)
gestern **mittag**	yesterday	lunchtime	(midday)
gestern **nachmittag**	yesterday	afternoon	
gestern **abend**	yesterday	evening	
gestern **nacht**	last*	night	

* There is potential ambiguity in this expression, given that a night stretches over yesterday *and* today. **Heute nacht** can mean the night to come or the night just past, and **gestern nacht** the night just past or the night before that. Usually the context will make the meaning clear.

Also, you might be wondering why the second word in each of the expressions above is written with a small letter rather than a capital: after all, **der Morgen** (the morning), **die Nacht** (the night) etc. are also correctly spelt! The reason for the small letter is that it is felt that e.g. **nacht** in an expression such as **heute nacht** is no longer a noun but part of an adverbial phrase, and adverbs aren't normally written with capitals.

Übung 9H

Events in sequence. Replace each of the numbers in the short text below with one of the following adverbs: **danach** – **dann** – **dort** – **zuerst**. Three of these adverbs are adverbs of time, one is an adverb of place. Check their meanings in the Notes to the Text (**dann** and **danach** are often interchangeable).

Ich bin von Hull nach Hamburg mit dem Schiff gefahren. [1] habe ich in Hamburg einen Zug genommen. In Berlin bin ich [2] in ein Café gegangen. Ich habe [3] eine Tasse Kaffee getrunken. Ich bin [4] in ein Schreibwarengeschäft gegangen und habe einen Stadtplan gekauft. [5] bin ich zum Hotel gegangen.

Übung 9J

The sentences below no longer mean what they were supposed to mean because the past participles are mixed up! Can you unscramble them, i.e. decide which past participle should be in which sentence?

1 **Berlin hat mir ausgezeichnet *geschmeckt.***
2 **Wir sind gestern zu Fuß von Potsdam nach Berlin *gefahren.***
3 **In Potsdam habe ich einen Berliner *getrunken.***
4 **Die Überfahrt hat sehr lange *gekostet.***
5 **Das gemischte Eis hat köstlich *gefallen.***

6 **Meine Frau ist gestern mit dem Zug von Berlin nach Bonn *geflogen.***
7 **In einem Schreibwarengeschäft habe ich einen Stadtplan, Ansichtskarten und Briefmarken *genommen.***
8 **Das Hotelzimmer hat nur vierzig Mark *gedauert.***
9 **Haben Sie den Bus oder den Zug *gekauft?***
10 **Ich bin oft von New York nach London *gegangen.***
11 **Haben Sie schon Berliner Weiße *gegessen?***

Übung 9K

Text 9 has been reprinted below with all the verbs missing: auxiliaries, past participles and **war**. You should be able to supply most of the missing items from memory if you worked through **Lektion neun** reasonably conscientiously!

PETER B: Wie [1] Sie nach Berlin [2], Frau Dettmann? Mit dem Bus oder mit dem Zug?

HEIDI D: Mit dem Bus. Und Sie, Herr Bennett? [3] Sie [4]?

PETER B: Nein, ich [5] vorgestern mit dem Schiff von Hull nach Hamburg [6]. Ich [7] auf dem Schiff [8] , und in Hamburg [9] ich den Zug [10] .

HEIDI D: Wie [11] die Fahrt?

PETER B: Oh, sie [12] nicht sehr gut. Die lange Überfahrt [13] leider naß und stürmisch. Aber die Zugfahrt [14] in Ordnung.

HEIDI D: Um wieviel Uhr [15] Sie [16]?

PETER B: Ich [17] gestern vormittag gegen elf Uhr in Berlin [18]. Ich [19] dann in ein Café [20]. Ich [21] ein Stück Torte [22] und eine Tasse Kaffee [23].

HEIDI D: Ach nein! Ich [24] gegen halb zwölf [25] und [26] auch zuerst in ein Café [27]. Ich [28] auch eine Tasse Kaffee [29].

PETER B: [30] Sie dann vielleicht einen Stadtplan [31]?

HEIDI D: Ja, ich [32] einen großen Stadtplan von Berlin [33] – und Ansichtskarten und Briefmarken.

PETER B: Na so was! Sie auch?! Typische Touristen! [34] Sie danach zum Hotel [35] oder was [36] Sie [37]?

HEIDI D: Ich [38] zum Hotel [39].

PETER B: Nicht etwa zum Hotel Müller!?

HEIDI D: Nein, nicht zum Hotel Müller sondern zum Hotel Schmidt. . . .

10 Herkunft

Where it all began

Language activities

- describing your background
- talking about the weather
- questioning

Language focus

- word order in statements
- how to say how often
- more possessive pronouns: *our, his, her,* etc.

Text 10

Dienstag abend (2)

Having sorted out the immediate past, Peter and Heidi now go further back – to their **Herkunft**, their origins. Although Peter now lives in York in the north east, he originally comes from Cockermouth in the north west of England, and shares his birthplace with William Wordsworth, the ever-popular 'Lakeland' poet. Heidi wasn't born where she is currently living, either: she started life in Rostock, a port on the Baltic. Peter moved to York when he was ten, Heidi to Dorfmark when she was three.

They then discuss schooling. Heidi had to travel to Fallingbostel, a neighbouring town, for her education (cycling in summer), whereas Peter had an easy stroll round the corner to his school. Neither professes to have had a particularly successful school career . . .

HEIDI D: Sind Sie in York geboren, Herr Bennett?

PETER B: Nein, ich bin in Cockermouth geboren. Das ist eine hübsche[1] kleine Stadt in Nordwestengland. In Cockermouth ist der Dichter[2] Wordsworth geboren. Er ist 1850[3] gestorben und bei uns[4] in Großbritannien immer noch[5] sehr beliebt.[6] Sind Sie in Dorfmark geboren, Frau Dettmann?

HEIDI D: Nein, ich bin in Rostock geboren. Das ist eine große Hafenstadt[7] an der Ostsee.[8] Sind Sie in Cockermouth aufgewachsen?[9]

PETER B: Nicht ganz.[10] Ich habe bis zu[11] meinem zehnten Lebensjahr[12] dort gewohnt, aber dann sind wir nach York gezogen.[13] Wie lange wohnen Sie schon in Dorfmark?

HEIDI D: Ich wohne seit[14] meinem dritten Lebensjahr in Dorfmark, aber ich bin in Fallingbostel zur Schule gegangen.[15] Fallingbostel ist eine kleine Stadt mit etwa[16] sechstausend Einwohnern.[17] Im Sommer bin ich jeden[18] Morgen die sechs Kilometer mit dem Fahrrad[19] zur Schule gefahren. Im Winter bin ich meistens[20] mit dem Zug oder manchmal mit dem Bus zur Schule gefahren.

PETER B: Und in York bin ich im Frühling,[21] Sommer, Herbst und Winter bei[22] Sonne, Regen und Schnee zu Fuß zur Schule gegangen. Aber das waren nur einige[23] hundert Meter – die Schule war ja[24] um die Ecke von unserem Haus.

HEIDI D: Waren Sie ein guter Schüler?

PETER B: Leider[25] nicht.

HEIDI D: Ich war auch keine gute Schülerin.

Notes

1 **hübsch** = 'pretty'
2 'poet, writer'
3 note that the year is given without 'in'
4 literally: 'with us', cf. French *chez nous*. **Bei** is a preposition that takes the dative case
5 literally: 'always still'. The **immer** is used to stress 'still'
6 'popular'
7 **der Hafen** ('harbour, port') + **die Stadt** ('town') = **die Hafenstadt**
8 **die Nordsee**, **die Ostsee** = 'the North Sea, the Baltic Sea'

9 **aufwachsen** (separable verb) = 'to grow up'
10 'not quite'
11 **bis zu** preposition + dative = 'until'
12 **das Leben** ('life') + **das Jahr** = **das Lebensjahr**
13 past participle of **ziehen** = 'to move' in the sense of change place of residence (also means: 'to pull')
14 **seit** preposition + dative = 'since'
15 past participle of **gehen**. **Zur Schule gehen** is a general expression meaning 'to go to school': at this stage it isn't clear whether she walked or travelled
16 'approximately'. Often used with numbers
17 **der Einwohner** is singular, **die Einwohner** the normal plural form. But here the plural follows the preposition **mit** which takes the dative, and the dative plural of most nouns has to have **-n** as an ending, hence here: **mit . . . sechstausend Einwohner*n***
18 'every'
19 **fahren** 'to travel' + **das Rad** ('wheel') = 'cycle'
20 **meistens . . . manchmal** = 'mostly/usually . . . sometimes/occasionally'
21 the seasons of the year, starting with 'spring'
22 literally: 'with', i.e. 'in'. **bei** is a very versatile preposition: see Note 4 above
23 'some, a few'
24 this **ja** is, unlike **Ja!** = 'yes', unstressed and used here for emphasis, suggesting e.g. 'after all, in fact . . .'
25 'unfortunately'

Übung 10A

Find equivalents in Text 10 (and in the Notes above) for the following nouns. Write them, each with a capital letter, in three columns and preceded by **der**, **das** or **die**. When you have finished, your German nouns should appear in alphabetical order in each column.

masculine	*neuter*	*feminine*
bus	cycle	corner
poet, writer	house	seaport
inhabitant	year	origin(s)
spring	life	North Sea
foot	year of one's life	Baltic Sea
harbour	wheel	school
autumn		pupil [female]

kilometre
metre
morning
rain
snow
pupil [male]
summer
winter
train
sun
town

Übung 10B

The two common adverbs **meistens** ('usually') and **manchmal** ('sometimes') are used in Text 10. Write out the answer to both questions in one sentence.

1 Who did what **meistens?**
2 Who did what **manchmal?**

Übung 10C

Find and write out the German equivalents in Text 10 of the following sentences/phrases. Don't try to translate the English sentences word for word: look for 'whole-sentence' equivalents and stick to the original German word order.

1 Were you born in York?
2 The poet Wordsworth was born in Cockermouth.
3 He is still very popular in Great Britain.
4 That's a port on the Baltic.
5 Did you grow up in Cockermouth?
6 Not quite.
7 I lived there until I was ten.
8 How long have you been living in Dorfmark?
9 In summer I cycled the six kilometres to school every morning.
10 In winter I usually went to school by train.
11 Were you good at school?
12 I'm afraid not!

Word order

Word order in German statements (i.e. sentences which are *not* questions and *not* commands) is more flexible than in English statements. (See **Lektion zwei** for a preliminary discussion of this point.) The rule-of-thumb is:

> the main **verb** in a German statement acts as a **pivot**: other parts of the statement revolve around the verb

Next to the verb – either on the right or on the left – is generally the subject.

Key sentence patterns

Columns 1 and 3 below can be switched, but the verb in the second column stays put, as do the items in the final column.

position 1 [or 3]	*position* 2	*position* 3 [or 1]	*position final*	
Ich	***nehme***	**die Suppe**		I('ll) take the soup.
Die Suppe	***nehme***	**ich.**		
Der Zug	***fährt***	**um neun Uhr**	***ab.***	The train leaves at nine.
Um neun Uhr	***fährt***	**der Zug**	***ab.***	
Ich	***möchte***	**am Fenster**	***sitzen.***	I'd like to sit by the window.
Am Fenster	***möchte***	**ich**	***sitzen.***	
Meine Frau	***ist***	**am 15. Juli**	***geboren.***	My wife was born on 15 July.
Am 15. Juli	***ist***	**meine Frau**	***geboren.***	

A longer sentence can often be broken up into more positions than the three/four above, e.g. the following sentence from Text 10 has eight segments, any one of which can appear in first position *except* **bin** which must stay in second position:

1 | 2 | 3 | 4 | 5

• **Im Sommer** | ***bin*** | **ich** | **jeden Morgen** | **die sechs Kilometer**

| 6 | 7 | *final*

| **mit dem Fahrrad** | **zur Schule** | ***gefahren.***

What you choose to put first in such a sentence is largely a question of style or of what you wish to emphasize. Some choices are less likely than others, but all the statements below – plus one or two not mentioned! – are possible:

- **Ich *bin* im Sommer jeden Morgen die sechs Kilometer mit dem Fahrrad zur Schule *gefahren.***
- **Im Sommer *bin* ich jeden Morgen die sechs Kilometer mit dem Fahrrad zur Schule *gefahren.***
- **Jeden Morgen *bin* ich im Sommer die sechs Kilometer mit dem Fahrrad zur Schule *gefahren.***
- **Die sechs Kilometer *bin* ich im Sommer jeden Morgen mit dem Fahrrad zur Schule *gefahren.***
- **Mit dem Fahrrad *bin* ich im Sommer jeden Morgen die sechs Kilometer zur Schule *gefahren.***

Übung 10D

The sentences below will appear familiar to you because they all contain the same words and therefore the same information as sentences you have met in Text 10. However, the sequence of words and phrases is different. Write out the equivalent original sentences from the Text and compare them with the following:

1. Der Dichter Wordsworth *ist* in Cockermouth *geboren.*
2. Wir *sind* dann nach York *gezogen.*
3. Ich *bin* im Sommer jeden Morgen die sechs Kilometer mit dem Fahrrad zur Schule *gefahren.*
4. Ich *bin* im Winter meistens mit dem Zug oder manchmal mit dem Bus zur Schule *gefahren.*
5. Ich *bin* in York im Frühling, Sommer, Herbst und Winter bei Sonne, Regen und Schnee zu Fuß zur Schule *gegangen.*
6. In Cockermouth *bin* ich *geboren.*
7. 1850 *ist* er *gestorben.*
8. Bei uns in Großbritannien *ist* er immer noch sehr *beliebt.*
9. Bis zu meinem zehnten Lebensjahr *habe* ich dort *gewohnt.*
10. Seit meinem dritten Lebensjahr *wohne* ich in Dorfmark.
11. In Fallingbostel *bin* ich zur Schule *gegangen.*

It is particularly common, for emphasis, to put an adverb or phrase indicating time (when), manner (how) or place (where) first in the sentence in place of the subject – as is the case in sentences 6 to 11 in **Übung 10D** above. English does this, too, of course, particularly with words or phrases of time, e.g.

(a) I bought a new car *yesterday.*
(b) *Yesterday* I bought a new car

But regardless of where 'yesterday' appears in the English sentence, *I* precedes 'bought'.

However, if **gestern** is put at the beginning of the German sentence, **ich** and **habe** have to switch places:

(a) ***Ich HABE gestern*** **ein neues Auto** ***gekauft.***
(b) ***Gestern HABE ich*** **ein neues Auto** ***gekauft.***

Übung 10E

Using the pattern above, re-write the following sentences with the *time word/phrase* at the beginning:

1 **Ich bin *meistens* zu Fuß zur Schule gegangen.**
2 **Ich habe *manchmal* den Zug genommen.**
3 **Ich habe *heute* schon zehn Tassen Kaffee getrunken!**
4 **Peter Bennett wohnt *seit seinem zehnten Lebensjahr* in York.**
5 **Wordsworth ist *1770* geboren.**
6 **Frau Dettmann hat *nur drei Jahre* in Rostock gewohnt.**
7 **Wir fahren *jetzt* zum Brandenburger Tor.**
8 **Wir essen *heute abend um acht Uhr* im Hotel.**
9 **Ich möchte nicht *heute abend* im Hotel essen.**
10 **Der Zug fährt *erst um 23 Uhr* ab.**

Questions

Essentially, there are two types of questions:

1 Those starting with question words, such as 'when? where? how?'
2 Those starting with the verb.

The latter can be answered with 'yes' or 'no', but the former require detailed information.

Übung 10F

Here are four type 1 questions from Text 9 and four from Text 8. Find the actual answers:

1 ***Wie*** **sind Sie nach Berlin gekommen, Frau Dettmann?**
2 ***Wie*** **war die Fahrt?**

3 ***Um wieviel Uhr*** **sind Sie angekommen?**
4 ***Was*** **haben Sie gemacht?**
5 ***Woher*** **kommen Sie?**
6 ***Was für*** **eine Stadt ist York?**
7 ***Seit wann*** **sind Sie hier in Berlin?**
8 ***Wie*** **heißen Sie?**

Personal pronouns

We first met the *possessive* forms of **ich** = **mein**, and of **Sie** = **Ihr** in **Lektion vier**. We can now extend the set (the appropriate form of the verb **haben** has been included after **ich** etc. for reference):

	I	***ich***	**habe**	→	***mein***	my
singular	he/it	***er***	**hat**	→	***sein***	his/its
	it	***es***	**hat**	→	***sein***	its
	she/it	***sie***	**hat**	→	***ihr***	her/its
plural	we	***wir***	**haben**	→	***unser***	our
	they	***sie***	**haben**	→	***ihr***	their
singular or plural	you	***Sie***	**haben**	→	***Ihr***	your

Note that there are two **sie/ihr** pairs and one **Sie/Ihr**. This is less confusing in practice than appears at first sight.

Possessive forms of the personal pronoun, like the indefinite article **ein**, are used in front of nouns, so they sometimes need endings. Also, any adjectives or ordinal numbers which *follow* **mein** etc. need endings. All the possessive pronouns work on the pattern given in the table below, i.e. they have the basic form as listed above, plus endings as necessary.

	masculine	*neuter*	*feminine*
nominative	**mein dritt*er***	**mein dritt*es***	**mein*e* dritt*e***
accusative	**mein*en* dritt*en***	**mein dritt*es***	**mein*e* dritt*e***
dative	**mein*em* dritt*en***	**mein*em* dritt*en***	**mein*er* dritt*en***

In the following sentences the words printed in italic have 'dative neuter' endings as in the table above:

Ich wohne seit *meinem dritten* Lebensjahr in Dorfmark.
Ich habe bis zu *meinem zehnten* Lebensjahr in Cockermouth gewohnt.

This is because the prepositions involved, **seit** and **zu**, always take the dative case (as do **aus**, **bei**, **mit**, **nach**, **von**) – and because **Jahr** (and therefore **Lebensjahr**) is a neuter noun.

Übung 10G

Supply the missing possessives and ordinal numbers (in words) with the appropriate endings.

1 Ich wohne seit ______ [4.] ______ Lebensjahr in London.
2 Peter wohnt seit ______ [11.] ______ Lebensjahr in York.
3 Heidi hat bis zu ______ [3.] ______ Lebensjahr in Rostock gewohnt.
4 Beethoven hat bis zu ______ [22.] ______ Lebensjahr in Bonn gewohnt.
5 Georg I. (der Erste), König von Großbritannien, hat bis zu ______ [54.] ______ Lebensjahr in Deutschland gewohnt.
6 Charlie Chaplin hat bis zu ______ [24.] ______ Lebensjahr in England gewohnt.
7 Marlene Dietrich hat bis zu ______ [29.] ______ Lebensjahr in Berlin gewohnt.
8 Wir sind Zwillinge [*twins*] und wohnen seit ______ [12.] ______ Lebensjahr in Amerika.

Seasons of the year

Plural	***die Jahreszeiten***
Singular	***die Jahreszeit***
In context	**im *Winter*, im *Frühling*, im *Sommer*, im *Herbst*** (all masculine) 'in the winter . . ., spring . . ., summer . . ., autumn'

Weather

Singular (no plural)	***das Wetter***
In context	***Wie ist das Wetter bei Ihnen* (in England, Deutschland . . .)?** What is the weather like (with you) . . .? 'How's the weather . . .?'

There are of course lots more ways of describing seasonal weather patterns, and the highly generalized UK-inspired visual overview on the next page contains but a few. Note:

noun		**der *Grad***	degree (like **Mark** it doesn't change after numbers)
verbs	**schneien**	***es schneit***	it snows, is snowing
	scheinen	***die Sonne scheint***	the sun shines, is shining
	regnen	***es regnet***	it rains, is raining
adjectives		***kalt***	cold
		warm	warm
		heiß	hot
		kühl	cool
		windig	windy

Übung 10H

Spend some time memorizing the text accompanying the drawings, and then, without looking back, provide the missing words below. When you have finished, check your answers against the text.

1 Im ______ ist es kalt.
Es ______.
Es ist ______ 5 ______.

2 Im Frühling ______ es warm.
______ regnet.
Es ______ 14 ______.

3 Im Sommer ist es ______.
Die Sonne ______.
______ haben 26 ______.

4 Im ______ ist es ______.
Es ist ______.
Wir ______ 12 Grad.

Wie ist das Wetter bei Ihnen?

1 Im *Winter* ist es kalt.
Es schneit.
Es sind minus 5 Grad.

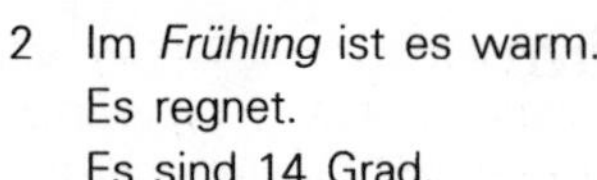

2 Im *Frühling* ist es warm.
Es regnet.
Es sind 14 Grad.

3 Im *Sommer* ist es heiß.
Die Sonne scheint.
Wir haben 26 Grad.

4 Im *Herbst* ist es kühl.
Es ist windig.
Wir haben 12 Grad.

Wie ist das Wetter bei Ihnen im Winter/Frühling/Sommer/Herbst?
Wieviel Grad sind es? Wieviel Grad haben Sie?

The following table is less impressionistic: it gives some hard data about average day temperatures and rainfall in various towns around the world in July and December. The accompanying exercises provide typical expressions relating to the weather but also practise word order and revision of numbers.

Land	*Stadt*	*Tagestemperatur [Grad Celsius]*		*Regen [Zentimeter]*	
		Dezember	*Juli*	*Dezember*	*Juli*
Deutschland	**Berlin**	1	23	5	8
Österreich	**Wien**	1	24	5	8
Schweiz	**Genf**	4	25	6	7
England	**Manchester**	8	20	8	8
Schottland	**Fort William**	8	18	22	10
Irland	**Dublin**	9	18	7	7
Indien	**Kalkutta**	28	32	1	32
USA	**New Orleans**	18	30	12	16
Kanada	**Winnipeg**	-10	25	2	8
Südafrika	**Kapstadt**	24	18	2	9
Australien	**Alice Springs**	34	19	3	1
Neuseeland	**Auckland**	21	15	8	14

Übung 10J

Answer the following questions about average day temperatures, using data from the table above. In your answers, stick to the Berlin model provided below, replacing the italicized words as appropriate.

> **Wieviel Grad sind es im Juli in Berlin?**
> Literally: 'How many degrees are there (it) in July in Berlin?' (i.e. 'How hot/cold is it . . .?')
> **Im *Juli* sind es in Berlin etwa** [= 'approx.'] ***dreiundzwanzig* Grad.**

1 Wieviel Grad sind es im Dezember in Alice Springs?
2 Wieviel Grad sind es im Juli in Wien?
3 Wieviel Grad sind es im Juli in Winnipeg ?
4 Wieviel Grad sind es im Dezember in Manchester?
5 Wieviel Grad sind es im Juli in Genf?
6 Wieviel Grad sind es im Dezember in Kapstadt?

7 Wieviel Grad sind es im Juli in Kalkutta?
8 Wieviel Grad sind es im Juli in Alice Springs?
9 Wieviel Grad sind es im Juli in Dublin?
10 Wieviel Grad sind es im Dezember in Dublin?
11 Wieviel Grad sind es im Dezember in Winnipeg?

Übung 10K

Answer the following questions about average rainfall, using data from the table above. In your answers, stick to the Berlin model provided below, replacing the italicized words as appropriate.

Wieviel Regen fällt im Juli in Berlin?
How much rain falls in July in Berlin?
Im *Juli* fallen in *Berlin* etwa *acht* Zentimeter Regen.

1 Wieviel Regen fällt im Dezember in Alice Springs?
2 Wieviel Regen fällt im Juli in Alice Springs?
3 Wieviel Regen fällt im Juli in Genf?
4 Wieviel Regen fällt im Dezember in New Orleans?
5 Wieviel Regen fällt im Juli in New Orleans?
6 Wieviel Regen fällt im Dezember in Fort William?
7 Wieviel Regen fällt im Juli in Fort William?
8 Wieviel Regen fällt im Juli in Kalkutta?
9 Wieviel Regen fällt im Dezember in Kalkutta?
10 Wieviel Regen fällt im Juli in Auckland?
11 Wieviel Regen fällt im Dezember in Kapstadt?

Übung 10L

Answer the following questions about the weather in general, using data from the table above. In your answers, stick to the Berlin model provided, describing temperatures in terms of:

(sehr) heiß	**warm**	**milde**	**kühl**	**(sehr) kalt**
(*very*) *hot*	*warm*	*mild*	*cool*	(*very*) *cold*

and how often it rains in terms of:

sehr stark	**(fast) immer**	**meistens**	**oft**
very heavily	(*almost*) *always*	*usually*	*often*

(nur) manchmal	**selten**	**fast nie**
(*only*) *occasionally*	*rarely*	*hardly ever*

Ask the question ten times and in your answers replace the italicized words as broadly appropriate:

Wie ist das Wetter im Juli in Berlin?
In *Berlin* ist es im *Juli warm* und es regnet *nur manchmal.*

1 Wie ist das Wetter im Dezember in Auckland?
2 Wie ist das Wetter im Juli in Alice Springs?
3 Wie ist das Wetter im Dezember in Winnipeg?
4 Wie ist das Wetter im Juli in Kalkutta?
5 Wie ist das Wetter im Dezember in Fort William?
6 Wie ist das Wetter im Dezember in Dublin?
7 Wie ist das Wetter im Juli in New Orleans?
8 Wie ist das Wetter im Dezember in Wien?
9 Wie ist das Wetter im Juli in Kapstadt?
10 Wie ist das Wetter im Dezember in Berlin?

Übung 10M

Now talk in general terms about the weather in your own part of the world. Ask four questions and give four answers.

Wie ist das Wetter *bei Ihnen* im [Winter–Frühling–Sommer–Herbst]?

1 **Bei uns** ist es im Winter ______ und es regnet ______
2 **Bei uns** ist es im Frühling ______ und es regnet ______
3 **Bei uns** ist es im Sommer ______ und es regnet ______
4 **Bei uns** ist es im Herbst ______ und es regnet ______

Übung 10N

Here are lots of questions which can be answered with **Ja!** or **Nein!** Use this **Übung** as an opportunity for *revision*: read through all the Texts before answering any of the questions! The questions all relate to information contained in the first ten **Lektionen** of the book. When answering, assume that the **Sie** in the early **Lektionen** is the Peter Bennett of the later ones. Note that there is no 'Does ...?' or equivalent in German questions, so 'Does Peter drink ...?' is simply and literally 'Drinks Peter ...?'

		JA	NEIN
1.1	Trinkt Peter Tee mit Zitrone?	☐	☐
1.2	Zahlt er acht Mark?	☐	☐

2.1 Kauft er einen kleinen Stadtplan von Berlin? ☐ ☐
2.2 Kostet der Stadtplan vier Mark fünfzig? ☐ ☐
2.3 Kostet eine Postkarte nach Amerika zwei Mark zwanzig? ☐ ☐
2.4 Kauft er fünf Ansichtskarten? ☐ ☐
3.1 Nimmt er die dritte Straße rechts? ☐ ☐
3.2 Ist das Hotel Müller auf der rechten Straßenseite? ☐ ☐
4.1 Nimmt er ein Doppelzimmer? ☐ ☐
4.2 Nimmt er ein Zimmer mit Dusche? ☐ ☐
4.3 Ist sein Zimmer im dritten Stock? ☐ ☐
4.4 Bucht er das Zimmer für sechs Nächte? ☐ ☐
4.5 Wohnt Peter Bennett in New York? ☐ ☐
4.6 Ist seine Paßnummer 22 45 12 13 D? ☐ ☐
4.7 Möchte er mit Kreditkarte zahlen? ☐ ☐
4.8 Hat er viel Gepäck? ☐ ☐
4.9 Nimmt er den Fahrstuhl? ☐ ☐
5.1 Hat das Hotel ein Restaurant? ☐ ☐
5.2 Sitzt er in der Ecke? ☐ ☐
5.3 Bestellt er einen Nachtisch? ☐ ☐
5.4 Trinkt er eine Flasche Wein? ☐ ☐
5.5 Trinkt er einen Sylvaner? ☐ ☐
5.6 Ißt er den Obstsalat ohne Sahne? ☐ ☐
5.7 Schmeckt ihm das Abendessen? ☐ ☐
6.1 Macht Peter seine Stadtrundfahrt am Mittwoch? ☐ ☐
6.2 Dauert die große Stadtrundfahrt eineinhalb Stunden? ☐ ☐
6.3 Kostet die Stadtrundfahrt zwanzig Mark? ☐ ☐
6.4 Fährt der Bus vom Brandenburger Tor ab? ☐ ☐
6.5 Kennt Peter das Europa-Center in der Budapester Straße? ☐ ☐
6.6 Fährt er zum Europa-Center? ☐ ☐
7.1 Ist Jochen Richter Hamburger? ☐ ☐
7.2 Ist er fünfundzwanzig Jahre alt? ☐ ☐
7.3 Ist er Ingenieur? ☐ ☐
7.4 Ist Berlin die Hauptstadt Deutschlands? ☐ ☐
7.5 Ist Berlin eine alte Stadt? ☐ ☐
7.6 Kann Peter den Reisebegleiter gut hören? ☐ ☐
7.7 Ist der Kurfürstendamm in Charlottenburg? ☐ ☐
7.8 Ist Charlottenburg das historische Zentrum Berlins? ☐ ☐
7.9 Fährt der Bus durch das Brandenburger Tor? ☐ ☐

pronunciation practice, dialogues and role-playing exercises recorded by native speakers of German and are an invaluable aid to improving your language skills.

If you have been unable to obtain the course pack, the double cassette (ISBN 0–415–02800–0) can be ordered separately through your bookseller or, in case of difficulty, send payment with order to Routledge Ltd, ITPS, Cheriton House, North Way, Andover, Hants SP10 5BE, price (1995) £10.99* including VAT, or to Routledge Inc., 29 West 35th Street, New York, NY 10001, USA, price $17.95 (Can. $23.95)*.

* *The publishers reserve the right to change prices without notice.*

CASSETTES ORDER FORM

Please supply one/two/ .... double cassette(s) of

Colloquial German, Hatherall and Hatherall.
ISBN 0–415–02800–0

Price £10.99* incl. VAT
$17.95 (Can. $23.95)*

☐ I enclose payment with order.
☐ Please debit my Access/Mastercharge/Mastercard/Visa/American Express. Account number:

☐☐☐☐☐☐☐☐☐☐☐☐☐☐☐☐ Expiry date ....

Name ....

Address ....

....

....

7.10 Heißt der Architekt vom Brandenburger Tor Rauch? ☐ ☐
7.11 Heißt Friedrichs Pferd 'Fritz'? ☐ ☐
7.12 Hat Berlin zwei Opernhäuser? ☐ ☐
7.13 Ist das Operncafé hinter dem Prinzessinenpalais? ☐ ☐
7.14 Empfiehlt Jochen die Sachertorte? ☐ ☐
8.1 Gefällt Peter Bennett Berlin? ☐ ☐
8.2 Kommt Heide Dettmann aus Süddeutschland? ☐ ☐
8.3 Hat Dorfmark eine Kathedrale? ☐ ☐
8.4 Hat York ein Eisenbahnmuseum? ☐ ☐
8.5 Liegt Berlin zwischen Hamburg und Hannover? ☐ ☐
8.6 Ist Dorfmark eine historische Stadt? ☐ ☐
9.1 Ist Heidi mit dem Zug nach Berlin gekommen? ☐ ☐
9.2 Ist Peter von Harwich nach Hamburg gefahren? ☐ ☐
9.3 Hat er auf dem Schiff geschlafen? ☐ ☐
9.4 War die Überfahrt schön? ☐ ☐
9.5 Ist er am Vormittag in Berlin angekommen? ☐ ☐
9.6 Ist er zuerst in ein Café gegangen? ☐ ☐
9.7 Wohnt Heidi im Hotel Müller? ☐ ☐
10.1 Ist Cockermouth in Südwestengland? ☐ ☐
10.2 Ist Wordsworth in York geboren? ☐ ☐
10.3 Ist Heidi in Fallingbostel geboren? ☐ ☐
10.4 Ist Heidi in Dorfmark zur Schule gegangen? ☐ ☐
10.5 Ist Peter mit dem Fahrrad zur Schule gefahren? ☐ ☐
10.6 Hat York nur sechstausend Einwohner? ☐ ☐
10.7 Liegt Rostock an der Ostsee? ☐ ☐
10.8 Waren Heidi und Peter gute Schüler? ☐ ☐

Übung 10P

Read through Text 10 again, then describe yourself and where you come from in similar terms: where you were born, where you grew up, how you got to school, whether you were a good pupil, etc.

11 Familie und Beruf

Home and work

Language activities

- describing your job
- marital status
- children: yes or no

Language focus

- direct and indirect objects
- fun with the dative
- lots of personal pronouns

Text 11

Dienstag abend [3]

Peter and Heidi exchange information on jobs and discover that they both do more or less the same thing: sell books. He works in a university bookshop in York, she in a general bookshop in Lüneburg. They then probe each other's marital status. He has been divorced for five years; his ex-wife, a doctor, lives in Scotland with the two children, a nine-year-old boy and a seven-year-old girl. Heidi is divorced, too, but there are no children, and her former husband, an American GI – they first bumped into each other on the Hamburg underground/subway – is now back in the States. Peter first met his ex-wife in a Manchester bookshop.

PETER B: Was sind Sie eigentlich[1] von Beruf,[2] Frau Dettmann?
HEIDI D: Ich bin Buchhändlerin.[3]
PETER B: Ach nein![4] Wissen[5] Sie, ich bin auch Buchhändler.
HEIDI D: Das gibt's doch nicht![6] Wo arbeiten[7] Sie?

PETER B: Ich arbeite in einer großen Universitätsbuchhandlung[8] in York. Arbeiten Sie auch in einer Universitätsbuchhandlung?

HEIDI D: Nein, nein! Ich arbeite in einer hübschen kleinen Buchhandlung in Lüneburg. Haben Sie Familie,[9] Herr Bennett?

PETER B: Ja und nein! Ich bin wieder alleinstehend:[10] das heißt,[11] ich bin seit fünf Jahren geschieden.[12] Meine Frau – meine ehemalige[13] Frau – wohnt in Schottland. Aber sie ist Engländerin.

HEIDI D: Haben Sie Kinder?

PETER B: Ich habe zwei Kinder – einen Sohn und eine Tochter.

HEIDI D: Wie alt sind sie?

PETER B: Der Sohn ist neun Jahre alt, meine Tochter ist sieben Jahre alt. Sie leben beide[14] bei meiner Frau. Und Sie? Sind Sie verheiratet?[15]

HEIDI D: Ich bin leider[16] auch geschieden, aber ich habe keine[17] Kinder. Mein Mann ist vor drei Jahren[18] nach Amerika zurückgegangen.[19]

PETER B: Ist er Amerikaner?

HEIDI D: Ja. Er war in der amerikanischen Armee und ist als Offizier[20] nach Deutschland gekommen. Ich habe ihn[21] in Hamburg in der U-Bahn[22] kennengelernt.[23]

PETER B: Meine Frau habe ich in Manchester in einer Buchhandlung kennengelernt – Manchester hat keine U-Bahn.

HEIDI D: Was ist sie von Beruf?

PETER B: Sie hat in Manchester Medizin studiert[24] und ist seit etwa zehn Jahren Ärztin.[25]

Notes

1 'actually, in fact'
2 literally: 'by profession'
3 literally: 'book trader/dealer' (female)
4 showing surprise: 'Really?!'
5 'to know', in the sense to have/acquire knowledge (see also Note 23)
6 even more surprised: literally: 'That gives it not', i.e. 'Well, I never! You don't say!' **Es gibt** = 'There is' is discussed in detail in **Lektion sechzehn**
7 'to work'
8 **die Universität** = 'university'. **Die Buchhandlung** is the shop in which

der/die Buchhändler(in) works. The **-s-** in the compound noun is not a plural: **-s-** is often used to link nouns in this way. The plural of **Universität** would be **Universitäten**

9 literally: 'do you have family', not '*a* family'

10 **wieder** = 'again', **alleinstehend** = 'single'. The English word 'single' is also used in this context. The word **ledig** is used to mean single in the sense of never married

11 'i.e.' Can also be written in German **d.h.**

12 'divorced', literally: separated

13 'former, ex-'

14 'they both live': **leben** is more existential than **wohnen**. 'Life' is **das Leben**, **eine Wohnung** is what you live in, your 'accommodation', typically a flat/apartment

15 'married'

16 'unfortunately'

17 'no'

18 **vor** in front of a stated number of years, months, days, etc. means 'ago';

19 here it takes the dative separable verb **zurückgehen**, 'to go back, return' ('for good', i.e. 'to live there': if the focus was on the journey as such, then **zurückfahren** would be used – assuming he didn't actually walk!)

20 'as (an) officer': note there is *no indefinite article here in German*

21 'him'; **er** ('he') is nominative, **ihn** ('him') is accusative

22 **U** stands for **(der) Untergrund**, meaning 'underground', **(die) Bahn** means 'track' or 'railway'

23 separable verb **kennenlernen**, 'to learn', i.e. 'get, to know' (in the sense of get acquainted with)

24 this **studiert** is, somewhat surprisingly, the past participle of **studieren**, 'to study': verbs ending in **-ieren** do not use **ge-** to form their past participles

25 the male form is **der Arzt**

Übung 11A

Find equivalents in Text 11 (and in the Notes above) for the following nouns. Write them all in their singular form with a capital letter, in three columns and preceded by **der**, **das** or **die**. When you have finished, your German nouns should appear in alphabetical order in each column.

masculine	*neuter*	*feminine*
American	year	army

doctor
profession, job
bookseller
Mr
man, husband
officer
son
underground [*not* the railway]

child
life

doctor
railway, track
bookseller
bookshop
English(woman)
family
woman, wife
medicine
daughter
underground [railway], subway
university
university bookshop
flat, apartment

Übung 11B

Find and write out the German equivalents in Text 11 of the following sentences/phrases. Don't try to translate the English sentences word for word: look for 'whole-sentence' equivalents and stick to the original German word order.

1 What is your job (actually)?
2 Well I never!
3 Do you work in a university bookshop, too?
4 Have you got a family?
5 I've been divorced for five years.
6 I have two children – a son and a daughter.
7 My husband went back to America three years ago.
8 In the American army.
9 Manchester doesn't have an underground/subway?
10 She studied medicine.
11 She's been a doctor for about ten years.

Übung 11C

In Text 11 the following German verbs occur, but not necessarily in the infinitive form given below. Match the German verbs with the English translations.

1 **sein**	A to study
2 **geben**	B to come
3 **wissen**	C to know
4 **arbeiten**	D to go back

5	**haben**	E	to be
6	**wohnen**	F	to have
7	**leben**	G	to give
8	**zurückgehen**	H	to live [focus on *reside*]
9	**kommen**	J	to live [focus on *exist*]
10	**kennenlernen**	K	to work
11	**studieren**	L	to get to know

Übung 11D

In the following sentences, supply the missing past participle from:

gewohnt studiert gewußt gekommen kennengelernt gehabt zurückgegangen gemacht gearbeitet gelebt

1 Peter und Heidi haben beide in einer Buchhandlung ______.
2 Sie hat keine Kinder ______.
3 Ihr Mann ist nach Amerika ______.
4 Er ist als Offizier nach Deutschland ______.
5 Peter hat in Cockermouth ______.
6 Er hat im Hotelrestaurant seine Zimmernummer nicht ______.
7 Er hat seine Frau in Manchester ______.
8 Sie hat dort Medizin ______.
9 Seine Kinder haben bei seiner Frau ______.
10 In Berlin haben Peter und Heidi eine große Stadtrundfahrt ______.

Übung 11E

Now, using the same ten verbs, write the sentences below in the present tense.

1 Sie__________beide in einer Buchhandlung.
2 Heidi_________keine Kinder.
3 Ihr Mann___________nach Amerika_________.
4 Er__________als Offizier nach Deutschland.
5 Peter________in York.
6 Er_________im Hotelrestaurant seine Zimmernummer nicht.
7 Er___________seine Frau in Manchester________.
8 Sie__________dort Medizin.
9 Seine Kinder__________bei seiner Frau.
10 In Berlin_______Peter und Heidi eine große Stadtrundfahrt.

Übung 11F

Translate the answers to the questions given, then compare your translations with the original replies in the text.

1 **Was sind Sie eigentlich von Beruf?**
I'm a bookseller.
2 **Wo arbeiten Sie?**
I work in a big university bookshop in York.
3 **Arbeiten Sie auch in einer Universitätsbuchhandlung?**
No, no! I work in a nice little bookshop in Lüneburg.
4 **Haben Sie Familie?**
Yes and no! I'm single again – I've been divorced for five years.
5 **Haben Sie Kinder?**
I have two children, a son and a daughter.
6 **Was ist Ihre ehemalige Frau von Beruf?**
She studied medicine in Manchester and has been a doctor for about ten years.

Pronouns

You have now met in context most of the pronoun forms that you will be using in this book, so it's a good time for an overview. But before tackling the table below, you might find it helpful to refresh your memory regarding 'Relationships within sentences' in **Lektion zwei** and the preliminary discussion on 'Pronouns' in **Lektion sechs**.

	I	he/it	she/it	it	we	they	you
nominative	**ich**	**er**	**sie**	**es**	**wir**	**sie**	**Sie**
	me	him/it	her/it	it	us	them	you
accusative	**mich**	**ihn**	**sie**	**es**	**uns**	**sie**	**Sie**
	me	him/it	her/it	it	us	them	you
dative	**mir**	**ihm**	**ihr**	**ihm**	**uns**	**ihnen**	**Ihnen**

Sentence relationships

An overview of sentence relationships, i.e. the use of 'cases', is given below using pronouns.

The NOMINATIVE case
is used when the pronoun is SUBJECT of a sentence, e.g.

***Ich* bin verheiratet**	*I*'m married
***Ich* habe keine Kinder**	*I* don't have children

The ACCUSATIVE case
is used when the pronoun is the DIRECT OBJECT of a sentence, e.g.

Können Sie *mich* hören?	Can you hear *me*?
Peter versteht *mich* nicht.	Peter doesn't/can't understand *me*.

The DATIVE case
is used when the pronoun is the INDIRECT OBJECT of a sentence, e.g.

Er hat *mir* zwei Mark gegeben.	He gave *me* 2 Marks.

In this last example, *what* he gave was not 'me' but the money, so Marks is the *direct* object. In other words, he gave the money (*direct* object, so *accusative* case in German) *to* me (I was the *indirect* object of the action described by the verb – so have to be in the *dative* case in German).

In English, no distinction is made between the meanings of **mich** and **mir** – both are 'me'. This uniformity applies to *all* the English OBJECT pronouns (see table above), regardless of whether they are DIRECT or INDIRECT objects in a sentence. In German, a distinction between direct and indirect objects is made for all pronouns *except* for the object forms of **wir**, which are *both* **uns** (again, check this out in the table above).

On the other hand, German, more frequently than English, does *not* distinguish between nominative and accusative (see table). Neither language changes 'you' (**Sie**) or 'it' (**es**) in the accusative, but English changes 'she' to 'her' in the accusative (German uses **sie** for both) and 'they' to 'them' (again, German uses **sie** for both).

More on direct and indirect objects

If you don't need more, please go straight on to p. 180.

In the sentence

Er hat mir (= dative) **zwei Mark** (= accusative) **gegeben**,

it is not the fact that the one object is a 'thing' and the other object a person which makes the thing accusative and the person dative: it is their relationship to the action expressed in the verb that matters. Let's take an example where there are both direct and indirect objects in the same sentence, and both are people. In some wedding ceremonies, the priest requires one of the participants to state in effect: 'I give this woman to this man' (or vice versa). Here 'I' is the subject, 'this woman' the direct object, and 'this man' the indirect object. The meaning of the sentence would still be clear if the word order were changed and the preposition 'to' left out: 'I (subject) give this man (indirect object) this woman (direct object)'.

The following sentences, therefore, mean the same because the case relationships are clearly the same even though the word order has changed:

I (subject) *give this woman* (direct object) *to this man* (indirect object)
I (subject) *give this man* (indirect object) *this woman* (direct object)

In German such a statement would require 'I' to be in the nominative case form, 'this woman' to be in the accusative and 'this man' to be in the dative case. For the record, literally translated that would be:

subject	verb	indirect object	direct object
nominative		*dative*	*accusative*
Ich	**gebe**	**diesem Mann**	**diese Frau**

If we use pronouns throughout, i.e. say 'I give him her' (or 'her to him'), then German would require a different word order, but the case relationships, and hence the meaning, of course remain the same:

subject	verb	direct object	indirect object
nominative		*accusative of* ***sie***	*dative of* ***er***
Ich	**gebe**	**sie**	**ihm**
I	give	her	to him

Let's change the meaning, and give him rather than her :

subject	verb	direct object	indirect object
nominative		*accusative of* ***er***	*dative of* ***sie***
Ich	**gebe**	**ihn**	**ihr**
I	give	him	to her

Cases with prepositions

The fact that prepositions 'take' cases has nothing to do with sentence relationships as such, i.e. with direct or indirect objects: it is a separate fact of life! Many prepositions take only the accusative or the dative, but some can take both: in the **Lektionen** to date we have concentrated on 'one-case' prepositions. Here are two common examples:

anything which follows **für** must be in the *accusative*,
anything which follows **bei** must be in the *dative* case.

The case is not always obvious to the ear or eye: with personal names it isn't obvious: **für Peter** and **bei Peter**. But with pronouns it usually is:

für *mich*	**für *ihn***	**für *es***	**für *sie***
bei *mir*	**bei *ihm***	**bei *ihm***	**bei *ihr***
für *uns*	**für *sie***	**für *Sie***	
bei *uns*	**bei *ihnen***	**bei *Ihnen***	

Cases with verbs

Most verbs naturally take a direct object (in the ACCUSATIVE) but you have also met some which take only the DATIVE: with these there is little to be gained from thinking in terms of indirect objects – it's best to learn such verbs as DATIVE VERBS and use them frequently. Two common examples to date are **gefallen** and **schmecken**, as in:

Berlin hat *mir* sehr gut gefallen.
Die Sachertorte hat *mir* gut geschmeckt.

Übung 11G

Using the pronoun table above for reference, supply the correct pronoun below and state which case it is in.

		Case
1	______ bin in Cockermouth aufgewachsen.	____
2	Wo sind ______ geboren?	____
3/4	[*We*] ______ danken [*you*] ______	____

5 Die Zwiebelsuppe schmeckt [*her*] ______ nicht. _____
6 Können Sie [*me*] ______ alle gut hören? _____
7 Wie ist das Wetter bei [*you*] ______? _____
8/9 Bei [*us*] ______ in Fallingbostel _____
regnet [it] ______ heute. _____
10/11 Heidi und Peter haben eine Stadtrundfahrt
gemacht. [*It*] ______ hat _____
[*them*] ______ ausgezeichnet gefallen. _____
12 Für [*her*] ______ war die Fahrt _____
mit dem Bus nach Berlin in Ordnung.
13 Für [*him*] ______ war die Überfahrt von Hull _____
nach Hamburg naß und stürmisch.
14 [*He*] ______ hat auf dem Schiff geschlafen. _____
15 [*They*] ______ sind beide geschieden. _____
16 Kalte Zwiebelsuppe schmeckt [*me*] ______ nicht. _____
17 Darf ich [*you*] ______ zu einem Glas Wein
einladen? _____

Übung 11H

Replace the personal names with pronouns. Where there are two names within a bracket, use a German equivalent of 'they/them'.

1 [Heidi und Peter] waren beide verheiratet.
2 [Peter] hat zwei Kinder.
3 [Heidi] hat keine Kinder.
4 Berlin gefällt [Heidi und Peter].
5 Das Hotelessen hat [Peter] ausgezeichnet geschmeckt.
6 Hotel Schmidt gefällt [Heidi] sehr gut.
7 Für [Peter und Heidi] war die Stadtrundfahrt sehr interessant.
8 Für [Jochen Richter], den Reisebegeleiter, war die Stadtrundfahrt anstrengend.
9 Für [Heidi] ist Dorfmark die Hauptstadt Deutschlands!

Übung 11J

Replace the italicized nouns or noun phrases with pronouns.

1 Wie lange dauert *die Fahrt?*
2 Sie sehen, *der Bus* fährt vom Europa-Center ab.
3 Kennen Sie *das Europa-Center?*
4 Ich möchte *den Kaffee* bestellen.
5 Ich kaufe *die Briefmarken.*

6 *Das Operncafé* ist hinter der Staatsoper.
7 Sehen Sie *das Brandenburger Tor?*
8 Ich habe *meinen Mann* in der U-Bahn kennengelernt.
9 Was ist *Ihre Frau* von Beruf?
10 Bei *Peter* in York ist das Wetter nicht immer sonnig und heiß.

Prepositions mit *and* bei

Mit and **bei** both take the dative case and can sometimes both be translated as 'with', but **mit** means 'with' in the sense of 'in the company of' and **bei** means 'at my place, in my home, in my country' etc., depending on context. The difference is clearly illustrated in the following two examples:

(a) **Möchten Sie *mit mir* eine Berliner Weiße trinken?**
Ja, ich möchte gern *mit Ihnen* eine Berliner Weiße trinken!
(b) **Möchten Sie *bei mir* eine Berliner Weiße trinken?**
Ja, ich möchte gern *bei Ihnen* eine Berliner Weiße trinken!

In (a), **mit mir/mit Ihnen** could be anywhere but it is likely that e.g. a café is the proposed venue. In (b), **bei mir/bei Ihnen** makes it clear that this is an invitation to a more private venue, e.g. your own home, hotel room, etc.

More generally, **bei uns in Deutschland** could be translated as 'Back home (in Germany)' or simply 'In Germany' (implying: '. . . which is where I come from'):

Tennis ist *bei uns* in Deutschland sehr beliebt!
Wordsworth ist *bei uns* in England immer noch sehr beliebt!
***Bei uns* in Miami scheint die Sonne.**
***Bei Peter* in York regnet es im Moment.**
***Bei uns* in Berlin schneit es oft im Winter.**
Wie ist das Wetter *bei Ihnen* in Australien?

Übung 11K

Insert the following German words in appropriate positions in the text:

Nouns: **Tochter; Medizin; Universitätsbuchhandlung; Jahre; Kinder**
Verbs: **leben; kennengelernt; arbeitet**
Prepositions: **bei; in; seit**

Pronouns:	**er; sie**
Adverbs:	**dort; jetzt**
Adjectives:	**verheiratet; geschieden; ehemaligen; großen**

Herr Bennett arbeitet in York in einer [adjective] [noun]. Er war [adjective], aber [adverb] ist er [preposition] fünf Jahren [adjective]. Sein Sohn ist neun [noun] alt, und seine [noun] ist sieben Jahre alt. Seine [noun] [verb] [preposition] seiner [adjective] Frau. Sie [verb] als Ärztin [preposition] Schottland. [Pronoun] hat in Manchester [noun] studiert. [Adverb] hat [pronoun] sie auch [verb].

Question word Wo?

Wo? means 'Where?' and the answer is always in the dative – though the dative doesn't always show:

Wo arbeiten Sie?	**Ich arbeite in Berlin.**

If the place you work at or in has an article in front of it, the article has to end in **-m** (masculine and neuter) or **-r** (feminine), e.g.

***der* Zoo:**

Der Tierarzt (*vet*) **arbeitet**	**i*m* Zoo.**
	in eine*m* Zoo.

***das* Hotel:**

Die Empfangsdame arbeitet	**i*m* Hotel.**
	in eine*m* Hotel.

***das* Reisebüro:**

Jochen Richter arbeitet	**i*m* Reisebüro.**
	in eine*m* Reisebüro.

***die* Buchhandlung:**

Peter arbeitet	**in de*r* Buchhandlung.**
	in eine*r* Buchhandlung.

***die* Universität:**

Professor Schmidt arbeitet/ist	**an de*r* Universität.**
	an ein*er* Universität.
Jochen Richter studiert/ist	**an/auf d*er* Universität.**
	an/auf ein*er* Universität.

Note that, as in English, where you work is not always expressed in terms of 'in' but with a variety of other prepositions, depending on the context. Another example: **Ich bin *bei* der Post** – which could be translated as 'I'm with . . .' or 'I work for the post office'.

Übung 11L

Translate the English words in brackets in each sentence below into German. To get this right you first need to know the genders of the German nouns: if necessary, check them in the Glossary.

Was sind Sie von Beruf? Wo arbeiten Sie?

1 Ich bin Kellner – ich arbeite in [a] Restaurant in Berlin.
2 Ich bin Studentin – ich studiere an [the] Technischen Universität in Charlottenburg.
3 Ich bin Kellnerin – ich arbeite [in the] Operncafé in Unter den Linden.
4 Ich bin Verkäufer – ich arbeite in [a] Schreibwarengeschäft am Kurfürstendamm.
5 Ich bin Buchhändlerin – ich arbeite in [a] hübschen kleinen Buchhandlung in Lüneburg.
6 Ich bin Arzt – ich arbeite in [a] Krankenhaus in Edinburg.
7 Ich bin Ärztin – ich arbeite in [a] Klinik in Berlin-Mitte.
8 Ich bin Schüler – ich bin auf [the] Beethoven-Schule in Bonn.
9 Ich bin Musiker – ich bin bei [the] Berliner Staatsoper.
10 Ich bin Offizier – ich bin bei [the] amerikanischen Armee in Washington.

Übung 11M

Revision. Replace the noun with a pronoun and slot in the appropriate separable verb (one for each sentence):

aufmachen	**ankommen**	**abfahren**	**ausgehen**	**zumachen**
open	arrive	depart	go out	close

1 **Bus**; 2 **Zug**; 3 **Restaurant**; 4 **Post**; 5 **Peter**

	pronoun	*verb (present)*		*verb prefix*
1	______	__________	um zehn vom Europa-Center	______
2	______	__________	um vierzehn Uhr in Berlin	______
3	______	__________	heute morgen um elf Uhr	______
4	______	__________	am Samstag um halb eins	______
5	______	__________	heute abend mit Heidi	______

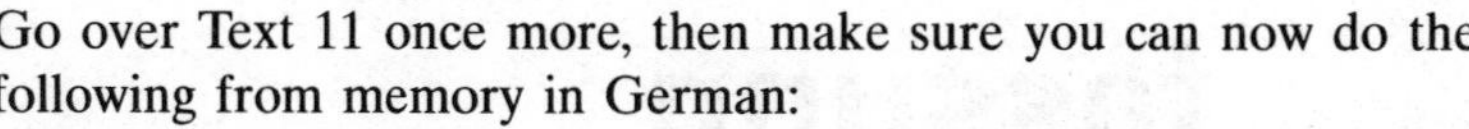

Übung 11N

Go over Text 11 once more, then make sure you can now do the following from memory in German:

1 Tell someone what your job is and where you work.
2 Elicit similar information from them.
3 Say whether or not you are married or divorced.
4 Say how long you have been in either condition!
5 Say where you met (got to know) your partner or whoever.
6 State how many children you have – or none, as the case may be.
7 If you have children, say how old they are. If you haven't, say how old you are!

12 Zusammen-fassung

The story so far

Language activities

- fact-finding
- telling a story
- testing your memory
- a mini 'CV'

Language focus

- past tense practice
- reflexive verbs
- *no* bananas etc.
- how to say 'ago'

Text 12

Sonntag bis Dienstag

The text differs from preceding ones: it is a summary (**eine Zusammenfassung**) in diary form of events and facts to date. Information is presented from a new angle, i.e. it is not given by the participants in a conversation using the first person pronouns ('I', 'we') but by an outside observer, a narrator using the third person ('he', 'she', 'they'). You will be familiar from preceding **Lektionen** with the basic content of the narrative below. Since any events described are now in the past, expect lots of practice here in the use of the past tense.

Peter Bennett ist in England aufgewachsen. Er ist vor vierzig Jahren in Cockermouth geboren und vor dreißig Jahren nach York gezogen. Er ist Buchhändler und arbeitet in einer Universitätsbuchhandlung in der nordenglischen Universitätsstadt York.

Er hat zwei Kinder – einen Sohn und eine Tochter. Sie leben bei seiner ehemaligen Frau in Schottland. Frau Dettmann ist Ärztin an einem Krankenhaus in Edinburg.

Herr Bennett ist also[1] geschieden. Er wohnt jetzt allein.[2]

SONNTAG 5. Mai[3]
Er ist am Sonntag in York abgefahren. Er ist mit dem Schiff von Hull nach Hamburg gefahren und hat auf dem Schiff geschlafen. Für eine Überfahrt war das Wetter leider nicht sehr gut: es war naß und stürmisch. Von Hamburg ist er dann mit dem Zug nach Berlin gefahren.

MONTAG 6. Mai
Er ist am Montag vormittag in Berlin angekommen. Zuerst ist er in ein Café gegangen. Dort hat er Kaffee getrunken und ein Stück Torte gegessen. Danach[4] ist er in ein Geschäft gegangen. Er hat dort einen kleinen Stadtplan, Ansichtskarten und Briefmarken gekauft. Anschließend[5] hat er nach[6] dem Weg zum Hotel Müller gefragt.

Im Hotel Müller hat er ein Einzelzimmer mit Dusche gebucht. Er hat das Zimmer für fünf Nächte vom 6. Mai bis zum 11. Mai reserviert. Sein Zimmer ist im ersten Stock, Nummer 18. Er hat sich im Zimmer sofort gewaschen.[7]

Am ersten Abend ist er dann ins[8] Hotelrestaurant gegangen. Im Restaurant hat er am Fenster gesessen. Er hat französische Zwiebelsuppe, Rührei mit Schinken und einen grünen Bohnensalat gegessen. Dazu hat er ein Viertel Weißwein getrunken. Zum Nachtisch hat er frischen Obstsalat mit Sahne bestellt.

DIENSTAG 7. Mai
Um halb drei (vierzehn Uhr dreißig) hat er eine Stadtrundfahrt gemacht. Im Bus hat er Heidi Dettmann kennengelernt. Anschließend ist er mit Frau Dettmann in ein Café gegangen. Sie haben zusammen[9] dort Berliner Weiße getrunken.

Herr Bennett und Frau Dettmann haben sich lange und lebhaft[10] im Café unterhalten.[11] Sie ist in der Hafenstadt Rostock an der Ostsee geboren aber in Dorfmark, einem[12] hübschen kleinen Ort in der Lüneburger Heide, aufgewachsen.

Frau Dettmann und Herr Bennett haben festgestellt, sie haben sehr viel gemeinsam[13] – beide sind zum Beispiel[14] Buchhändler, sie sind beide nicht mehr[15] verheiratet.

Wer weiß?[16] – Am Mittwoch gehen sie eventuell[17] zusammen[18] ins Theater. Oder vielleicht in ein Konzert . . .

Notes

1 **also** = 'therefore'. In German 'also, too' = **auch**
2 'alone, on his own'
3 pronounced: **der fünfte Mai**. 'On 5 May' = **am fünften Mai**
4 literally: 'thereafter', i.e. 'then, next'
5 'subsequently', i.e. yet another word for 'next'
6 'to ask the way' is 'to ask after the way' in German: ***nach dem Weg fragen***
7 **sich waschen** 'to wash (oneself)'
8 **ins** = **in** + **das** (accusative because the meaning here is 'into'). Once he is there, **im** (**in** + **dem** = dative) applies, as in the next line
9 'together'
10 'long and lively': both these words could be adjectives or adverbs in German – here they are adverbs since they say something about the action of the verb, i.e. about how Peter and Heidi talked
11 **sich unterhalten** is a reflexive verb ('to chat, converse'): see below for discussion of 'reflexives'
12 this is in the dative because **Dorfmark**, the noun it is dependent on, is in the dative after **in**. Grammatically, the phrase relating to **Dorfmark** is described as being 'in apposition to' **Dorfmark**
13 'in common', but German doesn't need an 'in': **wir haben viel gemeinsam** = 'we have a lot in common'
14 standard expression for 'for example'. Literally: 'to the example', often abbreviated as **z.B.** = 'e.g.'
15 literally: 'no more', idiomatically: 'no longer'
16 'Who knows?' **weiß** comes from the verb **wissen**
17 **eventuell** and **vielleicht** both mean 'perhaps' – beware: the former does *not* mean 'eventually'
18 'together'

Übung 12A

Find equivalents in Text 12 for the following nouns. Write them all in their singular form with a capital letter, in three columns and preceded by **der**, **das** or **die**. When you have finished, your German nouns should appear in alphabetical order in each column.

masculine	*neuter*	*feminine*
evening	example	postcard
bean salad	café	doctor (female)
bookseller	single room	postage stamp
bus/coach	window	shower
Tuesday	shop	Mrs/Ms
coffee	hotel	seaport town
May	hotel restaurant	heath
Wednesday	year	night
Monday	child	number
dessert	concert	Baltic Sea
fruit salad	hospital	cream
place	restaurant	sightseeing tour
ham	scrambled egg	daughter
son	ship	gateau
Sunday	piece	crossing
street plan	theatre	university bookshop
floor	quarter (litre)	university town
way	weather	summary
white wine	room	onion soup
train		

Übung 12B

Find and write out the German equivalents in Text 12 of the following sentences/phrases. Don't try to translate the English sentences word for word: look for 'whole-sentence' equivalents, stick to the original German word order, but leave any bits of the original out that obviously aren't required below.

1 Mr Bennett is divorced.
2 He grew up in England.
3 He slept on the boat.
4 Forty years ago.
5 After that he went to a café with Ms Dettmann.
6 They have a lot in common.
7 His room is on the first floor.
8 On the first evening.
9 For five nights.
10 Who knows?

Übung 12C

Find the past tense forms used in Text 12 for the verbs below. They are all considered to be *regular* verbs: their past participles all end in **-t**. For each verb give:

(a) the subject of the verb, (b) the form of **haben** used, (c) the past participle.

1 **kaufen** to buy
2 **fragen** to ask
3 **buchen** to book
4 **reservieren** to book, reserve
5 **bestellen** to order
6 **machen** to do
7 **kennenlernen** to get to know, make the acquaintance of
8 **feststellen** to establish, find out

Übung 12D

The following three verbs are in the present tense in Text 12. They are regular verbs like those above. What would their past participles be?

1 **arbeiten** to work
2 **wohnen** to live, reside
3 **leben** to live, spend one's life

Übung 12E

Find the past tense forms used in Text 12 for the verbs below. They are all considered to be *irregular* verbs: *none* of their past participles ends in **-t**. For each verb give:

(a) the subject of the verb, (b) the form of **haben** or **sein** used, (c) the past participle.

1 **aufwachsen** to grow up
2 **ziehen** to move (change place of residence)
3 **abfahren** to leave (by transport)
4 **schlafen** to sleep
5 **ankommen** to arrive
6 **gehen** to go (on foot)
7 **trinken** to drink
8 **sitzen** to sit

9	**essen**	to eat
10	**sich unterhalten**	to chat, converse

Übung 12F

Five of the verbs from **Übung 12C** and **Übung 12E** are separable. Write the infinitive and past participle of each.

Übung 12G

The three nouns in each set below have something in common. The letters of the third noun, however, have been scrambled. Can you unscramble them?

1	**Sonntag**	**Mittwoch**	***Sganidet***
2	**Bohnsalat**	**Rührei**	***Puwelpsbizee***
3	**Zug**	**Bus**	***Ffisch***
4	**Milch**	**Berliner Weiße**	***Niewßiew***
5	**Dorfmark**	**Lüneburg**	***Torckos***
6	**Sohn**	**Frau**	***Rottech***
7	**geboren**	**verheiratet**	***ischedenge***
8	**Medizin**	**Ärztin**	***Skuhnkerana***
9	**dann**	**danach**	***sclendießahn***

Plural nouns in the dative case

The easiest set of German endings to remember is probably those for the dative plural: almost everything has to end in **-n**. When a noun is involved, it takes its plural ending in the usual way and an **-n** is also added if:

(a) the plural of the noun doesn't already have an **-n**;
(b) the plural of the noun isn't **-s**, as in e.g. **Autos**.

Let's take the German for days, weeks, months and years as an example of 'dative plural **-n**':

Nominative singular	*Nom./Acc. plural*	*Dative plural*
der Tag	**die Tage**	***den* Tage*n***
die Woche	**die Wochen**	***den* Woche*n***
der Monat	**die Monate**	***den* Monate*n***
das Jahr	**die Jahre**	***den* Jahre*n***

Here is an overview of the forms of the definite article, with the dative plural in the bottom right-hand corner.

	Masculine singular	*Neuter singular*	*Feminine singular*	*all three plural*	
Nominative	**der**	**das**	**die**	**die**	
Accusative	**den**	**das**	**die**	**die**	
Dative	**dem**	**dem**	**der**	***den***	[noun + ***-n***]

You have already met the dative plural in operation in the following sentences:

Text 10: **Fallingbostel ist eine kleine Stadt *mit* etwa sechstausend Einwohner*n*.**
Fallingbostel is a small town of about 6000 inhabitants.

Text 11: **Ich bin *seit* fünf Jahre*n* geschieden.**
I've been divorced for five years.

Text 11: **Mein Mann ist *vor* drei Jahre*n* nach Amerika zurückgegangen.**
Three years ago my husband went back to America.

Text 12: **Peter Bennett ist *vor* vierzig Jahre*n* in Cockermouth geboren und *vor* dreißig Jahre*n* nach York gezogen.**
Peter Bennett was born in Cockermouth forty years ago and moved to York thirty years ago.

Prepositions vor – seit – mit

The prepositions **mit** and **seit** always take the dative.

Vor does, too, more often than not, and it always does when it means 'ago'. Then it is used *in front of* the noun, not after the noun as 'ago' is in English. It can also mean 'before', but the difference is invariably clear in context:

vor Mittwoch	before Wednesday
vor fünf Jahren	five years ago

Übung 12H

Translate the English into German.

1 **Ich habe** [three days ago] **ein ruhiges Einzelzimmer** [booked].
2 **Peter hat** [four hours ago] **eine Stadtrundfahrt** ['made, done'].

3 **Er hat** [eleven years ago] **seine Frau** [got to know].
4 **Ich habe *Colloquial German*** [two months ago] [bought].
5 [Two days ago] **bin ich mit dem Zug in Berlin** [arrived].
6 [Ten years ago] **bin ich nach Amerika** [travelled].
7 **Es hat** [twenty minutes ago] [rained].
8 **Es hat seit** [four years] **nicht** [snowed].
9. **Ich bin seit** [five weeks] [married].
10 **Meine Frau wohnt mit** [the children] **in Schottland.**
11 **York ist eine mittelgroße Stadt mit etwa** [100,000 inhabitants].

Kein

Kein is the one-word negative form of the indefinite article **ein**, and means in English 'no' or 'not a' or 'not any' etc. In effect, German speakers don't say 'I do *not* have *a banana*' but 'I have *no banana*.'

Ich habe *keine* Banane.	'I have no banana' or 'I don't have a banana!'
Wir haben *keine* Bananen.	'We have no bananas' or 'We don't have bananas.'

> A rule of thumb for learners of German is:
> Don't say **nicht** . . . **ein**: say ***kein!***

Übung 12J

Translate the following German sentences into idiomatic English. As you do so, you will see that there are many variations in English, depending on context, for the simple word **kein**. We could find space for only a few of them in the Key.

1 **Ich esse kein Eis.**
2 **Möchten Sie ein Bier? Danke, ich trinke kein Bier.**
3 **York hat keine U-Bahn.**
4 **Ich habe keinen Appetit.**
5 **Heidi Dettmann hat keine Kinder.**
6 **Das Restaurant hat keinen Rotwein mehr!**
7 **Herr Ober, ich habe keinen Sylvaner sondern einen Riesling bestellt!**

8 **Ich schlafe in keinem Doppelzimmer! Ich möchte ein ruhiges Einzelzimmer!**
9 **Haben Sie schöne Briefmarken? Nein, wir haben leider gar keine Briefmarken.**
10 **Ich kann keinen Kaffee mehr trinken!**

Übung 12K

Find the various forms of **kein** in **Übung 12J** above and locate them in the table below. Explain each form in each sentence in grammatical terms. For example, in the first sentence, **Eis** is neuter (**das**), it is also singular and it is the direct object of the verb – it's *what* you (don't) *eat* – so **Eis** is in the accusative and is preceded by that form of **kein** which is starred* in the table. The first answer is, therefore:

1 **kein** = accusative neuter singular.

	Masculine singular	*Neuter singular*	*Feminine singular*	*all three plural*
Nominative	**kein**	**kein**	**keine**	**keine**
Accusative	**keinen**	**kein***	**keine**	**keine**
Dative	**keinem**	**keinem**	**keiner**	***keinen*** [noun + -*n*]

Übung 12L

Slot the appropriate forms of **kein** into the sentences below.

1 **Frau Dettmann hat _______ Sohn.**
2 **Sie hat auch _______ Tochter.**
3 **Herr Ober, ich habe _______ Kaffee bestellt sondern Tee!**
4 **Möchten Sie die Sachertorte mit Sahne? Nein, danke, ich möchte _______ Sahne.**
5 **Nehmen Sie Zucker? Danke, ich nehme _______ Zucker.**
6 **Kennen Sie ein gutes Restaurant in Berlin? Nein, ich bin _______ Berliner!**
7 **Ich kenne leider _______ Restaurants in Berlin.**
8 **Sind Sie Schotte? Nein, ich bin _______ Schotte sondern Waliser!**
9 **Ist ein Konzert heute abend? Nein, heute ist _______ Konzert.**
10 **Haben Sie einen Stadtplan für mich? Leider nicht, wir haben _______ Stadtpläne mehr!**

Reflexive verbs: sich waschen, sich unterhalten

In essence, reflexive verbs in German are verbs

(a) which always have both subject and an object;
(b) whose subject and object are the same person (or, less frequently, thing).

In English, a sentence such as 'I washed myself' satisfies condition (b): there is a subject and an object, both relating to the same person. Such 'reflexivity' is both more common in German (and e.g. French) than it is in English – and in German mostly *non-*optional! If you wish to indicate that A washed A (and not B or the dishes, etc.), you cannot in German choose to say 'I washed', you have to add 'myself'.

'Reflexivity' is indicated by 'reflexive pronouns', i.e. pronouns that 'reflect' back to the subject of the verb. The subject can, of course, be a noun or a pronoun.

subj.	*verb*	*reflex.*	*past participle*	
ich	**habe**	***mich***		myself
er				him/itself
sie	**hat**	***sich***	**gewaschen**	her/itself
es				itself
wir		***uns***		ourselves
sie	**haben**	***sich***		themselves
Sie		***sich***		yourself

From the point of view of English, a verb with the meaning of 'to converse, chat' would not appear to be reflexive. But the German verb **sich unterhalten** can *also* mean 'to entertain oneself'. To chat 'to' someone is in German to chat with (**mit**). **Mit** always takes the dative, so the pronouns in the fifth column below are in their dative form.

subj.	*verb*	*reflex.*	*prep.*	*+ dative*		*past participle*
ich	**habe**	***mich***		**Ihnen**	you	
Peter	**hat**	***sich***		**ihr**	her	
Heidi	**hat**	***sich***	**mit**	**ihm**	him	**unterhalten**
wir		***uns***		**ihnen**	them	
sie	**haben**	***sich***		**uns**	us	
Sie		***sich***		**mir**	me	

In the present tense, the two verbs **sich waschen** and **sich unterhalten** have the forms you would expect, except for the **er/sie/es** form which is: ***wäscht sich*** and ***unterhält sich***.

Übung 12M

Using the information above, translate the following sentences into German.

1 I chatted to her.
2 She's chatting to him.
3 Peter Bennett chatted with me.
4 Heidi chatted with you.
5 We chatted to the children.
6 Ms. Dettmann and Mr Bennett had a long and lively chat. [find the original of this sentence in Text 12].
7 They chatted to the inhabitants [NB dative pl. ends in **-n**].
8 The inhabitants chatted with them.

Übung 12N

Read the following sentences out loud, step by step, in the sequences indicated. The aim is to memorize each whole sentence and to be able, without hesitation, to ring changes within it.

Ich habe
Ich habe mich
Ich habe mich lange und lebhaft
Ich habe mich lange und lebhaft *mit ihnen*
Ich habe mich lange und lebhaft *mit ihnen* unterhalten
(I had a long and lively chat with them.)

Repeat the above, but replacing ***mit ihnen*** ('them') with (a) ***mit ihm*** ('him'), (b) ***mit ihr*** ('her').

Anschließend
Anschließend bin ich
Anschließend bin ich *mit ihr*
Anschließend bin ich *mit ihr* in ein Café
Anschließend bin ich *mit ihr* in ein Café gegangen.
(Afterwards I went (in)to a café with her.)

Repeat the above, but replacing ***mit ihr*** ('her') with (a) ***mit ihm*** ('him'), (b) ***mit ihnen*** ('them').

Übung 12P

Read through the ZUSAMMENFASSUNG (Text 12) again, paying attention to both the language and the information given.

Übung 12Q

Test yourself (A). Answer the following questions in German without looking back at the text. Give as many answers as you can in complete sentences.

1 Wo ist Peter Bennett aufgewachsen?
2 Wann ist Peter nach York gezogen?
3 Was ist er von Beruf?
4 Wo arbeitet er?
5 Wie viele Kinder hat er?
6 Wo leben seine Kinder?
7 Wie ist er nach Hamburg gefahren?
8 Was für ein Zimmer hat er im Hotel Müller gebucht?
9 Für wie lange hat er das Zimmer reserviert?
10 Wo hat er an seinem ersten Abend in Berlin gegessen?
11 Wo hat er im Restaurant gesessen?
12 Was hat er gegessen?
13 Was hat er dazu getrunken?
14 Was hat er zum Nachtisch bestellt?
15 Wie haben sich Herr Bennett und Frau Dettmann im Café unterhalten?

When you have done as much as you can, compare your answers with the original text. Give yourself 3 points maximum for an answer:

for 1 point: the facts are correct and you think you could be understood;
for 2 points: both the facts and the word order are correct;
for 3 points: everything correct.

Interpret your points score out of 45 thus:

35 +	:	**ausgezeichnet!**	(excellent)
30–34	:	**sehr gut!**	
25–29	:	**gut!**	
20–24	:	**bestanden!**	(pass)
0–19	:	**sitzenbleiben!**	(stay down, *i.e.* revise hard before going on to the next **Lektion**)

If you had problems with the facts, you've probably been working through the book too quickly or too intermittently. You need a revision course: it would be an excellent idea to go back over all the **Texte**.

If you had major problems with getting the verb in the right place, go back to **Lektion neun** and **Lektion zehn** and check out the sections entitled Word order.

If your spelling is not perfect, don't worry. If it's totally chaotic, put in some practice by using the cassettes for dictation exercises. Stop the tape after every few words, write down what you are hearing, and finally check what you have written against the texts. If you do this consistently, little by little your spelling will improve!

If your endings are *sometimes* wrong, you already understand enough to know how to put them right. If your endings are *always* wrong, accept it as a fact of life and concentrate on learning German words and their meanings.

Übung 12R

Test yourself (B). Ask the questions in German for which we have given the answers. The section in italics in the answer is the key information you are seeking, so you need to start each question with the appropriate question word from the following list:

Wo? Was? Wie? Wie viele? Für wie lange?

1 Er ist *in England* aufgewachsen.
2 Er ist *vor dreißig Jahren* nach York gezogen.
3 Er ist *Buchhändler*.
4 Er arbeitet *in einer Universitätsbuchhandlung* in der Universitätsstadt York.
5 Er hat *zwei* Kinder – einen Sohn und eine Tochter.
6 Sie leben *bei seiner Frau in Schottland*.
7 Er ist *mit dem Schiff* von Hull nach Hamburg gefahren.
8 Im Hotel Müller hat er *ein ruhiges Einzelzimmer mit Dusche* gebucht.
9 Er hat das Zimmer für *fünf* Nächte vom 6. Mai bis zum 11. Mai reserviert.

10 Am ersten Abend hat er *im Hotelrestaurant* gegessen.
11 Im Restaurant hat er *am Fenster* gesessen.
12 Er hat *französische Zwiebelsuppe, Rührei mit Schinken und einen grünen Bohnensalat* gegessen.
13 Dazu hat er *ein Viertel Weißwein* getrunken.
14 Zum Nachtisch hat er *frischen Obstsalat mit Sahne* bestellt.
15 Herr Bennett und Frau Dettmann haben sich *lange und lebhaft* unterhalten.

When you have done as much as you can, compare your answers with **Übung 12Q**. Give yourself 3 points maximum for an answer:

for 1 point: the question word is correct and you think you could be understood;
for 2 points: the question word and the word order are correct;
for 3 points: everything correct.

> To interpret your points score out of 45, use the same scheme as for **Übung 12Q** above. If you had problems with *forming questions*, check out **Lektion neun** and the section entitled QUESTIONS in **Lektion zehn**.

Übung 12S

Write the questions in **12Q** and the answers in **12R** on index cards (or strips of paper): you will need 2 x 15 cards/strips. Shuffle them, lay them out on a table, and collect matching pairs. Do this as often as you think you need to before embarking on the next stage, which is to take the answer cards one by one and give the question from memory. Stage three is to ask the questions one by one and give the answers from memory. Again: ***Übung macht den Meister!***

Übung 12T 

Tell as much of your own life story as you can on the basis of the German vocabulary you already know. You could say, e.g.:

1 I'm [nationality].
2 I grew up in. . . ..
3 I was born X years ago in. . . .
4 X years (months, weeks, days) ago I moved to. . . .

5 Your profession/job.
6 Where you work.
7 I am (not) married. (I am divorced.)
8 I have X (no) children.
9 I'm X years old.
10 My wife/husband/daughter/son is X years old.
11 My wife/husband is [nationality].
12 S/he grew up in. . . . *and round you go again!*

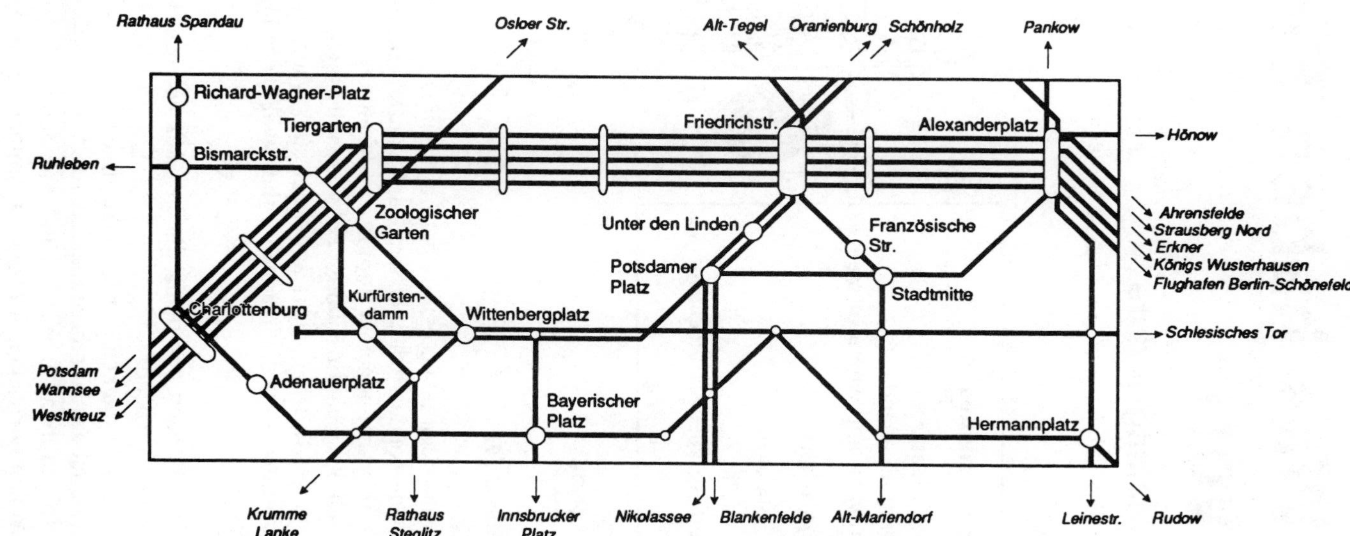

Map 6 Berlin
Central area with selected U-Bahn and S-Bahn stations

13 Was haben Sie vor?

Making a date

Language activities

- making a date
- agreeing an agenda
- fixing when and where to meet

Language focus

- separable verbs
- 'into' vs. 'in'
- 'something special': adjectives as nouns

Text 13

Dienstag abend [4]

The evening has been a success, so both are happy and grateful. Heidi Dettmann wonders whether they can't continue in this vein and suggests they get together tomorrow evening, too – for a concert in Schloß Charlottenburg. Peter readily agrees. They discuss how to get to the concert and when and where to meet. Tomorrow morning, though, it appears they will be going their separate ways. . . .

HEIDI D: Herr Bennett, ich danke Ihnen[1] ganz herzlich[2] für den schönen Abend.
PETER B: Nichts zu danken[3] – ich danke Ihnen!
HEIDI D: Was haben Sie morgen abend vor?[4]
Peter D. Morgen abend habe ich nichts Besonderes[5] vor. Und Sie?
HEIDI D: Wollen wir vielleicht etwas[6] zusammen unternehmen?[7]

PETER B: Ja, gern! Was schlagen Sie vor?[8]

HEIDI D: Ich habe folgenden Vorschlag:[9] da ist ein schönes Mozartkonzert im Schloß Charlottenburg. Mozart höre ich besonders gern[10] und Schloß Charlottenburg ist bestimmt[11] sehenswert. *Ich* möchte also[12] gern ins[13] Schloßkonzert gehen – aber lieber[14] nicht allein. Haben Sie Lust,[15] mitzukommen?[16]

PETER B: Ja, ich komme gern mit.[17] Wo liegt[18] das Schloß?

HEIDI D: Am Spandauer Damm,[19] glaube[20] ich. Die U-Bahn-Station[21] ist aber garantiert[22] Richard-Wagner-Platz:[23] Linie 1, Richtung[24] Rathaus Spandau.

PETER B: Um wieviel Uhr fängt das Konzert an?[25]

HEIDI D: Es fängt um halb acht an. Wo wollen[26] wir uns treffen?[27] Vor[28] dem Bahnhof? Oder vielleicht am Schloßeingang?[29]

PETER B: Gute Idee![30] Sagen wir[31] am Schloßeingang um Viertel vor sieben?

HEIDI D: Abgemacht![32] Also: morgen, Mittwoch, achtzehn Uhr fünfundvierzig.

PETER B: Richtig. Und viel Spaß morgen früh!

HEIDI D: Danke, gleichfalls.[33] Gute Nacht!

PETER B: Gute Nacht! Bis morgen abend!

HEIDI D: Gute Nacht! Bis morgen!

Notes

1 **danken** takes the dative [see **Lektion elf** 'Cases with verbs']
2 literally: 'quite (i.e. very) heartily'; idiomatically: 'very much'
3 literally: 'nothing to (be) thank(ed)', i.e. 'don't mention it, my pleasure, you're welcome', etc.
4 **vorhaben** (separable verb) = 'to intend, to have planned'. Idiomatically the sentence might in English be 'What are you doing tomorrow evening?'
5 'nothing special, nothing in particular'
6 'something' (the opposite of **nichts**)
7 literally: 'undertake', i.e. 'do'. She could have said **machen** instead of **unternehmen**
8 **vorschlagen** (separable verb) = 'propose, suggest, put forward'
9 **der Vorschlag** = 'proposal, suggestion', **folgend** = 'following'. Note that no **den** ('the') is required here
10 literally: 'I hear willingly' (**gern**), i.e. 'I like listening to, I like to listen to', or simply: 'I like'

11 **bestimmt** = 'definitely', but with a high degree of probability and not quite 100% certainty: Heidi has never been to the palace, so she is predicting it will be 'worth seeing' (**sehenswert**)
12 **also** = 'therefore'; **auch** = 'too, also'
13 **ins (in** + **das)** = '(in)to'
14 'rather, preferably'
15 **die Lust** = 'pleasure, enjoyment' (nothing stronger!). **Haben Sie Lust?** = 'Would you like to . . .?'
16 **mitkommen** is a separable verb, meaning here 'to join me, to come with me' (the pronoun 'me' is omitted if the sense is clear without it)
17 see previous Note: here 'you' is not needed to make the sense clear, so is left out
18 **liegen** = 'to lie', i.e. here 'to be situated'. In English we would simply say 'is' in this context
19 another Berlin street called a **Damm**, cf. **Kurfürstendamm**. A **Damm (der)** is 'a causeway' and suggests that the road was originally built higher than the surrounding (probably marshy) terrain
20 **glauben** = 'to believe'
21 **die Station** was originally 'stop' rather than 'station'. **Der Bahnhof** can mean only 'station', not 'stop'
22 'guaranteed', i.e. 'I can guarantee, I know, I assure you'
23 **Richard Wagner, deutscher Komponist, 1813 in Leipzig geboren, 1883 in Venedig** (Venice) **gestorben**. The word **Platz** in this context is usually translated as 'Square', but there is in fact no 'Square' as such here. **Platz** can be any shape or simply a point where roads meet.
24 'the line' (**die Linie**) is No. 1, 'the direction' (**die Richtung**) Spandau Town Hall (**das Rathaus**). Before 1920 Spandau was an independent town to the west and is arguably older than the original Berlin
25 **anfangen** is a separable verb = 'to begin'
26 **wollen** is stronger than **möchten**, it suggests wanting + intention. Nevertheless, an idiomatic translation would simply be 'Where shall/do we meet?'
27 **sich treffen** is here a reflexive verb clearly indicating that they meet each other, not someone else
28 'before, in front'
29 **der Eingang** = 'entrance (on foot)'. **die Einfahrt** = 'entrance (by transport)'
30 **die Idee** = 'idea'
31 literally: 'say we', idiomatically: 'let's say'
32 **abmachen** is a separable verb meaning 'to agree'. **Abgemacht!** = 'agreed, done!'
33 **gleichfalls** = 'equally, the same to you!'

Übung 13A

Find equivalents in Text 13 and in the Notes above for the following nouns. Write them all in their singular form with a capital letter, in three columns and preceded by **der**, **das** or **die**. When you have finished, your German nouns should appear in alphabetical order in each column.

masculine	*neuter*	*feminine*
evening	concert	entrance [for vehicles]
railway station	town hall	idea
causeway	palace	line, route
entrance [pedestrian]	quarter	pleasure
composer		night
Wednesday		direction
square		underground/subway station
fun		clock, o'clock
proposal, suggestion		

Übung 13B

Find and write out the German equivalents in Text 13 of the following sentences/phrases. Don't try to translate the English sentences word for word: look for 'whole-sentence' equivalents and stick to the original German word order.

1. What are your plans for tomorrow evening?
2. I've nothing special on!
3. I'd like to go to the concert in the palace.
4. But preferably not on my own!
5. At what time does the concert start?
6. Where shall we meet?
7. Let's say at the palace entrance at a quarter to seven!
8. Agreed!
9. Enjoy yourself tomorrow morning!
10. Thanks, you too!

Separable verbs

In this lesson you almost double your stock of indispensable separable verbs. In **Lektion sechs** there were five examples of such verbs, each with a different prefix:

ab|fahren	→	**ich fahre ______**	**ab**	leave/depart
an|kommen	→	**ich komme ______**	**an**	arrive
auf|machen	→	**ich mache ______**	**auf**	open
zu|machen	→	**ich mache ______**	**zu**	shut/close
aus|gehen	→	**ich gehe ______**	**aus**	go out

We can now add four new verbs. including two new prefixes:

vor|haben	→	**ich habe ______**	**vor**	intend, plan to
vor|schlagen	→	**ich schlage ______**	**vor**	suggest, propose
mit|kommen	→	**ich komme ______**	**mit**	join, come with (e.g. you)
an|fangen	→	**ich fange ______**	**an**	start, begin

Übung 13C

Complete the following sentences in the present tense. If you need the **er/sie/es** form of the verb and are not sure whether it should have an ***Umlaut*** (two dots over a vowel) or not, the Glossary will help.

begin 1 **Wann _______ das Konzert ____?**
leave 2 **Wann _______ der Bus nach Hamburg ____?**
plan 3 **Was _______ Sie am Sonntag ____?**
arrive 4 **Der Zug _______ um 18 Uhr 44 in Berlin ____.**
suggest 5 **Ich _______ ____, wir gehen morgen ins Kino.**
come 6 **OK, ich _______ gern ____!**
begin 7 **Der Film _______ um acht Uhr ____.**
close 8 **Um wieviel Uhr _______ die Post am Samstag ____?**
open 9 **Ich weiß nicht. Ich weiß, sie _______ um acht Uhr ____.**
go out 10 **Morgen _______ Peter mit Heidi ____ .**

Übung 13D

Now try more or less the same in the past tense: you only need to supply the past participle, which in separable verbs is formed like this: *prefix + -ge- + appropriate verb form*. Again, the Glossary will help out if required. The answer to 1 has been provided.

begin 1 **Wann *hat* das Konzert *angefangen*?**
leave 2 **Wann *ist* der Bus nach Hamburg____________?**
plan 3 **Was *haben* Sie am Sonntag__________?**
arrive 4 **Der Zug *ist* um 18 Uhr 44 in Berlin____________.**
suggest 5 **Ich *habe* __________ , wir gehen jetzt ins Kino.**

begin	6	**OK, aber der Film *hat* schon um acht Uhr________.**
close	7	**Um wieviel Uhr *hat* die Post am Samstag____ ?**
open	8	**Ich weiß nicht. Ich weiß, sie *hat* um acht Uhr________.**
go out	9	**Gestern *ist* Peter mit Heidi__________.**
get to know	10	**Sie *haben* sich in Berlin_________________.**

etwas / **nichts** → **Besonderes**

'Something special' in German is **etwas Besonderes**, 'nothing special' **nichts Besonderes**. The second word, **Besonderes**, is essentially an adjective which has been turned into a noun (hence the capital letter, since all nouns in German have capital letters). Most adjectives after **etwas** and **nichts** follow this pattern:

etwas *Gutes*	something good, a good thing
nichts Gutes	no good, not a good thing
etwas *Interessantes*	something interesting
nichts Interessantes	nothing interesting/of interest
etwas *Amerikanisches*	something American
nichts *Sehenswertes*	nothing worth seeing

> Erich Maria Remarque's famous anti-war novel, written in 1929, was entitled in its original German ***Im Westen nichts Neues***, literally: 'nothing new in the west'. It was published in English as *All Quiet on the Western Front.*

Übung 13E

Translate the following phrases into German, turning the adjectives into nouns (with initial capitals!) and giving them the necessary **-es** ending. Guess as many meanings as possible before looking up the words in the Glossary.

alkoholisch; **besser**; **deutsch**; **elegant**; **eßbar**; **genau**; **großartig**; **neu**; **ungewöhnlich**; **wahr**; **wichtig**; **witzig**.

1	something German	7	something new
2	nothing unusual	8	nothing important
3	something wonderful	9	something funny
4	something smart	10	something true
5	nothing alcoholic	11	nothing better
6	something edible	12	nothing exact/specific

Two-case prepositions

In our last overview of prepositions (**Lektion acht**) we said that 'Some German prepositions always require that anything which follows them should be in the dative case; others require the accusative case. A third group requires sometimes the one case and sometimes the other.'

It is time to touch on this third group. From e.g. **Lektion elf** (see particularly the section on the question word **Wo?**) you will be accustomed to sentences such as:

Jochen arbeitet *in einem* Reisebüro.
Die Empfangsdame arbeitet *im* Hotel.

But if you are blessed with hyper-perception you will have more recently noted with curiosity sentences such as these:

Text 12 **Zuerst ist er *in ein* Café gegangen.**
Danach ist er *in ein* Geschäft gegangen.
Am ersten Abend ist er *ins* Hotelrestaurant gegangen.
Am Mittwoch gehen Heidi und Peter eventuell *ins* Theater . . . oder vielleicht *in ein* Konzert.
Text 13 **Ich möchte gern *ins* Schloßkonzert gehen.**

Clearly, the behaviour of the definite and indefinite articles following the preposition **in** in the sentences above differs. There are two reasons for this:

(a) **in** can take the dative *or* accusative;
(b) **in** + ***dative*** means 'in' = *location*
i.e. there *is no* movement towards a destination involved;
in + ***accusative*** means or implies 'into' = *direction*
i.e. there *is* movement *towards* a destination.

English used to have 'Whither?' (= Where to?) and 'Where?' (static). Now 'Where?' can be locational or directional. In German two different question words are still needed:

Question:	***Wohin* gehen Sie?** Where are you going (to)?	***Wo* arbeiten Sie?** Where do you work?
Answers:	***in*** + *accusative*	***in*** + *dative*
masculine	**Ich gehe *in den* Zoo.** **Ich gehe *in einen* Zoo.**	**Ich arbeite *im* Zoo.** **Ich arbeite *in einem* Zoo.**
neuter	**Ich gehe *ins* Hotel.** **Ich gehe *in ein* Hotel.**	**Ich arbeite *im* Hotel.** **Ich arbeite *in einem* Hotel.**
feminine	**Ich gehe *in die* Apotheke.** **Ich gehe *in eine* Apotheke.**	**Ich arbeite *in der* Apotheke.** **Ich arbeite *in einer* Apotheke.**

In condensed form these are the two sets of articles you need in order to be able to make the 'in/into' distinction in German:

	masculine	*neuter*	*feminine*	*plural*
acc.	***den*/einen**	***das*/ein**	***die*/eine**	***die*/keine***
dat.	***dem*/einem**	***dem*/einem**	***der*/einer**	***den*/keinen***

* There is, of course, no plural of 'a' = **ein**, so we have used 'not any/no' = **kein** here in order to demonstrate a plural ending.

Übung 13F

In each of the sentences below ***in*** + 'the' is missing, sometimes in the accusative, sometimes in the dative case. Supply the missing words and state whether each definite article is accusative or dative.

1 **Ich gehe_________Park. Kommen Sie mit?**
2 **Die Sonne scheint. Ich schlage vor, wir gehen______ Tiergarten.**
3 **Es ist schon ein Uhr. Ich gehe______Restaurant.**
4 **Haben Sie Lust, heute abend______Oper zu gehen?**
5 **Ich gehe eigentlich lieber______Theater!**
6 **Wo spielen die Berliner Philharmoniker heute?______ Philharmonie?**
7 **Wohin gehen Sie? Heute ist Sonntag. Ich gehe______Kirche.**
8 **Morgen arbeite ich_________Rathaus.**

9 **Ich esse heute abend_______Hotelrestaurant.**
10 **Wo ist die nächste U-Bahn-Sation? ______Bismarckstraße.**

The four commonest prepositions which can take the accusative or dative depending on the meaning intended are:

in – an – auf – vor

To indicate where you want to meet as being not 'in' but 'at' or 'by' a particular venue, the preposition **an** is generally used (with a few nouns it is **auf**). If you wish to meet 'in front of' something, use **vor**.

Übung 13G

'Where shall we meet?' The answer – in the dative – is ***am*** or ***an der*** 'at/by' one of the following places in Berlin. Supply the missing word/words:

masculine	*neuter*	*feminine*
Kurfürstendamm	Brandenburger Tor	Philharmonie
Spandauer Damm	Pergamonmuseum	U-Bahn-Station
Reichstag	Schloß Charlottenburg	Staatsoper
Zoo	Spandauer Rathaus	Nationalgalerie
Hauptbahnhof		
Richard-Wagner-Platz		

1 **Wo wollen wir uns treffen?**
Sagen wir __________ Staatsoper.
2 **Wo wollen wir uns treffen?**
Sagen wir __________Zoo.
3 **Wo wollen wir uns treffen?**
Sagen wir __________Philharmonie.
4 **Wo wollen wir uns treffen?**
Sagen wir __________Pergamonmuseum.

5 **Wo wollen wir uns treffen?**
Sagen wir ___________Nationalgalerie.
6 **Wo wollen wir uns treffen?**
Sagen wir ___________Richard-Wagner-Platz.
7 **Wo wollen wir uns treffen?**
Sagen wir ___________Spandauer Rathaus.
8 **Wo wollen wir uns treffen?**
Sagen wir ___________Hauptbahnhof.
9 **Wo wollen wir uns treffen?**
Sagen wir ___________U-Bahn-Station.
10 **Wo wollen wir uns treffen?**
Sagen wir ___________Kurfürstendamm.

Übung 13H

Answer the following questions, spelling out the time and putting the subject first as in the model sentence provided.

Um wieviel Uhr fängt das Konzert an? = eight o'clock
Das Konzert fängt um acht Uhr an.

1 **Um wieviel Uhr fängt das Theater an?** = half past eight
2 **Um wieviel Uhr fängt der Film an?** = ten to seven
3 **Um wieviel Uhr fängt die Oper an?** = half past seven
4 **Um wieviel Uhr kommt der Zug an?** = 20.53
5 **Um wieviel Uhr fängt die Schule an?** = quarter past ten
6 **Um wieviel Uhr fährt der Bus ab?** = quarter to nine

Übung 13J

In the text below, two dashes represent words of two letters, three dashes words of three. Can you reconstruct the sentences below by slotting in all the following words (it's probably best to put a line through 'used' words as you proceed)?

am – am – am – am – am – an – das – das – der – der – ein – er – er – es – im – in – in – in – in – in – ins – ist – ist – ist – nur – sie – um – um – und – Uhr – von – vor

1 **– – – Komponist Wolfgang Amadeus Mozart – – – – – 21. Januar 1756 – – Salzburg geboren.**
2 **– – – – – – – 5. Dezember 1791 – – Wien gestorben.**
3 **Heute – – – – – nicht – – – – – Österreich beliebt sondern – – – – – ganzen Welt.**

4 -- **Mittwoch abend gibt -- --- schönes Mozartkonzert -- Schloß Charlottenburg -- Berlin.**
5 --- **Schloß liegt -- Spandauer Damm.**
6 --- **Konzert fängt -- acht --- --.**
7 **Heidi Dettmann --- Peter Bennett wollen zusammen --- Konzert gehen.**
8 --- **wollen sich -- Viertel --- sieben -- Schloßeingang treffen.**

Übung 13K

Reconstruct the following compound nouns. The missing parts are listed below the exercise but it would be useful first to cover up the list and complete as many of the compounds as you can without it!

1 **der** ______ **schlüssel**		11 **die** ______ **rundfahrt**	
2 **der** ______ **salat**		12 **die** ______ **karte**	
3 **der** ______ **begleiter**		13 **die** ______ **marke**	
4 **der** ______ **stil**		14 **die** ______ **suppe**	
5 **der** ______ **eingang**		15 **die** ______ **haltestelle**	
6 **der** ______ **hof**		16 **die** ______ **torte**	
7 **das** ______ **museum**		17 **die** ______ **küste**	
8 **das** ______ **zimmer**		18 **die** ______ **handlung**	
9 **das** ______ **bild**		19 **die** ______ **nummer**	
10 **die** ______ **karte**		20 **die** ______ **stadt**	

Bahn – Bau – Brief – Buch – Bus – Eisenbahn – Hafen – Hotel – Nuß – Obst – Ostsee – Post – Reise – Schloß – Speise – Stadt – Stand – Zimmer – Zimmer – Zwiebel

Übung 13L

In the dialogue below, all the capital letters except those at the beginning of sentences have been changed to lower case letters. Highlight all the small letters that according to the rules of German spelling should be large, and then check with the original text at the beginning of the **Lektion**.

HEIDI D: Herr Bennett, ich danke ihnen ganz herzlich für den schönen abend.
PETER B: Nichts zu danken – ich danke ihnen!
HEIDI D: Was haben sie morgen abend vor?

Peter D. Morgen abend habe ich nichts besonderes vor. Und sie?
HEIDI D: Wollen wir vielleicht etwas zusammen unternehmen?
PETER B: Ja, gern! Was schlagen sie vor?
HEIDI D: Ich habe folgenden vorschlag: da ist ein schönes mozartkonzert im schloß charlottenburg. Mozart höre ich besonders gern und schloß charlottenburg ist bestimmt sehenswert. Ich möchte also gern ins schloßkonzert gehen – aber lieber nicht allein. Haben sie lust, mitzukommen?
PETER B: Ja, ich komme gern mit. Wo liegt das schloß?
HEIDI D: Am spandauer damm, glaube ich. Die u-bahn-station ist garantiert richard-wagner-platz: linie 1, richtung rathaus spandau.
PETER B: Um wieviel uhr fängt das konzert an?
HEIDI D: Es fängt um halb acht an. Wo wollen wir uns treffen? Vor dem bahnhof? Oder vielleicht am schloßeingang?
PETER B: Gute idee! Sagen wir am schloßeingang um viertel vor sieben?
HEIDI D: Abgemacht! Also: morgen, mittwoch, achtzehn uhr fünfundvierzig.
PETER B: Richtig! Und viel spaß morgen früh!
HEIDI D: Danke, gleichfalls! Gute nacht!

Übung 13M

Now, in German:

1 Ask someone whether they have any plans for tomorrow.
2 Say you particularly like listening to Beethoven.
3 Ask where the Kurfürstendamm is situated.
4 Say you would like to go to a concert.
5 Say you have a suggestion.
6 Ask what your partner suggests.
7 Ask where you want to arrange to meet.
8 Say 'in front of the station'.
9 Say 'Agreed!'
10 Thank someone profusely for a lovely evening.

14 Wirklich hervorragend!

Music has charms

Language activities

- expressing enthusiasm
- contradicting
- stating your interests

Language focus

- verbs
- **wäre / hätte**
- **Wofür? Für wen?**

Text 14

Mittwoch abend

The concert was first class, the venue ideal for Heidi's kind of music: Mozart. To maintain the mood – musical and otherwise – they plan to visit Berlin's famous museum of musical instruments the next morning. Heidi, when she was younger, played the harp and piano, so the museum visit is her suggestion. Peter doesn't play an instrument. He listens to music, and mostly 'lighter' kinds of music than she does, but he is open-minded and certainly willing to meet up outside the museum the next morning. As an early riser, he is confident he will be there on time . . .

HEIDI D: Das Konzert war wirklich[1] hervorragend,[2] nicht wahr?[3]
PETER B: Ja, das stimmt,[4] ganz ausgezeichnet! Der Konzertsaal ist für Mozart einfach[5] ideal. Wunderschön!
HEIDI D: Sagen Sie, hätten[6] Sie Lust, mit mir morgen vormittag ein Museum zu besuchen?[7]

PETER B: Ja, warum[8] nicht? Aber welches?[9] Berlin hat viele Museen.[10]

HEIDI D: Wie wär's mit mehr[11] Musik? Das Musikinstrumenten-Museum[12] am[13] Tiergarten[14] ist weltberühmt[15] – besonders für Instrumente aus der Renaissance[16] und aus dem Barock.[17]

PETER B: Interessieren Sie sich schon lange[18] für Musikinstrumente?

HEIDI D: Ja, sehr.[19] Ich interessiere mich vor allem[20] für alte Harfen. Als Kind[21] habe ich Harfe und Klavier[22] gespielt.[23]

PETER B: Gut, ich komme gern mit. Ich spiele kein Instrument und ich habe noch nie[24] ein Musikinstrumenten-Museum besucht. Aber ich höre gern Musik, manchmal klassische, meistens gute Unterhaltungsmusik[25] – und auch Schlagermusik.

HEIDI D: Ich höre *viel* lieber klassische Musik!

PETER B: OK! Wann und wo wollen wir uns treffen?

HEIDI D: Nach[26] meinem Stadtplan ist das Musikinstrumenten-Museum in der Tiergartenstraße hinter[27] der Philharmonie.

PETER B: Wie kommt man[28] dorthin?[29]

HEIDI D: Wollen wir mal sehen![30] Ich glaube, da gibt[31] es keine U-Bahn. . . . Die nächste S-Bahn-Station[32] ist Potsdamer Platz: Linie 1 Richtung Oranienburg oder Linie 2 Richtung Schönholz. Alles klar?[33]

PETER B: Linie 1 oder 2 . . .mit der S-Bahn. . . .

HEIDI D: Bis Potsdamer Platz.

PETER B: Bis Potsdamer Platz. Alles klar.

HEIDI D: Wollen wir uns um zehn Uhr vor dem Museum treffen – oder ist das vielleicht zu früh?

PETER B: Kein Problem. Ich bin Frühaufsteher.[34] Gute Nacht, Heidi! Bis morgen dann!

HEIDI D: Gute Nacht, Peter! Bis morgen!

Notes

1 'really'
2 'outstanding'
3 literally: 'not true?' i.e. in this context: 'wasn't it?' **Nicht wahr?** can be tagged on to any statement to turn it into a question.
4 'that's correct'

5 'simply'
6 **hätten Sie Lust** = literally: 'Would you have pleasure?' i.e. 'Would you like to?' **Hätten** is an alternative to **haben** (discussed later in this **Lektion**)
7 'to visit'. Note that the infinitive is at the end of the sentence
8 'why?'
9 'which?'
10 singular **Museum**, plural **Museen**. Not many German nouns end in **-um**, but those that do often have an unusual plural form
11 literally: 'how would it be with?' **Mehr** = 'more . . .?' i.e. 'How about some more . . .?'
12 **das Instrument**, **die Instrument***e* (plural). The **-n-** in **Musikinstrumente***n***-Museum** is not part of the plural but used here to link **Instrumente** and **Museum** together as a compound noun
13 it's not 'in' the **Tiergarten**, it's 'by/alongside it'
14 **der Tiergarten** is a large park in the centre of Berlin, now laid out in the informal 'English style'. It literally means 'animal garden' and was once used to stock deer, wild boar, etc. for hunting (**das Tier** and English 'deer' are historically related)
15 'world-famous'
16 15th/16th century
17 17th/early 18th century. **Barock** can be neuter *or* masculine!
18 literally: 'already a long time'. Idiomatically, we would probably say in English in a similar situation: 'Have you always been interested in musical instruments?'
19 i.e. **sehr lange**
20 'above all'
21 'as (a) child': neuter in German = **das Kind**
22 genders: **die Harfe**, **das Klavier**
23 the verb **spielen**, 'to play', is regular
24 **nie**, even on its own, means 'never', but **noch** often keeps it company!
25 the German music industry distinguishes between **E-Musik** and **U-Musik**, the first being **ernste Musik** = 'serious music' (classical), the second **Unterhaltungsmusik** = literally 'entertainment music' ('lighter' and pop music). **Ein Schlager** (masc.) is a 'hit', from the verb **schlagen**, 'to beat'
26 **nach** = (here) 'according to' (+ dative)
27 **hinter** = 'behind' (+ dative or accusative, here + dative)
28 **man** = 'one' but is used much more frequently than 'one' is in English: like French *on*, German **man** is stylistically completely neutral: there is no social stigma (or kudos) attached to using it!
29 in older forms of English this would have been 'thither'. **Dort** is static

(ich wohne dort), whereas **dorthin** suggests movement towards a point **(ich gehe dorthin)**

30 a common set expression = 'Let's see. . . .' The small word **mal** occurs frequently between words in conversation and stretches the utterance rather than giving it extra meaning!

31 literally: 'there gives it no' = 'there is no' (**es gibt** is discussed in **Lektion sechzehn**). Heidi needs a new map: the underground station at Potsdamer Platz was reopened after the Berlin wall came down.

32 **S** = **schnell** ('fast'). The **S-Bahn** is the 'overground' suburban/metropolitan railway

33 literally: 'Everything clear?'

34 a noun formed from **früh** = 'early' + **aufstehen** = 'to get up'.

Übung 14A

Find equivalents in Text 14 and in the Notes above for the following nouns. Write them all in their singular form with a capital letter, in three columns and preceded by **der**, **das** or **die**. When you have finished, your German nouns should appear in alphabetical order in each column.

masculine	*neuter*	*feminine*
Baroque	Baroque	harp
early riser	instrument	line
garden	child	[literally] 'pleasure'
concert room/hall	piano	music
square	concert	night
hit	museum	Renaissance
street plan	problem	direction
	animal	suburban railway
		stop/station
		subway/underground
		clock
		entertainment

Übung 14B

Find and write out the German equivalents in Text 14 of the following sentences/phrases. Don't try to translate the English sentences word for word: look for 'whole-sentence' equivalents, stick to the original German word order, but leave any bits of the original out that obviously aren't required below.

1 Tell me, do you fancy going to a museum with me tomorrow morning?
2 How about some more music?
3 From the Renaissance and Baroque.
4 I'm particularly interested in old harps.
5 I enjoy listening to music.
6 I much prefer (to listen to) classical music.
7 According to my street plan the museum is behind the Philharmonie.
8 The nearest S-Bahn stop is. . . .
9 Or is that too early perhaps?
10 Let's see. . . .

Reflexive verbs

We met our first reflexive verbs in **Lektion zwölf**. Altogether we now have four such verbs:

sich waschen	**sich unterhalten**	**sich treffen**	**sich interessieren**
to wash (oneself)	to talk, chat	to meet (each other)	to be interested

Since the direct object of these verbs is the reflexive pronoun ('myself' etc.), they need a preposition to connect the action of the verb to any other noun or pronoun in the sentence. The preposition needed varies, as it might in English, e.g. 'I'm meeting up with . . . I'm interested in . . .,' etc.

Ich wasche mich.	**Sie** [she] **w*ä*scht sich.**
Ich unterhalte mich (***mit*** . . . + dative)	**Sie unterh*ä*lt sich mit ihm** [him].
Ich treffe mich (***mit*** . . . + dative)	**Sie tr*i*fft sich mit ihm** [him].
Ich interessiere mich (***für*** . . . + accusative)	**Sie interessiert sich für alte Harfen.**

Note that in the **er/sie/es** form, three of the four verbs above are irregular: their vowel changes.

Übung 14C

Read the following sentences out loud, step by step, in the sequences indicated. The aim is to memorize whole sentences and to be able, without hesitation, to ring changes within them. In addition to **Harfen**, use any nouns after **alte** as long as they are in the plural form.

Ich
Ich interessiere mich
Ich interessiere mich *schon lange*
Ich interessiere mich *schon lange* für *alte Harfen*
[Filme? Ansichtskarten? Autos? . . .]

Repeat the above, step by step, but replacing **schon lange** when you reach line three with (a) **seit Jahren** (for years) (b) **vor allem** (above all), (c) **ganz besonders** (specially)

Wofür?

If you wish to ask someone in German *what* they are interested *in*, then the equivalent of 'what . . . in' is a *single* word at the beginning of the sentence:

***Wofür* interessieren Sie sich? Ich interessiere mich *für* Musik.**

If you wish to ask someone in German *who* they are interested *in*, then the equivalent of 'who . . . in' is *two words*, literally 'for whom', also at the beginning of the sentence:

***Für wen* interessieren Sie sich? Ich interessiere mich *für* Mozart.**

The preposition will of course vary according to the verb. Instead of **für**, which takes the accusative of **wer? = wen?**, the two verbs below require **mit**, hence the dative of **wer? = wem?**

***Mit wem* treffen Sie sich?**	**Ich treffe mich *mit* dem Hotelmanager.**
***Mit wem* unterhalten Sie sich?**	**Ich unterhalte mich *mit* meinem Sohn.**

But if you want to ask someone *what* (not who!) they wash (themselves) *with*, then 'what . . . with' is a single word as in:

***Womit* waschen Sie sich?**	**Ich wasche mich nur *mit* Wasser.**

Übung 14D

Write out personal sets of statements in reply to pairs of questions, following the patterns given but choosing your own preferred people/teams to replace the items underlined. We have listed some suggestions for replacements – only to inspire/provoke you!

(a) ***Wofür* interessieren Sie sich?** [say for what]
    e.g. **Ich interessiere mich für <u>Jazz</u>.**
(b) ***Für wen* interessieren Sie sich *besonders*?** [say for whom]
    e.g. **Ich interessiere mich besonders für <u>Charlie Parker</u>.**

(a) ***Wofür* interessieren Sie sich?**	(b) ***Für wen* interessieren Sie sich *besonders*?**
... **für Kunst** (art)	... **für Picasso.**
... **für Fußball** (football)	... **für Manchester United.**
... **für Literatur** (literature)	... **für Graham Greene.**
... **für Krimis** (detective stories)	... **für Agatha Christie.**
... **für Lyrik** (poetry)	... **für Emily Dickinson.**
... **für Film**	... **für Alfred Hitchcock.**
... **für Rockmusik**	...
... **für Schlagermusik**	...
... **für klassische Musik**	...
... **für Ballett**	...

... **für Country Music, Baseball, amerikanischen Fußball ...**
... für Kricket, Rugby, Tennis ...... etc. etc.

Dafür!

Dafür is a kind of 'answer-version' of the question word **Wofür?** If what you might be interested in is already specified in the question, then there are two possible ways of replying in the affirmative, beyond simply saying yes, e.g.

Q: **Interessieren Sie sich *für Musik*?**

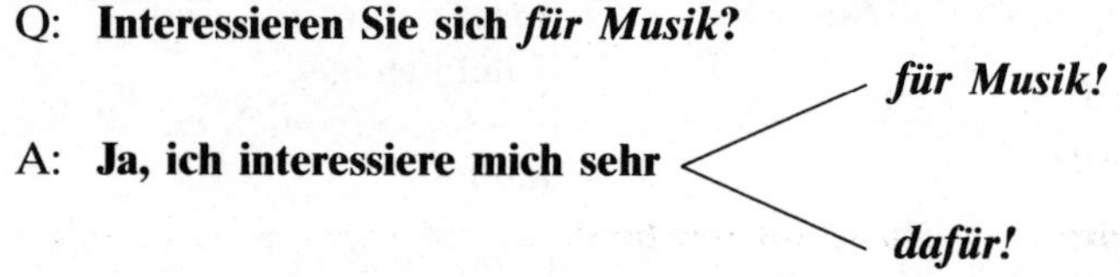

We won't go into them here but there are lots of pairs like **wofür/dafür** in German

e.g. **Womit? – damit** **Woran? – daran** **Worauf? – darauf.**

There is also the uncooperative interchange frequently engaged in by children:

Warum? Why? **Darum!** Because!/That's why!

Übung 14E

Text 14 contains three examples of adjectives preceded by what might be called an 'intensifier'. Can you find them? If so, you will be able to complete the following sentences.

	intensifier	*adjective*
1 **Für Heidi war das Konzert**	________	________
2 **Für Peter war das Konzert**	________	________
3 **Für Mozart war der Konzertsaal**	________	________

Which (of several)?

The endings of **Welch**-? follow the same pattern as for the definite article.

	masculine	*neuter*	*feminine*	*plural*
nominative	**welch*er***	**welch*es***	**welch*e***	**welch*e***
accusative	**welch*en***	**welch*es***	**welch*e***	**welch*e***
dative	**welch*em***	**welch*em***	**welch*er***	**welch*en***

In the three sentences below there is a choice to be made. The thing that is going to be seen/done/visited is the direct object of the verb, i.e. accusative – and so the form of **Welch**-? has to be accusative, too.

(a) **Hätten Sie Lust, mit mir heute abend einen Film zu sehen?**
Are you interested in seeing a film with me this evening?
Ja, gern! Aber *welchen*?

(b) **Hätten Sie Lust, mit mir morgen vormittag ein Museum zu besuchen?**
Are you interested in visiting a museum with me tomorrow morning?
Ja, gern! Aber *welches*?

(c) **Wollen wir morgen eine Stadtrundfahrt machen?**
Shall we take in a city tour tomorrow?
Ja, *welche*? Die große oder die kleine?

Übung 14F

Contradict in German the English statements given below, using information and vocabulary from Text 14. First do as much as you can without referring back to the Text. **Wie bitte?!** said with a note of surprise in the voice suggests 'Surely not! Come off it . . .' etc.

1 The concert was really terrible! **Wie bitte!? Es war** ___
2 Nobody has ever heard of the museum. **Wie bitte!? Es ist** ___
3 Berlin has very few museums. **Wie bitte!? Berlin** ___
4 Did Heidi play the violin as a child? **Nein, sie hat als Kind** ___
5 Heidi much prefers rock music. **Wie bitte?! Sie hört** ___
6 Are Heidi and Peter meeting at nine? **Nein, sie treffen sich** ___
7 The concert hall is quite unsuited to Mozart. **Wie bitte?! Der** ___
8 Isn't Heidi into old pianos? **Nein, sie** ___
9 Is there an underground/subway station at Potsdamer Platz? **Nein, sie glaubt, da** ___
10 Peter has difficulty in getting up early. **Wie bitte?! Er** ___
11 Peter plays the guitar. **Wie bitte!? Er** ___
12 The museum is in Unter den Linden. **Das stimmt nicht, es** ___

Wäre/hätte

These so-called conditional forms of the verbs 'to be' **sein** and 'to have' **haben** are very commonly heard, hence their introduction here. Their literal meanings might be described as: 'would be . . .' and 'would have . . .'

ich **er/sie/es**	***wäre***	***hätte***
wir **sie** **Sie**	***wären***	***hätten***

It's best to remember them in context, of course – not least because you would often translate them differently there. The following two sentences mean more or less the same:

(a) ***Haben* Sie Lust, mit mir morgen vormittag ein Museum zu besuchen?**
(b) ***Hätten* Sie Lust, mit mir morgen vormittag ein Museum zu besuchen?**

The first sentence is slightly more direct, the second slightly more tentative. In English, the difference might be conveyed by:

(a) Are you interested in visiting a museum with me tomorrow morning?
(b) Would you be interested in visiting a museum with me tomorrow morning?

In e.g. a shop or a restaurant, **Ich hätte gern** ... is often used instead of **Ich möchte** ...

Ich *möchte* (bitte)	**... ein Kännchen Kaffee.**
Ich *hätte gern*	**... ein Kännchen Kaffee.**

Sentences containing **wäre/wären**, the conditional forms of **sein**, are generally hypothetical in meaning, cf.

Das *ist* schön!	That's nice!
Das *wäre* schön!	That would be nice!
Das *wär*'s?	That would be it?/Is that all? (see Text 1B)

In Text 14 we met:

Wie *wär's* mit ...? (= **Wie *wäre es* mit ...?**)

This is a colloquial expression, meaning literally 'How would it be with ...?' i.e. 'How about ...?' In the spoken language the **-e** of **wäre** is often dropped.

Übung 14G

Say 'How about ...?' with the nouns indicated. With some sentences you will need to think about endings: as you know, **mit** takes the dative!

1 **Wie wär's mit** [more coffee]**?**
2 **Wie wär's mit** [an ice-cream]**?**
3 **Wie wär's mit** [a cup of tea]**?**
4 **Wie wär's mit** [a piece of cake]**?**
5 **Wie wär's mit** [a Berliner Weiße]**?**
6 **Wie wär's mit** [a museum]**?**
7 **Wie wär's mit** [a Riesling]**?**
8 **Wie wär's mit** [a red wine]**?**
9 **Wie wär's mit** [a window seat]**?**
10 **Wie wär's mit** [an opera]**?**

Übung 14H

Read through Text 14 again and then reconstruct the dialogue below. The incomplete words (each dash = one missing letter) are all verbs for which only the first letter of each verb has been provided. It would be better not to write in the book, because you could then use this exercise for revision at a later date to establish how much has stuck.

HEIDI D: Das Konzert w – – wirklich hervorragend, nicht wahr?
PETER B: Ja, das s – – – – –, ganz ausgezeichnet! Der Konzertsaal i – – für Mozart einfach ideal. Wunderschön!
HEIDI D: Sagen Sie, h – – – – – Sie Lust, mit mir morgen vormittag ein Museum zu b – – – – – – – ?
PETER B: Ja, warum nicht? Aber welches? Berlin h – – viele Museen.
HEIDI D: Wie w – – 's mit mehr Musik? Das Musikinstrumenten-Museum am Tiergarten i – – weltberühmt, besonders für Instrumente aus der Renaissance und aus dem Barock.
PETER B: I – – – – – – – – – – – – – – Sie sich schon lange für Musikinstrumente?
HEIDI D: Ja, sehr. Ich i – – – – – – – – – – – – mich vor allem für alte Harfen. Als Kind h – – – ich Harfe und Klavier g – – – – – – – .
PETER B: Gut, ich k – – – – gern mit. Ich s – – – – – – kein

Instrument und ich h --- noch nie ein Musikinstrumenten-Museum b ------- . Aber ich h --- gern Musik, manchmal klassische, meistens gute Unterhaltungsmusik – und auch Schlagermusik.

HEIDI D: Ich h --- viel lieber klassische Musik.

PETER B: OK! Wann und wo wollen wir uns t ------- ?

HEIDI D: Nach meinem Stadtplan i -- das Musikinstrumenten-Museum in der Tiergartenstraße hinter der Philharmonie.

PETER B: Wie k ---- man dorthin?

HEIDI D: Wollen wir mal s ---- ! Ich glaube, da g --- es keine U-Bahn. ... Die nächste S-Bahn-Station i -- Potsdamer Platz: Linie 1 Richtung Oranienburg oder Linie 2 Richtung Schönholz. Alles klar?

PETER B: Alles klar.

HEIDI D: Wollen wir uns um zehn Uhr vor dem Museum t ------- oder i -- das vielleicht zu früh?

PETER B: Kein Problem. Ich b -- Frühaufsteher.

15 Freizeit

Time out

Language activities

- talking about hobbies and leisure activities
- switching from formal to familiar
- expressing likes and preferences

Language focus

- from **Sie** to **du**
- **gern, ungern**
- **lieber**

Text 15

Donnerstag mittag

Heidi and Peter enjoyed the museum but it's time for some fresh air. Heidi readily agrees to go for a walk along the Wannsee, particularly in view of the marvellous weather. She suggests it's time they were on familiar speaking terms, which means changing the word for 'you' in German from **Sie** to **du**, and Peter makes his first tentative steps in this direction. They then discuss what they usually do in their (limited) **Freizeit**, their spare time. . . .

HEIDI D: Das Museum hat mir gut gefallen.[1] Ihnen doch auch, nicht wahr?

PETER B: Ja, sehr! Aber ich brauche[2] jetzt frische Luft. Hätten Sie Lust, mit mir einen Spaziergang[3] am Wannsee[4] zu machen? Das Wetter ist einmalig,[5] die Sonne scheint so schön . . .

HEIDI D: Tolle Idee![6] Ich bin auch für Wasser und Wald. Sagen Sie, wollen wir uns nicht duzen?[7] Ich finde, das Siezen ist inzwischen[8] doch[9] ein bißchen steif.[10]

PETER B: Ja, gern! Ich danke Ihnen. Oh Entschuldigung! – *dir* natürlich, ich danke *dir*, Heidi.

HEIDI D: Ja, man muß sich dran gewöhnen,[11] aber ich glaube,[12] du lernst es schnell. Was für Hobbys[13] hast du eigentlich?

PETER B: Ich habe viele. Ich lese[14] viel, höre[15] Musik, ich spiele manchmal Tennis, ich wandere gern, ich schwimme gern, und ich besuche Museen – nicht nur in Berlin. Ich habe eigentlich zu viele Hobbys und zu wenig Freizeit.[16] Und du? Schwimmst du gern?

HEIDI D: Nicht besonders, ich schwimme nicht gut. Ich spiele auch furchtbar schlecht[17] Tennis. Ich kann nur wandern. Und ich wandere gern. Außerdem lese ich gern und höre viel Musik. Wie oft wanderst du, Peter?

PETER B: So oft wie möglich.[18] Ich mache eine lange Wanderung drei- bis viermal[19] im Monat, also fast jeden[20] Sonntag. Man kann in der Nähe von[21] York herrlich wandern. Das Wetter ist aber leider nicht immer ideal. . . .

Notes

1 see dative verbs: **Lektion elf**

2 **brauchen**: regular verb, 'to need'

3 'a (generally gentle) walk', as opposed to **eine Wanderung** (see below) which is longer, more of 'a hike'

4 **der See** = 'lake'. **Der Wannsee** refers to lake-like expanses of the River Havel in west Berlin, where it meanders through woods from north to south before eventually flowing into the Elbe

5 literally: unique, i.e. 'superb, fantastic' (choose your own hyperbole!)

6 'great, brilliant idea!' **Toll** used to mean 'mad' (and still does in **die Tollwut** = 'rabies') but colloquially it now expresses a very positive reaction to something, cf. English 'Crazy!'

7 **duzen** is a verb meaning 'to use' the more familiar ***du*** (rather than the more formal **Sie**) form.

8 **inzwischen** = 'meanwhile'

9 **doch** is frequently included in German sentences for emphasis. Here it hardly needs to be translated but could be as e.g. 'after all'

10 literally: a bit stiff, i.e. 'too formal'
11 **man muß sich dran gewöhnen** = literally: 'one has to accustom oneself to it', i.e. (here): 'You'll get used to it!' The expression is used colloquially in many contexts. The impersonal pronoun **man** could refer to the speaker or the person addressed, or the world in general! The context makes clear who is meant
12 **glauben**, 'to believe', is regular, and so is **lernen**, 'to learn', in the next line
13 several English nouns ending in '-y' have been imported into German (e.g. also **das Baby**), but in German they usually end **-ys** in the plural rather than **-ies**
14 **lesen**, 'to read', is irregular: **ich lese**, **er liest**, past participle: **gelesen**
15 **hören**, 'to hear, listen to', is regular
16 **die Freizeit** = 'free time' and is also used for 'leisure'
17 **schlecht** = 'bad, badly'; **furchtbar** = 'terrible, terribly'
18 'as often as possible'
19 a number + **mal** = 'times', as in **zweimal** = 'twice', **dreimal** = 'three times'
20 'every, each'
21 'near', in a geographical sense, is usually expressed in German by the phrase **in der Nähe von**

Übung 15A

Find equivalents in Text 15 and in the Notes above for the following nouns. Write them all in their singular form with a capital letter, in three columns and preceded by **der**, **das** or **die**. When you have finished, your German nouns should appear in alphabetical order in each column.

masculine	*neuter*	*feminine*
month	baby	sorry!
lake	hobby	spare/leisure time
Sunday	museum	idea
walk, stroll	tennis	air
wood, forest	water	music
	weather	vicinity
		sun
		rabies
		walk, ramble, hike

Übung 15B

Find and write out the German equivalents in Text 15 of the following sentences/phrases. Don't try to translate the English sentences word for word: look for 'whole-sentence' equivalents, stick to the original German word order, but leave any bits of the original out that obviously aren't required below.

1 I enjoyed the museum.
2 Now I need fresh air!
3 Actually I have too many hobbies and too little spare time.
4 You'll get used to it!
5 I read a lot, I listen to music.
6 I do a long walk three or four times a month.
7 Near York.
8 I play tennis very badly.
9 I'm not a good swimmer.
10 The weather's glorious!

Übung 15C

Match the questions (numbers) and answers (letters):

1 **Wollen wir uns nicht duzen?**
2 **Hätten Sie Lust, mit mir einen Spaziergang zu machen?**
3 **Was für Hobbys hast du?**
4 **Wie oft wanderst du?**
5 **Schwimmst du gern?**
A **Nicht besonders, ich schwimme nicht gut.**
B **So oft wie möglich!**
C **Tolle Idee!**
D **Ja, gern!**
E **Ich habe viele.**

Du – Sie

Many languages have separate 'familiar' and 'formal' terms of address (e.g. French *tu* vs. *vous*, Spanish *tú* vs. *usted*). When to use which term of address can be a complicated and delicate matter – the 'rules' vary somewhat from speaker to speaker. Broadly, as far as German is concerned, the so-called familiar form is used to address (no hierarchy intended!):

animals
children
not too distant relations
fellow students
workmates and closer colleagues
friends

Clearly, there is some scope for interpretation as far as this list is concerned. When is a child not a child? What is a non-distant relative? How close a colleague?, etc. The speaker's age is a factor, too: the younger s/he is, the more likely s/he is to use **du**. Elderly German speakers may well use **Sie** with some of their longest-standing friends.

Du has been called the 'pronoun of solidarity'. **Sie** might be described as the 'pronoun of respect'. If in doubt, use **Sie** – it is much easier to give a negative impression using **du** than it is using **Sie**. Remember: **Sie** is in the first instance *neutral*, it is *not unfriendly*.

It's probably best to let a native German-speaker take the lead on the choice of pronouns.

Verbs with Sie *and* du

The form of the verb used after **Sie** is the same as the infinitive, but the verb **sein** 'to be' is an exception in almost all things:

sein: *to be* **Sie *sind*** **er/sie *ist*** **du *bist***

The form of the verb after **du** is generally the same as the form used after **er/sie/es** with the addition of **-s-** before the final **-t**:

to learn	**Sie lernen**	**er/sie lern*t***	**du lern*st***
to have	**Sie haben**	**er/sie ha*t***	**du ha*st***
to swim	**Sie schwimmen**	**er/sie schwimm*t***	**du schwimm*st***

If the verb stem already ends in **-s** or **-ß**, then the **du** form and **er/sie/es** form are the same, simply because it would be impossible to pronounce an additional **-s-**:

to read	**Sie lesen**	**er/sie lies*t***	**du lies*t***
to kiss	**Sie küssen**	**er/sie küß*t***	**du küß*t***

The **er/sie/es** form of some verbs, however, does not have a final **-t**; so for the **du** form of these verbs, **-st** rather than just **-s-** has to be added. If there is already a final **-s** or **-ß**, then only **-t** need be added for the **du** form.

to be able	**Sie können**	**er/sie kann**	**du kann*st***
to know	**Sie wissen**	**er/sie weiß**	**du weiß*t***

Übung 15D

The list below contains only verbs which form their **du** form according to the commonest pattern. Can you supply the forms required?

	Sie		*er/sie/es*	*du*
1	**brauchen**	need	**braucht**	________
2	**machen**	do, make	**macht**	________
3	**sagen**	say	**sagt**	________
4	**finden**	find	**findet**	________
5	**glauben**	believe	**glaubt**	________
6	**hören**	hear, listen	**hört**	________
7	**spielen**	play	**spielt**	________
8	**wandern**	walk, hike	**wandert**	________
9	**besuchen**	visit	**besucht**	________
10	**gefallen**	please	**gefällt**	________
11	**scheinen**	shine, appear	**scheint**	________
12	**danken**	thank	**dankt**	________
13	**gehen**	go, walk	**geht**	________
14	**fahren**	go, travel	**fährt**	________
15	**schlafen**	sleep	**schläft**	________

Übung 15E

Replace the words in *italics* in the sentences below in order to change the formal to the familiar, i.e. the **Sie** form to the **du** form, using the appropriate case from the diagram and changing the verb form where indicated.

	formal		*familiar*	*cf.*
nominative	***Sie***		***du***	**ich**
accusative	***Sie***	YOU	***dich***	**mich**
dative	***Ihnen***		***dir***	**mir**

1 **Wie gefällt *Ihnen* Berlin?**
2 **Ich gehe gern mit *Ihnen* ins Konzert.**
3 ***Spielen Sie* gern Tennis?**
4 **Wo *haben Sie* gestern das Mozartkonzert gehört?**
5 **Ich bringe *Sie* zum Bahnhof.**
6 ***Haben Sie* noch nie ein Musikinstrumenten-Museum besucht?**
7 **Um wievel Uhr *fahren Sie* nach Hamburg?**
8 **Was *glauben Sie*?**
9 **Ich danke *Ihnen*!**
10 **Kann ich *Sie* morgen besuchen?**

Gern

In isolation, **gern** means 'yes' or 'gladly/willingly', e.g.

Möchtest du Kaffee? **Gern! (Ja, gern!)**

It can be used to stress **möchten**, as e.g.

Ich möchte gern Tee! I'd like tea.

Used in conjunction with other verbs **gern** indicates enjoyment of whatever action the verb describes, e.g.

Ich trinke gern Kaffee. I like drinking coffee, *i.e.* I enjoy coffee.
Ich schwimme gern. I enjoy swimming
Ich höre gern Musik. I enjoy (listening to) music
Ich wandere gern. I like going for long walks

The opposite of **gern** is **ungern** or **nicht gern**:

Ich schwimme gut aber *ungern*
I'm a good swimmer but I don't swim for pleasure
Ich höre nicht *gern* Rockmusik.
I don't like (listening to) rock music

Übung 15F

Answer the questions in German:

(a) **Was macht Peter gern?**
1 He likes playing tennis.
2 He likes visiting museums.

3 He likes swimming.
4 He likes going for long walks.
5 He likes reading.
6 He likes listening to music.
(b) **Was macht Heidi *nicht* gern?**
7 She doesn't like swimming.
8 She doesn't like playing tennis.
(c) **Was machen Heidi *und* Peter gern?**
9–12 They. . . .

Lieber

is used to express preferences and is therefore often met in the environment of **gern**, e.g.

Ich trinke *gern* Kaffee
I like coffee

Meine Frau trinkt *lieber* Tee
My wife prefers tea

Übung 15G

Express your preferences using a verb plus **lieber**:

1 **Ich** [prefer to drink] **Berliner Weiße.**
2 **Ich** [prefer to play] **Klavier.**
3 **Ich** [prefer to listen to/hear] **Musik.**
4 **Ich** [prefer to go] **ins Konzert.**
5 **Ich** [prefer to visit] **Museen.**
6 **Ich** [prefer to 'do'] **einen Spaziergang am Wannsee.**
7 **Ich** [prefer going for long walks] **in der Nähe von York.**
8 **Ich** [prefer travelling] **mit dem Bus.**
9 **Ich** [prefer reading] **ein gutes Buch.**
10 **Ich** [prefer sleeping].

Übung 15H

In the following sentences the adjectives or adverbs have been omitted. Can you remember any of them? If you need help, they are listed below the exercise, but try the exercise first with them covered up.

1 **Das Museum hat mir _______ gefallen.**
2 **Aber ich brauche jetzt _______ Luft!**

3 **Das Wetter ist ______!**
4 **Die Sonne scheint so ______!**
5 **______ Idee!**
6 **Ich glaube, du lernst es ______.**
7 **Ich habe ______ zu viele Hobbys.**
8 **Ich spiele ______ ______ Tennis.**
9 **Ich wandere so oft wie ______.**
10 **Man kann in der Nähe von York ______ wandern.**

eigentlich – einmalig – frische – furchtbar – gut – herrlich – möglich – schlecht – schnell – schön – tolle

Übung 15J

An impossible scenario! The dialogue below is topsy-turvy in that the participants, instead of moving from the **Sie** to the **du** form, move perfectly amicably in the wrong direction! Can you restore the dialogue to its original form? The italics indicate where restoration is needed.

HEIDI D: Das Museum hat mir gut gefallen. *Dir* doch auch, nicht wahr?

PETER B: Ja, sehr! Aber ich brauche jetzt frische Luft! *Hättest du* Lust, mit mir einen Spaziergang am Wannsee zu machen? Das Wetter ist einmalig, die Sonne scheint so schön . . .

HEIDI D: Tolle Idee! Ich bin auch für Wasser und Wald. Wollen wir uns nicht *siezen*? Ich finde, das *Duzen* ist inzwischen doch ein bißchen *familiär*.

PETER B: Ja, gern! Ich danke *dir*! Oh Entschuldigung! – *Ihnen* natürlich, ich danke *Ihnen*, Heidi!

HEIDI D: Ja, man muß sich dran gewöhnen, aber ich glaube, *Sie lernen* es schnell! Was für Hobbys *haben Sie* eigentlich?

PETER B: Ich habe viele! Ich lese viel, höre Musik, ich spiele manchmal Tennis, ich wandere gern, ich schwimme gern, und ich besuche Museen – nicht nur in Berlin! Ich habe eigentlich zu viele Hobbys und zu wenig Freizeit! Und *Sie*? *Schwimmen Sie* gern?

HEIDI D: Nicht besonders, ich schwimme nicht gut. Ich spiele auch furchtbar schlecht Tennis. Ich kann nur wandern! Und ich wandere gern! Außerdem lese ich gern und höre viel Musik. Wie oft *wandern Sie*, Peter?

PETER B: So oft wie möglich. . . .

Übung 15K

Was für Hobbys haben *Sie*? Was machen Sie gern in *Ihrer* Freizeit? What are *your* hobbies? What do *you* like doing in your spare time? Build your own profile from the words in Text 15 and selected from the suggestions below. Write out the resulting sentences and learn them for future use.

1 First check out the list of activities below, adding to each statement *where the blank lines are* the word from this set which applies to you: **gern** | **ungern** | **nicht**. For example, you like watching television so you write: **Ich sehe *gern* fern.**

2 In the second stage repeat only those items in the list which *you* do or have done, slotting in an appropriate word or phrase from this set:

jeden Tag | **jede Woche** | **oft** | **manchmal** | **selten**
every day | every week | often | sometimes | rarely
einmal | **zweimal** (etc.) **in der Woche** | **im Monat** | **im Jahr**
once | twice . . . per week | per month | per year
e.g. you watch television daily, so you write: **Ich sehe *jeden Tag* fern.**

Ich tanze ______(dance)
Ich bastele _____(make things)
Ich angele _____(fish)
Ich nähe _______(sew)
Ich stricke ______(knit)
Ich studiere ____(study)

Ich fotografiere _________ (take photographs)
Ich filme __________('video')
Ich singe __________(sing)
Ich reite _____________ (go horse-riding)
Ich koche _________(cook)
Ich male __________(paint)

Ich höre ___________**Musik**, **Radio** (listen to music, radio)
Ich spiele __________**Klavier**, **Gitarre** (play piano, guitar)
Ich spiele __________**Golf**, **Fußball**, **Bridge**, **Schach** (chess)
Ich sehe ___________**fern** (watch television)
Ich fahre __________**Rad** (go cycling)
Ich gehe ___________**spazieren** (go for walks)
Ich führe __________**den Hund aus** (take the dog out)
Ich fahre __________**(mit dem Auto) aufs Land** (drive into the countryside)
Ich sehe ___________**Fußball**, **Rugby**, **Baseball**, **Kricket** (watch football etc.)
Ich arbeite _________**im Garten** (work in the garden)

Ich arbeite ________**am Haus** (work on the house)
Ich gehe ___________**ins Kino**, **Theater**, **Konzert** (go to the cinema etc.)
Ich gehe ___________**in ein Restaurant**, **Lokal**, **Museum** (pub, museum)
Ich gehe ___________**in die Oper**, **in eine Kunstgalerie** (art gallery)
Ich mache _________**Aerobic**, **Fitneßtraining** (keep fit etc.)
Ich lerne __________**Deutsch** (learn German)
Ich schreibe _______**Briefe**, **Bücher** (letters, books)

Apologies for any leisure pursuits omitted. Collect any others you need from a large English–German dictionary!

16 Gute Besserung!

Off to the doctor's

Language activities

- phoning
- health matters
- using the familiar **du**

Language focus

- modal verbs
- **Es gibt . . .**
- **Sagen Sie!/Sag!**
- **mir, dir, Ihnen**

Text 16

Freitag früh

Friday, Heidi and Peter's last full day in Berlin, looks like being particularly busy. It begins with a bump: he falls down outside the hotel and hurts his ankle. So the morning is a write-off. He phones her to say he has to go to the doctor's. She offers her assistance which he gratefully declines, but he asks her to phone him back in the early afternoon . . .

EMPFANG: Hotel Schmidt, guten Morgen!
PETER B: Guten Morgen! Kann ich bitte mit Frau Dettmann sprechen?[1]
EMPFANG: Einen Moment, ich verbinde[2] Sie.
HEIDI D: Dettmann am Apparat.[3]
PETER B: Guten Morgen, Heidi, hier ist Peter! Wie geht's?[4] Gut geschlafen?[5]

HEIDI D: Danke. Und wie geht's dir?

PETER B: Es tut mir furchtbar leid,[6] aber wir können uns heute vormittag nicht treffen.[7] Ich muß sofort zum Arzt.[8]

HEIDI D: Warum? Geht's dir schlecht?[9] Bist du krank?[10]

PETER B: Nein, nicht direkt. Dummerweise[11] bin ich vor dem Hotel hingefallen.[12] Mein Knöchel[13] ist stark angeschwollen.[14] Ich glaube, er ist verstaucht[15] aber bestimmt nicht gebrochen.[16]

HEIDI D: Armer[17] Peter, kannst du noch gehen?

PETER B: Ja, ich kann noch gehen – aber nur mit Mühe.[18] Zum Glück[19] gibt es eine Praxis[20] gleich um die Ecke.

HEIDI D: Kann ich dir irgendwie[21] helfen?[22]

PETER B: Das ist lieb von dir[23], aber du kannst mir im Moment nicht helfen – vielleicht heute nachmittag.

HEIDI D: Bist du sicher?[24]

PETER B: Ja, ganz sicher. Ruf mich vielleicht um zwei Uhr wieder an![25]

HEIDI D: Gut! Um zwei. Und gute Besserung![26] Ich wünsche dir viel Glück[27] beim Arzt.

PETER B: Danke. Bis später. . . .[28]

Notes

1 'speak': **er/sie spricht**, **(hat) gesprochen**. If she were phoning him, she would have said: **Kann ich bitte mit Herr*n* Bennett sprechen (Herr** requires an -***n*** in the dative (as here) and the accusative

2 'connect': **er/sie verbindet**, **(hat) verbunden**

3 **der Apparat** means 'apparatus' generally but is also used for a phone line. The standard way in German of saying 'Speaking!' in reply to a caller's request to speak to you is **Am Apparat!** 'Phone number' is **die Telefonnummer** (but **das Telefon**), 'extension number' **die Apparatnummer**

4 literally: 'How goes it?' (**es** is abbreviated to **'s** here)

5 literally: 'Well slept?' i.e. 'Did you sleep well?'

6 **Es tut mir leid** = 'I'm sorry' (literally: 'it does me injury'). **Tun**: **er/sie tut**, **(hat) getan**

7 'to meet': **er/sie trifft**, **(hat) getroffen**

8 'have to go to the doctor immediately': **gehen** is left off the end of the sentence as being self-explanatory

9 **gut** $\neq$ **schlecht**

10 **krank** = 'ill', cf. **Krankenhaus** = 'hospital'

11 **dumm** = 'stupid/stupidly', **dummerweise** = 'stupidly'. 'Dumb' meaning not able to speak = **stumm**

12 **hinfallen**, 'to fall down', is a variant of **fallen**, 'to fall', **fällt**, **(bin) gefallen**
13 **der Knöchel** = 'ankle' (the related word **der Knochen** = 'bone')
14 'swollen'
15 'sprained'
16 'broken'
17 **arm** = 'poor'
18 **die Mühe** = 'effort, trouble'
19 'fortunately'. **Das Glück** = 'happiness, good fortune'
20 **die Praxis** = 'doctor's practice, surgery'
21 'in some way'
22 **helfen**, 'to help', is a dative verb, like **danken**, hence ***mir*** . . . **helfen**
23 'that's sweet/kind of you'
24 'sure'
25 'call me again at about two!' **Anrufen** is an irregular separable verb: **ruft . . . an, (hat) angerufen**
26 a standard expression, used to wish someone a 'good improvement' i.e. 'a speedy recovery'. Note that **Gesundheit!** means 'health!' but it is used after a person sneezes and is not interchangeable with **Gute Besserung!**
27 'I wish you much good fortune at the doctor's'. See Note 19.
28 literally: 'till later'

Übung 16A

Find equivalents in Text 16 and in the Notes above for the following nouns. Write them all in their singular form with a capital letter, in three columns and preceded by **der**, **das** or **die**. When you have finished, your German nouns should appear in alphabetical order in each column.

masculine	*neuter*	*feminine*
apparatus [phone]	happiness, fortune	improvement, recovery
doctor	hotel	corner
moment	hospital	Mrs, woman
success	telephone	health ['Bless you!']
foot		effort, trouble
Mr, gentleman		number
ankle		practice, surgery
bone		second
moment		clock, o'clock
morning		

Übung 16B

Find and write out the German equivalents in Text 16 of the following sentences/phrases. Don't try to translate the English sentences word for word: look for 'whole-sentence' equivalents, stick to the original German word order, but leave any bits of the original out that obviously aren't required below.

1 Just a moment, I'll put you through!
2 Can I speak to Mrs Dettmann?
3 How are you?
4 I'm terribly sorry!
5 This morning.
6 Are you ill?
7 I think it's sprained but not broken.
8 I was stupid enough to fall in front of the hotel.
9 Poor Peter!
10 Fortunately the surgery is just round the corner.
11 Call me back at two.
12 Get better soon!

Pronouns in general

If you need to revise pronouns, check out **Lektion elf**. With the **du** forms included, the pronoun table now looks like this:

	I	*you [famil.]*	*he/it*	*she/it*	*it*	*we*	*they*	*you [formal]*
nom.	**ich**	**du**	**er**	**sie**	**es**	**wir**	**sie**	**Sie**
	me	*you*	*him/it*	*her/it*	*it*	*us*	*them*	*you*
acc.	**mich**	**dich**	**ihn**	**sie**	**es**	**uns**	**sie**	**Sie**
	me	*you*	*him/it*	*her/it*	*it*	*us*	*them*	*you*
dat.	**mir**	**dir**	**ihm**	**ihr**	**ihm**	**uns**	**ihnen**	**Ihnen**

Dative pronouns

By now you have met quite a few common expressions containing dative pronouns, so it might be useful to bring them together. In the German sentences below, the words in square brackets could be omitted.

Das Museum hat mir gut gefallen.	I liked the museum (it pleased me . . .)
Hat es [dir/Ihnen] geschmeckt?	Did you enjoy the meal?
Danke, es hat [mir] gut geschmeckt.	Yes, thank you, I did.
[Ich wünsche dir/Ihnen]. . . .	I wish you . . .
. . . **viel Glück!**	. . . the best of luck!
. . . **viel Spaß!**	. . . 'much fun' (i.e. have fun/a good time!)
. . . **gute Besserung!**	. . . 'a good recovery' (i.e. get better soon!)
. . . **guten Appetit!**	. . . 'a good appetite' (i.e. enjoy your meal!)
Das ist lieb von dir/Ihnen!	That's kind/sweet of you!
Ich danke dir/Ihnen!	Thank you!
Wie kann ich dir/Ihnen helfen?	How can I help you?
Es tut mir leid!	I'm sorry!
Wie geht es [dir/Ihnen]?	How are you?

Übung 16C

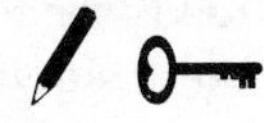

If **Es tut *mir* leid!** means 'I'm sorry!', how would you, adapting the same expression, say:

1 We are sorry.
2 Heidi is sorry.
3 She is sorry.
4 Peter is sorry.
5 He is sorry.
6 They are sorry.
7 You [familiar] are sorry.
8 You [formal] are sorry.

Übung 16D

Put the following descriptors in order from best to worst. Then label them from *(a)* = *best* to *(e)* = *worst.*

furchtbar schlecht – sehr gut – ausgezeichnet – einmalig gut – nicht so gut

Now answer the questions below, first adding the dative pronoun required and then the descriptor from your list as per the letters in brackets.

1 **Wie geht es dir? Danke, es geht** ______ (d) ______
2 **Wie geht es Ihnen? Es geht** ______ **leider** (e) ________
3 **Wie geht es Peter? Ich glaube, es geht** ______ (c) ______
4 **Wie geht es Heidi? Ich glaube, es geht** ______ (a) ______
5 **Wie geht es Heidi und Peter?**
Ich glaube, es geht ______ (b) ______

A well-known saying which illustrates in succinct form the use of the nominative and dative of two personal pronouns is:

Wie du mir, so ich dir!

Literally: 'As you to me, so I to you!', i.e. 'You haven't been nice to me, so I'm not going to be nice to you!' We hope you will never want to use this expression. . . .

Modal verbs

Modal verbs were first discussed with reference to **möchten** in **Lektion fünf** where we said that the English equivalents of the German modals cover meanings such as:

would, should, could, can, may, might, must,
would like/want (to), ought to

You have met several other German modals in the meantime, so we now bring them together in a table below, plus **sollen** which occurs later (in **Lektion siebzehn**).

	would like	be able/ can	must/ have to	may/ can	want/ intend	should/ ought
	möchten	***können***	***müssen***	***dürfen***	***wollen***	***sollen***
ich	**möchte**	**kann**	**muß**	**darf**	**will**	**soll**
du	**möchtest**	**kannst**	**mußt**	**darfst**	**willst**	**sollst**
er / sie / es	**möchte**	**kann**	**muß**	**darf**	**will**	**soll**
wir / sie / Sie	**möchten**	**können**	**müssen**	**dürfen**	**wollen**	**sollen**

Note that the **er/sie/es** form for these verbs is the same as the **ich** form. For most German verbs these forms differ, e.g. **ich mach*e***, **er mach*t*.**

Übung 16E

The following sentences contain modals which have occurred in previous **Lektionen**. Can you remember what the sentences mean and in what context they were used, who said what and why? After you have made notes on as many of the sentences as you possibly can, go back to the **Lektionen** (an excellent revision exercise!) and check out what you may or may not have forgotten.

1 **Lektion 15**
1.1 **Sagen Sie, *wollen* wir uns nicht duzen?**
1.2 **Ja, man *muß* sich dran gewöhnen!**
1.3 **Ich *kann* nur wandern.**
1.4 **Man *kann* in der Nähe von York herrlich wandern.**
2 **Lektion 14**
2.1 **Wann und wo *wollen* wir uns treffen?**
2.2 ***Wollen* wir mal sehen!**
3 **Lektion 13**
3.1 ***Wollen* wir vielleicht etwas zusammen unternehmen?**
3.2 **Ich *möchte* also gern ins Schloßkonzert gehen.**
3.3 **Wo *wollen* wir uns treffen?**
4 **Lektion 8**
4.1 ***Darf* ich Sie vielleicht nachher zu einem Glas Bier oder Wein oder Saft einladen?**
5 **Lektion 7**

5.1 ***Können* Sie mich alle gut hören?**

The most obvious shared characteristic of German modals is that in sentences in which they are used, a second verb (in its infinitive form) is frequently needed for the sentence to make sense, e.g.

Ich möchte	**am**	**Fenster sitzen.**
I would like	at the	window to sit.

The modal (the finite verb) is in standard second position in the sentence above, and the infinitive lives at the end.

Übung 16F

Complete these sentences from Text 16, using (a) a modal verb and (b) an infinitive. The infinitives, in random order, are:

helfen × 2	**sprechen**	**treffen**	**gehen** × 3
help	speak	meet	go, walk

1 (a) **ich bitte mit Frau Dettmann** (b)?
2 **Wir** (a) **uns heute vormittag nicht** (b).
3 **Ich** (a) **sofort zum Arzt!**
[the infinitive is omitted here as being understood: see **Lektion fünf**]
4 **Armer Peter,** (a) **du noch** (b)?
5 **Ja, ich** (a) **noch** (b) – **aber nur mit Mühe!**
6 **Wie** (a) **ich dir** (b)?
7 **Das ist lieb von dir aber du** (a) **mir im Moment nicht** (b).

Questions and commands

See the section headed 'Questions and commands' in **Lektion drei** for a first discussion of this topic. In grammar books, incidentally, questions are often called 'interrogatives' and commands 'imperatives'.

Questions and commands using Sie

look very much the same: it is the context and the tone of voice which tell you what is meant:

Sagen Sie 'Munich' auf Englisch?
Do you say 'Munich' in English?

Sagen Sie 'München'!
Say (*i.e.* pronounce) 'München'!

In everyday conversation, direct imperatives are used with care – people don't usually want to be 'ordered around' – but they certainly occur (a) when orders/instructions are expected or invited and (b) in 'formulaic' expressions, like 'Tell me . . .':

Instructions
Go straight ahead . . .
***Gehen Sie* geradeaus!**
Take the third street on the right . . .
***Nehmen Sie* die dritte Straße rechts!**
Take the lift just here on the left . . .
***Nehmen Sie* hier links den Fahrstuhl!**
Give me a ring this evening . . .
***Rufen Sie* mich heute abend an!**

'Formulaic' expressions
Sorry! (Forgive me!)
***Entschuldigen Sie*, bitte!**
Tell me, shall we use the **du** form?
***Sagen Sie!* Wollen wir uns nicht duzen?**
Tell me, do you fancy visiting a museum with me tomorrow morning?
***Sagen Sie!* Hätten Sie Lust, mit mir morgen vormittag ein Museum zu besuchen?**

Questions and commands using du

differ from one other in form:

***Rufst du* mich an?**
***Ruf* mich vielleicht um zwei Uhr wieder an!**

To form this imperative it's generally helpful to know the standard present tense **du** form of the verb – and then leave off the **-st**. Thus:

to work	**arbeiten**	**Du arbeitest**	→ ***Arbeite!***
to say	**sagen**	**Du sagst**	→ ***Sag!***
to come	**kommen**	**Du kommst**	→ ***Komm!***

Some verbs change their vowel to **-i** in the **du** form but here the rule still applies:

to speak	**sprechen**	**Du sprichst**	→ ***Sprich!***
to give	**geben**	**Du gibst**	→ ***Gib!***
to help	**helfen**	**Du hilfst mir**	→ ***Hilf mir!***

The rule does not, however, work for irregular verbs which change their vowel to **ä**, e.g.

to drive	**fahren**	**Du fährst**	→ ***Fahr!***
to sleep	**schlafen**	**Du schläfst**	→ ***Schlaf!***

There are a few relatively rare exceptions to these general statements.

Es gibt . . .

'There is . . .' and 'There are . . .' are generally both expressed in German by the single expression **Es gibt** . . . (literally: 'It gives . . .') followed by the accusative case.

Es gibt zwei Stadtrundfahrten heute.
There are two city tours today.
Gibt es einen Arzt (hier) in der Nähe?
Is there a doctor in the vicinity?
— Ja, gleich um die Ecke!
Gibt es ein Restaurant (hier) in der Nähe?
— Es gibt *viele* Restaurants hier in der Nähe.
Gibt es (hier) in der Nähe eine U-Bahn-Station?
— Nein, es gibt keine U-Bahn-Station hier in der Nähe.

Wo gibt es in Berlin Wald und Wasser?
Where can one find trees and water . . .?
— Am Wannsee natürlich.
Wo gibt es in Berlin ein großes Kaufhaus?
Where in Berlin is there a big department store?
— Am Wittenbergplatz.
Gibt es in Berlin einen Zoo?
Is there (Does Berlin have . . .)?
—Es gibt *zwei* Zoos in Berlin – einen in Charlottenburg und einen in Lichtenberg.
Gibt es in Berlin einen Alexanderplatz?
Is there an Alexanderplatz in Berlin?
— Aber sicher, der Alexanderplatz liegt in Berlin-Mitte

Übung 16G

Answer questions in relation to your own nearest town/village, sticking closely to the following answer patterns:

(1) masculine nouns
Gibt es bei Ihnen *einen* Bahnhof?
(a) **Nein, bei uns gibt es keinen Bahnhof.**
(b) **Ja, bei uns gibt es einen Bahnhof.**
(c) **Ja, bei uns gibt es zwei/drei . . . viele Bahnhöfe.**

(2) neuter nouns
Gibt es bei Ihnen *ein* Hallenbad?
(a) **Nein, bei uns gibt es kein Hallenbad.**
(b) **Ja, bei uns gibt es ein Hallenbad.**
(c) **Ja, bei uns gibt es zwei/drei . . . viele Hallenbäder.**

(3) feminine nouns
Gibt es bei Ihnen *eine* Apotheke?
(a) **Nein, bei uns gibt es keine Apotheke.**
(b) **Ja, bei uns gibt es eine Apotheke.**
(c) **Ja, bei uns gibt es zwei/drei . . . viele Apotheken.**

Choose the appropriate answer in each case from (a) or (b) or (c) above for the nouns below. If you need to make the noun plural, you may of course need to look the plural form up in the Glossary.

Gibt es bei Ihnen **einen internationalen Flughafen?**
einen Zoo?
einen Konzertsaal?
einen Tennisplatz?
einen Golfplatz?

Gibt es bei Ihnen **ein Theater?**
ein großes Kaufhaus?
ein Krankenhaus?
ein Kino?
ein Museum?

Gibt es bei Ihnen **eine Kunstgalerie?**
eine U-Bahn?
eine Universität?
eine Apotheke?
eine Kathedrale?

An early 1960s German hit in 3/4 time, still heard at carnivals, beer festivals, etc., is the following (mostly tongue-in-cheek) dotty ditty:

Es gibt kein Bier auf Hawaii, es gibt kein Bier,
drum fahre ich nicht nach Hawaii, drum bleib' ich hier!

There's no beer in Hawaii, there's no beer,
that's why I'm not going to Hawaii, that's why I'm staying home!

Übung 16H

We have re-written some of Text 16 in the third person (he/she/they form), as a sort of dramatic narrative! Without looking at the original, try to rewrite what we have written as a real dialogue again! Start with Peter speaking. What Heidi has to say is in italics.

Es tut Peter furchtbar leid, aber sie können sich heute vormittag nicht treffen, er muß sofort zum Arzt.

Geht's ihm schlecht? Ist er krank?

Nein, nicht direkt! Dummerweise ist er vor dem Hotel hingefallen. Sein Knöchel ist stark angeschwollen.

Armer Peter! Kann er noch gehen?

Ja, er kann noch gehen – aber nur mit Mühe.

Wie kann Heidi ihm helfen?

Sie kann ihm im Moment nicht helfen.

Ist er sicher?

Ja, ganz sicher.

Sie wünscht ihm viel Glück beim Arzt.

17 Nichts Schlimmes!

No bones broken

Language activities

- health and general well-being
- relativities: 'better' and 'best'
- shopping

Language focus

- adjectives
- comparatives and superlatives
- **ich kaufe *mir/dir* einen Hut**

Text 17

Freitag nachmittag [1]

Heidi phones Hotel Müller as promised to enquire after Peter's health. He has indeed sprained his ankle, though not seriously, and the doctor's prescription is to remain active rather than sit back and rest. While Peter was at the doctor's, Heidi visited a famous department store and emerged with three new articles of clothing. Before Peter can go shopping (he wants to buy a hat), he has to get hold of some money. He also needs some help. Heidi is happy to escort him – slowly – to the bank. . . .

EMPFANG: Hotel Müller, guten Tag!
HEIDI D: Guten Tag, kann ich bitte mit Herrn[1] Bennett, Zimmer 18, sprechen?
EMPFANG: Augenblick,[2] ich verbinde Sie.
PETER B: Hier Bennett.
HEIDI D: Ach Peter, hier ist Heidi. Wie geht es dir?

PETER B: Danke, es geht mir viel besser.
HEIDI D: Aber was hat der Arzt gesagt?
PETER B: Es ist nichts Schlimmes.[3] Ich habe mir tatsächlich[4] den Knöchel leicht[5] verstaucht und nicht gebrochen.
HEIDI D: Gott sei Dank![6]
PETER B: Ich soll[7] mich auch nicht ausruhen[8] – ich soll den Fuß bewegen.[9]
HEIDI D: Ja, ja, das ist die neueste Methode.[10] Es soll besser für die Durchblutung[11] sein.
PETER B: Ja, das sagt der Arzt auch. Nun, Heidi, hast du heute morgen etwas Interessantes gemacht?
HEIDI D: Ich habe natürlich vor allem[12] an dich gedacht.[13] Ich bin aber auch einkaufen gegangen.[14] Ich war im KaDeWe.[15]
PETER B: Und hast du dir was[16] Schönes gekauft?
HEIDI D: Oh ja, ich habe mir eine schicke graue Hose[17] gekauft und ein süßes schwarzes Kleid und eine sehr preiswerte[18] weiße Jacke.
PETER B: Ich gratuliere![19] Du warst ja[20] heute erfolgreicher[21] als[22] ich! Vielleicht kaufe ich mir morgen einen großen breiten Hut.[23] Was meinst du?[24] Ich muß aber vorher[25] Geld wechseln.[26] Kannst du mir dabei[27] helfen?
HEIDI D: Ja, gern. Soll ich dich jetzt sofort vom Hotel abholen? Die Banken machen in einer Stunde zu.
PETER B: Ja, das wäre lieb. Gehen wir dann zusammen[28] zur Bank – aber langsam, bitte, sehr langsam.[29]
HEIDI D: Selbstverständlich.[30] Also: Tschüs[31] bis dann!

Notes

1 nominative: **Herr**, dative: **Herrn** (very few German nouns change like this in the dative singular)
2 **[einen] Augenblick** = 'just a moment, second'. Alternatives: **[einen] Moment! eine Sekunde!**
3 **schlimm** = 'serious, bad'
4 'in actual fact, indeed'
5 **leicht** = 'lightly', i.e. (here): 'slightly, not seriously'
6 literally: '[to] God be thanks!' i.e. 'Thank goodness' (*or similar*)!
7 'I shouldn't, I am not to' (i.e. 'the doctor has told me not to . . .')
8 regular separable reflexive verb: **sich ausruhen** = 'to rest'
9 regular verb = 'to move, to make [something] move'
10 'that's the newest/latest method/technique'

11 **das Blut** = 'blood', **die Durchblutung** is its circulation
12 'above all'
13 'thought of you'. **Denken**, **denkt**, **gedacht**. 'To think of' = **denken an** + accusative
14 'to go shopping' = **einkaufen gehen**, 'to go to shop'
15 **KaDeWe** is an abbreviation for **Kaufhaus des Westens**, literally 'department store of the west'. It is Berlin's biggest and most up-market store, situated at Wittenbergplatz near the Kurfürstendamm. (**des** is a genitive case form of the masculine singular **der**: see any German grammar book for further information.)
16 **was** is here a shortened, colloquial version of **etwas**
17 **schick** is from the French *chic*, **grau** = 'grey'. **Die Hose** ('trousers' Am. 'pants') is singular in German
18 **preiswert** = 'worth the price' i.e. not expensive and good value. **Billig** ≠ **teuer** = cheap ≠ expensive
19 literally: 'I congratulate', i.e. 'Congratulations!'
20 **ja** is not stressed here and would not be translated as 'yes', its 'basic' meaning. It is frequently used within sentences for positive emphasis
21 'more successful'
22 **als** has many meanings, but after 'more . . .' it is bound to mean 'than'
23 'broad hat', i.e. with a broad brim
24 **meinen** (regular) more frequently means 'to think' than 'to mean'
25 'before, beforehand, before that'
26 'change'
27 literally: 'thereby', i.e. 'with that'
28 'together'
29 **langsam** ≠ **schnell**
30 'of course, it goes without saying'
31 see **Lektion eins!**

Übung 17A

Find equivalents in Text 17 and in the Notes above for the following nouns. Write them all in their singular form with a capital letter, in three columns and preceded by **der**, **das** or **die**. When you have finished, your German nouns should appear in alphabetical order in each column.

masculine	*neuter*	*feminine*
doctor	blood	bank
moment	money	circulation
thanks	hotel	trousers/pants

reception	department store	jacket, cardigan
foot	dress	method
God	room	second
Mr [nominative case]		hour
hat		
ankle		
moment		
day		

Übung 17B

Find and write out the German equivalents in Text 17 of the following sentences/phrases. Don't try to translate the English sentences word for word: look for 'whole-sentence' equivalents, stick to the original German word order, but leave any bits of the original out that obviously aren't required below.

1 Thank goodness!
2 Just a moment, I'll put you through!
3 Did you buy anything nice?
4 Congratulations!
5 Can I speak to Mr Bennett?
6 The banks close in an hour.
7 I went shopping.
8 I feel a lot better.
9 What did the doctor say?
10 What do you think?

Übung 17C

Find the questions to match the following answers. The answers are listed in chronological order.

1 **Sie möchte mit Herrn Bennett sprechen.**
2 **Nummer achtzehn.**
3 **Es geht ihm viel besser.**
4 **Nein, er hat ihn leicht verstaucht.**
5 **Nein, er soll den Fuß bewegen.**
6 **Sie ist einkaufen gegangen.**
7 **Ja, sie hat eine Hose, ein Kleid und eine Jacke gekauft.**
8 **Einen Hut.**
9 **In einer Stunde.**
10 **Ja, aber sehr langsam!**

11 **Nein, Heidi holt ihn vom Hotel ab.**
A **Hat er sich den Knöchel gebrochen?**
B **Hat sie Erfolg gehabt?**
C **Wann machen die Banken zu?**
D **Mit wem möchte Heidi sprechen?**
E **Was hat Heidi Freitag früh gemacht?**
F **In welchem Zimmer wohnt er?**
G **Geht er alleine zur Bank?**
H **Was möchte Peter vielleicht kaufen?**
J **Kann Peter eigentlich gehen?**
K **Wie geht es ihm?**
L **Er muß sich bestimmt ausruhen!**

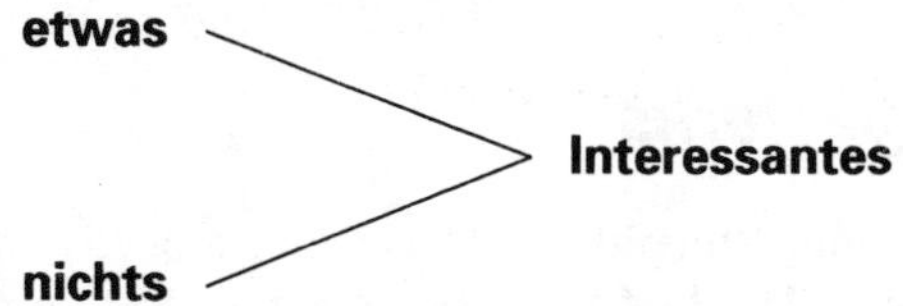

'Something interesting/of interest' in German is **etwas Interessantes**, 'nothing interesting/of interest' **nichts Interessantes**. The second word, **Interessantes**, is essentially an adjective which has been turned into a noun (hence the capital letter, since all nouns in German have capital letters).

Übung 17D

Translate the following phrases into English. The exercise is a follow-up to **Übung 13E**.

1 **etwas Gutes**
2 **etwas Sehenswertes**
3 **etwas Neues**
4 **etwas Schickes**
5 **etwas Alkoholisches**
6 **etwas Eßbares**
7 **nichts Schlimmes**
8 **nichts Wichtiges**
9 **etwas Schönes**
10 **etwas Wahres**
11 **nichts Besseres**
12 **nichts Besonderes**

Übung 17E

Match the following adjectives with their meanings. If you get them right, the German words should appear in alphabetical order.

1	wide	A	**herrlich**
2	fresh	B	**toll**
3	grey	C	**schwarz**
4	large	D	**lang**
5	good	E	**groß**
6	magnificent	F	**preiswert**
7	outstanding	G	**frisch**
8	long	H	**hervorragend**
9	inexpensive	J	**breit**
10	smart, elegant	K	**süß**
11	black	L	**weiß**
12	sweet	M	**gut**
13	great!	N	**schick**
14	white	P	**grau**

Case and gender patterns

The table below gives the complete sets of article and adjective endings practised in this book. The first two sets you have met in stages already, i.e. the endings for the

1 indefinite articles: **ein**, **kein**, and possessives: **mein**, **dein/Ihr**, **sein/sein/ihr**, **unser**, **ihr**
2 definite article: **der**, **das**, **die**, etc.

		masculine singular		*neuter* singular		*feminine* singular		*all three* plural	
1	*nominative*	**kein**	**-er**	**kein**	**-es**	**keine**	**-e**	**keine**	**-en**
	accusative	**keinen**	**-en**	**kein**	**-es**	**keine**	**-e**	**keine**	**-en**
	dative	**keinem**	**-en**	**keinem**	**-en**	**keiner**	**-en**	**keinen**	**-en**
2	*nominative*	**der**	**-e**	**das**	**-e**	**die**	**-e**	**die**	**-en**
	accusative	**den**	**-en**	**das**	**-e**	**die**	**-e**	**die**	**-en**
	dative	**dem**	**-en**	**dem**	**-en**	**der**	**-en**	**den**	**-en**
3	*nominative*	**guter**		**gutes**		**gute**		**gute**	
	accusative	**guten**		**gutes**		**gute**		**gute**	
	dative	**gutem**		**gutem**		**guter**		**guten**	

The third set gives the endings of adjectives 'on their own' in front of nouns, i.e. when they are *not* preceded by a definite or indefinite article or a possessive etc.

You will see that the endings of the adjectives in 3 are to all intents and purposes the same as the various forms of **der**, **das**, **die**, etc. – so you don't need to learn another set of endings, but only have to remember the rule that *adjectives 'on their own' in front of nouns have the same endings as the definite article*. And if, by the way, there are several adjectives 'on their own' in front of a particular noun, they all have the same ending, e.g.

preiswert*er* englisch*er* Tee	inexpensive English tea
klar*es* sonnig*es* Wetter	clear sunny weather
sehr schön*e* neu*e* Kleider	beautiful new dresses

Übung 17F

Complete these sentences in German. The missing words – indicated in English – are all in the *accusative* case but the gender of the noun varies, of course, so the article and adjective endings will, too.

1 **Ich habe mir** [a smart grey] **Hose gekauft.**
2 **Ich habe mir** [a 'sweet' black] **Kleid gekauft.**
3 **Ich habe mir** [a very inexpensive white] **Jacke gekauft.**
4 **Ich möchte morgen** [a large wide(-rimmed)] **Hut kaufen.**
5 **Heute haben wir** [magnificent] **Wetter!**
6 **Ich habe gestern** [an outstanding German] **Riesling getrunken!**
7 **Nehmen Sie** [the third] **Straße rechts!**
8 **Ich mache** [a long] **Wanderung einmal im Monat.**
9 **Ich wünsche dir** [good] **Besserung!**
10 **Ich brauche jetzt** [fresh] **Luft!**
11 **Ich habe** [a great] **Idee!**
12 **Ja, du hast oft** [great] **Ideen!**

Comparatives and superlatives: better – best

The common origin of English and German comes through particularly clearly in the 'good – better – best' sequence of adjectives:

Das ist eine	***gute***	**Idee!**
Das ist eine	***bessere***	**Idee!**
Das ist	**die *beste***	**Idee!**

Comparatives

The basic rule for the formation of comparatives in German is to add *-er* to the adjective, e.g.

beautiful	**schön**	**schön*er***
smart, elegant	**schick**	**schick*er***
successful	**erfolgreich**	**erfolgreich*er***
happy	**glücklich**	**glücklich*er***

This rule applies in German, *however long the adjective.* Don't be influenced by English, which often uses 'more . . .' rather than '-er', e.g. 'more successful' rather than 'successfuler'; or it sometimes offers a choice, e.g. 'more happy' or 'happier', depending on context.

With a very limited number of very common *short* German adjectives, the comparative requires not only the addition of *-er* but also a change in pronunciation of the vowel, e.g.

old	**alt**	***ä*lt*er***
long	**lang**	**l*ä*ng*er***
near	**nah(e)**	**n*ä*h*er***
big, great, tall	**groß**	**gr*ö*ß*er***
young	**jung**	**j*ü*ng*er***
short [e.g. time]	**kurz**	**k*ü*rz*er***

NB 'short/tall' relating to stature = **klein/groß.**

If the comparative form of an adjective is in any way irregular, this will be indicated in the Glossary.

Comparisons using adjectives are made using **als** for 'than' and **so** . . . **wie** for 'as . . . as', e.g.

älter *als* . . .	older than . . .
nicht *so* alt *wie* . . .	not as old as . . .
genau *so* alt *wie* . . .	just as old as . . .

Übung 17G

Let's assume:

(a) **Martina ist zehn Jahre alt;**
(b) **Oliver ist elf Jahre alt;**
(c) **Steffi ist zwölf Jahre alt;**
(d) **Hans ist auch zwölf Jahre alt;**

(e) **Jochen, der Reisebegleiter, ist achtundzwanzig Jahre alt.**

Compare their relative ages, slotting in **jünger**, **älter**, **nicht so alt**, **genau so alt**, as appropriate:

1 **Oliver ist** ______	**als Martina.**
2 **Martina ist** ______	**als Oliver.**
3 **Steffi ist** ______	**als Jochen.**
4 **Jochen ist viel** ______	**als Steffi.**
5 **Oliver ist** ______	**wie Steffi.**
6 **Steffi ist** ______	**wie Hans.**
7 **Hans ist** ______	**als Martina.**
8 **Martina ist** ______	**wie Oliver.**

Superlatives

The basic rule for the formation of superlatives in German is to add *-st* + *ending* to the adjective, e.g.

beautiful	**schön**	**schön*st*-**
smart, elegant	**schick**	**schick*st*-**
successful	**erfolgreich**	**erfolgreich*st*-**
happy	**glücklich**	**glücklich*st*-**

Again, this rule applies in German, *however long the adjective*. For longer adjectives, English, of course, uses 'most . . .' e.g. 'most successful' rather than 'successfulest', or it sometimes offers a choice, e.g. 'most happy' or 'happiest', depending on context.

Those short German adjectives which change their vowel in the comparative do the same for the superlative:

alt	***ä*lt*est*-**	oldest
lang	**l*ä*ngst-**	longest
nahe(e)	**n*ä*ch*st*-**	nearest, next
groß	**gr*ö*ß*t*-**	biggest, tallest
jung	**j*ü*ng*st*-**	youngest
kurz	**k*ü*rz*est*-**	shortest [e.g. time]

Note here that

(a) **ältest**- has an extra -**e**- to make it easier to pronounce;
(b) the superlative ending of **größt**- is -**t**- rather than -**st**-;
(c) **nächst**- is irregular (it acquires -**c**- in the superlative);
(d) **kürzest**- follows the same pattern as **ältest**-.

As in English, there are two ways in German of expressing the superlative:

(a) **Jochen ist *der älteste.*** Jochen is the oldest.
Martina ist *die jüngste.* Martina is the youngest.
(b) **Jochen ist *am ältesten.*** Jochen is oldest.
Martina ist *am jüngsten.* Martina is youngest.

Note that with type (a), the gender/sex needs to be specified in front of the adjective, whereas in type (b) ***am*** never changes.

Übung 17H

In order to learn the superlative, you will have to indulge in some hyberbole: whether any of the following statements are actually true is neither here nor there! Translate the items in brackets, following the type (a) pattern above.

1 **Der Kurfürstendamm ist** [the most distinguished] **Einkaufsstraße in Berlin.**
2 **Unter den Linden ist** [the most interesting] **Straße in Berlin.**
3 **Berlin ist** [the biggest] **Stadt Deutschlands.***
4 **Dorfmark ist** [the most beautiful] **Dorf Niedersachsens.***
5 **York ist** [the oldest] **Stadt in Yorkshire.**
6 **Wordsworth ist** [the most popular] **Dichter Englands.***
7 [The nearest] **Hotel heißt Hotel Müller.**
8 **Um wieviel Uhr fährt** [the next] **Zug nach Postdam?**
9 **Die** [latest] **Methode heißt: Nicht ruhen! Den Fuß bewegen!**
10 **In Frankreich habe ich starken Kaffee getrunken, aber in Deutschland** [the strongest]**!**

* The **-s** ending on the starred words above suggests 'of '... Germany etc.

Übung 17J

Answer the questions, using data from the following table.

Land	*Stadt*	*Tagestemperatur [Grad Celsius]*		*Regen [Zentimeter]*	
		Dezember	*Juli*	*Dezember*	*Juli*
Deutschland	**Berlin**	1	23	5	8
Österreich	**Wien**	1	24	5	8
Schweiz	**Genf**	4	25	6	7
England	**Manchester**	8	20	8	8
Schottland	**Fort William**	8	18	22	10
Irland	**Dublin**	9	18	7	7
Indien	**Kalkutta**	28	32	1	32
USA	**New Orleans**	18	30	12	16
Kanada	**Winnipeg**	–10	25	2	8
Südafrika	**Kapstadt**	24	18	2	9
Australien	**Alice Springs**	34	19	3	1
Neuseeland	**Auckland**	21	15	8	14

warm: hot/warm **kühl**: cool **kalt**: cold **trocken**: dry **naß**: wet

1 **Wo ist es im Juli am wärmsten?** **In** ______
2 **Wo ist es im Juli am kühlsten?** **In** ______
3 **Wo ist es im Dezember am wärmsten?** **In** ______
4 **Wo ist es im Dezember am kältesten?** **In** ______
5 **Wo ist es im Juli am trockensten?** **In** ______
6 **Wo ist es im Dezember am trockensten?** **In** ______
7 **Wo ist es im Dezember am nassesten*?** **In** ______
8 **Wo ist es im Juli am nassesten*?** **In** ______

* **am nässesten** is also used for the superlative

Reflexive verbs: sich waschen × *2*

See **Lektion zwölf** for an overview of reflexives to date. There we said that in essence reflexive verbs in German are verbs

(a) which always have both subject and an object;
(b) whose subject and object are the same person (or, less frequently, thing).

Reflexives in this sense follow this pattern:

Ich habe mich unterhalten	I talked/chatted
Ich habe mich ausgeruht	I rested
Ich habe mich gewaschen	I washed

Now, 'I' might of course wish to indicate specifically e.g. that 'I washed my hair' rather than 'myself' generally, in which case **die Haare** becomes the accusative direct object instead of **mich**.

nom.	*acc.*	
Ich habe	***mich***	**gewaschen**
Ich habe	***meine Haare***	**gewaschen**

In the latter sentence, the verb is no longer reflexive in the original sense: the subject and object are no longer identical. But there is clearly some reflexivity here – after all, the hair belongs to me! – and German can express this very clearly with sentences such as this:

nom.	*dat.*	*acc.*	
Ich habe	***mir***	***die Haare***	**gewaschen**

As long as it makes sense, this sort of construction is possible with a large number of verbs, two of which you have met in this **Lektion**:

Ich habe	***mir***	***den Fuß***	**verstaucht**
Ich habe	***mir***	***eine Hose***	**gekauft**

Also, as long as it makes sense, it is of course possible to change the dative pronoun (see list of dative pronouns in **Lektion sechzehn**) or exchange it for a noun, e.g.

Ich habe ***dir / ihm / meinem Mann*** **eine Hose gekauft**
I('ve) bought you / him / my husband (etc.). . . .

Finally, it is perfectly possible not to use a dative at all and to say instead:

Ich habe meinen Fuß verstaucht
Ich habe eine Hose gekauft

In the second sentence it is not clear, however, for whom the item was bought.

Here in tabulated form are the two 'reflexive' patterns discussed above:

		either: *acc.*	or: *dat.* + *acc..*	
ich	**habe**	***mich***	***mir***	***die Haare*** **gewaschen**
du	**hast**	***dich***	***dir***	
er / sie / es	**hat**	***sich*** **gewaschen**	***sich***	

		either: *acc.*	or: *dat.* + *acc..*	
wir	**haben**	***uns***	***uns***	***die Haare*** **gewaschen**
sie		***sich***	***sich***	
Sie		***sich***	***sich***	

Übung 17K

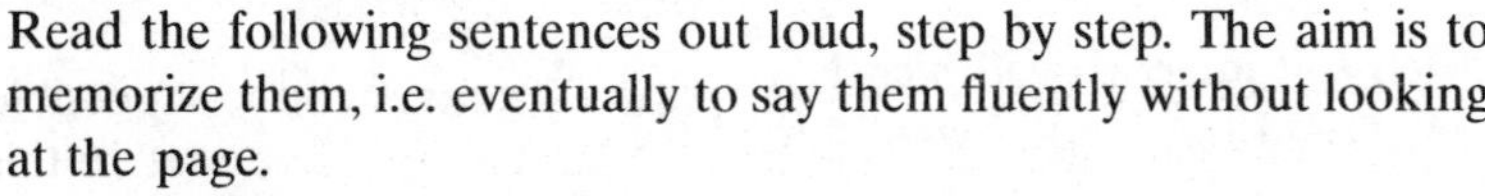

Read the following sentences out loud, step by step. The aim is to memorize them, i.e. eventually to say them fluently without looking at the page.

Vielleicht
Vielleicht kaufe *ich*
Vielleicht kaufe *ich mir*
Vielleicht kaufe *ich mir* morgen
Vielleicht kaufe *ich mir* morgen einen großen breiten Hut

Vielleicht
Vielleicht kauft *sie*
Vielleicht kauft *sie sich*
Vielleicht kauft *sie sich* heute nachmittag
Vielleicht kauft *sie sich* heute nachmittag ein schönes neues Kleid

Vielleicht
Vielleicht kaufst *du*
Vielleicht kaufst *du dir*
Vielleicht kaufst *du dir* am Samstag
Vielleicht kaufst *du dir* am Samstag eine neue schwarze Hose

Vielleicht
Vielleicht kaufen *wir*

Vielleicht kaufen *wir uns*
Vielleicht kaufen *wir uns* nächstes Jahr
Vielleicht kaufen *wir uns* nächstes Jahr ein schickes neues Auto

Sollen

Sollen is our last modal verb, the one we signalled in **Lektion sechzehn** as being forthcoming. In Text 17 it occurs on three occasions:

Ich soll mich nicht ausruhen
I'm not supposed to rest
Ich soll den Fuß bewegen
I'm supposed to/should move/use my foot
Soll ich dich vom Hotel abholen?
Should I fetch you at/from the hotel?

As the English translations indicate, **sollen** conveys a kind of 'moral obligation' – which is, of course, sometimes not fulfilled, as in e.g.

Ich soll aber ich will nicht!
I should but I don't want/intend to!

How to cure an ankle sprain?

Ein verstauchter Fuß gehört nicht ins Bett sondern auf die Treppe!

These often-heard words of wisdom mean 'Keep moving!' or literally: 'A sprained foot belongs not in(to) the bed but on(to) the stairs'. Do check, if the circumstance ever arises, that *your* doctor agrees.

18 Auf der Bank

Cashing a cheque

Language activities

- cashing a cheque
- using the telephone: an overview
- spelling aloud

Language focus

- naming letters
- pronunciation

Text 18

Freitag nachmittag [2]

Auf der Bank, at the bank, Peter wishes to change a traveller's cheque. The counter clerk asks to see some identification (ID or passport), tells him how much in Marks he can expect for his cheque, asks him to sign, and tells him which cashpoint to go to in order to collect the money.

ANGESTELLTE:[1] Guten Tag! Bitte schön?
PETER B: Guten Tag! Ich möchte einen Reisescheck wechseln.[2]
ANGESTELLTE: Ja, darf ich Ihren Ausweis[3] oder Reisepaß sehen?
PETER B: Bitte schön.
ANGESTELLTE: Danke schön. Einen kleinen Moment bitte. . . . Das sind[4] zweihundertfünfunddreißig Mark fünfundsechzig Pfennig. Unterschreiben[5] Sie bitte hier! . . .

	Danke. Sie bekommen die Auszahlung[6] hier gleich links an der ersten Kasse.[7]
PETER B:	Vielen Dank.

Notes

1 literally: 'employed' i.e. 'employee', with the feminine ending **-e**. If the employee were male, **Angestellter** would be used here
2 regular verb: = 'to change/exchange' (something). **Das Wechselgeld** is 'change' in the sense of money you get back or that you need for, e.g., the phonebox. If the weather is described as **wechselhaft**, then it's changeable
3 **ein Ausweis** is any form of written certification but here quite specifically an official 'identity card', for which 'a passport' (**der Paß** or **Reisepaß**) is an acceptable alternative
4 literally: 'that are . . .' rather than 'that is . . .' because the Marks (plural) are felt to be the subject of the German sentence, rather than 'that'
5 non-separable irregular verb: **er/sie, unterschreibt, (hat) unterschrieben**, literally: *to* 'underwrite', i.e. 'sign'
6 literally; 'you get the pay-out', i.e. 'Collect your money. . . .'
7 'till' or 'cashpoint'

Übung 18A

Find equivalents in Text 18 and in the Notes above for the following nouns. Write them all in their singular form with a capital letter, in three columns and preceded by **der, das** or **die**. When you have finished, your German nouns should appear in alphabetical order in each column.

masculine	*neuter*	*feminine*
employee (male)	change	employee (female)
identification card		pay-out
thanks		bank
moment		cash-point
Pfennig		Mark
passport		
traveller's cheque		
cheque		
day		

Übung 18B

Find in the above list, and write out, the German equivalents of the following sentences/phrases. Don't try to translate the English sentences word for word: look for 'whole-sentence' equivalents, stick to the original German word order, but leave any bits of the original out that obviously aren't required below.

1 Sign here please.
2 I'd like to change a traveller's cheque.
3 May I see your ID or passport?
4 At the bank.
5 At the first cash point.
6 Friday afternoon.
7 Just a second, please.
8 That's two hundred and thirty five Marks!

Spelling aloud

In this **Lektion** we want to look at how to spell in spoken German, because

(a) sustained practice in pronouncing German letters helps a great deal with pronunciation generally. Most German letters in their spoken form consist of one or two very clearly focused sounds only: it makes good sense, if a 'useful' reason can be found for doing it, to concentrate occasionally on shorter stretches of sound than on whole words and sentences;

(b) communication over the phone in particular can be easier if one can spell out, as is frequently required, one's name, address, etc. wholly unambiguously to the person on the line. Our personal and place names can be difficult for German speakers to spell correctly unseen: why *should* they know, for example, that Bennett has two e's, two n's and two t's? And as for Carlisle, Gloucester, Tucson or Poughkeepsie . . .!?

The ***Buchstabiertafel der* Deutschen Post***, literally '*the spelling table of the German Post Office*', is reproduced below and can be heard on the recordings accompanying this book. It is of course more important to remember how a letter is pronounced than its actual spelling name, but the names are useful, are fun and they may well help you to remember how to pronounce the letters.

(*This is the genitive case form of the feminine singular ***die***: *see* any German grammar book for further information.)

In the table, note that e.g. 'A for Anton' is expressed in German as **A *wie Anton,* wie** meaning 'like, as'. Both **ch** and **sch** are here pronounced like English 'sh', hence **Ch *wie Charlotte*** and **Sch *wie Schule.***

A letter with which you will be very familiar is not included in the table: **ß**. It is really a 'double letter' (the Swiss always use **ss** instead). The name of the symbol **ß** is most commonly **'ess-tset'**, i.e. **sz**, this being the combination of letters from which **ß** was originally formed. So although on paper **ß** looks like a single letter, when spelt out loud it becomes two: **S (wie Samuel)**, **Z (wie Zacharias)**.

Die Buchstabiertafel der Deutschen Post

1 **A *wie* Anton**

2	**Ä**	**Ärger**	17	**O**	**Otto**
3	**B**	**Berta**	18	**Ö**	**Ökonom**
4	**C**	**Cäsar**	19	**P**	**Paul**
5	**Ch**	**Charlotte**	20	**Q**	**Quelle**
6	**D**	**Dora**	21	**R**	**Richard**
7	**E**	**Emil**	22	**S**	**Samuel**
8	**F**	**Friedrich**	23	**Sch**	**Schule**
9	**G**	**Gustav**	24	**T**	**Theodor**
10	**H**	**Heinrich**	25	**U**	**Ulrich**
11	**I**	**Ida**	26	**Ü**	**Übermut**
12	**J**	**Julius**	27	**V**	**Viktor**
13	**K**	**Kaufmann**	28	**W**	**Wilhelm**
14	**L**	**Ludwig**	29	**X**	**Xanthippe**
15	**M**	**Martha**	30	**Y**	**Ypsilon**
16	**N**	**Nordpol**	31	**Z**	**Zacharias**

Übung 18C

Listen to and repeat the above alphabet until you can easily remember at least half of it. Practise listening and pronouncing *both* while looking *and* without looking at the table above – in whichever order you feel happiest with.

Übung 18D

Supply the missing information from the table:

1 *e.g.* ***Der zweite Buchstabe*** *[letter]* ***ist Ä wie Ärger.***
2 **Der dreißigste Buchstabe ist _____ wie ______.**
3 **Der sechsundzwanzigste Buchstabe ist _____ wie ______.**
4 **Der fünfundzwanzigste Buchstabe ist _____ wie ______.**
5 **Der zwölfte Buchstabe ist _____ wie ______.**
6 **Der siebenundzwanzigste Buchstabe ist _____ wie _____.**
7 **Der siebte Buchstabe ist _____ wie ______.**
8 **Der achtzehnte Buchstabe ist _____ wie ______.**
9 **Der vierte Buchstabe ist _____ wie ______.**
10 **Der elfte Buchstabe ist _____ wie ______.**
11 **Der neunundzwanzigste Buchstabe ist _____ wie ______.**
12 **Der erste Buchstabe ist _____ wie ______.**
13 **Der einundzwanzigste Buchstabe ist _____ wie ______.**
14 **Der vierzehnte Buchstabe ist _____ wie ______.**
15 **Der sechzehnte Buchstabe ist _____ wie ______.**
16 **Der zweiundzwanzigste Buchstabe ist _____ wie ______.**
17 **Der dritte Buchstabe ist _____ wie ______.**
18 **Der dreizehnte Buchstabe ist _____ wie ______.**
19 **Der achte Buchstabe ist _____ wie ______.**
20 **Der letzte Buchstabe ist _____ wie ______.**

Übung 18E

Supply the missing information from the table, writing out the ordinal number in full:

1 **Der __________ Buchstabe ist D wie __________.**
2 **Der __________ Buchstabe ist W wie __________.**
3 **Der __________ Buchstabe ist P wie __________.**
4 **Der __________ Buchstabe ist H wie __________.**
5 **Der __________ Buchstabe ist T wie __________.**
6 **Der __________ Buchstabe ist O wie __________.**
7 **Der __________ Buchstabe ist L wie __________.**
8 **Der __________ Buchstabe ist Q wie __________.**

Übung 18F

The words used in the ***Buchstabiertafel*** fall into three distinct groups: (a) 17 male personal names, (b) 6 female personal names, and (c) 8 other words. Guess which words belong in which categories. Some of the names, by the way, are rather dated.

Übung 18G

The words in the table which are *not* personal names are translated below. Match the translations (by inspired guesswork!) with the German originals.

1 North Pole
2 school
3 economist
4 businessman
5 annoyance, bother
6 (the name of a letter of the alphabet)
7 high spirits
8 source

Übung 18H

Write down the spelling pronunciations of the following places. If you can do this without looking at the table, so much the better.

*e.g. **Bonn*** = **B wie Berta**; **O wie Otto**; **Doppel-N wie Nordpol**

1 **Wien**
2 **Görlitz**
3 **Meißen**
4 **Fallingbostel**
5 **Mühlwärts**
6 **New Jersey**
7 **Melbourne**
8 **Cockermouth**
9 **Vancouver**
10 **Chicago**

Übung 18J

If you are asked to spell something in German, the question may be one of several:

Wie schreibt man das?	How does one write that (. . . is that written)?
Wie schreiben Sie das?	How do you write it?
Wie buchstabiert man das?	How does one spell that (. . . is that spelt)?
Wie buchstabieren Sie das?	How do you spell it?

Answer the following pairs of questions following this pattern:

(a) **Wie heißt *aber* auf Englisch?** Answer: ***But.***
(b) **Wie schreibt man das?** Answer: ***B wie Berta, U wie Ulrich, T wie Theodor.***

If necessary, check the Glossary and spelling table for the answers.

1a **Wie heißt *Knöchel* auf Englisch?**
1b **Wie schreibt man das?**
2a **Wie heißt *verstauchen* auf Englisch?**
2b **Wie schreibt man das?**
3a **Wie heißt *Tochter* auf Englisch?**
3b **Wie schreibt man das?**
4a **Wie heißt *Hafen* auf Englisch?**
4b **Wie schreibt man das?**
5a **Wie heißt *sofort* auf Englisch?**
5b **Wie schreibt man das?**
6a **Wie heißt *hervorragend* auf Englisch?**
6b **Wie schreibt man das?**
7a **Wie heißt *Spaziergang* auf Englisch?**
7b **Wie schreibt man das?**
8a **Wie heißt *verheiratet* auf Englisch?**
8b **Wie schreibt man das?**
9a **Wie heißt *geschieden* auf Englisch?**
9b **Wie schreibt man das?**
10a **Wie heißt *früh* auf Englisch?**
10b **Wie schreibt man das?**

Übung 18K

This appears to be the shortest exercise in this **Lektion**, but it is also the most important. Write down – and remember – the German spelling pronunciation of your own name and address.

Using the telephone

Here is an overview of the sort of expressions you are most likely to meet when establishing contact by phone in a German-speaking country:

You hear: surname/business name with or without a form of greeting, e.g.

- **Dettmann!**
- **Hotel Müller, guten Tag!**

NB You will *not* be told the number that you have called unless you ask.

If you know and ***siezen*** the person who has answered, then you might say in reply:

- **Guten Tag, Frau Dettmann, hier (ist) Peter Bennett.**

If you know and ***duzen*** the person who has answered, then you could say:

- **Hallo, Heidi, hier (ist) Peter.**
- **Tag, Heidi. . . .**

If you are in a more formal business situation, you might wish to give your business address with or without your surname and a greeting:

- **Buchhandlung Lüneburg. (Dettmann.) (Guten Tag!)**

If you want to speak to a particular person, you could ask:

- **Kann ich bitte mit Frau Dettmann/Herrn Bennett sprechen?**
  Can I please speak to Ms Dettmann/Mr Bennett?

The reply can clearly take many forms. Let's assume you have to be connected, then you might hear:

- **Ich verbinde Sie.** Connecting you!
- **Bleiben Sie am Apparat!** Stay on the line!
- **(Einen) Moment, bitte!** Just a second, please!
- **Augenblick, bitte!** ditto

If you are in fact already speaking to the person you need, the reply could well be:

- **Am Apparat.** On the line (i.e. Speaking!)

If the person you want is not there, then you might hear:

- **Frau . . ./Herr . . . ist im Augenblick/heute/diese Woche nicht da.**
  Ms . . ./Mr . . . isn't there/available at the moment/today/this week.

This could be followed immediately by:

- **Soll/Kann ich (ihr/ihm) etwas ausrichten?**
  Can I take (actually: *pass on*) a message (to her/him/her)?

Your options would then be e.g.

- **Nein, danke! Ich rufe später zurück.**
  No, thank you, I'll call back later.
- **Um wieviel Uhr kann ich sie/ihn erreichen?**
  At what time can I reach her/him?

If the answer is that you would indeed like to pass on a message, then start with

- **Ja, bitte!**

At this point you might need to:

(a) spell your name – and sometimes even the name of the person you are trying to contact;
(b) state a time using the 24-hour clock;
(c) give broader indications of 'when', e.g. **später**, **heute nachmittag**, **morgen früh**, etc.

Finally, to thank and take your leave of the person you have been speaking to say e.g.:

- **Vielen Dank/Danke schön!** **Auf Wiederhören!**

Since **Auf Wieder*sehen*!** means 'see (you) again' and you may never have seen the person you have been talking to, it is standard to say **Auf Wieder*hören*!** 'hear (you) again' on the phone.

Übung 18L

Let's assume you are Peter Bennett and that you want to speak to a Frau Dettmann and tell her that you cannot meet her this morning as you have to go to the doctor's. Since she's not in her hotel room, you leave a message with the receptionist to the effect that you would like her to call you back at 2 p.m., and you give your number. Translate the English cues into German (you might like to look over Text 16 to get you in the right mood!).

— **Hotel Schmidt. Guten Morgen!**
Good morning. Can I speak to Mrs Dettmann?
— **Ich verbinde Sie. Einen Moment, bitte. . . . (Es) tut mir leid, Frau Dettmann ist nicht da. Soll ich etwas ausrichten?**
Yes, please. My name is Bennett. I cannot meet Mrs Dettmann this morning. I have to go to the doctor. Mrs Dettmann can

contact ('reach') me at 2 this afternoon in the hotel. The phone number is 8 32 33 21.
— **Entschuldigen Sie bitte, wie buchstabieren Sie Ihren Namen?**
(Spell out your name: Bennett)
— **Gut, Herr Bennett, (das) geht in Ordnung.**
Many thanks. Goodbye!
— **Nichts zu danken. Auf Wiederhören!**

Übung 18M

Cover up the previous exercise. Now translate the English cues below as idiomatically as you can into German.

— Hotel Schmidt. Good morning!
Guten Morgen! Kann ich bitte mit Frau Dettmann sprechen?
— I'll put you through. Just a moment, please. . . . I'm sorry, Frau Dettmann isn't answering ('isn't there'). Can I take a message?
Ja, bitte. Mein Name ist Bennett/Ich heiße Bennett. Ich kann Frau Dettmann heute früh nicht treffen. Ich muß zum Arzt. Sie kann mich um 14 Uhr im Hotel erreichen. Die Telefonnummer ist acht – zweiunddreißig – dreiunddreißig – einundzwanzig.
— Sorry, how do you spell your name?
B wie Berta, E wie Emil, Doppel-N wie Nordpol, E wie Emil, Doppel-T wie Theodor
— Fine, Mr Bennett! I'll pass that on! [very idiomatically, not literally]
Vielen Dank! Auf Wiederhören!
— Don't mention it! [again, idiomatically, not literally] Goodbye!

Übung 18N

Repeat **Übung 18B**. If it causes you any problems, check out Text 18 again, and also re-do **Übung 18A**.

This phone card was issued two years after German re-unification and celebrates the re-introduction of a single dialling code for East and West Berlin, after decades of partition. Literally, the text says 'Berlin is telephonically united'.

19 Unterschiede

Making comparisons

Language activities
expressing

- similarities
- differences
- preferences

Language focus

- comparatives and superlatives
- adjectives and adverbs
- separable verbs
- **ihr** and **euch**

[1] (see Notes)

Text 19

Freitag nachmittag [3]

His ankle having survived the walk to the bank, Peter doesn't wish to overdo the doctor's 'keep moving' prescription, so he and Heidi take to the nearest café for a rest and a further exchange of views on similarities and differences (**Unterschiede**) between this, that and the other. The weather is at the top of the agenda, and likes/dislikes *vis-à-vis* the seasons of the year also emerge. They then get on to food, a topic quickly exhausted because Peter is far from choosy, and end up comparing the compact, medieval city of York with the more expansive, largely nineteenth-century Berlin . . .

HEIDI D: Peter, wie ist es eigentlich bei euch in England?[2] Wie ist das Wetter zum Beispiel?[3]

PETER B: In York? – kühl bis warm, selten richtig[4] heiß.
HEIDI D: Bei uns ist es im Sommer bestimmt wärmer als bei euch – aber im Winter wahrscheinlich auch kälter. Ich ziehe den Herbst in Deutschland vor.[5]
PETER B: In England ist die grüne[6] Jahreszeit die schönste Jahreszeit: ich ziehe den Frühling vor.
HEIDI D: Wie schmeckt dir das deutsche Essen eigentlich? Besser als das englische oder nicht so gut?
PETER B: Genauso[7] gut, genauso schlecht. Ich esse[8] alles. Aber der deutsche Kaffee ist mir[9] manchmal zu stark.
HEIDI D: Ich nehme an,[10] Berlin ist anders[11] als York. Sag mal,[12] was ist für dich der größte Unterschied?
PETER B: Ganz klar: in York spricht[13] man Englisch, in Berlin spricht man Deutsch.
HEIDI D: Nein, wirklich?[14] Was sonst?[15]
PETER B: Ja, sonst die breiten Straßen. In York ist die Innenstadt[16] sehr eng.[17] In Berlin sind die Straßen viel breiter.
HEIDI D: Wahrscheinlich sind die Straßen von York viel älter als z.B.[18] der Kurfürstendamm . . .

Notes

1 this ubiquitous sticker, issued by Berlin's municipal transport company (BVG), was aimed at lowering stress levels on the trains and buses. The slogan succinctly suggests that things go better if people are nice(r) to each other
2 literally: 'How is it with you?' i.e. 'What are things like in England? What is England like?' **Bei euch** is the plural equivalent of **bei dir**. You met **bei uns** in Text 4. German speakers often use **England** to mean Britain
3 'for example'
4 literally: '*real* hot', rather than '*really* hot': see **Lektion neun** on German adverbs and adjectives
5 **vorziehen** = 'prefer, favour' is an irregular separable verb: **ich ziehe . . . vor**, **ich habe . . . vorgezogen**
6 'green'
7 'just as, equally'
8 **essen** 'eat' is irregular: **ich esse**, **du ißt**, **er ißt**, **ich habe gegessen**
9 literally: 'is to me sometimes too strong', i.e. 'I find . . .'
10 **annehmen** = (here) 'suppose, assume' (sometimes: 'accept') is separable
11 'different from, other than'

12 the little word **mal** occurs a lot in conversation and often its exact meaning is difficult to pin down. Here, **Sag** ('say'), the imperative **du**-form of **sagen**, is felt to be perhaps too direct when used on its own. The imperatives are often 'softened' in this way with **mal** or with **doch**
13 irregular verb: **sprechen, spricht, gesprochen**
14 literally: 'no really?' but with the right intonation, it means 'Go on! You don't say!' etc.
15 'what else? otherwise?'
16 = **das Stadtzentrum**
17 'narrow'
18 **zum Beispiel**

Übung 19A

Find equivalents in Text 19 and the Notes above for the following nouns. Write them all in their singular form with a capital letter, in three columns and preceded by **der, das** or **die**. When you have finished, your German nouns should appear in alphabetical order in each column.

masculine	*neuter*	*feminine*
spring	example	town centre
autumn	German	season
coffee	English	street
summer	food	
difference	town centre	
winter	weather	

Übung 19B

Find and write out the German equivalents in Text 19 of the following sentences/phrases. Don't try to translate the English sentences word for word: look for 'whole-sentence' equivalents, stick to the original German word order, but leave any bits of the original out that obviously aren't required below.

1 What's the weather like?
2 For example.
3 What else?
4 How do you like German food?
5 Berlin is different from York.
6 I prefer spring.

7 Not as good.
8 Just as bad.
9 What is the biggest difference?
10 German coffee is sometimes too strong for me!

Übung 19C

Match the German questions with the English answers.

1 **Wie ist das Wetter in York?**
2 **Wie ist das Wetter in Dorfmark?**
3 **Wer zieht den Frühling vor?**
4 **Wer zieht den Herbst vor?**
5 **Wie findet Peter den deutschen Kaffee?**
6 **Ist Berlin anders als York?**
A Heidi prefers autumn.
B Cool to warm, rarely really hot.
C Yes, in Berlin the streets are much wider.
D Peter prefers spring.
E Sometimes he finds the coffee too strong.
F In summer warmer than in York but probably colder in winter, too.

Übung 19D

Cover up **Übung 19C** and write German questions which match the following answers. The words in italics indicate the specific information you are seeking.

1 ***Peter* zieht den Frühling vor.**
2 ***Heidi* zieht den Herbst vor.**
3 **Peter findet den deutschen Kaffee *manchmal zu stark.***
4 **In York ist das Wetter kühl bis warm, selten richtig heiß.**
5 **Im Sommer ist das Wetter in Dorfmark *wärmer als in York aber im Winter wahrscheinlich auch kälter.***
6 **Ja, ganz *anders als York*: in Berlin spricht man Deutsch und die Straßen sind viel breiter.**

Bei uns . . . Bei euch

'What's it like in your country?' – or words to that effect – is something that almost everyone gets asked when abroad. The standard

German query on this score is: ***Wie ist es bei euch?*** The table below indicates where **euch** 'comes from'.

Whereas the more formal **Sie** can refer to *either* singular *or* plural 'you', the familiar **du** is only singular. Its plural counterpart is **ihr** in the nominative case and **euch** in both the accusative and dative. We have put ***für*** in front of the accusative pronouns below because it always takes the accusative, and ***bei*** in front of the dative pronouns because it always takes the dative.

	singular	*plural*	*sing./plural*	*plural*
	you	you	you	we
nominative	**du**	**ihr**	**Sie**	**wir**
accusative	***für* dich**	***für* euch**	***für* Sie**	***für* uns**
dative	***bei* dir**	***bei* euch**	***bei* Ihnen**	***bei* uns**

Comparatives and superlatives

See **Lektion siebzehn** for an overview of how to form the comparative and superlative of adjectives and adverbs.

Übung 19E

The forms missing from the following table are all contained in Text 19. Plug the gaps!

	positive	*comparative*	*superlative* (takes endings according to context)
1 old	**alt**	*	**ältest-**
2 broad	**breit**	*	**breitest-**
3 narrow	*	**enger**	**engst-**
4 good	*	*	**best-**
5 big, great	**groß**	**größer**	*
6 hot	*	**heißer**	**heißest-**
7 cool	*	**kühler**	**kühlst-**
8 cold	**kalt**	*	**kältest-**
9 bad	*	**schlechter**	**schlechtest-**
10 strong	*	**stärker**	**stärkst-**
11 beautiful	**schön**	**schöner**	*
12 warm	*	*	**wärmst -**

Übung 19F

Use your imagination to make comparisons between towns and/or countries. The comparisons do not have to be based on fact: invent sentences, however speculative! But don't depart from the structure given below. Each sentence you create will consist of four parts, as indicated. The sort of sentence that should emerge if you stick to the pattern is:

Part 1	*Part 2*	*Part 3*	*Part 4*
Bei euch in Österreich ...	**ist der Kaffee ...**	**meistens stärker als ...**	**bei uns in Amerika.**
Bei uns in London ...	**sind die Häuser ...**	**vielleicht kleiner als ...**	**bei euch in Hamburg.**

We have listed some adverb qualifiers for slotting into Part 3. You will find more adjectives both in **Lektion siebzehn** and in the Glossary if you need them. Use the Glossary, too, or a dictionary, for any additional nouns you wish to use.

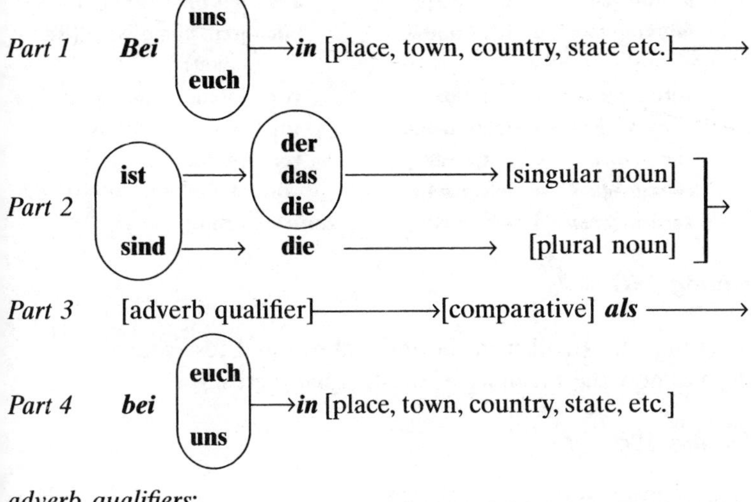

adverb qualifiers:

immer	always	**vielleicht**	perhaps, possibly
meistens	usually	**wahrscheinlich**	probably
oft	often	**bestimmt**	certainly
manchmal	sometimes	**sicherlich**	surely
selten	seldom, rarely	**eigentlich**	actually, in fact
nie	never	**viel**	much

Separable verbs

Lektionen sechs, elf, dreizehn and **siebzehn** contained separable verbs, which we list below for reference together with two new separable verbs from **Lektion neunzehn**.

ab|*fahren* → **ich fahre ________ ab** leave/depart
ab|*holen* → **ich hole ___________ab** fetch/collect
an|*fangen* → **ich fange ________ an** start, begin
an|*kommen* → **ich komme _______ an** arrive
an|*nehmen* → **ich nehme an** assume, suppose (also: accept)
an|*rufen* → **ich rufe __________ an** phone, call (on phone)
auf|*machen* → **ich mache _______ auf** open
auf|*wachsen* → **ich wachse ______ auf** grow up
aus|*führen* → **ich führe _______ aus** take out (dog)
aus|*gehen* → **ich gehe ________ aus** go out
aus|*richten* → **ich richte _______ aus** pass on a message
sich aus|*ruhen* → **ich ruhe mich aus** rest
aus|*steigen* → **ich steige _______ aus** get off (e.g. bus)
mit|*kommen* → **ich komme ______ mit** join, come with (e.g. you)
vor|*haben* → **ich habe ________ vor** intend, plan to
vor|*schlagen* → **ich schlage ______ vor** suggest, propose
vor|*ziehen* → **ich ziehe ________ vor** prefer
zu|*machen* → **ich mache _______ zu** shut/close
zurück|*gehen* → **ich gehe _____ zurück** return

Übung 19G

Cover up the English in the table above and test yourself to see if you know the meaning of the German verbs.

Übung 19H

Cover up the German words in the table above and see if you can translate the English meanings.

Übung 19J

Go back to the **Lektionen** indicated to remind yourself how the separable verbs were used in sentences.

Preferences

We now have two common ways of expressing the notion of preferring:

1 using **vorziehen**
2 using a verb + **lieber** (see **Lektion fünfzehn**)

Vorziehen often, but certainly not invariably, relates to a specific choice rather than to a general preference, e.g.

Fahren wir nach Berlin mit dem Zug oder mit dem Bus?
Shall we go to Berlin by train or by coach?
Was ziehst du vor? / Was ziehen Sie vor?
Which do you prefer?
Ich ziehe den Zug vor.
I prefer the train.

On the whole, when you want to make general comparisons, **lieber** is to be recommended as being more flexible – but you have to know a suitable verb, e.g.

Ich fahre *gern* mit der U-Bahn.
I like travelling by underground
(or simply: I like the underground).
Ich fahre *lieber* mit der U-Bahn *als* mit dem Bus.
I prefer the underground to the bus.
Ich fahre *am liebsten* mit dem Auto.
Best of all I prefer to go by car!

Übung 19K 

Using the pattern immediately above, express 'your' likes/preferences below by replacing the English in brackets with German. The English translations are not idiomatic: they are designed to remind you that you need to find a verb as well as to select from **gern – lieber – am liebsten.**

1 **Ich** [like to drink] **Weißwein.**
2 **Ich** [prefer to drink] **Weißwein als Rotwein.**
3 **Ich** [most prefer to drink] **Tee.**
4 **Ich** [like playing] **Klavier.**
5 **Ich** [prefer playing] **Klavier als Harfe.**
6 **Ich** [most prefer to play] **Fußball.**

7 **Ich** [like eating] **Bohnensalat.**
8 **Ich** [prefer to eat] **Tomatensalat als Bohnensalat.**
9 **Ich** [most prefer to eat] **Eis.**
10 **Ich** [like to go] **ins Theater.**
11 **Ich** [prefer to go] **ins Theater als in ein Konzert.**
12 **Ich** [most prefer to go] **ins Kino.**
13 **Ich** [like listening to] **klassische Musik.**
14 **Ich** [prefer listening to] **Jazz.**
15 **Ich** [most prefer listening to] **Volksmusik.**

Übung 19L

Revision: times and numbers. You have phoned the information service for times of trains from Ostend to Vienna and what you hear over the phone is printed out below. Change the times in words to figures and enter them in the timetable.

Abfahrt	**Ostende:**	**siebzehn Uhr sieben**
Ankunft	**Aachen:**	**zwanzig Uhr dreißig**
Abfahrt	**Aachen:**	**zwanzig Uhr vierundvierzig**
Ankunft	**Köln:**	**einundzwanzig Uhr dreiundzwanzig**
Abfahrt	**Köln:**	**einundzwanzig Uhr fünfunddreißig**
Ankunft	**Bonn:**	**einundzwanzig Uhr fünfundfünfzig**
Abfahrt	**Bonn:**	**einundzwanzig Uhr siebenundfünfzig**
Ankunft	**Koblenz:**	**zweiundzwanzig Uhr zweiunddreißig**
Abfahrt	**Koblenz:**	**zweiundzwanzig Uhr fünfunddreißig**
Ankunft	**Mainz:**	**dreiundzwanzig Uhr achtundzwanzig**
Abfahrt	**Mainz:**	**dreiundzwanzig Uhr zweiunddreißig**
Ankunft	**Frankfurt:**	**vierundzwanzig Uhr**
Abfahrt	**Frankfurt:**	**null Uhr achtzehn**
Ankunft	**Nürnberg:**	**drei Uhr elf**
Abfahrt	**Nürnberg:**	**drei Uhr achtundzwanzig**
Ankunft	**Passau:**	**fünf Uhr zweiundfünfzig**
Abfahrt	**Passau:**	**sechs Uhr vierzehn**
Ankunft	**Wien Westbahnhof (Endstation):**	**neun Uhr fünfundvierzig**

Ankunft	*Ostende–Wien–Express*	Abfahrt
	Ostende	_____
_____	***Aachen* Hbf***	_____
_____	***Köln* Hbf**	_____
_____	***Bonn* Hbf**	_____
_____	***Koblenz* Hbf**	_____
_____	***Mainz* Hbf**	_____
_____	***Frankfurt (Main)* Hbf**	_____
_____	***Nürnberg* Hbf**	_____
_____	***Passau* Hbf**	_____
_____	***Wien* Westbf**†	

* **Hauptbahnhof** = *main/central station* † **Westbahnhof** = *west station*

When you have filled in the above timetable, check it against the one given in **Lektion sieben**.

Übung 19M 

Revision: grammatical terms. We said at the beginning of the book that grammatical terms were no more than 'handy labels' for describing how a language works. We have reprinted below (with adjustments) some of the contexts in which these 'handy labels' occurred in *Colloquial German*. Can you supply the missing words (each question mark = one word)? If you can't but have still learnt some German *en route*, congratulations: it's your German, not our labels, that really matters!

1 [?] are much easier to spot in German than in English because German [?], regardless of where they come in a sentence, are written with a capital letter.
2 [?] are often words which indicate some kind of action. In English they can immediately follow e.g. 'I, you, we, they,' etc.
3 In English, the [??] has two forms, 'a' and 'an'. In German the [??] in its dictionary form is **ein**, but it frequently acquires endings which tell us about its relationship to other words in a sentence.

4 Immediately in front of the word they describe, [?] must have appropriate endings; away from their noun they do not, e.g.

Der Stadtplan ist zu *klein*. Ich möchte ein*en* groß*en* Stadtplan.

5 The general rule for forming an [??] is:

cardinal + **t** + ending e.g. **die zweite [zwei + t + e] Tasse.**

6 [??] and their relatives are extremely common in English and German. The English equivalents of the German [??] cover meanings such as 'would, should, could, can, may, might, must, would like/want (to), ought to'.

7 Words are more often written together in German than in English to produce [?]. English is more likely to keep words separate or use hyphens to connect them, e.g.

room key	*double room*	*room number*
Zimmerschlüssel	**Doppelzimmer**	**Zimmernummer**

8 [?] are generally found in front of nouns and pronouns, and are mostly used to indicate when, how or where. English examples: '*in* London; *to* Berlin; *on* Tuesday; *with* great difficulty; *before* breakfast; *after* you . . .'

9 They are called [??] because they can and often have to be divided up. They are marked in the Glossary thus: **ab|fahren.**

10 The first part of **ab|fahren** is called a [?].

11 In essence, [?] verbs in German are verbs (a) which always have both a subject and an object; (b) whose subject and object are the same person (or, less frequently, thing).

12 The easiest set of German endings to remember is probably those for the [??]: almost everything has to end in -**n**.

13 The most common way of talking about the past in English and German is to use a *past tense* of the verb. In spoken German, the most common past tense by far is called the [?] tense.

14 All German *regular* verbs form their [??] like this:

schmeck*|en** → **ge** + ***schmeck + **t** → ***geschmeckt***

15 The basic rule for formation of [?] in German is to add =***er*** to the adjective, e.g. **schön** → **schön*er***. This rule applies in German, *however long the adjective*.

16 The basic rule for the formation of [?] in German is to add -***st*** + *ending* to the adjective, e.g. **schön** → **schön*st*-**. Again, this rule applies in German, *however long the adjective*.

17 Provide the missing [?] verb form in the following sentences taken from Text 9: **Wie ____ Sie nach Berlin gekommen?**

18 **Sie *hat* in Potsdam einen Berliner *gekauft*.** *She (has) bought a doughnut in Potsdam.* The doughnut is the [??] of the verb **kaufen**, i.e. the doughnut is 'what' she bought.

19 In the same way that adjectives describe nouns, an [?] will say something extra about the action of the verb, e.g.

when it happened	→	[?] of time	e.g. **heute**
how it happened	→	[?] of manner	e.g. **gut**
where it happened	→	[?] of place	e.g. **hier**

20 The DATIVE case is used when e.g. a pronoun is the [??] of a verb, e.g.

Er hat *mir* zwei Mark gegeben.	He gave me 2 Marks.

20 Rückblick und Zukunftspläne

Looking back . . . and forwards

This final unit is a 'revision and reinforcement' unit.
It contains no new grammar and very few new words.
The story line also pauses to take stock and then reaches a forward-looking conclusion.

Text 20

Freitag abend

All good things have to come to an end, it seems – and it *was* good, as is clear from the conversation that takes place over a Berliner Weiße on Heidi and Peter's final evening in Berlin. They take **einen Rückblick**, a look back together (very much together) over the four days which have left them wanting more. They may well return in September, which they drink to now. Their plans for the future, **ihre Zukunftspläne**, in fact begin to snowball: they may even meet up before too long in York – next year perhaps, in spring? Heidi receives advice on how best to get there and comments positively on Peter's new hat. . .

PETER B: Wie wär's[1] mit einer Berliner Weiße? Und wie wär's mit einem kleinen Imbiß[2] dazu?[3]

HEIDI D: Danke, ich möchte nichts essen, ich habe keinen Appetit. Unser letzter Abend in Berlin! Ja, Peter, ich glaube, Berliner Weiße ist genau richtig. Natürlich nur mit Schuß.

PETER B: Herr Ober, zwei Berliner Weiße, bitte. Mit Waldmeister.[4]

KELLNER: Das wär's?[5]

PETER B: Danke. Ja, Heidi, wie die Zeit vergeht![6] Vier Tage in Berlin – vier Tage mit dir – sind leider viel zu schnell vorbei.[7] Ich muß bald wiederkommen.

HEIDI D: Ich auch. Sag[8] mir nur wann!

PETER B: Ich weiß nicht genau,[9] aber ich habe noch[10] eine Woche Urlaub[11] in diesem[12] Jahr. Hast du im September Zeit?

HEIDI D: Ich weiß auch nicht genau, aber ich glaube ja.[13]

PETER B: Was hat dir besonders gut an Berlin gefallen?[14] Für mich war das Schloßkonzert besonders schön.

HEIDI D: Für mich war das Konzert sehr schön, aber der Spaziergang am Wannsee war noch[15] schöner. Und am schönsten war für mich die Stadtrundfahrt. Dadurch habe ich Berlin und dich kennengelernt.

PETER B: Ich danke dir für das schöne Kompliment. Nur eins[16] hat mir an Berlin *nicht* gefallen: mein verstauchter Fuß. Aber das war natürlich meine eigene Schuld.[17]

KELLNER: Zwei Berliner Weiße mit Schuß.

PETER B: Vielen Dank. Heidi, wir trinken auf uns.[18] Zum Wohl![19]

HEIDI D: Zum Wohl! Auf uns!

PETER B: Komm doch auch mal 'rüber nach England![20] Am besten fliegst du von Hannover oder Hamburg nach Manchester oder London. Dann nimmst[21] du den Intercity. Mit dem Schiff dauert[22] es natürlich länger.

HEIDI D: Danke für die Einladung,[23] Peter. Deine Heimat[24] interessiert mich wirklich sehr.[25] Vielleicht schon nächstes[26] Jahr im Frühling?[27]

PETER B: Die schönste Jahreszeit, nicht wahr?[28] Ich freue mich schon![29]

HEIDI D: Ich mich auch.[30] Übrigens,[31] Peter, der neue Hut steht dir[32] unwahrscheinlich gut[33]. . . .

Notes

1 for **wäre/hätte** see **Lektion vierzehn**
2 **der Imbiß** = 'snack'
3 literally: 'thereto', i.e. 'to accompany it, to go with it'
4 the two types of **Schuß**: a dash (shot) of raspberry (**Himbeere**) or of woodruff (**Waldmeister**)
5 see Text 1B
6 literally: 'How the time passes!'
7 'over, gone'

8 see **Lektion sechzehn** for discussion of the **du** form of the imperative
9 literally: 'exactly', i.e. 'I'm not sure, certain'
10 **noch** has many uses: with a number it means 'another'
11 holidays from work are **der** (sing.) **Urlaub**; school holidays are **die** (pl.) **Ferien**
12 'this'
13 'I believe so' is **Ich glaube ja** or **Ich glaube schon**
14 for **gefallen** (a dative verb) see **Lektion acht**: Verbs 'of liking'
15 the versatile **noch** again: with a comparative it acts as an intensifier, so **noch schöner** = 'even nicer, better', etc.
16 'one (thing)'
17 'my own fault'
18 'to drink to' is **trinken auf** + accusative
19 both **Zum Wohl!** and **Prost!** are used to mean 'cheers! Your health!'
20 Approximate translation: 'How about coming over to England sometime, too?' **doch** occurs frequently in conversation as a kind of filler: here it adds a little persuasion to Peter's suggestion. **'rüber** is the colloquial abbreviation of **herüber**. **(He)rüberkommen** is separable
21 **nehmen**, 'to take', is irregular: **ich nehme**, **er/sie nimmt**, **hat genommen**
22 lierally: 'It lasts', i.e. 'it takes' (of time)
23 the verb 'to invite' is **einladen**, the noun **die Einladung** (all nouns formed in this way are feminine)
24 **die Heimat** is where you feel you belong: where you feel 'home' is
25 'very' on its own, i.e. without 'much', is standard with the reflexive verb **sich interessieren**
26 **nächstes Jahr** ≠ **dieses Jahr** ('next' ≠ 'this')
27 the sentence literally means: 'Perhaps already next year in spring?' **Schon** has 'already' as its first meaning in dictionaries, but is often simply confirmatory, as in **Ich glaube schon** = 'I believe so', or **Das mache ich schon!** = 'I'll do that!'
28 a tag question = (here) 'isn't it?' Unlike English tag questions, **nicht wahr?** never needs to change according to context. It is often abbreviated to **Nicht?** or even **Nich'?**
29 **sich freuen**: 'to be pleased, to look forward to'
30 i.e. **Ich freue mich auch**
31 'by the way, incidentally'
32 **stehen** + dative of the person = 'suits' (you etc.)
33 literally: 'improbably well'. Heidi is in fact showing great enthusiasm!

Übung 20A

Find equivalents in Text 19 and in the Notes above for the following nouns. Write them all in their singular form with a capital letter, in three columns and preceded by **der**, **das** or **die**. When you have finished, your German nouns should appear in alphabetical order in each column.

masculine	*neuter*	*feminine*
evening	year	invitation
appetite	compliment	home (town, country, etc.)
thank(s)	concert	raspberry
spring	ship	season
foot	health, well-being	fault, guilt
Mr		city tour
hat		week
snack		time
waiter		future
plan		
retrospect, review, look back		
shot, dash		
September		
walk		
day		
holiday, leave		
woodruff		
plan for the future		

Übung 20B

Find and write out the German equivalents in Text 20 of the following sentences/phrases. Don't try to translate the English sentences word for word: look for 'whole-sentence' equivalents, stick to the original German word order, but leave any bits of the original out that obviously aren't required below.

1 How about a Berliner Weiße?
2 And how about a snack to go with it?
3 By the way. . . .
4 The new hat really suits you!
5 I still have a week's holiday this year.
6 Why don't you come to England?
7 But that was my own fault, of course!

8 I think Berliner Weiße is just the thing!
9 How time flies!
10 Just tell me when!

Übung 20C

Match the German verbs with English equivalents.

1		**danken**	A	be interested in
2		**dauern**	B	be pleased, look forward to
3		**essen**	C	believe
4		**fliegen**	D	come
5	(sich)	**freuen**	E	drink
6		**gefallen**	F	eat
7		**glauben**	G	fly
8	(sich)	**interessieren (für)**	H	get to know, become acquainted
9		**kennenlernen**	J	know [things]
10		**kommen**	K	last [of time]
11		**nehmen**	L	please, like
12		**sagen**	M	pass [of time]
13		**stehen**	N	return
14		**trinken**	P	say
15		**vergehen**	Q	stand, suit
16		**wiederkommen**	R	take
17		**wissen**	S	thank

Übung 20D

Can you put together German sentences by matching items in the two columns below?

1	**Ich glaube** . . .	A	. . . **doch auch mal rüber nach England!**
2	**Deine Heimat** . . .	B	. . . **vergeht!**
3	**Am besten** . . .	C	. . . **wiederkommen.**
4	**Ich weiß** . . .	D	. . . **ja.**
5	**Ich muß bald** . . .	E	. . . **gefallen?**
6	**Der Hut steht** . . .	F	. . . **dir für das schöne Kompliment.**
7	**Ich danke** . . .	G	. . . **mir nur wann!**
8	**Wir trinken** . . .	H	. . . **dir unwahrscheinlich gut.**
9	**Komm** . . .	J	. . . **auch nicht genau.**
10	**Was hat dir besonders** . . .	K	. . . **fliegst du.**

11	**Durch die Stadtrundfahrt . . .**	L	**. . . dauert es länger.**
12	**Du nimmst . . .**	M	**. . . nichts essen.**
13	**Wie die Zeit . . .**	N	**. . . interessiert mich sehr.**
14	**Ich freue . . .**	P	**. . . noch eine Woche Urlaub.**
15	**Ich möchte . . .**	Q	**. . . den Intercity.**
16	**Ich habe . . .**	R	**. . . auf uns.**
17	**Mit dem Schiff . . .**	S	**. . . habe ich dich kennengelernt.**
18	**Sag, . . .**	T	**. . . mich schon.**

Übung 20E

Below we have changed the familiar **du**-forms to the more formal **Sie**-forms. Change them back again without (initially) looking at the original text.

1. **Vier Tage in Berlin – vier Tage mit *Ihnen* – sind leider viel zu schnell vorbei.**
2. ***Sagen Sie* mir nur wann!**
3. ***Haben Sie* im September Zeit?**
4. **Was hat *Ihnen* besonders gut an Berlin gefallen?**
5. **Dadurch habe ich Berlin und *Sie* kennengelernt.**
6. **Ich danke *Ihnen* für das schöne Kompliment.**
7. ***Kommen Sie* doch auch mal 'rüber nach England!**
8. **Am besten *fliegen Sie* von Hannover oder Hamburg nach Manchester oder London.**
9. **Dann *nehmen Sie* den Intercity.**
10. ***Ihre* Heimat interessiert mich wirklich sehr.**
11. **Übrigens, *Herr Bennett*, der neue Hut steht *Ihnen* unwahrscheinlich gut.**

Übung 20F

Write out a translation of the following into English. Afterwards check your translation against that given in the Key for *accuracy and completeness of information* – the exact wording of the translation is not important – and make adjustments if necessary.

1. *Am Sonntag* . . . ist Peter Bennett in York abgefahren.
2. *Am Montag vormittag* . . . ist er in Berlin angekommen. Er hat zuerst in einem Café etwas getrunken und in einem Schreibwarengeschäft einen Stadtplan und Ansichtskarten gekauft. Dann ist er zum Hotel gegangen.

3 *Am Montag abend* . . . hat er im Hotelrestaurant gegessen.

4 *Am Dienstag nachmittag* . . . hat er eine Stadtrundfahrt gemacht und Heidi Dettmann kennengelernt.

5 *Am Dienstag abend* . . . haben Peter und Heidi sich lange und lebhaft unterhalten und zusammen Berliner Weiße getrunken.

6 *Am Mittwoch abend* . . . waren sie im Schloß Charlottenburg. Sie haben dort ein hervorragendes Mozartkonzert gehört.

7 *Am Donnerstag vormittag* . . . haben sie das weltberühmte Berliner Musikinstrumenten-Museum besucht.

8 *Am Donnerstag nachmittag* . . . haben sie einen Spaziergang am Wannsee gemacht. Das Wetter war einmalig schön!

9 *Am Freitag morgen* . . . ist Peter vor dem Hotel hingefallen und hat sich den Fuß leicht verstaucht. Heidi hat erfolgreich eingekauft.

10 *Am Freitag nachmittag* . . . sind sie zusammen zur Bank gegangen. Peter hat sich dann einen Hut gekauft.

11 *Am Freitag abend* . . . haben sie in einem Café am Kurfürstendamm eine zweite Fahrt nach Berlin geplant. Peter hat Heidi auch nach England eingeladen.

Übung 20G

Did you check, and where necessary amend, your English translation as suggested above? If so, without initially referring to the above German text, now try to translate your English version back into German. Alternatively, try to translate the English version in the Key back into German.

Übung 20H

Here is a second set (remember **Übung 10N**?) of questions and statements which can be answered with **Ja!** or **Nein!** Use this exercise as an opportunity for *revision*, i.e. read through **Texte 11** to **20** before answering the questions even if you do already know some of the answers. The first two digits of each question indicate the **Lektion** number.

11.1 **Ist Heidi Dettmann Buchhändlerin von Beruf?**
11.2 **Arbeitet sie in einer Universitätsbuchhandlung?**
11.3 **Hat Peter Bennett Kinder?**
11.4 **Ist Heidi verheiratet?**

11.5 **Peter hat seine Frau in York kennengelernt?**
11.6 **Seine Frau ist auch Buchhändlerin.**
13.1 **Hat Peter Lust, ins Konzert zu gehen?**
13.2 **Ist das ein Beethovenkonzert?**
13.3 **Liegt Schloß Charlottenburg am Kurfürstendamm?**
13.4 **Wollen sie sich am Bahnhof treffen?**
14.1 **Gefällt ihnen das Konzert?**
14.2 **Sie wollen am Donnerstag nachmittag ein Museum besuchen.**
14.3 **Peter hat als Kind Klavier gespielt.**
14.4 **Spielt Heidi noch Harfe?**
14.5 **Peter hört besonders gern Mozart.**
14.6 **Heidi zieht Unterhaltungsmusik vor.**
14.7 **Das Musikinstrumenten-Museum liegt am Zoo.**
14.8 **Gibt es eine U-Bahn-Station am Museum?**
14.9 **Ist zehn Uhr zu früh für Peter?**
15.1 **Am frühen Morgen fahren Heidi und Peter zum Wannsee.**
15.2 **Heidi möchte schwimmen.**
15.3 **Spielt Peter oft Tennis?**
15.4 **Kann man in der Nähe von York gut wandern?**
15.5 **Peter macht eine Wanderung fast jeden Samstag.**
16.1 **Am Freitag gehen Peter und Heidi zur Bank.**
16.2 **Vor der Bank ist er hingefallen . . .**
16.3 **. . . und hat sich den Knöchel verstaucht.**
17.1 **Der Arzt meint, er soll sich ausruhen.**
17.2 **Heidi kauft sich eine schwarze Hose, ein weißes Kleid und eine graue Jacke.**
17.3 **Die Jacke war teuer.**
17.4 **Möchte Peter auch eine Hose kaufen?**
17.5 **Holt ihn Heidi vom Hotel ab?**
19.1 **In York ist es im Sommer wärmer als in Dorfmark aber im Winter kälter.**
19.2 **Der Sommer ist die grüne Jahreszeit.**
19.3 **Heidi hat den Herbst besonders gern.**
19.4 **In Berlin sind die Straßen viel enger als in York.**
20.1 **Am letzten Abend trinken Peter und Heidi wieder Weißwein.**
20.2 **Heidi hat Hunger.**
20.3 **Peter möchte erst in zwei Jahren nach Berlin wiederkommen.**
20.4 **Hat er noch Urlaub in diesem Jahr?**
20.5 **Für Heidi war der Spaziergang am Wannsee am schönsten.**
20.6 **Heidi und Peter trinken Berliner Weiße ohne Schuß.**
20.7 **Fährt Heidi vielleicht nach York?**
20.8 **Freut sie sich schon?**

Übung 20J

Amend the above statements and questions so that all of them could be answered truthfully with **Ja!**

Übung 20K

Finally, a bumper quiz! How much attention did you pay to our Notes sections? If you can supply *any* of the information missing below, you've a right to feel pleased – not least for having reached the final page of the final **Lektion** in this book! The first number against each Note refers to the **Lektion** in which the original Note appeared. **Viel Erfolg!**

1.1 a variety of chocolate gateau, invented in 1832 by Metternich's Viennese cook
2.1 **eine Postkarte** is strictly a postcard with space for writing on both sides but is also used loosely for **eine** _______, a 'view card', i.e. one with a photograph on the front.
3.1 to stop someone politely you can either use a verb – as here (literally: 'excuse!') – or a noun – _______ **!**
3.2 **rechts** ≠ _______ 'right ≠ left'
4.1 there are three possibilities here in German: **der Fahrstuhl, der Aufzug, der** _______
4.2 literally: 'Englishman'. A woman would say **Ich bin** _______.
5.1 **Herr Ober!** is the standard form of address for a waiter, with _______**!** the equivalent for a waitress. Outside this professional context, _______ is used for 'Miss' but it is impolite to use it without the person's name attached
5.2 **S** _______ and **R** _______ are varieties of grape
5.3 **lieblich** suggests not dry (_______) without being too sweet (_______)
5.4 a set use of the (regular) verb **stimmen**. _______ = 'That's correct'
6.1 _______ here means 'o'clock', but **die/eine** _______ is 'the/a clock' or 'watch'
6.2 a large shopping complex near the eastern end of the Kurfürstendamm
7.1 this German expression is used much more widely than the English 'Ladies and Gentlemen'
7.2 often abbreviated **z.B.** = *e.g.*

7.3 literally: 'middle', but ______ is also the actual name of Berlin's central district
7.4 means 'under the lime trees'
7.5 An alternative to e.g. **Mein Name ist Jochen** would be **Ich** ______
7.6 = 'time'. There is a quality German weekly newspaper called ***Die*** ______
8.1 the first speaker is German and female, hence **Deutsch*e***. The male form would be ______
8.2 A female foreigner would be **Ausländerin. Das** ______ is 'abroad'
8.3 a light, fizzy beer, usually drunk (through a straw!) outdoors in hot weather, with a **Schuß** ('shot') of raspberry or woodruff syrup!
8.4 **der** ______ = 'fruit juice' (historically related to the English word 'sap')
8.5 ______ = 'I may', from the irregular modal verb **dürfen**
9.1 ______ is the most common (and the official) term of address for a woman these days, whether married or not. The use of ______ for an unmarried woman is felt by many to be antiquated
9.2 **gestern** is 'yesterday', so ______ is 'the day before yesterday'
10.1 **die** ______, **die Ostsee** = 'the North Sea, the ______ Sea'
11.1 = 'i.e.'______ can also be abbreviated in German as **d.h.**
11.2 **U** stands for **(der)** ______, meaning 'underground', **(die)** ______ means 'track' or 'railway'
11.3 ______ is the female form: the male form is **der Arzt**
12.1 pronounced: **der fünfte Mai**. 'On 5 May' = ______
12.2 **eventuell** and ______ both mean 'perhaps' – beware: the former does NOT mean 'eventually'
13.1 **also** = 'therefore'; ______ = 'also, too'
13.2 A ______ **(der)** is 'a causeway' and suggests that the road was originally built higher than the surrounding (probably marshy) terrain
13.3 ______, **deutscher Komponist, 1813 in Leipzig geboren, 1883 in Venedig gestorben.**
13.4 **abmachen** is a separable verb meaning 'to agree'. ______**!** = 'agreed, done!'
14.1 singular **Museum**, plural ______**.** Not many German nouns end in **-um**, but those that do often have an unusual plural form
14.2 **der** ______ is a large park in the centre of Berlin, now laid out

in the informal 'English style'. It literally means 'animal garden' and was once used to stock deer, wild boar, etc. for hunting (**das** ______ and English 'deer' are historically related)

15.1 **Der** ______ refers to large lake-like expanses of the River Havel in west Berlin, where it meanders through woods from north to south before eventually flowing into the Elbe

16.1 On the phone the standard way in German of saying 'Speaking!' in reply to a caller's request to speak to you is **Am** ______**!**

16.2 **der Knöchel** = 'ankle' (the related word **der** ______ = 'bone')

16.3 a standard expression used to wish someone a 'good improvement' i.e. 'a speedy recovery'. Note that **Gesundheit!** means 'health!' but it is used after a person sneezes and is not interchangeable with ______**!**

17.1 ______ is an abbreviation for **Kaufhaus des Westens**, literally 'department store of the west', situated at Wittenbergplatz near the Kurfürstendamm

17.2 ______ ≠ **teuer** = 'cheap' ≠ 'expensive'

18.1 **ein** ______ is any form of written certification but here quite specifically an official 'identity card', for which a 'passport' (**der Paß** or **Reisepaß**) is an acceptable alternative

19.1 German speakers often use ______. to mean Britain

19.2 **essen** 'to eat' is irregular: **ich esse**, **du ißt**, **er ißt**, **ich habe** ______

20.1 there are two types of ______ a 'dash' (shot) of 'raspberry' (______) or of 'woodruff' (**Waldmeister**)

20.2 holidays from work are **der** (sing.) ______; school holidays are **die** (pl.) **Ferien**

20.3 both ______ and **Prost!** are used to mean 'cheers!', 'Your health!'

20.4 **nehmen**, 'to take', is irregular: **ich nehme**, **er/sie nimmt**, **hat** ______

20.5 **die** ______ is where you feel you belong: where you feel 'home' is

20.6 a tag question = (here) 'isn't it?' Unlike English tag questions, **nicht** ______**?** (literally: 'not true?') never needs to change according to context. It is often abbreviated to **Nicht?** or even **Nich'?**

Don't stop now!
Keep your German going if you can.
The more you learn, the more rewarding it gets.

Key to exercises

1A 1 Guten Tag! 2 Bitte sehr? 3 Tee, bitte! 4 Mit Zitrone. 5 Mit Milch, bitte! 6 Möchten Sie sonst noch etwas? 7 Nein, Danke. 8 Ich möchte bitte zahlen! 9 Zwei Mark sechzig. 10 Drei Mark! 11 Und sieben Mark zurück! 12 Auf Wiedersehen!

1C 1 DM 5,50. 2 DM 7,80. 3 DM 3,30. 4 DM 1,90. 5 DM 6,70. 6 DM 8,40. 7 DM 2,60. 8 DM 9,20. 9 DM 4,30. 10 DM 1,60.

1E 1 sechs Mark siebzig. 2 eine Mark zwanzig. 3 fünf Mark fünfzig. 4 vier Mark dreißig. 5 drei Mark neunzig. 6 sieben Mark sechzig. 7 drei Mark sechzig. 8 vier Mark vierzig. 9 zwei Mark neunzig. 10 sechs Mark zwanzig. 11 neun Mark achtzig. 12 eine Mark fünfzig. 13 zwei Mark dreißig. 14 neun Mark zwanzig. 15 sieben Mark vierzig.

1F 1 Was bekommen Sie? 2 Kaffee, bitte. 3 Eine Tasse oder ein Kännchen? 4 Das wär's? 5 Und ein Stück Sachertorte. 6 Ich möchte gleich zahlen. 7 Das macht neun Mark fünfzig, bitte. 8 Stimmt so! 9 Ich danke Ihnen. 10 Auf Wiederschauen!

1H *First column*: Dank; Kaffee; Kellner; Tag; Tee. *Second*: Kännchen; Stück; Wiederschauen, Wiedersehen. *Third*: Kellnerin; Mark; Milch; Sachertorte; Tasse; Zitrone.

1K 1 möchten: would like. 2 zahlen: pay. 3 bekommen: get. 4 sein: to be. 5 möchten: would like. 6 machen: make, do. 7 stimmen: to be correct. 8 danken: thank.

1L 1 DM 2,60. 2 DM 9,50. 3 'Sachertorte' (chocolate gateau), one piece/slice.

1M 1E. 2H. 3D. 4A. 5G. 6C. 7B. 8F.

1N 1 Guten Tag! 2 Kaffee, bitte! 3 Ein Kännchen, bitte! 4 Nein, danke! 5 Ich möchte bitte zahlen! 6 Stimmt so! 7 Danke schön! Auf Wiedersehen/Wiederschauen!

1Q 1 Seven: Sachertorte; Apfelstrudel; (Berliner) Pfannkuchen; (Schwarzwälder) Kirschtorte; (Basler) Leckerli; (Thüringer) Mohnkuchen; (Dresdner) Stollen. 2 Deutschland; Österreich; Schweiz. 3 Eight: Wien (Vienna); Berlin; Schwarzwald (Black Forest); Baden-Württemberg; Basel; Thüringen. 4 chocolate. 5 apricot jam. 6 honey, almonds, sugar, flour. 7 schnapps (Schnaps). 8 Hauptstadt. 9 'Whoever has the choice, has the torment'.

1R in Deutschland, in Österreich *but* in der Schweiz.

1S 1 Torte: gateau. 2 kosten: cost. 3 ein: a. 4 fein: fine. 5 deutsch: German. 6 bieten: offer. 7 frisch: fresh. 8 warm: warm. 9 schmecken: taste. 10 Mandel: almond. 11 klein: small. 12 Fall: case.

1T (a) Torten; Mandeln, Fälle. (b) kostet; bietet; schmeckt.

2A (der) Pfennig, Stadtplan, Tag, Verkäufer. (die) Ansichtskarte, Briefmarke, Mark, Postkarte.

2B 1 Das macht zusammen zehn Mark fünfzig. 2 Was kostet eine Postkarte nach Großbritannien? 3 Möchten Sie einen großen oder einen kleinen Stadtplan? 4 Ich möchte zwei Briefmarken zu achtzig Pfennig. 5 Möchten Sie sonst noch etwas? 6 Ja, die vier schwarzweißen Ansichtskarten. 7 Ja, wir haben auch Briefmarken. 8 Und neun Mark fünfzig zurück.

2C 1 einen Stadtplan. 2 eine Mark. 3 einen Pfennig. 4 eine Briefmarke. 5 ein Stück Sachertorte. 6 einen Schnaps. 7 eine Tasse Tee. 8 eine Ansichtskarte.

2D 1 großen. 2 guten. 3 starken. 4 neuen.

2E 1 Ich bestelle Kaffee. 2 Er zahlt 3 Vier Briefmarken kosten zwei Mark. 4 Eine Tasse Tee kostet neunzig Pfennig. 5 Das macht zehn Mark fünfzig. 6 Bestellen Sie Tee mit Milch? 7 Ja, ich bestelle Tee mit Milch. 8 Sie bestellt Tee mit Zitrone.

2F 1 Drei Ansichtskarten von Berlin kosten zwei Mark siebzig. 2 Eine Postkarte nach England kostet achtzig Pfennig. 3 Drei Briefe nach Australien kosten neun Mark. 4 Ein Stadtplan von Frankfurt kostet vier Mark achtzig.

2G kostet: 1, 2, 4, 7. kosten: 3, 5, 6, 8.

2J 1 DM 1,64. 2 DM 5,22. 3 DM 3,38. 4 DM 10,97. 5 DM 6,36. 6 DM 8,49. 7 DM 2,65. 8 DM 9,34. 9 DM 4,22. 10 DM 7,99.

2L 1 sechs Mark siebenundsiebzig. 2 eine Mark fünfundzwanzig. 3 fünf Mark fünfundfünfzig. 4 vier Mark einunddreißig. 5 drei Mark neunundneunzig. 6 zwei Mark dreiundvierzig. 7 sieben Mark sechsundsechzig. 8 neun Mark achtunddreißig. 9 zehn Mark zweiundachtzig. 10 acht Mark einundzwanzig.

2M 1 DM 5,40: fünf Mark vierzig. 2 DM 10,–: zehn Mark. 3 DM 5,80: fünf Mark achtzig. 4 DM 54,40: vierundfünfzig Mark vierzig.

2N 1C. 2A. 3E. 4D. 5B.

3A (der) Dank, Moment, Spaß. (das) Hotel. (die) Seite, Straße.

3B 1 Gehen Sie geradeaus! 2 Viel Spaß in Berlin! 3 Nehmen Sie die zweite Straße rechts! 4 Entschuldigen Sie, bitte! 5 Ja, genau. 6 Das Hotel Müller ist auf der linken Seite. 7 Nicht die zweite sondern die dritte Straße. 8 Wie komme ich zum Hotel Müller? 9 Richtig. 10 Vielen Dank.

3C 1(o). 2 (k). 3(a). 4(v). 5(b). 6(i). 7(n). 8(p). 9(g). 10(m). 11(z). 12(j). 13(q). 14(s). 15(u). 16(t). 17(l). 18(c). 19(d). 20(e). 21(h). 22(w). 23(f). 24(x). 25(ß). 26(r). 27(y).

3D 1(i). 2(c). 3(j). 4(d). 5(a). 6(h). 7(k). 8(l). 9(f). 10(g). 11(e). 12(b).

3E Brandenburger Tor. 2 Theater. 3 Jugendherberge. 4 U-Bahn. 5 Reisebüro. 6 Flughafen. 7 Bushaltestelle. 8 Oper.

3F 1 zum Museum? 2 zur Post? 3 zum Flughafen? 4 zur Apotheke? 5 zum Brandenburger Tor? 6 zur Telefonzelle? 7 zur U-Bahn? 8 zum Pergamonmuseum? 9 zum Kaufhaus? 10 zur Jugendherberge?

3G *Questions* (?): 2, 4, 6, 8, 10, 12, 15, 16 *Commands* (!): 1, 3, 5, 7, 9, 11, 13, 14, 17

3H 1 der Kurfürstendamm? 2 der Flughafen? 3 die Jugendherberge? 4 das Pergamonmuseum? 5 der Flohmarkt? 6 der Hafen?

3J 1 eine Telefonzelle? 2 eine Tankstelle? 3 ein Kino? 4 ein Campingplatz? 5 das nächste Hotel? 6 die nächste Post? 7 der nächste Bahnhof? 8 das nächste Freibad/Hallenbad/Schwimmbad?

3L 1 erste. 2 fünfte. 3 dritte. 4 siebte. 5 vierte. 6 neunte. 7 zehnte. 8 achte. 9 sechste. 10 zweite.

3M (a) (b) (c) fünfundvierzig.

3N (a) 0 77 20 16 (b) 5 11 18 38 (c) 7 72 17 47 (d) 1 46 35 09 (e) 3 64 90 12

4A (der) Dank, Engländer, Fahrstuhl, Koffer, Mai, Nachname, Name, Stock, Vorname, Wohnort, Zimmerschlüssel. (das) Bad, Doppelzimmer, Einzelzimmer, Gepäck, Zimmer. (die) Dusche, Empfangsdame, Kreditkarte, Nacht, Nationalität, Nummer, Paßnummer, Seite, Treppe, Unterschrift.

4B 1 Woher kommen Sie? 2 Wo wohnen Sie? 3 Wie möchten Sie zahlen? 4 Haben Sie ein ruhiges Zimmer frei? 5 Mein Nachname ist . . . 6 Ihre Unterschrift, bitte. 7 Ich habe einen sehr schweren Koffer. 8 Das ist Ihr Zimmerschlüssel. 9 Die Treppe ist geradeaus. 10 Möchten Sie (ein Zimmer) mit Bad oder mit Dusche?

4C 1 Wie ist Ihre Kreditkartennummer? 4552 9118 5727 6336: 2 Wie ist Ihre Telefonnummer? 0 54 89 31 19: 3 Wie ist Ihre Paßnummer? 22 45 12 13 E.

4D 1 kleinen . . . großen. 2 starken. 3 zweite . . . dritte. 4 Guten. 5 ruhiges. 6 schweren. 7 schwarzweiße. 8 freundliches. 9 nette.

4E 1 nach. 2 zu. 3 zum. 4 auf der. 5 mit . . . mit. 6 für . . . bis zum. 7 Von . . . bis zum. 8 im. 9 mit. 10 zur.

4F 1 vierten Januar. 2 achtzehnten Februar. 3 dritten April. 4 achtzehnten Mai. 5 zwanzigsten Juni. 6 ersten August. 7 ersten November. 8 einundzwanzigsten Oktober. 9 zwanzigsten Dezember. 10 ersten Januar.

4G 1 zwölften achten. 2 siebten neunten. 3 zweiundzwanzigsten zehnten. 4 einunddreißigsten zwölften. 5 vierzehnten dritten. 6 dreißigsten vierten. 7 fünfzehnten siebten. 8 zehnten sechsten. 9 neunundzwanzigsten zweiten. 10 neunzehnten elften. 11 fünften fünften. 12 ersten ersten.

4K 1C. 2E. 3F. 4J. 5K. 6A. 7B. 8D. 9H. 10G.

4M 1 Haben Sie ein ruhiges Zimmer frei? 2 Ich möchte ein Zimmer mit Dusche. 3 Was kostet das Zimmer? 4 Vom neunundzwanzigsten Mai bis zum ersten Juni. 5 Nummer dreiundzwanzig im ersten Stock auf der rechten Seite. 6 Ich habe einen sehr schweren Koffer. 7 Haben Sie einen Fahrstuhl?

5A (der) Abend, Bohnensalat, Dank, Hotelgast, Kaffee, Nachtisch, Obstsalat, Rotwein, Schinken, Weißwein, Zimmerschlüssel. (das) Eis, Fenster, Kännchen, Restaurant, Rührei, Viertel, Zimmer. (die) Ecke, Entschuldigung, Flasche, Mitte, Nummer, Person, Sahne, Seite, Speisekarte, Zimmernummer, Zwiebelsuppe.

5B 1 Es ist auf der rechten Seite. 2 Lieber am Fenster. 3 Hier ist die Speisekarte. 4 Ich weiß nicht. 5 Hat es (Ihnen) geschmeckt? 6 Ich nehme den Obstsalat. 7 Haben Sie schon gewählt? 8 Das stimmt! 9 Die Nummer steht auf dem Schlüssel. 10 Möchten Sie einen Nachtisch? 11 Wie bitte?

5C 1 Ich möchte ein Zimmer mit Bad. 2 Möchten Sie am Fenster sitzen? 3 Möchten Sie ein Einzelzimmer oder ein Doppelzimmer? 4 Möchten Sie einen großen oder einen kleinen Stadtplan? 5 Ich möchte zwei Briefmarken zu achtzig Pfennig. 6 Möchten Sie Kaffee bestellen? 7 Ich möchte mit Kreditkarte zahlen. 8 Ich möchte den trockenen Wein. 9 Ich möchte einen starken, schwarzen Kaffee. 10 Möchten Sie den frischen Obstsalat?

5D 2 Nein, der Bohnensalat hat mir gar nicht gut geschmeckt! 3 Ja, das Eis hat mir geschmeckt. 4 Ja, der Wein hat mir ausgezeichnet geschmeckt! 5 Nein, die französische Zwiebelsuppe hat mir gar nicht geschmeckt! 6 Nein, die Sachertorte hat mir nicht gut geschmeckt. 7 Ja, der Kaffee hat mir sehr gut geschmeckt! 8 Nein, die Schwarzwälder Kirschtorte hat mir nicht geschmeckt.

5E Ich habe schon (1 . . . . 10) gewählt. 1 einen Bohnensalat. 2 eine Flasche Weißwein. 3 den frischen Obstsalat. 4 Rührei mit Schinken. 5 eine französische Zwiebelsuppe. 6 ein Viertel Rotwein. 7 einen Nachtisch. 8 ein gemischtes Eis.

5F 1 ein Einzelzimmer bestellt. 2 ein Doppelzimmer bestellt. 3 Tee getrunken. 4 Kaffee getrunken. 5 Rührei gegessen. 6 Schinken gegessen. 7 einen kleinen Stadtplan gekauft. 8 einen großen Stadtplan gekauft. 9 den frischen Obstsalat genommen. 10 ein gemischtes Eis genommen.

5H 1: 234. 2: 769. 3: 373. 4: 616. 5: 7523. 6: 8949. 7: 1 350 781. 8: 5 000 005 555. 9: 4711. 10: 12 001 031.

5J 1: 1871. 2: 1919. 3: 1564. 4: 1492. 5: 1867. 6: 1894. 7: 1632. 8: 1776. 9: 1066. 10: 2001.

5M 1D: 21.1.1756–5.12.1791. 2E: 5.5.1818–14.4.1883. 3F: 17.12.1770–26.3.1827. 4A: 28.4.1749–22.3.1832. 5J: 18.12.1913–8.10.1992 6B: 4.1.1785–20.9.1863. 7K: 14.3.1879–18.4.1955. 8C: 24.2.1786–16.12.1859. 9H: 27.12.1901–6.5.1992. 10G: 21.5.1471–6.4.1528.

5N 1 Ulm/Princeton. 2 Berlin/Paris. 3 Salzburg/Wien. 4 Trier/London. 5 Nürnberg/Nürnberg. 6 Lübeck/Unkel am Rhein. 7 Hanau/Berlin. 8 Hanau/Berlin. 9 Frankfurt am Main/Weimar. 10 Bonn/Wien.

5P 1 Er ist in Nürnberg geboren. 2 Er ist in Wien gestorben. 3 Er ist in Trier geboren. 4 Sie ist in Paris gestorben. 5 Er ist in Princeton gestorben. 6 Er ist in Lübeck geboren. 7 Er ist in Berlin gestorben. 8 Er ist (auch) in Berlin gestorben. 9 Er ist in Weimar gestorben. 10 Er ist in Bonn geboren.

5Q 1J. 2H. 3G. 4L. 5F. 6D. 7M. 8K. 9A. 10C. 11B. 12E.

5R 1a. kaufe. 1b. kaufen. 2a. nimmt. 2b. nehme. 3a. sitzt. 3b. sitzt. 4a. habe. 4b. hat. 5a. Gehen. 5b. gehe. 6a. kostet. 6b. schmeckt. 7a. trinkt. 7b. trinkt. 8a. schmeckt. 8b. ist. 9a. bin. 9b. Sind. 10a. kaufen. 10b. kostet.

5S 1E. 2D. 3F. 4B. 5C. 6A.

5T 1 Guten Abend! 2 Ich möchte am Fenster sitzen. 3 Die Speisekarte, bitte. 4 Ich möchte einen trockenen Weißwein. 5 Ich möchte Rührei mit Schinken und einen Salat dazu. 6 Es hat (mir) (sehr) gut geschmeckt. 7 Was haben Sie heute? 8 (Ich möchte) ein Kännchen Kaffee (bitte). 9 Ich möchte (bitte) zahlen. 10 Auf Wiedersehen/Wiederschauen!

6A (der) Bus, Dienstag, Donnerstag, Fuß, Mittwoch, Morgen, Name, Tag, Vorname. (das) Center, Hotel, Problem. (die) Fahrt, Karte, Mark, Minute, Stadtrundfahrt, Straße, Stunde, Uhr.

6B 1 Guten Morgen! 2 Für welchen Tag, bitte? 3 Mittwoch, Donnerstag? 4 Für heute, Dienstag, wenn's geht. 5 Auf welchen Namen, bitte? 6 Vorname Peter, wie Peter. 7 Danke, Herr Bennett. 8 Sie sehen, der Bus fährt vom Europa-Center in der Budapester Straße ab. 9 Das Europa-Center ist nur acht Minuten zu Fuß vom Hotel entfernt. 10 Vielen Dank.

6C 1 Wie lange dauert eine Fahrt? 2 Kennen Sie das Europa-Center? 3 Kein Problem! 4 Es gibt zwei Stadtrundfahrten heute. 5 Können Sie für mich bestellen? 6 Für heute, Dienstag, wenn's geht. 7 Hier ist Ihre Karte. 8 Noch nicht. 9 Vierzehn Uhr dreißig. 10 Um halb elf.

6D 1 Ich möchte zehn Karten zu zwölf Mark neunzig. 2 Nur fünfzehn Minuten zu Fuß. 3 Die Stadtrundfahrt dauert vier Stunden und zwanzig Minuten. 4 Ich möchte vier Postkarten und Briefmarken. 5 Berlin hat fünfhundert Kirchen und zweihundert Apotheken. 6 Die Straßen von London. 7 Zwei Ansichtskarten kosten nur eine Mark.

6F Stadtrundfahrten ... heute morgen ... halb zwölf ... große ... heute abend ... halb acht.

6G 1: 4.30. 2: 10.30. 3: 1.30. 4: 3.30. 5: 5.30. 6: 12.30 or 00.30.

6H Es ist . . . 1 halb zehn. 2 halb sieben. 3 halb zwölf. 4 halb neun. 5 halb fünf. 6 halb eins.

6K 1 Sie dauert dreieinhalb Stunden. 2 Er dauert fünfundneunzig Minuten. 3 Es dauert zwei Wochen. 4 Sie dauert vierundzwanzig Stunden. 5 Sie dauert fünfeinhalb Stunden! 6 Es dauert nur neunundsiebzig Minuten. 7 Er dauert nur drei Minuten.

6L 1 mit dem Schiff. 2 mit dem Zug. 3 mit dem Taxi. 4 mit dem Motorrad. 5 mit der S-Bahn. 6 mit der Straßenbahn. 7/8 mit dem Auto/Wagen. 9 mit der U-Bahn. 10 mit dem Fahrrad. 11 mit der Bahn. 12 mit dem Bus.

6M 1 mit dem Zug. 2 mit der U-Bahn. 3 zu Fuß. 4 mit dem Fahrrad. 5 mit dem Schiff. 6 mit dem Bus. 7 mit der S-Bahn.

6P 1 Karten für. 2 Oper. 3 am Dienstag. 4 Bus. 5 um. 6 vom Rathaus. 7 Stunde mit. 8 zum. 9 um. 10 Opernhaus. 11 Minuten zu. 12 vom. 13 Oper. 14 um. 15 Stunde. 16 Minuten für. 17 im.

6Q 1 Guten Morgen! Ich möchte eine Fahrkarte/Karte für eine Stadtrundfahrt. 2 Ich möchte eine Karte für heute, Dienstag. 3 Ich möchte eine Karte für heute nachmittag um halb drei. 4 Wie lange dauert die (Stadtrund)fahrt? 5 [Your name] 6 (Sie bekommen) zehn Mark fünfzig zurück. 7 Das Europa-Center ist nur zwanzig Minuten zu Fuß vom Hotel entfernt. 8 Gute Fahrt! 9 Vielen Dank/Danke schön/Danke sehr/Ich danke Ihnen.

7A (der) Appetit, Architekt, Baustil, Berliner, Bezirk, Bus, Einwohner, Fahrgast, Herr, Kaffee, König, Kuchen, Kurfürstendamm, Mann, Meter, Moment, Quadratkilometer, Reisebegleiter, Student. (das) Beispiel, Brandenburger Tor, Jahr, Lieblingspferd, Meisterwerk, Operncafé, Opernhaus, Pferd, Prinzessinnenpalais, Standbild, Wahrzeichen, Zentrum. (die) Dame, Einkaufsstraße, Hauptstadt, Kopie, Kultur, Linde, Million, Mitte, Nußtorte, Oper, Quadriga, Stadt, Stadtrundfahrt, Straße, Straßenmitte, Straßenseite, Uhr, Welt, Zeit.

7B 1 (Herzlich) willkommen in Berlin! 2 Ich bin achtundzwanzig Jahre alt. 3 Können Sie mich alle gut hören? 4 Berlin ist wieder die Hauptstadt Deutschlands. 5 Berlin hat heute mehr als drei Millionen Einwohner. 6 Berlin ist über siebenhundertfünfzig Jahre alt. 7 Wir stehen im Moment am Kurfürstendamm. 8 Das Brandenburger Tor, das Wahrzeichen Berlins. 9 Meine Damen und Herren. 10 Die Deutsche Staatsoper. 11 Hinter der Staatsoper. 12 Guten Appetit!

7C 1 bin. 2 ist. 3 sind. 4 glaube. 5 hat. 6 haben. 7 können. 8 stehen. 9 wissen. 10 sagen. 11 fahren. 12 sehen. 13 heißt. 14 hält. 15 empfehle. 16 wünsche.

7D bin, ist, sind, hat, kann, weiß, fährt, sieht, hält, empfiehlt.

7E Wien: 9.00; 10.20; 12.21; 21.19 Leipzig: 11.30; 12.17; 14.31; 23.02 Berlin: 14.01; 16.11; 16.15; 0.55

7F Ostende ab: siebzehn Uhr sieben. Aachen an: zwanzig Uhr dreißig, ab: ... vierundvierzig. Köln an: einundzwanzig Uhr dreiundzwanzig, ab: ... fünfunddreißig. Bonn an: einundzwanzig Uhr fünfundfünfzig, ab: ... siebenundfünfzig. Koblenz an: zweiundzwanzig Uhr zweiunddreißig, ab: ...fünfunddreißig. Mainz an: dreiundzwanzig Uhr achtundzwanzig, ab: ... zweiunddreißig. Frankfurt an: vierundzwanzig Uhr (Mitternacht), ab: null Uhr (und) achtzehn (Minuten). Nürnberg an: drei Uhr elf, ab: ... achtundzwanzig. Passau an: fünf Uhr zweiundfünfzig, ab: sechs Uhr vierzehn. Wien an: neun Uhr fünfundvierzig.

7G 1 um zehn Uhr. 2 um halb elf. 3 um Viertel nach zwölf. 4 um halb zehn. 5 um halb drei. 6 um Viertel vor eins. 7 um Viertel vor acht.

7H : 1.45. 2: 1.00. 3: 4.30. 4: 3.15. 5: 5.45. 6: 2.30. 7: 9.30. 8: 9.15

7K Es ist ... 1 sechs Uhr. 2 zwei Minuten nach sechs. 3 Viertel nach sechs. 4 dreiundzwanzig Minuten nach sechs. 5 halb sieben. 6 sechzehn Minuten vor sieben. 7 Viertel vor sieben. 8 zehn (Minuten) vor sieben. 9 vier Minuten vor sieben. 10 sieben Uhr.

7M 2 neuter nominative. 3 feminine accusative. 4 masculine nominative. 5 feminine nominative. 6 feminine dative. 7 feminine dative. 8 masculine dative. 9 neuter dative. 10 masculine nominative.

7P 1 die Dame. 2 der Herr. 3 der Name. 4 der Reisebegleiter. 5 das Jahr. 6 der Student. 7 der Gast. 8 die Welt. 9 die Hauptstadt. 10 die Stadt. 11 der Quadratkilometer. 12 die Million. 13 der Einwohner. 14 der Stadtbezirk. 15 das Beispiel. 16 der Moment. 17 der Kurfürstendamm. 18 die Einkaufsstraße. 19 die Mitte. 20 das Zentrum. 21 das Tor. 22 das Wahrzeichen/Symbol. 23 der Baustil. 24 der Architekt. 25 die Quadriga. 26 die Linde. 27 die Straßenmitte. 28 das Standbild. 29 der Meter. 30. der Mann. 31 das Pferd. 32 der König. 33 das Lieblingspferd. 34 das Meisterwerk. 35 die Stadt. 36 die Stadtrundfahrt. 37 die Zeit. 38 der Kaffee. 39 der Kuchen. 40. der Bus. 41 die Straßenseite. 42 die Oper. 43 das Opernhaus. 44 das Café. 45 die Kopie. 46 die Kultur. 47 die Nußtorte. 48 der Appetit. 49 (der) Herr. 50. (die) Uhr.

7Q 1 große. 2 alte. 3 vornehme. 4 historische. 5 klassizistisch. 6 schöne. 7 breite, berühmte 8 schöne. 9 großes, hoch. 10 Große. 11 anstrengend. 12 rechten. 13 Deutsche. 14 herrliche. 15 original. 16 köstliche. 17 Guten.

8A (der) Amerikaner, Ausländer, Engländer, Name, Saft, Waldmeister, Wein. (das) Ausland, Bier, Dorf, Eisenbahnmuseum, Glas, Norddeutschland, Nordengland. (die) Ausländerin, Berliner Weiße, Deutsche, Himbeere, Kathedrale, Lüneburger Heide, Stadt, Stadtrundfahrt, Universität.

8B 1 Berlin gefällt mir sehr gut. 2 Sind Sie vielleicht Ausländer? 3 Woher kommen sie? 4 Ich komme aus Norddeutschland. 5 York ist eine mittelgroße Stadt. 6 Seit wann sind Sie hier in Berlin? 7 Wie ist Ihr Name? 8 Eine Stadtrundfahrt ist tatsächlich anstrengend, nicht wahr? 9 Darf ich Sie (vielleicht) nachher zu einem Glas Bier oder Wein einladen? 10 Wie wär's mit Berliner Weiße?

8C 1 Da. 2 Ae. 3 Bf. 4 Cb. 5 Ed. 6 Fc.

8E 1 Engländer(in). 2 Inder(in). 3 Amerikaner(in). 4 Schotte/ Schottin. 5 Österreicher(in). 6 Neuseeländer(in). 7 Deutscher/ Deutsche. 8 Australier(in). 9 Schweizer(in). 10 Waliser(in). 11 Südafrikaner(in). 12 Ire/Irin. 13 Kanadier(in).

8K Es ist . . . 1 ein modernes Hotel. 2 ein ruhiges Zimmer. 3 eine sehr alte Kathedrale. 4 eine lange Straße. 5 eine historische Stadt. 6 ein deutsches Auto. 7 eine französische Zwiebelsuppe.

8M 1: 82. 2: 78. 3: 73. 4: 35. 5: 64. 6: 56. 7: 56. 8: 90. 9: 78. 10: 76.

9A (der) Bus, Kaffee, Stadtplan, Sturm, Tourist, Zug. (das) Café, Fräulein, Hotel, Schiff, Stück. (die) Ansichtskarte, Briefmarke, Fahrt, Frau, Ordnung, Tasse, Torte, Überfahrt, Uhr, Zugfahrt

9B 1 Wie sind Sie nach Berlin gekommen? 2 Ich bin vorgestern mit dem Schiff von Hull nach Hamburg gefahren. 3 In Hamburg habe ich den Zug genommen. 4 Wie war die Fahrt? 5 Die lange Überfahrt war leider naß und stürmisch. 6 Um wieviel Uhr sind Sie angekommen? 7 Ich bin gestern vormittag gegen elf Uhr angekommen. 8 Ich bin zuerst in ein Café gegangen. 9 Na so was! 10 Ich bin zum Hotel gegangen.

9C 1 gekauft. 2 gefahren. 3 geflogen. 4 gegangen. 5 gekommen. 6 angekommen. 7 gemacht. 8 genommen. 9 geschlafen. 10 getrunken.

9D 1 hat . . . gekauft. 2 habe . . . getrunken. 3 hat . . . gegessen. 4 hat . . . gekauft. 5 habe . . . geschlafen. 6 hat . . . genommen.

9E 1 sind. 2 Sind. 3 bin. 4 sind. 5 bin. 6 bin. 7 Sind. 8 bin.

9F 1 Sind sie von Dallas nach Berlin geflogen? 2 Sind Sie gestern zum Hotel gegangen? 3 Sind Sie mit dem Bus von Dorfmark nach Berlin gefahren? 4 Sind Sie auch am Montag gegen elf Uhr angekommen? 5 Haben sie den ersten Zug genommen? 6 Hat Ihnen Berlin gefallen? 7 Wie hat Ihnen die Berliner Weiße geschmeckt? 8 Haben Sie den großen Stadtplan gekauft?

9H 1 dann. 2 dann/zuerst. 3 dort. 4 dann/danach. 5 dann/danach.

9J 1 gefallen. 2 gegangen. 3 gegessen. 4 gedauert. 5 geschmeckt. 6 gefahren. 7 gekauft. 8 gekostet. 9 genommen. 10 geflogen. 11 getrunken.

9K 1 sind. 2 gekommen. 3 sind. 4 geflogen. 5 bin. 6 gefahren. 7 habe. 8 geschlafen. 9 habe. 10 genommen. 11 war. 12 war. 13 war. 14 war. 15 sind. 16 angekommen. 17 bin. 18 angekommen. 19 bin. 20 gegangen. 21 habe. 22 gegessen. 23 getrunken. 24 bin. 25 angekommen. 26 bin. 27 gegangen. 28 habe. 29 getrunken. 30 haben. 31 gekauft. 32 habe. 33 gekauft. 34 sind. 35 gegangen. 36 haben. 37 gemacht. 38 bin. 39 gegangen.

10A (der) Bus, Dichter, Einwohner, Frühling, Fuß, Hafen, Herbst, Kilometer, Meter, Morgen, Regen, Schnee, Schüler, Sommer, Winter, Zug. (das) Fahrrad, Haus, Jahr, Leben, Lebensjahr, Rad. (die) Ecke, Hafenstadt, Herkunft, Nordsee, Ostsee, Schule, Schülerin, Sonne, Stadt.

10B 1 In the winter, Heidi Dettmann usually went to school by train. 2 She sometimes went by bus.

10C 1 Sind sie in York geboren? 2 In Cockermouth ist der Dichter Wordsworth geboren. 3 Er ist (bei uns) in Großbritannien immer noch sehr beliebt. 4 Das ist eine Hafenstadt an der Ostsee. 5 Sind Sie in Cockermouth aufgewachsen? 6 Nicht ganz. 7 Ich habe bis zu meinem zehnten Lebensjahr dort gewohnt. 8 Wie lange wohnen Sie (schon) in Dorfmark? 9 Im Sommer bin ich jeden Morgen die sechs Kilometer mit dem Fahrrad zur Schule gefahren. 10 Im Winter bin ich meistens mit dem Zug zur Schule gefahren. 11 Waren Sie ein guter Schüler? 12 Leider nicht!

10E 1 Meistens bin ich zu Fuß zur Schule gegangen. 2 Manchmal habe ich den Zug genommen. 3 Heute habe ich schon zehn Tassen Kaffee getrunken! 4 Seit seinem zehnten Lebensjahr wohnt Peter Bennett in York. 5 1770 ist Wordsworth geboren. 6 Nur drei Jahre hat Frau Dettmann in Rostock gewohnt. 7 Jetzt fahren wir zum Brandenburger Tor. 8 Heute abend um acht Uhr essen wir im Hotel. 9 Heute abend möchte ich nicht im Hotel essen. 10 Erst um 23 Uhr fährt der Zug ab.

10F 1 Mit dem Bus. 2 Sie war nicht sehr gut. 3 Gegen elf Uhr. 4 Ich bin in ein Café gegangen. 5 Ich komme aus York. 6 York ist eine mittelgroße Stadt. 7 Ich bin erst seit gestern hier. 8 Ich heiße Bennett, Peter Bennett.

10G 1 meinem vierten. 2 seinem elften. 3 ihrem dritten. 4 seinem zweiundzwanzigsten. 5 seinem vierundfünfzigsten. 6 seinem vierundzwanzigsten. 7 ihrem neunundzwanzigsten. 8 unserem zwölften.

10J 1 Im Dezember sind es in Alice Springs etwa vierunddreißig Grad. 2 Im Juli sind es in Wien etwa vierundzwanzig Grad. 3 Im Juli sind es in Winnipeg etwa fünfundzwanzig Grad. 4 Im Dezember sind es in Manchester etwa acht Grad. 5 Im Juli sind es in Genf etwa fünfundzwanzig Grad. 6 Im Dezember sind es in Kapstadt etwa vierundzwanzig Grad. 7 Im Juli sind es in Kalkutta etwa zweiunddreißig Grad. 8 Im Juli sind es in Alice Springs etwa neunzehn Grad. 9 Im Juli sind es in Dublin etwa achtzehn Grad. 10 Im Dezember sind es in Dublin etwa neun Grad. 11 Im Dezember sind es in Winnipeg etwa minus zehn Grad.

10K 1 Im Dezember fallen in Alice Springs etwa drei Zentimeter Regen. 2 Im Juli fällt in Alice Springs etwa ein . . . 3 Im Juli fallen in Genf etwa sieben . . . 4 Im Dezember fallen in New Orleans etwa zwölf . . . 5 Im Juli fallen in New Orleans etwa sechzehn . . . 6 Im Dezember fallen in Fort William etwa zweiundzwanzig . . . 7 Im Juli fallen in Fort William etwa zehn . . . 8 Im Juli fallen in Kalkutta etwa zweiunddreißig . . . 9 Im Dezember fällt in Kalkutta etwa ein . . . 10 Im Juli fallen in Auckland etwa vierzehn . . . 11 Im Dezember fallen in Kapstadt etwa zwei . . .

10L 1 In Auckland ist es im Dezember warm und es regnet nur manchmal. 2 In Alice Springs ist es im Juli warm und es regnet fast nie. 3 In Winnipeg ist es im Dezember sehr kalt und es regnet selten. 4 Im Juli ist es in Kalkutta sehr heiß und es regnet sehr stark. 5 Im Dezember ist es in Fort William kühl und es regnet meistens. 6 Im Dezember ist es in Dublin kühl und es regnet manchmal. 7 Im Juli ist es in New Orleans heiß und es regnet oft. 8 Im Dezember ist es in Wien kalt und es regnet manchmal. 9 Im Juli ist es in Kapstadt warm und es regnet manchmal. 10 Im Dezember ist es in Kalkutta heiß und es regnet fast nie.

10N Ja: 2.1; 2.3; 3.1; 4.2; 4.7; 4.8; 4.9; 5.1; 5.3; 5.5; 5.7; 7.4; 7.5; 7.6; 7.7; 7.9; 8.1; 8.4; 9.3; 9.5; 9.6: 10.7. Nein: 1.1; 1.2; 2.4; 3.2; 4.1; 4.3; 4.4; 4.5; 4.6; 5.2; 5.4; 5.6; 6.1; 6.2; 6.3; 6.4; 6.5; 6.6; 7.1; 7.2; 7.3; 7.8; 7.10; 7.11; 7.12; 7.13; 7.14; 8.2; 8.3; 8.5; 8.6; 9.1; 9.2; 9.4; 9.7; 10.1; 10.2; 10.3; 10.4; 10.5; 10.6; 10.8

11A (der) Amerikaner, Arzt, Beruf, Buchhändler, Herr, Mann, Offizier, Sohn, Untergrund. (das) Jahr, Kind, Leben. (die) Armee, Ärztin, Bahn, Buchhändlerin, Buchhandlung, Engländerin, Familie, Frau, Medizin, Tochter, U-Bahn, Universität, Universitätsbuchhandlung, Wohnung.

11B 1 Was sind Sie eigentlich von Beruf? 2 Das gibt es nicht! 3 Arbeiten Sie auch in einer Universitätsbuchhandlung? 4 Haben Sie Familie? 5 Ich bin seit fünf Jahren geschieden. 6 Ich habe zwei Kinder – einen Sohn und eine Tochter. 7 Mein Mann ist vor drei Jahren nach Amerika zurückgegangen. 8 In der amerikanischen Armee. 9 Manchester hat keine U-Bahn. 10 Sie hat Medizin studiert. 11 Sie ist seit etwa zehn Jahren Ärztin.

11C 1E. 2G. 3C. 4K. 5F. 6H. 7J. 8D. 9B. 10L. 11A.

11D 1 gearbeitet. 2 gehabt. 3 zurückgegangen. 4 gekommen. 5 gewohnt. 6 gewußt. 7 kennengelernt. 8 studiert. 9 gelebt. 10 gemacht.

11E 1 arbeiten. 2 hat. 3 geht . . . zurück. 4 kommt. 5 wohnt. 6 weiß. 7 lernt . . . kennen. 8 studiert. 9 leben. 10 machen.

11G 1 ich: nom[inative]. 2 Sie: nom. 3 Wir: nom. 4 Ihnen: dat[ive]. 5 ihr: dat. 6 mich: acc[usative]. 7 Ihnen: dat. 8 uns: dat. 9 es: nom. 10 sie: nom. 11 ihnen: dat. 12 sie: acc. 13 ihn: acc. 14 er: nom. 15 sie: nom. 16 mir: dat. 17 Sie: acc.

11H 1 sie. 2 er. 3 sie. 4 ihnen. 5 ihm. 6 ihr. 7 sie. 8 ihn. 9 sie.

11J 1 sie. 2 er. 3 es. 4 ihn. 5 sie. 6 Es. 7 es. 8 ihn. 9 sie. 10 ihm.

11K Herr Bennett arbeitet in York in einer großen Universitätsbuchhandlung. Er war verheiratet, aber jetzt ist er seit fünf Jahren geschieden. Sein Sohn ist neun Jahre alt, und seine

Tochter ist sieben Jahre alt. Seine Kinder leben bei seiner ehemaligen Frau. Sie arbeitet als Ärztin in Schottland. Sie hat in Manchester Medizin studiert. Dort hat er sie auch kennengelernt.

11L 1 einem. 2 der. 3 im *or* in dem. 4 einem. 5 einer. 6 einem. 7 einer. 8 der. 9 der. 10 der.

11M 1 Er fährt . . . ab. 2 Er kommt . . . an. 3 Es macht . . . auf. 4 Sie macht . . . zu. 5 Er geht . . . aus.

12A (der) Abend, Bohnensalat, Buchhändler, Bus, Dienstag, Kaffee, Mai, Mittwoch, Montag, Nachtisch, Obstsalat, Ort, Schinken, Sohn, Sonntag, Stadtplan, Stock, Weg, Weißwein, Zug. (das) Beispiel, Café, Einzelzimmer, Fenster, Geschäft, Hotel, Hotelrestaurant, Jahr, Kind, Konzert, Krankenhaus, Restaurant, Rührei, Schiff, Stück, Theater, Viertel, Wetter, Zimmer. (die) Ansichtskarte, Ärztin, Briefmarke, Dusche, Frau, Hafenstadt, Heide, Nacht, Ostsee, Sahne, Stadtrundfahrt, Tochter, Torte, Überfahrt, Universitätsbuchhandlung, Universitätsstadt, Zusammenfassung, Zwiebelsuppe.

12B 1 Herr Bennett ist geschieden. 2 Er ist in England aufgewachsen. 3 Er hat auf dem Schiff geschlafen. 4 Vor vierzig Jahren. 5 Anschließend ist er mit Frau Dettmann in ein Café gegangen. 6 Sie haben sehr viel gemeinsam. 7 Sein Zimmer ist im ersten Stock. 8 Am ersten Abend. 9 Für fünf Nächte. 10 Wer weiß?

12C 1 Er hat . . . gekauft. 2 Er hat . . . gefragt. 3 Er hat . . . gebucht. 4 Er hat . . . reserviert. 5 Er hat . . . bestellt. 6 Er hat . . . gemacht. 7 Er hat . . .kennengelernt. 8 Frau Dettmann und Herr Bennett haben . . . festgestellt.

12D 1 gearbeitet. 2 gewohnt. 3 gelebt.

12E 1 Peter Bennett ist . . . aufgewachsen. 2 Er ist . . . gezogen. 3 Er ist . . . abgefahren. 4 Er hat . . . geschlafen. 5 Er ist . . . angekommen. 6 Er ist . . . gegangen. 7 Er hat . . . getrunken. 8 Er hat . . . gesessen. 9 Er hat . . . gegessen. 10 Frau Dettmann und Herr Bennett haben sich . . . unterhalten.

12F kennenlernen > kennengelernt; feststellen > festgestellt;

aufwachsen > aufgewachsen; abfahren > abgefahren; ankommen > angekommen.

12G 1 Dienstag. 2 Zwiebelsuppe. 3 Schiff. 4 Weißwein. 5 Rostock. 6 Tochter. 7 geschieden. 8 Krankenhaus. 9 anschließend.

12H 1 vor drei Tagen . . . gebucht. 2 vor vier Stunden . . . gemacht. 3 vor elf Jahren . . . kennengelernt.4 vor zwei Monaten . . . gekauft. 5 Vor zwei Tagen . . . angekommen. 6 Vor zehn Jahren . . . gefahren. 7 vor zwanzig Minuten . . . geregnet. 8 vor vier Jahren . . . geschneit. 9 fünf Wochen verheiratet. 10 den Kindern. 11 (ein)hunderttausend Einwohnern.

12J (e.g.) 1 I don't eat ice-cream. 2 I don't drink beer. 3 . . . doesn't have an underground/subway. 4 I'm not hungry. 5 . . . doesn't have (any)/has no children. 6 . . . has run out of red wine! 7 . . . didn't order Sylvaner . . . 8 I'm not sleeping in a double room . . . 9 I'm afraid we haven't any at all. 10 I've had enough (of) coffee . . .

12K 2 kein: acc. neut. sing. 3 keine: acc. fem. sing. 4 keinen: acc. masc. sing. 5 keine: acc. pl. 6 keinen: acc. masc. sing. 7 keinen: acc. masc. sing. 8 keinem: dat. neut. sing. 9 keine: acc. pl. 10 keinen: acc. masc. sing.

12L 1 keinen. 2 keine. 3 keinen. 4 keine. 5 keinen. 6 kein. 7 keine. 8 kein. 9 kein. 10 keine.

12M 1 Ich habe mich mit ihr unterhalten. 2 Sie unterhält sich mit ihm. 3 Peter Bennett hat sich mit mir unterhalten. 4 Heidi hat sich mit Ihnen unterhalten. 5 Wir haben uns mit den Kindern unterhalten. 6 Frau Dettmann und Herr Bennett haben sich lange und lebhaft unterhalten. 7 Sie haben sich mit den Einwohnern unterhalten. 8 Die Einwohner haben sich mit ihnen unterhalten.

13A (der) Abend, Bahnhof, Damm, Eingang, Komponist, Mittwoch, Platz, Spaß, Vorschlag. (das) Konzert, Rathaus, Schloß, Viertel. (die) Einfahrt, Idee, Linie, Lust, Nacht, Richtung, U-Bahn-Station, Uhr

13B 1 Was haben Sie morgen abend vor? 2 Ich habe nichts Besonderes vor. 3 Ich möchte gern ins Schloßkonzert gehen. 4 Aber lieber nicht allein! 5 Um wieviel Uhr fängt das Konzert an? 6 Wo wollen wir uns treffen? 7 Sagen wir am Schloßeingang um Viertel vor sieben. 8 Abgemacht! 9 Viel Spaß morgen früh! 10 Danke, gleichfalls!

13C 1 fängt . . . an. 2 fährt . . . ab. 3 haben . . .vor. 4 kommt . . . an. 5 schlage vor . . . 6 komme . . . mit. 7 fängt . . . an. 8 macht . . .zu. 9 macht . . .auf. 10 geht . . . aus.

13D 2 abgefahren. 3 vorgehabt. 4 angekommen. 5 vorgeschlagen. 6 angefangen. 7 zugemacht. 8 aufgemacht. 8 ausgegangen. 9 kennengelernt.

13E 1 etwas Deutsches. 2 nichts Ungewöhnliches. 3 etwas Großartiges. 4 etwas Elegantes. 5 nichts Alkoholisches. 6 etwas Eßbares. 7 etwas Neues. 8 nichts Wichtiges. 9 etwas Witziges. 10 etwas Wahres. 11 nichts Besseres. 12 nichts Genaues.

13F 1 in den: acc. 2 in den: acc. 3 ins (in das): acc. 4 in die: acc. 5 ins (in das): acc. 6 in der: dat. 7 in die: acc. 8 im (in dem): dat. 9 im (in dem): dat. 10 in der: dat.

13G an der: 1, 3, 5, 9 am: 2, 4, 6, 7, 8, 10

13H 1 Das Theater fängt um halb neun an. 2 Der Film fängt um zehn (Minuten) vor sieben an. 3 Die Oper fängt um halb acht an. 4 Der Zug kommt um zwanzig Uhr dreiundfünfzig (sieben Minuten vor neun) an. 5 Die Kirche fängt um Viertel nach zehn an. 6 Der Bus fährt um Viertel vor neun ab.

13J 1 Der, ist, am, in. 2 Er, ist, am, in. 3 ist, er, nur, in, in, der. 4 Am, es, ein, im, in. 5 Das, am. 6 Das, um, Uhr, an. 7 und, ins. 8 Sie, um, vor, am.

13K 1 Zimmer . . . 2 Obst . . . 3 Reise . . . 4 Bau . . . 5 Schloß . . . 6 Bahn . . . 7 Eisenbahn . . . 8 Hotel . . . 9 Stand . . . 10 Post . . . 11 Stadt . . . 12 Speise . . . 13 Brief . . . 14 Zwiebel . . . 15 Bus . . . 16 Nuß . . . 17 Ostsee . . . 18 Buch . . . 19 Zimmer . . . 20. Hafen . . .

13M 1 Was haben Sie morgen vor? 2 Ich höre besonders gern Beethoven/Beethoven höre ich besonders gern. 3 Wo liegt/ist der Kurfürstendamm? 4 Ich möchte (gern) ins Konzert gehen. 5 Ich schlage vor . . . /Ich habe folgenden/einen Vorschlag. 6 Was schlagen Sie vor? 7 Wo wollen wir uns treffen? 8 Vor dem Bahnhof. 9 Abgemacht! 10 Ich danke Ihnen ganz herzlich für den schönen Abend.

14A (der) Barock, Frühaufsteher, Garten, Konzertsaal, Platz, Schlager, Stadtplan. (das) Barock, Instrument, Kind, Klavier, Konzert, Museum, Problem, Tier. (die) Harfe, Linie, Lust, Musik, Nacht, Renaissance, Richtung, S-Bahn, Station, U-Bahn, Uhr, Unterhaltung.

14B 1 Sagen Sie, hätten Sie Lust, mit mir morgen vormittag ein Museum zu besuchen? 2 Wie wär's mit mehr Musik? 3 Aus der Renaissance und (aus) dem Barock. 4 Ich interessiere mich vor allem für alte Harfen. 5 Ich höre gern Musik. 6 Ich höre viel lieber klassische Musik. 7 Nach meinem Stadtplan ist das Museum hinter der Philharmonie. 8 Die nächste S-Bahn-Station ist . . . 9 Oder ist das vielleicht zu früh? 10 Wollen wir mal sehen!

14E 1 wirklich hervorragend. 2 ganz ausgezeichnet. 3 einfach ideal.

14F 1 hervorragend. 2 weltberühmt. 3 hat viele Museen. 4 Harfe und Klavier gespielt. 5 viel lieber klassische Musik. 6 um zehn Uhr. 7 Konzertsaal ist für Mozart einfach ideal! 8 interessiert sich vor allem für alte Harfen. 9 gibt es keine U-Bahn(-Station). 10 ist Frühaufsteher. 11 spielt kein Instrument. 12 ist in der Tiergartenstraße hinter der Philharmonie.

14G 1 mehr Kaffee. 2 einem Eis. 3 einer Tasse Tee. 4 einem Stück Kuchen. 5 einer Berliner Weiße. 6 einem Museum. 7 einem Riesling. 8 einem Rotwein. 9 einem Fensterplatz. 10 einer Oper.

15A (der) Monat, See, Sonntag, Spaziergang, Wald. (das) Baby, Hobby, Museum, Tennis, Wasser, Wetter. (die) Entschuldigung, Freizeit, Idee, Luft, Musik, Nähe, Sonne, Tollwut, Wanderung.

15B 1 Das Museum hat mir gut gefallen. 2 Ich brauche jetzt frische Luft. 3 Ich habe eigentlich zu viele Hobbys und zu wenig Freizeit. 4 Man muß sich dran gewöhnen. 5 Ich lese viel, höre Musik. 6 Ich mache eine lange Wanderung drei- bis viermal im Monat. 7 In der

Nähe von York. 8 Ich spiele furchtbar schlecht Tennis. 9 Ich schwimme nicht gut. 10 Das Wetter ist einmalig!

15C 1D. 2C. 3E. 4B. 5A.

15D 1 brauchst. 2 machst. 3 sagst. 4 findest. 5 glaubst. 6 hörst. 7 spielst. 8 wanderst. 9 besuchst. 10 gefällst. 11 scheinst. 12 dankst. 13 gehst. 14 fährst. 15 schläfst.

15E 1 dir. 2 dir. 3 Spielst du. 4 hast du. 5 dich. 6 Hast du. 7 fährst du. 8 glaubst du? 9 dir! 10 dich.

15F 1 Er spielt gern Tennis. 2 Er besucht gern Museen. 3 Er schwimmt gern. 4 Er wandert gern. 5 Er liest gern. 6 Er hört gern Musik. 7 Sie schwimmt nicht gern. 8 Sie spielt nicht gern Tennis. 9 Sie besuchen gern Museen. 10 Sie wandern gern. 11 Sie lesen gern. 12 Sie hören gern Musik.

15G 1 trinke lieber. 2 spiele lieber. 3 höre lieber. 4 gehe lieber. 5 besuche lieber. 6 mache lieber. 7 wandere lieber/mache lieber lange Wanderungen. 8 fahre lieber. 9 lese lieber. 10 schlafe lieber.

15H 1 gut. 2 frische. 3 einmalig. 4 schön. 5 Tolle. 6 schnell. 7 eigentlich. 8 furchtbar schlecht. 9 möglich. 10 herrlich.

16A (der) Apparat, Arzt, Augenblick, Erfolg, Fuß, Herr, Knöchel, Knochen, Moment, Morgen. (das) Glück, Hotel, Krankenhaus, Telefon. (die) Besserung, Ecke, Frau, Gesundheit, Mühe, Nummer, Praxis, Sekunde, Uhr.

16B 1 Einen Moment, ich verbinde Sie. 2 Kann ich (bitte) mit Frau Dettmann sprechen? 3 Wie geht's? 4 Es tut mir furchtbar leid. 5 Heute vormittag. 6 Bist du krank? 7 Ich glaube, er ist verstaucht aber nicht gebrochen. 8 Dummerweise bin ich vor dem Hotel hingefallen. 9 Armer Peter! 10 Zum Glück gibt es eine Praxis gleich um die Ecke. 11 Ruf mich um zwei Uhr wieder an! 12 Gute Besserung!

16C 1 Es tut uns leid. 2 Es tut Heidi leid. 3 Es tut ihr leid. 4 Es tut Peter leid. 5 Es tut ihm leid. 6 Es tut ihnen leid. 7 Es tut dir leid. 8 Es tut Ihnen leid.

16D 1 mir nicht so gut. 2 mir . . . furchtbar schlecht. 3 ihm . . . sehr gut. 4 ihr einmalig gut. 5 ihnen ausgezeichnet.

16F 1 Kann . . . sprechen? 2 können . . . treffen. 3 muß. 4 kannst . . . gehen? 5 kann . . . gehen. 6 kann . . . helfen. 7 kannst . . . helfen.

17A (der) Arzt, Augenblick, Dank, Empfang, Fuß, Gott, Herr, Hut, Knöchel, Moment, Tag. (das) Blut, Geld, Hotel, Kaufhaus, Kleid, Zimmer. (die) Bank, Durchblutung, Hose, Jacke, Methode, Sekunde, Stunde.

17B 1 Gott sei Dank! 2 Augenblick, ich verbinde Sie. 3 Hast du (dir) was Schönes gekauft? 4 Ich gratuliere! 5 Kann ich (bitte) mit Herrn Bennett sprechen? 6 Die Banken machen in einer Stunde zu. 7 Ich bin einkaufen gegangen. 8 Es geht mir viel besser. 9 Was hat der Arzt gesagt? 10 Was meinst du?

17C 1D. 2F. 3K. 4A. 5L. 6E. 7B. 8H. 9C. 10J. 11G.

17D 1 something good. 2 sg. worth seeing. 3 sg. new. 4 sg. smart. 5 sg. alcoholic. 6 sg. edible. 7 nothing bad/serious. 8 ng. important. 9 sg. nice. 10 sg. true. 11 ng. better. 12 ng. special.

17E 1J. 2G. 3P. 4E. 5M. 6A. 7H. 8D. 9F. 10N. 11C. 12K. 13B. 14L.

17F 1 eine schicke graue. 2 ein süßes schwarzes. 3 eine sehr preiswerte weiße. 4 einen großen breiten. 5 herrliches. 6 einen hervorragenden deutschen. 7 die dritte. 8 eine lange. 9 gute. 10 frische. 11 eine tolle. 12 tolle.

17G 1 älter. 2 jünger. 3 jünger. 4 älter. 5 nicht so alt. 6 genau so alt. 7 älter. 8 nicht so alt.

17H 1 die vornehmste. 2 die interessanteste. 3 die größte. 4 das schönste. 5 die älteste. 6 der beliebteste. 7 das nächste. 8 der nächste. 9 die neueste. 10 den stärksten.

17J 1 Kalkutta. 2 Auckland. 3 Alice Springs. 4 Winnipeg. 5 Alice Springs. 6 Kalkutta. 7 Fort William. 8 Kalkutta.

18A (der) Angestellte [ein Angestellter], Ausweis, Dank, Moment, Pfennig, Reisepaß, Reisescheck, Scheck, Tag. (das) Wechselgeld. (die) Angestellte, Auszahlung, Bank, Kasse, Mark.

18B 1 Unterschreiben Sie bitte hier! 2 Ich möchte einen Reisescheck wechseln. 3 Darf ich Ihren Ausweis oder Reisepaß sehen? 4 Auf der Bank. 5 An der ersten Kasse. 6 Freitag nachmittag. 7 Einen kleinen Moment bitte! 8 Das sind zweihundertfünfunddreißig Mark.

18D 1 Ä wie Ärger. 2 Ypsilon. 3 Übermut. 4 Ulrich 5 Julius. 6 Viktor. 7 Emil. 8 Ökonom. 9 Cäsar. 10 Ida. 11 Xanthippe. 12 Anton. 13 Richard. 14 Ludwig. 15 Nordpol. 16 Samuel. 17 Berta. 18 Kaufmann. 19 Friedrich. 20. Zacharias.

18E 1 sechste ... Dora. 2 achtundzwanzigste ... Wilhelm. 3 neunzehnte ... Paul. 4 zehnte ... Heinrich. 5 vierundzwanzigste ... Theodor. 6 siebzehnte ... Otto. 7 vierzehnte ... Ludwig. 8 zwanzigste ... Quelle.

18F (a) Anton, Cäsar, Emil, Friedrich, Gustav, Heinrich, Julius, Ludwig, Otto, Paul, Richard, Samuel, Theodor, Ulrich, Viktor, Wilhelm, Zacharias. (b) Berta, Charlotte, Dora, Ida, Martha, Xanthippe. (c) Ärger, Kaufmann, Nordpol, Ökonom, Quelle, Schule, Übermut, Ypsilon.

18G Nordpol. 2 Schule. 3 Ökonom. 4 Kaufmann. 5 Ärger. 6 Ypsilon. 7 Übermut. 8 Quelle.

19A (der) Frühling, Herbst, Kaffee, Sommer, Unterschied, Winter. (das) Beispiel, Deutsch, Englisch, Essen, Stadtzentrum, Wetter. (die) Innenstadt, Jahreszeit, Straße.

19B 1 Wie ist das Wetter? 2 Zum Beispiel. 3 Was sonst? 4 Wie schmeckt dir das deutsche Essen? 5 Berlin ist anders als York. 6 Ich ziehe den Frühling vor. 7 Nicht so gut! 8 Genau so schlecht! 9 Was ist der größte Unterschied? 10 Der deutsche Kaffee ist mir manchmal zu stark.

19C 1B. 2F. 3D. 4A. 5E. 6C.

19E 1 älter. 2 breiter. 3 eng. 4 gut; besser. 5 größt–. 6 heiß. 7 kühl. 8 kälter. 9 schlecht. 10 stark. 11 schönst-. 12 warm; wärmer.

19K 1 trinke gern. 2 trinke lieber. 3 trinke am liebsten. 4 spiele gern. 5 spiele lieber. 6 spiele am liebsten. 7 esse gern. 8 esse lieber. 9 esse am liebsten. 10 gehe gern. 11 gehe lieber. 12 gehe am liebsten. 13 höre gern. 14 höre lieber. 15 höre am liebsten.

19M 1 Nouns (x2). 2 Verbs. 3 indefinite article (x2). 4 adjectives. 5 ordinal number. 6 Modal verbs. 7 compounds. 8 Prepositions. 9 separable verbs. 10 prefix. 11 reflexive. 12 dative plural. 13 perfect. 14 past participle. 15 comparatives. 16 superlatives. 17 auxiliary. 18 direct object. 19 adverb(s). 20. indirect object.

20A (der) Abend, Appetit, Dank, Frühling, Fuß, Herr, Hut, Imbiß, Kellner, Plan, Rückblick, Schuß, September, Spaziergang, Tag, Urlaub, Waldmeister, Zukunftsplan. (das) Jahr, Kompliment, Konzert, Schiff, Wohl. (die) Einladung, Heimat, Himbeere, Jahreszeit, Schuld, Stadtrundfahrt, Woche, Zeit, Zukunft.

20B 1 Wie wär's mit einer Berliner Weiße? 2 Und wie wär's mit einem Imbiß dazu? 3 Übrigens ... 4 Der neue Hut steht dir unwahrscheinlich gut. 5 Ich habe noch eine Woche Urlaub in diesem Jahr. 6 Komm doch auch mal 'rüber nach England! 7 Aber das war natürlich meine eigene Schuld. 8 Ich glaube, Berliner Weiße ist genau richtig. 9 Wie die Zeit vergeht! 10 Sag mir nur wann!

20C 1S. 2K. 3F. 4G. 5B. 6L. 7C. 8A. 9H. 10D. 11R. 12P. 13Q. 14E. 15M. 16N. 17J.

20D 1D. 2N. 3K. 4J. 5C. 6H. 7F. 8R. 9A. 10E. 11S. 12Q. 13B. 14T. 15M. 16P. 17L. 18G.

20F 1 On Sunday Peter Bennett left York. 2 On Monday morning he arrived in Berlin. First he drank something in a café and bought a street map and postcards in a stationer's shop. Then he went to the hotel. 3 On Monday evening he dined in the hotel restaurant. 4 On Tuesday afternoon he went on a sightseeing tour and made the acquaintance of Heidi Dettmann. 5 On Tuesday evening Peter and Heidi had a long and lively chat and drank Berliner Weisse together. 6 On Wednesday evening they were in Schloss Charlottenburg. There they heard an outstanding Mozart concert. 7 On Thursday morning they visited the world-famous Berlin museum of musical instruments. 8 On Thursday afternoon they went for a walk by the Wannsee. The weather was out of this world! 9 On Friday morning Peter fell down in front of the hotel and slightly sprained his foot. Heidi was successful with her shopping. 10 On Friday afternoon they went to the bank together. Then Peter bought himself a hat. 11 On Friday evening, in a café on the Kurfürstendamm, they planned a second trip to Berlin. Peter also invited Heidi to England.

20H Ja: 11.1; 11.3; 13.1; 14.1; 15.4; 15.5; 16.1; 16.3; 17.5; 19.3; 20.4; 20.7; 20.8 Nein: 11.4; 11.5; 11.6; 13.2; 13.3; 13.4; 14.2; 14.3; 14.4; 14.5; 14.6; 14.7; 14.8; 14.9; 15.1; 15.2; 15.3; 16.2; 17.1; 17.2; 17.3; 17.4; 19.1; 19.2; 19.4; 20.1; 20.2; 20.3; 20.5; 20.6.

20K 1.1 Sachertorte. 2.1 Ansichtskarte. 3.1 Entschuldigung! 3.2 links. 4.1 Lift. 4.2 Engländerin. 5.1 Fräulein (x2). 5.2 Sylvaner ... Riesling. 5.3 trocken ... süß. 5.4 Das stimmt! 6.1 Uhr... Uhr. 6.2 Europa-Center. 7.1 Meine Damen und Herren! 7.2 zum Beispiel. 7.3 Berlin-Mitte. 7.4 Unter den Linden. 7.5 heiße Jochen. 7.6 Zeit. 8.1 Deutscher. 8.2 Ausland. 8.3 Berliner Weiße. 8.4 Saft. 8.5 Darf. 9.1 Frau ... Fräulein. 9.2 vorgestern. 10.1 Nordsee ... Baltic. 11.1 das heißt. 11.2 Untergrund ... Bahn. 11.3 Ärztin. 12.1 am fünften Mai. 12.2 vielleicht. 13.1 auch. 13.2 Damm. 13.3 Richard Wagner. 13.4 Abgemacht! 14.1 Museen. 14.2 Tiergarten ... Tier. 15.1 Wannsee. 16.1 Apparat. 16.2 Knochen. 16.3 Gute Besserung! 17.1 KaDeWe. 17.2 billig. 18.1 Ausweis. 19.1 England. 19.2 gegessen. 20.1 Schuß ... Himbeere. 20.2 Urlaub. 20.3 Zum Wohl! 20.4 genommen. 20.5 Heimat. 20.6 wahr.

German–English glossary

Abbreviations

=	same as
acc.	accusative
adj.	adjective
adv.	adverb
art.	article
comp.	comparative
dat.	dative
interrog.	interrogative
irreg.	irregular
L	Lektion
n.	noun
nf.	noun feminine
nm.	noun masculine
nn.	noun neuter
num.	numeral, number
poss.	possessive
pp.	past participle
prep.	preposition
pron.	pronoun
refl.	reflexive
reg.	regular
sep.	separable
v.	verb

Nouns

The gender of nouns is indicated by the definite article in the nominative case before and by an abbreviation after each noun, e.g.:

der **Abend** *nm.*

The plural forms of most nouns have been given in full at the end of each entry, e.g.

der **Abend** *nm.* evening *Abende*

Plurals of 'professions' and 'peoples' have not been listed. Note that for 'peoples' the following pattern is very common:

Engländ*er*	*see*	*pl.* **Engländ*er***
Engländ*erin*	*see*	*pl.* **Engländ*erinnen***

Verbs

Verbs are entered under their infinitive form. At the end of each verb entry, the **er/sie/es** form of the present and of the perfect tense are given, e.g.

abfahren . . .	*fährt ab;*	*ist abgefahren*
fragen . . .	*fragt;*	*hat gefragt*

Many irregular verb forms have been given separate entries and cross-referenced with their infinitives, e.g.

abgefahren	*see*	*abfahren*
nimmt	*see*	*nehmen*

Adjectives and adverbs

Where a German word is commonly used as both adjective and adverb, this is generally indicated, e.g.

schnell *adj./adv.* quick(ly), fast

Almost all the German words occurring in *Colloquial German* are listed below with the English meanings that they have in the book. A good dictionary may give additional meanings or uses.

der **Abend** *nm.* evening *Abende*
das **Abendessen** *nn.* dinner, evening meal *–essen*
aber but
abfahren *v. irreg. sep.* leave (of or by vehicle) *fährt ab*; *ist abgefahren*
die **Abfahrt** *nf.* departure (by vehicle) *Abfahrten*
abgefahren *see abfahren*
abgemacht *adj./pp.* agreed
abholen *v. reg. sep.* fetch, collect *holt ab*; *hat abgeholt*
acht *num.* eight
achtzig *num.* eighty
acht– *ordinal* eighth
Aerobic *nn.* aerobics
aktiv *adj./adv.* active(ly), energetic(ally)
alkoholisch *adj.* alcoholic (drink)
alle *pron. plural/adj.* all
allein *adj.* (*not used in front of nouns*) alone
alleinstehend *adj.* single, unattached
alles *pron.* everything
als *adv.* than *mehr als*: more than
also *adv.* so, therefore
alt *adj.* old *comp. älter*
am = *an dem*
Amerika *nn.* America, United States of America
der **Amerikaner** *nm.*/die **Amerikanerin** *nf.* American
amerikanisch *adj.* American
an *prep.* + *acc./dat.* on, at . . .
anders *adv.* different(ly)
anderthalb = *eineinhalb num.* one and a half
anfangen *v. irreg. sep.* begin, start *fängt an*; *hat angefangen*
angefangen *see anfangen*
angekommen *see ankommen*
angeln *v. reg.* fish, go fishing *angelt*; *hat geangelt*
angeschwollen *adj./pp.* swollen
ankommen *v. irreg. sep.* arrive *kommt an*; *ist angekommen*
die **Ankunft** *nf.* arrival *Ankünfte*
annehmen *v. irreg. sep.* accept, suppose *nimmt an*; *hat angenommen*
anrufen *v. irreg. sep.* call by phone *ruft an*; *hat angerufen*
anschließend *adv.* after that, subsequently
die **Ansichtskarte** *nf.* picture postcard *-karten*
anstrengend *adj.* exhausting
der **Apfelstrudel** *nm.* apple strudel (cake)
die **Apotheke** *nf.* chemist's/drug-store *Apotheken*
der **Apparat** *nm. Am Apparat!* 'Speaking!'(on phone)
der **Appetit** *nm.* appetite *Guten Appetit!* 'Enjoy your meal!'
die **Aprikosenmarmelade** *nf.* apricot jam *–marmeladen*
April *nm.* April
arbeiten *v. reg.* work *arbeitet*; *hat gearbeitet*
arbeitslos *adj.* unemployed
der **Architekt** *nm.*/die **Architektin** *nf.* architect
der **Ärger** *nm.* annoyance, trouble, bother
arm *adj.* poor
die **Armee** *nf.* army *Armeen*
der **Arzt** *nm.*/die **Ärztin** *nf.* doctor (medical)
auch *adv.* also, as well, too
auf *prep.* + *acc./dat.* on, at . . .

aufgewachsen *see aufwachsen*
aufmachen *v. reg. sep.* open *macht auf; hat aufgemacht*
aufstehen *v. irreg. sep.* get up, rise *steht auf; ist aufgestanden*
aufwachsen *v. irreg. sep.* grow up *wächst auf; ist aufgewachsen*
der **Aufzug** *nm.* lift/elevator *Aufzüge*
der **Augenblick** *nm.* moment, second *Augenblicke*
August *nm.* August
aus *prep. + dat.* from, out of
ausführen *v. reg. sep.* take for walk *führt aus; hat ausgeführt*
ausgehen *v. irreg. sep.* go out *geht aus; ist ausgegangen*
ausgezeichnet *adj./pp.* excellent
das **Ausland** *nn.* abroad
der **Ausländer** *nm.*/die **Ausländerin** *nf.* foreigner
ausrichten *v. reg. sep.* pass on a message *richtet aus; hat ausgerichtet*
(sich) **ausruhen** *v. reg. (refl.) sep.* rest *ruht aus; hat ausgeruht*
außerdem *adv.* besides, in addition
aussteigen *v. irreg. sep.* get out/off (a vehicle) *steigt aus; ist ausgestiegen*
Australien *nn.* Australia
der **Ausweis** *nm.* identity card *Ausweise*
die **Auszahlung** *nf.* payment, pay-out *–zahlungen*
das **Auto** *nn.* car *Autos*

das **Bad** *nn.* bath *Bäder*
die **Bahn** *nf.* railway/railroad *Bahnen*
der **Bahnhof** *nm.* station (train) *–höfe*
bald *adv.* soon
das **Ballett** *nn.* ballet
die **Bank** *nf.* bank *Banken*
der/das **Barock** *nm./nn.* the Baroque
Basler Leckerli *nn.* honey cake from Basel
basteln *v. reg.* make things *bastelt; hat gebastelt*
der **Baustil** *nm.* building/architectural style *–stile*
ein **Beamter** *nm.*/eine **Beamtin** *nf.* civil servant
bei *prep. + dat.* with, at ... *bei mir*: at my place
beide *pron./adj.* both
das **Beispiel** *nn.* example *Beispiele*
bekannt *adj.* known, well known
bekommen *v. irreg.* get *bekommt; hat bekommen*
beliebt *adj.* popular
der **Berliner** *nm.*/die **Berlinerin** *nf.* Berliner
der **Beruf** *nm.* profession, job *Berufe*
berühmt *adj.* famous
besonder–/besonders *adj./adv.* special(ly)
besser *see gut*
die **Besserung** *nf.* improvement, recovery
bestanden *adj./pp.* passed (of test or exam)
bestellen *v. reg.* order (goods, a service) *bestellt; hat bestellt*
bestimmt *adv.* certainly, surely
bestrichen *adj./pp.* coated, spread
best– *see gut*
besuchen *v. reg.* visit *besucht; hat besucht*
das **Bett** *nn.* bed *Betten*

bewegen *v. reg.* move (something) *bewegt; hat bewegt*
bezahlen *v. reg.* pay *bezahlt*
der **Bezirk** *nm.* administrative district *Bezirke*
das **Bier** *nn.* beer
bieten *v. irreg.* offer *bietet; hat geboten*
billig *adj./adv.* cheap, inexpensive
bin *see sein v.*
bis *prep. + acc.* until
(ein) **bißchen** *adv.* a little, a bit, rather
bist *see sein v.*
bitte please, don't mention it, etc.
bleiben *v. irreg.* remain, stay *bleibt; ist geblieben*
der **Bohnensalat** *nm.* bean salad *–salate*
brauchen *v. reg./irreg.* need *braucht; hat gebraucht*
brechen *v. irreg.* break *bricht; hat gebrochen*
breit *adj.* broad, wide
Bridge *nn.* bridge = card game
der **Brief** *nm.* letter *Briefe*
die **Briefmarke** *nf.* postage stamp *–marken*
das **Buch** *nn.* book *Bücher*
buchen *v. reg.* book *bucht; hat gebucht*
der **Buchhändler** *nm.*/die **Buchhändlerin** *nf.* book dealer, bookshop assistant
die **Buchhandlung** *nf.* bookshop *–handlungen*
buchstabieren *v. reg.* spell *buchstabiert*
die **Buchstabiertafel** *see Tafel, buchstabieren*
die **Bundesbahn** *nf.* Federal Railway
die **Bundespost** *nf.* Federal Post Office
ein **Büroangestellter** *nm.*/eine **Büroangestellte** *nf.* office employee
der **Bus** *nm.* bus, coach *Busse*
der **Busfahrer** *nm.*/die **Busfahrerin** *nf.* bus driver
die **Busfahrt** *see Fahrt, Bus*
die **Bushaltestelle** *nf.* bus stop *–stellen*

das **Café** *nn.* café *Cafés*
der **Campingplatz** *nm.* camp(ing) site *–plätze*
circa *adv.* approximately, about (*with nos.*)
cis C sharp (music)
clever *adj.* clever, smart

da *adv.* there, here
dabei *see* L17
dadurch *adv.* through that, thereby
dafür *see* L14
die **Dame** *nf.* lady *Damen*
damit *see* L14
der **Damm** *nm.* causeway *Dämme*
danach *adv.* then, thereafter
danke thanks, thank you
danken (für) *v. reg. + dat.* thank (for) *dankt; hat gedankt*
dann *adv.* then, next
daran *see* L14
darauf *see* L14
darf *see dürfen*
darum *see* L14
dauern *v. reg.* last (of time) *dauert; hat gedauert*
dazu *adv.* in addition, with it
dein *poss.* your (relates to *du*)
denken (an) + *acc. v. irreg.* think (of) *denkt; hat gedacht*

denn for, because
deutsch *adj./adv.* German
Deutsch *nn.* German (language)
ein **Deutscher** *nm.*/eine **Deutsche** *nf.* German (person)
Deutschland *nn.* Germany
Dezember *nm.* December
der **Dichter** *nm.*/die **Dichterin** *nf.* poet
Dienstag *nm.* Tuesday
dies– *art./pron.* this
direkt *adj./adv.* direct(ly) *Nicht direkt*: Not exactly!
die **D-Mark** *nf.* Deutsche Mark German currency
doch *adv.* 'after all' etc. (*used for emphasis*)
der **Dolmetscher** nm./die **Dolmetscherin** *nf.* interpreter
die **Donau** *nf.* the Danube
Donnerstag *nm.* Thursday
das **Doppelzimmer** *nn.* double room *–zimmer*
das **Dorf** *nn.* village *Dörfer*
dort *adv.* there
dorthin *adv.* (to) there, 'thither'
dran *see daran see* L14
drei *num.* three
dreißig *num.* thirty
der **Dresdner** *nm.*/die **Dresdnerin** *nf.* Dresdener
dritt– *ordinal* third
drum *see darum see* L14
du *pron.* you (singular, informal)
dumm *adj.* stupid *comp. dümmer*
dummerweise *adv.* stupidly
durch *prep. + acc.* through
die **Durchblutung** *nf.* blood circulation
dürfen *v. modal irreg.* be allowed, can, may *darf*
die **Dusche** *nf.* (bath-)shower *Duschen*
(sich) **duzen** *v. reg.* (*refl.*) use the 'du' form *duzt*; *hat geduzt*

die **Ecke** *nf.* corner *Ecken*
ehemalig *adj.* former
das **Ei** *nn.* egg *Eier*
eigen *adj.* own
eigentlich *adv.* actually, in actual fact
ein, ein– *art./num.* a/one
eineinhalb *see anderthalb*
einfach *adj./adv.* simple, simply
der **Eingang** *nm.* entrance *Eingänge*
einig– adj. a few, some
einkaufen *v. reg. sep.* go shopping *kauft ein*; *hat eingekauft*
die **Einkaufsstraße** *see Straße, einkaufen*
einladen (zu) *v. irreg. sep.* invite (to) *lädt ein*; *hat eingeladen*
einmalig *adj./adv.* unique, superb
eins *num.* one
der **Einwohner** *nm.* inhabitant *Einwohner*
das **Einzelzimmer** *nn.* single room *–zimmer*
das **Eis** *nn.* ice, ice-cream
die **Eisenbahn** *nf.* railway/railroad *–bahnen*
elegant *adj.* elegant, smart
der **Empfang** *nm.* reception *Empfänge*
die **Empfangsdame** *nf.* (female) receptionist *–damen*
empfehlen *v. irreg.* recommend *empfiehlt*; *hat empfohlen*
eng *adj./adv.* narrow
England *nn.* England, UK

der **Engländer** *nm.*/die **Engländerin** *nf.* Englishman/woman
Englisch *nn.* English (language)
englisch *adj.* English
entfernt *adj./adv./pp.* away, at a distance
entlang *prep.* (*follows noun*) along the street: *die Straße entlang*
entschuldigen *v. reg.* excuse, pardon *entschuldigt*; *hat entschuldigt*
die **Entschuldigung** *nf.* apology, excuse *Entschuldigungen*
er *pron.m.* he, it
der **Erfolg** *nm.* success *Erfolge*
erfolgreich *adj./adv.* successful
erreichen *v. reg.* reach, get hold of (on the phone) *erreicht*; *hat erreicht*
erst *adv.* only *erst morgen*: not until tomorrow
erst– *ordinal* first
es *pron. n.* it (also *see es gibt*)
es gibt . . . there is . . ., there are . . .
eßbar *adj.* edible
essen *v. irreg.* eat *ißt*; *hat gegessen*
das **Essen** *nn.* food, meal
etwa *adv.* approximately (*with nos.*) (also *see* Text 9, Note 24)
etwas *pron.* something
euch *see ihr pron.*
euer *poss.* your (*relates to ihr*)
eventuell *adv.* perhaps, possibly

fahren *v. irreg.* go, travel *fährt*; *ist gefahren*
der **Fahrgast** *nm.* passenger *–gäste*
das **Fahrrad** *nn.* bicycle *Fahrräder*
der **Fahrstuhl** *nm.* lift/elevator *–stühle*
die **Fahrt** *nf.* trip, journey *Fahrten*
der **Fall** *nm.* case *auf alle Fälle*: in any case, at any rate
fallen *v. irreg. fall fällt*; *ist gefallen*
familiär *adj.* informal, familiar
die **Familie** *nf.* family *Familien*
fast *adv.* almost
Februar *nm.* February
fein *adj./adv.* fine, refined, distinguished
das **Fenster** *nn.* window *Fenster*
die **Ferien** *n.plural.* school/college vacation(s)
fernsehen *v. irreg. sep.* watch television *sieht fern*; *hat ferngesehen*
feststellen *v. reg. sep.* ascertain, find out *stellt fest*; *hat festgestellt*
der **Film** *nm.* film *Filme*
filmen *v. reg.* film, use a film/video camera *filmt*; *hat gefilmt*
finden *v. irreg.* find *findet*; *hat gefunden*
der **Finger** *nm.* finger *Finger*
das **Fitneßtraining** *nn.* fitness training, keep-fit
die **Flasche** *nf.* bottle *Flaschen*
fliegen *v. irreg.* fly, travel by air *fliegt*; *ist geflogen*
der **Flohmarkt** *nm.* flea market *–märkte*
der **Flughafen** *nm.* airport *–häfen*
der **Fluß** *nm.* river *Flüsse*
fotografieren *v. reg.* take photographs *fotografiert*; *hat fotografiert*
fragen *v. reg.* ask *nach dem Weg fragen*: ask the way *fragt*; *hat gefragt*
der **Franken** *nm.* Swiss currency 100 Rappen

Frankreich *nn.* France
französisch *adj.* French
die **Frau** *nf.* woman, Mrs/Ms (+ *name*) *Frauen*
das **Fräulein** *nn.* waitress, Miss (+ *name*) *Fräulein*
frei *adj./adv.* free
das **Freibad** *nn.* open-air swimming pool *–bäder*
Freitag *nm.* Friday
die **Freizeit** *nf.* free/leisure/spare time
sich **freuen** *v. reg. refl.* be pleased, look forward to *freut*; *hat gefreut*
freundlich *adj./adv.* friendly
frisch *adj./adv.* fresh
früh *adj/adv.* early *Dienstag früh*: Tuesday morning
der **Frühaufsteher** *nm.* early riser *Frühaufsteher*
früher *adj./adv.* previous(ly), earlier
der **Frühling** *nm.* Spring
fünf *num.* five
fünfzig *num.* fifty
für *prep. + acc.* for
furchtbar *adj./adv.* terrible, terribly, very
der **Fuß** *nm.* foot *zu Fuß*: on foot *Füße*
der **Fußball** *nm.* football *Fußbälle*

die **Galerie** *nf.* gallery *Galerien*
ganz *adv.* quite, completely, very
gar nicht *adv.* not at all
garantiert *adj./pp.* guaranteed
der **Garten** *nm.* garden *Gärten*
der **Gast** *nm.* guest *Gäste*
das **Gebäck** *nn.* biscuits, cake, pastries
geben *v. irreg.* give *es gibt*: there is/are *gibt*; *hat gegeben*
geboren *adj/pp.* born
der **Geburtstag** *nm.* birthday *–tage*
gefahren *see fahren*
gefallen *v. irreg. + dat.* please, like *gefällt*; *hat gefallen*
gefallen *see fallen*
geflogen *see fliegen*
gegangen *see gehen*
gegen *prep. + acc.* towards, against
gegessen *see essen*
gehen *v. irreg.* go, walk *wenn's geht*: if possible *wie geht's?* how are you? *geht*; *ist gegangen*
gehören *v. reg. + dat.* belong *gehört*; *hat gehört*
gekühlt *adj./pp.* chilled
das **Geld** *nn.* money
gemeinsam *adj./adv.* in common, together
gemischt *adj./pp.* mixed
genau *adj./adv.* exact(ly)
Genf Geneva
genommen *see nehmen*
genug *adv.* enough
geöffnet *adj./pp.* open(ed)
das **Gepäck** *nn.* luggage
gerade *adj./adv.* straight
geradeaus *adv.* straight ahead, straight on
gern(e) *adv.* willingly *ich esse gern*: I like food/eating
geschieden *adj./pp.* divorced
geschlafen *see schlafen*
geschlossen *adj./pp* shut
gesessen *see sitzen*
gestorben *adj./pp.* dead, died
die **Gesundheit** *nf.* health *Gesundheit!* Bless you!
getrunken *see trinken*

gewaschen *see waschen*

sich **gewöhnen** an + *acc. v. reg. refl.* get used to *gewöhnt sich*; *hat sich gewöhnt*

gewußt *see wissen*

gezogen *see ziehen*

gibt *see geben*

die **Gitarre** *nf.* guitar *Gitarren*

das **Glas** *nn.* glass *Gläser*

glauben *v. reg.* (+ *dat. obj. if person*) believe *glaubte*; *hat geglaubt*

gleich *adv.* immediately *gleich um die Ecke*: just round the corner

gleichfalls *adv.* equally, the same to you

das **Glück** *nn.* fortune, happiness *zum Glück*: fortunately

glücklich *adj.* happy

Golf *nn.* golf

der **Golfplatz** *nm.* golf course *–plätze*

der **Gott** *nm.* god, God *Grüß Gott!* Hello! (*used in south*) *Götter*

der **Grad** *nm. no plural with nums.* degree

gratulieren *v. reg.* + *dat.* congratulate *gratuliert*; *hat gratuliert*

grau *adj.* grey/gray

der **Groschen** *nm.* Austrian currency 100 = 1 Schilling. German coin = 10 Pfennig

groß *adj.* big, large, great *comp. größer*

großartig *adj./adv.* great, marvellous

Großbritannien *nn.* (Great) Britain

grün *adj.* green

grüßen *v. reg.* greet *Grüß Gott!* Hello! (used in south) *grüßt*; *hat gegrüßt*

gültig *adj.* valid

gut; besser; best–/am besten *adj./adv.* good/well; better; best

das **Haar** *nn., usually plural.* hair *Haare*

haben *v. irreg.* have *hat*; *hat gehabt*

der **Hafen** *nm.* harbour, dock, port *Häfen*

die **Hafenstadt** *nf.* seaport/town/city *–städte*

halb *adj./adv.* half, half past *halb drei*: half past two

das **Hallenbad** *nn.* indoor swimming pool *–bäder*

halten *v. irreg.* stop, hold *hält*; *hat gehalten*

die **Harfe** *nf.* harp *Harfen*

hat *see haben*

hätte, hätten *see haben*

der **Hauptbahnhof** *nm.* main station (rail) *–höfe*

die **Hauptstadt** *nf.* capital city *–städte*

das **Haus** *nn.* house *Häuser*

die **Hausfrau** *nf.* housewife *–frauen*

der Hausmann *nm.* houseman *–männer*

die **Heide** *nf.* heath(land)

die **Heimat** *nf.* home town/region

heiß *adj.* hot

heißen *v. irreg. ich heiße*: my name is *das heißt*: that means, i.e. *heißt*; *hat geheißen*

helfen *v. irreg.* + *dat.* help *hilft*; *hat geholfen*

der **Herbst** *nm.* Autumn/Fall

die **Herkunft** *nf.* origin(s)

der **Herr** *nm.* man, gentleman, Mr. (+ *name*) *Herren*

herrlich *adj./adv.* splendid(ly), magnificent(ly)
herüberkommen *v. irreg. sep.* come over, drop by *kommt (he)rüber; ist (he)rübergekommen*
hervorragend *adj.* outstanding
herzlich *adj./adv.* 'heart(il)y', very *Herzlich willkommen!*
heute *adv.* today
hier *adv.* here
hilft *see helfen*
die **Himbeere** *nf.* raspberry *Himbeeren*
hinfallen *v. irreg.* fall down *fällt hin; ist hingefallen*
hinter *prep. + acc./dat.* behind
historisch *adj./adv.* historical(ly)
das **Hobby** *nn.* hobby *Hobbys*
hoch (**hoh–** *before nouns*) *adj.* high *comp. höher*
der **Honig** *nm.* honey
hören *v. reg.* hear, listen to *hört; hat gehört*
die **Hose** *nf.* pair of trousers/pants *Hosen*
das **Hotel** *nn.* hotel *Hotels*
das **Hotelessen** *see Essen, Hotel*
hübsch *adj./adv.* pretty
der **Hund** *nm.* dog *Hunde*
hundert *num.* hundred
der **Hunger** *nm.* hunger
der **Hut** *nm.* hat *Hüte*

ich *pron.* I, me!
ideal *adj.* ideal
die **Idee** *nf.* idea *Ideen*
ihm *pron. dat. see er, es*
ihn *pron. acc. see er*
Ihnen *pron. dat. see Sie* you
ihnen *pron. dat. see sie* they
Ihr *poss.* your (*relates to Sie*)
ihr *poss.* her, its, their (*relates to sie*)
ihr *pron.* you (*plural of* du, *informal*)
ihr *pron. dat. see sie* she, it
im = *in dem*
der **Imbiß** *nm.* snack *Imbisse*
immer *adv.* always *immer geradeaus*: keep going, straight ahead *immer noch*: still
in *prep. + acc./dat.* (in)to, in
der **Inder** *nm.*/die **Inderin** *nf.* Indian (person from India)
Indien *nn.* India
der **Ingenieur** *nm.*/die **Ingenieurin** *nf.* engineer
die **Innenstadt** *nf.* town centre, downtown
die **Insel** *nf.* island *Inseln*
das **Instrument** *nn.* instrument *Instrumente*
interessant *adj.* interesting
sich **interessieren** (für) *v. reg. refl.* be interested in *interessiert sich; hat sich interessiert*
international *adj.* international
inzwischen *adv.* meanwhile, in the meantime
der **Ire** nm./die **Irin** *nf.* Irishman/woman
irgendwie *adv.* somehow (or other)
Irland *nn.* Ireland
ist *see sein v.*

ja yes *ich glaube ja*: I think so
die **Jacke** *nf.* jacket, cardigan *Jacken*
das **Jahr** *nn.* year *Jahre*
die **Jahreszeit** *nf.* season (of the year) *–zeiten*
Januar *nm.* January

der **Jazz** *nm.* jazz
jede– *art./pron.* every *jeden Sonntag*: every Sunday
jetzt *adv.* now
die **Jugendherberge** *nf.* youth hostel *–herbergen*
Juli *nm.* July
jung *adj.* young *comp. jünger*
Juni *nm.* June

der **Kaffee** *nm.* coffee
der **Kaiser** *nm.* emperor *Kaiser*
kalt *adj.* cold *comp. kälter*
Kanada *nn.* Canada
der **Kanadier** nm./die **Kanadierin** *nf.* Canadian (person)
kann *see können*
das **Kännchen** *nn.* pot (of coffee served in a café)
Kapstadt Capetown
die **Karte** *nf.* ticket, card *Karten*
die **Kasse** *nf.* till, check-out, cash desk *Kassen*
die **Kathedrale** *nf.* cathedral *Kathedralen*
kaufen *v. reg.* buy *kauft*; *hat gekauft*
das **Kaufhaus** *nn.* department store *–häuser*
der **Kaufmann** *nm.* businessman, trader, merchant *Kaufleute*
kein *art.* not a, no *ich trinke kein Bier*: I don't drink beer
der **Kellner** *nm.*/die **Kellnerin** *nf.* waiter
kennen *v. irreg.* know, be acquainted with *kennt*; *hat gekannt*
kennenlernen *v. reg. sep.* get to know, become acquainted with *lernt kennen*; *hat kennengelernt*
der **Kilometer** *nm.* kilometre Kilometer
das **Kind** *nn.* child *Kinder*
das **Kino** *nn.* cinema *Kinos*
die **Kirche** *nf.* church *Kirchen*
die **Kirschtorte** *nf.* chocolate gateau made with cherry schnapps *–torten*
klar *adj./adv.* clear *Alles klar?* OK?
klassisch *adj.* classical
klassizistisch *adj.* neo-classical
das **Klavier** *nn.* piano *Klaviere*
das **Kleid** *nn.* dress *Kleider*
klein *adj./adv.* small, little
die **Klinik** *nf.* clinic, hospital *Kliniken*
der **Knöchel** *nm.* ankle *Knöchel*
der **Knochen** *nm.* bone *Knochen*
kochen *v. reg.* cook, boil *kocht*; *hat gekocht*
koffeinfrei *adj.* decaffeinated
der **Koffer** *nm.* suitcase *Koffer*
kommen *v. irreg.* come, get to *kommt*; *ist gekommen*
das **Kompliment** *nn.* compliment *Komplimente*
der **Komponist** *nm.*/die **Komponistin** *nf.* composer
der **König** *nm.*/die **Königin** *nf.* king/queen
können *v. modal irreg.* be able, can *kann*
das **Konzert** *nn.* concert *Konzerte*
der **Konzertsaal** *nm.* concert hall *Konzertsäle*
die **Kopie** *nf.* copy *Kopien*
kosten *v. reg.* cost *kostet*; *hat gekostet*
köstlich *adj./adv.* delicious
krank *adj.* ill *comp. kränker*

das **Krankenhaus** *nn.* hospital *–häuser*
die **Kreditkarte** *nf.* credit card *–karten*
der **Krimi** *nm.* detective/crime story *Krimis*
der **Kuchen** *nm.* cake *Kuchen*
kühl *adj.* cool
die **Kultur** *nf.* culture *Kulturen*
die **Kunst** *nf.* art *Künste*
die **Kunstgalerie** *nf.* art gallery *–galerien*
kurz *adj.* short *comp.* kürzer

das **Land** *nn.* state, country, countryside *Länder*
lang(e) *adj./adv.* long *comp.* länger
langsam *adj./adv.* slow(ly)
leben *v. reg.* live, exist, spend one's life *lebt*; *hat gelebt*
das **Leben** *nn.* life *Leben*
das **Lebensjahr** *see Jahr, Leben*
lebhaft *adj./adv.* lively, in a lively manner
der **Lehrer** *nm.*/die **Lehrerin** *nf.* teacher
leicht *adj./adv.* easy, simple, slightly
leid *adv. es tut mir leid!* I'm sorry
leider *adv.* unfortunately
Leckerli *see Basler*
die **Lektion** *nf.* lesson, chapter, unit *Lektionen*
lernen *v. reg.* learn *lernt*; *hat gelernt*
lesen *v. irreg.* read *liest*; *hat gelesen*
letzt– *adj.* last
lieb *adj./adv.* sweet, kind, nice
lieber *adv.* rather, preferably *ich esse lieber Eis* I prefer ice-cream
lieblich *adj.* medium sweet (of wine)
das **Lieblingspferd** *nn.* favourite horse *–pferde*
liegen *v. irreg.* lie, be situated *liegt*; *hat gelegen*
liest *see lesen*
der **Lift** *nm.* lift, elevator *Lifte/Lifts*
die **Linde** *nf.* lime tree, linden *Linden*
die **Linie** *nf.* line *Linien*
links *adv.* left, to the left, on the left-hand side
link– *adj.* left, left-hand
die **Literatur** *nf.* literature *Literaturen*
das **Loch** *nn.* hole *Löcher*
das **Lokal** *nn.* pub, bar *Lokale*
die **Luft** *nf.* air
die **Lust** *nf. Haben Sie Lust?* Would you like to? Do you fancy . . .?
die **Lyrik** *nf.* poetry

machen *v. reg.* make, do *macht*; *hat gemacht*
das **Mädchen** *nn.* girl *Mädchen*
Mai *nm.* May
mal *adv. Moment mal!* Just a moment! *dreimal*: three times
malen *v. reg.* paint (pictures) *malt*; *hat gemalt*
der **Manager** *nm.*/die **Managerin** *nf.* manager
manchmal *adv.* sometimes
die **Mandel** *nf.* almond *Mandeln*
der **Mann** *nm.* man *Männer*
die **Mark** *nf.* German currency 100 Pfennig
März *nm.* March
die **Medizin** *nf.* medicine

das **Mehl** *nn.* flour
mehr *adv.* more *mehr als*: more than *nicht mehr*: no longer
mein *poss.* my
meinen *v. reg.* think, mean, have an opinion *meint*; *hat gemeint*
meistens *adv.* mostly, usually
der **Meister** *nm.*/die **Meisterin** *nf.* master, expert
das **Meisterwerk** *nn.* masterpiece *–werke*
der **Meter** *nm.* metre *Meter*
die **Methode** *nf.* method, technique *Methoden*
mich *pron. acc. see ich*
mild(e) *adj.* mild
die **Milliarde** *nf.* billion, thousand million *Milliarden*
die **Million** *nf.* million *Millionen*
minus *adv.* minus
die **Minute** *nf.* minute *Minuten*
mir *pron. dat. see ich*
mit *prep. + dat.* with
mitkommen *v. irreg. sep.* accompany, come/go with *kommt mit*; *ist mitgekommen*
der **Mittag** *nm.* midday, noon
die **Mitte** *nf.* middle, centre
mittelgroß *adj.* medium-sized
Mittwoch *nm.* Wednesday
möchten *v. modal irreg.* would like *möchte*
modern *adj.* modern
möglich *adj.* possible
der **Mohn** *nm.* poppy(-seed)
der **Mohnkuchen** *see Kuchen, Mohn*
der **Moment** *nm.* moment *Moment mal!* Just a second!
der **Monat** *nm.* months *Monate*
Montag *nm.* Monday
morgen *adv.* tomorrow *heute morgen*: this morning
der **Morgen** *nm.* morning *Morgen*
das **Motorrad** *nn.* motorbike *Motorräder*
müd(e) *adj.* tired
die **Mühe** *nf.* trouble, bother, effort, difficulty
das **Museum** *nn.* museum *Museen*
die **Musik** *nf.* music
muß *see müssen*
müssen *v. modal irreg.* have to, must *muß*

Na? Well? *Na also!* So there we/you are!
nach *prep. + dat.* to, according to
nachher *adv.* after(wards)
der **Nachmittag** nm. afternoon, p.m.
der **Nachname** *nm.* surname *Nachnamen*
nächst– *adj.* next
die **Nacht** *nf.* night *Nächte*
der **Nachtisch** *nm.* dessert, sweet course *Nachtische*
nah(e) *adj.* near *comp. näher*
die **Nähe** *nf.* proximity *in der Nähe von*: near
nähen *v. reg.* sew *näht*; *hat genäht*
der **Name** *nm.* name *Namen*
naß *adj.* wet *comp. nasser/nässer*
die **Nationalität** *nf.* nationality *Nationalitäten*
natürlich *adj./adv.* natural(ly), of course
nehmen *v. irreg.* take *nimmt*, *hat genommen*
nein no
nett *adj.* nice, pleasant
neu *adj.* new, recent
neun *num.* nine
neunzig *num.* ninety

Neuseeland *nn.* New Zealand
der **Neuseeländer** *nm.*/die **Neuseeländerin** *nf.* New Zealander
nicht *adv.* not
nichts *pron.* nothing *Nichts zu danken!* Don't mention it!
nie *adv.* never
nimmt *see nehmen*
noch *adv.* still *noch nicht*: not yet *immer noch*: still
Nordamerika *nn.* North America
der **Nordpol** *nm.* North Pole
die **Nordsee** *nf.* North Sea
normal *adj.* normal, ordinary
November *nm.* November
die **Nummer** *nf.* number *Nummern*
nun *adv.* now (also non-temporally)
nur *adv.* only
die **Nuß** *nf.* nut *Nüsse*

der **Ober** *nm.* waiter (male) *Ober*
der **Obstsalat** *nm.* fruit salad *–salate*
oder or
der **Offizier** *nm.* officer *Offiziere*
oft *adv.* often
ohne *prep.* + *acc.* without
der **Ökonom** *nm.* economist *Ökonomen*
Oktober *nm.* October
das **Oktoberfest** *nn.* Munich's 'October' beer festival *–feste*
der **Onkel** *nm.* uncle *Onkel/Onkels*
die **Oper** *nf.* opera, opera house *Opern*
das **Opernhaus** *nn.* opera house *–häuser*
die **Ordnung** *nf.* order *in Ordnung!* OK!
das **Orchester** *nn.* orchestra *Orchester*
original *adj.* original
Ostdeutschland *nn.* east Germany
Österreich *nn.* Austria
der **Österreicher** *nm.*/die **Österreicherin** *nf.* Austrian (person)
die **Ostsee** *nf.* Baltic Sea

paddeln *v. reg.* row, paddle (a boat)
das **Palais** (*antiquated*) *see Palast*
der **Palast** *nm.* palace *Paläste*
der **Park** *nm.* park *Parks*
das **Parkhaus** *nn.* (multi-storey) car park, parking lot *–häuser*
der **Parkplatz** *nm.* car park, parking lot, parking space *–plätze*
der **Paß** *nm.* passport *Pässe*
die **Paßnummer** *see Nummer, Paß*
perfekt *adj./adv.* perfect(ly)
die **Person** *nf.* person *Personen*
der **Pfannkuchen** *nm.* doughnut-like cake/pastry *–kuchen*
der **Pfau** *nm.* peacock *Pfauen*
der **Pfennig** *nm.* German currency 100 = 1 Mark
das **Pferd** *nn.* horse *Pferde*
Pik *nn.* spades (in cards)
der **Pilot** *nm.*/die **Pilotin** *nf.* pilot
das **Pils** *nn.* (variety of) beer
die **Pizza** *nf.* pizza *Pizzas*
der **Plan** *nm.* plan *Pläne*
der **Platz** *nm.* place, square *Plätze*
plus plus, and
der **Politiker** *nm.*/die **Politikerin** *nf.* politician
die **Post** *nf.* postal service, post office
die **Postkarte** *nf.* postcard *–karten*

die **Praxis** *nf.* practice, surgery *Praxen*
preiswert *adj./adv.* good value, cheap (for the quality)
der **Prinz** *nm.*/die **Prinzessin** *nf.* prince; princess
das **Problem** *nn.* problem *Probleme*
der **Professor** *nm.* professor *Professoren*
Prost! Cheers! Your health!
der **Punkt** *nm.* point, dot *Punkte*

der **Quadratkilometer** *nm.* square kilometre *–kilometer*
die **Quadriga** *nf.* quadriga: statue with four-horse chariot *Quadrigen*
die **Qual** *nf.* torment, pain *Wer die Wahl hat, hat die Qual!* Whoever has the choice, has . . .' *Qualen*
die **Quelle** *nf.* source *Quellen*

das **Rad** *nn.* wheel *Räder*
radfahren *v. irreg. sep. fährt Rad*; *ist radgefahren*
das **Radio** *nn.* radio *Radios*
der **Rappen** *nm.* Swiss currency 100 = 1 Franken
das **Rathaus** *nn.* town/city hall, municipal office *–häuser*
rechts *adv.* right, to the right, on the right-hand side
recht– *adj.* right, right-hand
der **Regen** *nm.* rain
regnen *v. reg.* rain *es regnet*; *hat geregnet*
der **Reisebegleiter** *nm.*/die **Reisebegleiterin** tour guide *Reisebegleiter*
das **Reisebüro** *nn.* travel agency/shop *–büros*
der **Reisepaß** *nm.* passport *–pässe*
der **Reisescheck** *nm.* traveller's cheque *–schecks*
reiten *v. irreg.* ride (a horse), go riding *reite*; *hat/ist geritten*
die **Renaissance** *nf.* the Renaissance
der **Rentner** *nm.*/die **Rentnerin** *nf.* retired person, pensioner
reservieren *v. reg.* reserve *reserviert*; *hat reserviert*
das **Restaurant** *nn.* restaurant *Restaurants*
richtig *adj./adv.* right, correct
die **Richtung** *nf.* direction *Richtungen*
der **Riesling** *nm.* Riesling (grape variety)
die **Rockmusik** *nf.* rock music
der **Roggen** *nm.* rye (cereal)
der **Rotwein** *nm.* red wine *–weine*
'rüber *see herüber*
der **Rückblick** *nm.* retrospective, look back *–blicke*
ruhen *v. reg.* rest (something) *ruht*; *hat geruht*
ruhig *adj./adv.* quiet, peaceful
das **Rührei** *nn.* scrambled egg *–eier*

die **S-Bahn** *nf.* metropolitan railway (S = *schnell*)
die **Sachertorte** *nf.* 'Sacher' cake *–torten*
Sachsen *nn.* Saxony
der **Saft** *nm.* juice *Säfte*
sagen *v. reg.* say, tell *sagt*; *hat gesagt*
die **Sahne** *nf.* cream
Samstag *nm.* **Sonnabend** Saturday
Schach *nn.* chess

scheinen *v. irreg.* shine *scheint; hat geschienen*
schick *adj.* chic, smart
das **Schiff** *nn.* ship, boat *Schiffe*
der **Schilling** *nm.* Austrian currency 100 Groschen
der **Schinken** *nm.* ham
schlafen *v. irreg.* sleep *schläft; hat geschlafen*
der **Schlager** *nm.* hit (record that 'makes the charts') *Schlager*
die **Schlagermusik** *see Musik, Schlager*
die **Schlagsahne** *nf.* whipped cream
schlecht *adj./adv.* bad(ly)
schlimm *adj./adv.* serious, bad, problematic
das **Schloß** *nn.* castle, palace *Schlösser*
der **Schlüssel** *nm.* key *Schlüssel*
schmecken *v. reg.* taste *Schmeckt es dir/Ihnen?* Do you like it? *schmeckt; hat geschmeckt*
der **Schnaps** *nm.* schnapps, spirits, liquor *Schnäpse*
der **Schnee** *nm.* snow
schneien *v. reg.* snow *schneit; hat geschneit*
schnell *adj./adv.* quick(ly), fast
die **Schokoladentorte** *nf.* chocolate gateau *–torten*
schon *adv.* already
schön *adj./adv.* beautiful, nice, 'very (much)'
der **Schotte** *nm.*/die **Schottin** *nf.* Scot
Schottland *nn.* Scotland
das **Schreibwarengeschäft** *nn.* stationery shop *–geschäfte*
die **Schuld** *nf.* guilt, fault, mistake
die **Schule** *nf.* school *Schulen*
der **Schüler** *nm.*/die **Schülerin** *nf.* schoolboy; schoolgirl
der **Schuß** *nm.* shot *Schüsse*
schwarz *adj.* black *comp. schwärzer*
Schwarzwälder *adj.* 'of the Black Forest'
schwarzweiß *adj.* black and white
die **Schweiz** *nf.* Switzerland
der **Schweizer** *nm.*/die **Schweizerin** *nf.* Swiss (person)
schwer *adj./adv.* heavy, difficult
schwimmen *v. irreg.* swim *schwimmt; hat/ist geschwommen*
das **Schwimmbad** *nn.* swimming pool *–bäder*
sechs *num.* six
sechzig *num.* sixty
der **See** *nm.* lake *Seen*
die **See** *nf.* sea *Seen*
sehen *v. irreg.* see *sieht; hat gesehen*
sehenswert *adj.* worth seeing
sehr *adv.* very
sei *see sein v.*
sein, sein– *poss.* his, its
sein *v. irreg.* to be *ist; ist gewesen*
seit *prep. + dat.* since
die **Seite** *nf.* side *Seiten*
die **Sekunde** *nf.* second *Sekunden*
selbstverständlich *adj./adv.* of course, it goes without saying
selten *adj./adv.* seldom, rare(ly)
September *nm.* September
Servus! 'Bye! (*used in south*)
sich *pron. refl. see er, es, sie*
sicher *adj./adv.* sure, secure
sicherlich *adv.* certainly, surely, probably
Sie *pron.* you (singular or plural, formal)
sie *pron.* she, it, they

sieben *num.* seven
siebt– *ordinal* seventh
siebzig *num.* seventy
(sich) **siezen** *v. reg.* (*refl.*) use the 'Sie' form *siezt*; *hat gesiezt*
sind *see sein v.*
singen *v. irreg.* sing *singt*; *hat gesungen*
sitzen *v. irreg.* sit *sitzt*; *hat gesessen*
sitzenbleiben *v. irreg.* not move up a class/grade, repeat the year
so *adv.* so, as *so oft wie möglich*: as often as possible
sofort *adv.* immediately
der **Sohn** *nm.* son *Söhne*
sollen *v. modal irreg.* ought, should *soll*
der **Sommer** *nm.* summer
sondern but *nicht . . . sondern*: not . . . but
Sonnabend *nm.* **Samstag** Saturday
die **Sonne** *nf.* sun *Sonnen*
sonnig *adj.* sunny
Sonntag *nm.* Sunday
sonst *adv.* otherwise, else *Was sonst?* What else?
die **Sparkasse** *nf.* savings bank *–kassen*
der **Spaß** *nm.* fun, joke *Viel Spaß!* Enjoy yourself! *Späße*
spät *adj.* late *Wie spät ist es?* What time is it?
spazierengehen *v. irreg. sep.* go for a walk *geht spazieren*; *ist spazierengegangen*
der **Spaziergang** *nm.* walk *Spaziergänge*
die **Speisekarte** *nf.* menu *–karten*
spielen *v. reg.* play *spielt*; *hat gespielt*
sprechen *v. irreg.* speak *spricht*; *hat gesprochen*
spricht *see sprechen*
der **Staat** *nm.* state, country *Staaten*
die **Stadt** *nf.* town, city *Städte*
der **Stadtbezirk** *nm.* borough, administrative district of town/city *–bezirke*
der **Stadtplan** *nm.* street map, map of town/city *-pläne*
die **Stadtrundfahrt** *nf.* sightseeing tour of town/city *–fahrten*
das **Standbild** *nn.* statue, monument *–bilder*
stark *adj./adv.* strong *comp. stärker*
die **Station** *nf.* stop, stage *Stationen*
stehen *v. irreg.* stand, suit *Der Hut steht dir gut!* The hat suits you. *steht*; *hat gestanden*
steif *adj./adv.* stiff, (too) formal
stimmen *v. reg.* to be correct *das stimmt*: that's right *Stimmt so!* Keep the change! *stimmt*; *hat gestimmt*
der **Stock** *nm.* storey, floor
die **Straße** *nf.* street, road *Straßen*
die **Straßenbahn** *nf.* tram, tramway, streetcar *Straßenbahnen*
die **Straßenmitte** *nf.* middle of the street/road
stricken *v. reg.* knit *strickt*; *hat gestrickt*
das **Stück** *nn.* piece (also *see Theater–*) *Stück(e)*
der **Student** *nm.*/die **Studentin** *nf.* student
studieren *v. reg.* study *studiert*; *hat studiert*

stumm *adj./adv.* dumb, mute
die **Stunde** *nf.* hour *Stunden*
der **Sturm** *nm.* storm, rough weather *Stürme*
stürmisch *adj.* stormy
Südafrika *nn.* South Africa
der **Südafrikaner** *nm.*/die **Südafrikanerin** *nf.* South African (person)
Südamerika *nn.* South America
Südwestdeutschland *nn.* south west Germany
die **Suppe** *nf.* soup *Suppen*
süß *adj./adv.* sweet(ly)
der **Sylvaner** *nm.* Sylvaner (grape variety)
das **Symbol** *nn.* symbol *Symbole*

die **Tafel** *nf.* table, chart *Tafeln*
der **Tag** *nm.* day Tage
die **Tagestemperatur** *see Temperatur*, *Tag*
täglich *ad./adv.* daily
die **Tankstelle** *nf.* petrol/gas station *–stellen*
tanzen *v. reg.* dance *tanzt*; *hat getanzt*
die **Tasse** *nf.* cup *Tassen*
tatsächlich *adv.* actually, in actual fact
tausend *num.* thousand
das **Taxi** *nn.* taxi *Taxis*
der **Taxifahrer** *nm.*/die **Taxifahrerin** *nf.* taxi driver
technisch *adj.* technical
der **Tee** *nm.* tea
die **Telefonnummer** *nf.* phone number *–nummern*
die **Telefonzelle** *nf.* phone/call box *–zellen*
die **Temperatur** *nf.* temperature *Temperaturen*

Tennis *nn.* tennis
der **Tennisplatz** *nm.* tennis court *–plätze*
teuer *adj./adv.* dear, expensive
der **Text** *nm.* text *Texte*
das **Theater** *nn.* theatre *Theater*
das **Theaterstück** *nn.* play *–stücke*
die **Themse** *nf.* the Thames
Thüringer *adj.* 'of Thuringia'
das **Tier** *nn.* animal *Tiere*
der **Tierarzt** *nm.*/die **Tierärztin** *nf.* vet(erinary) surgeon
der **Tiergarten** *nm.* zoo *–gärten*
der **Tisch** *nm.* table *Tische*
Tja! Well . . .
die **Tochter** *nf.* daughter *Töchter*
die **Toilette** *nf.* lavatory, toilet *Toiletten*
toll *adj./adv.* great, brilliant, fantastic
die **Tollwut** *nf.* rabies
der **Tomatensalat** *nm.* tomato salad *–salate*
das **Tor** *nn.* gate *Tore*
die **Torte** *nf.* cream cake, gateau *Torten*
der **Tourist** *nm.* tourist *Touristen*
(sich) **treffen** *v. irreg.* (*refl.*) meet, meet up *trifft*; *hat getroffen*
die **Treppe** *nf.* stairs, staircase *Treppen*
trinken *v. irreg.* drink *trinkt*; *hat getrunken*
trocken *adj.* dry
Tschüs! Tschüß! 'Bye!'
tun *see leid*
typisch *adj./adv.* typical(ly)

die **U-Bahn** *nf.* underground railway/subway *U-Bahnen* (*U* = *Untergrund*)

über *prep. + acc./dat.* above, over, via

die **Überfahrt** *nf.* crossing (by boat, ship) *–fahrten*

der **Übermut** *nm.* high spirits

der **Übersetzer** *nm.*/die **Übersetzerin** *nf.* translator

übrigens *adv.* incidentally, by the way

die **Übung** *nf.* exercise *Übungen*

die **Uhr** *nf.* clock, o'clock *Uhren*

um *prep. + acc. um zwei Uhr*: at 2 o'clock *um die Ecke*: around the corner

der **Umlaut** *nm.* umlaut (change of vowel sound indicated by two dots over letter) *Umlaute*

und and

ungewöhnlich *adj.* unusual, uncommon

ungern = *nicht gern see gern*

die **Universität** *nf.* university *Universitäten*

uns *pron. acc./dat. see wir*

unser *poss.* our

unter *prep. + acc./dat.* under

der **Untergrund** *nm.* underground

sich **unterhalten** *v. irreg. refl.* chat, discuss *unterhält sich*; *hat sich unterhalten*

die **Unterhaltungsmusik** *nf.* light music, 'easy listening'

unternehmen *v. irreg.* do, undertake *unternimmt*; *hat unternommen*

der **Unterschied** *nm.* difference *Unterschiede*

unterschreiben *v. irreg.* sign *unterschreibt*; *hat unterschrieben*

die **Unterschrift** *nf.* signature *Unterschriften*

der **Urlaub** nm. holidays, leave (from work)

die **USA** *nm. plural* the USA

Venedig *nn.* Venice

verbinden *v. irreg.* connect *verbindet*; *hat verbunden*

vergehen *v. irreg.* pass (of time) *vergeht*; *ist vergangen*

verheiratet *adj./pp.* married

der **Verkäufer** *nm.*/die **Verkäuferin** *nf.* sales assistant

verstauchen *v. reg.* sprain *verstaucht*; *hat verstaucht*

der **Vertreter** *nm.*/die **Vertreterin** *nf.* (sales) representative

viel *adj./pron.* much, a lot

vielleicht *adv.* perhaps, maybe

vier *num.* four

das **Viertel** *nn.* quarter

vierzig *num.* forty

die **Volksmusik** *nf.* folk music

vom = *von dem*

von *prep. + dat.* by, from

vor *prep. + acc./dat.* before, in front of *vor allem*: above all *vor drei Jahren*: three years ago

vorbei *adv.* past, over

vorgeschlagen *see vorschlagen*

vorgestern *adv.* the day before yesterday

vorhaben *v. irreg. sep.* intend, plan, have planned *hat vor*; *hat vorgehabt*

vorher *adv.* before(hand)

der **Vormittag** *nm.* morning, a.m.

der **Vorname** *nm.* forename, first name *Vornamen*

vornehm *adj./adv.* distinguished, 'posh'

der **Vorschlag** *nm.* suggestion, proposal *Vorschläge*

vorschlagen *v. irreg. sep.* propose, suggest *schlägt vor*: *hat vorgeschlagen*

vorziehen *v. irreg. sep.* prefer *zieht vor*; *hat vorgezogen*

der **Wagen** *nm.* car

die **Wahl** *nf.* choice, election *Wahlen*

wählen *v. reg.* choose, select *wählt*; *hat gewählt*

wahr *adj.* true *Nicht wahr?* Isn't it? (etc.)

wahrscheinlich *adv.* probably

das **Wahrzeichen** *nn.* symbol, emblem

der **Wald** *nm.* wood(s), forest *Wälder*

der **Waldmeister** *nm.* woodruff [Asperula odorata]

der **Waliser** *nm.*/die **Waliserin** *nf.* Welshman/woman

wandern *v. reg.* go rambling/hiking/for walks *wandert*; *ist gewandert*

die **Wanderung** *nf.* (long) walk, hike, ramble *Wanderungen*

wann *interrog.* when?

war *see sein v.* was

wär(e) *see sein v.* would be *Das wär's?* Is that all?

warm *adj.* warm, hot (of water) *comp. wärmer*

warum *interrog.* why?

was *interrog.* what?

was *see etwas*

was für *interrog.* what sort of?

(sich) **waschen** *v. irreg.* (*refl.*) wash *wäscht*; *hat gewaschen*

das **Wasser** *nn.* water

das **Wechselgeld** *nn.* change (from a financial transaction)

wechselhaft *adj.* changeable (of weather)

wechseln *v. reg.* change (e.g. money) *wechselt*; *hat gewechselt*

der **Weg** *nm.* way, path *Wege*

der **Wein** *nm.* wine *Weine*

weiß *adj.* white

weiß *see wissen*

Weiße, Berliner *nf.* variety of beer

der **Weißwein** *nm.* white wine *–weine*

weiter *adv.* further

welch– *adj./interrog.* which? *Auf welchen Namen?* In what name?

die **Welt** *nf.* world *Welten*

wem *dat. see wer*

wen *acc. see wer*

wenig *pron./adj.* little, few

wer *interrog.* who?

der **Westen** *nm.* the West

das **Wetter** *nn.* weather

wichtig *adj.* important

wie *interrog./adv.* how? what?/like, as *Wie heißen Sie?* What's your name? *Nicht so gut wie . . .* Not as good as . . .

wieder *adv.* again

Auf **Wiederhören!** *nn.* (*from v.*) Goodbye (used on phone)

wiederkommen *v. irreg. sep.* return, come back kommt *wieder*; *ist wiedergekommen*

Auf **Wiederschauen!** *nn.* (*from v.*) Goodbye (used more in the south)

Auf **Wiedersehen!** *nn.* (*from v.*) Goodbye

Wien *nn.* Vienna

Wiener *nm./adj.* Viennese

wieviel *interrog.* how much? *Wieviel Uhr ist es?* What time is it?

will *see wollen*
willkommen *adj.* welcome
windig *adj.* windy
der **Winter** *nm.* Winter
wir *pron.* we
wirklich *adv.* really
wissen *v. irreg.* know *weiß*; *hat gewußt*
witzig *adj.* funny, amusing
wo *interrog.* where?
die **Woche** *nf.* week *Wochen*
der **Wochentag** *nm.* weekday, day of the week *Wochentage*
wofür *interrog.* for what? what for?
woher *interrog.* where from?
das **Wohl** *nn.* health, well-being *Zum Wohl!* Cheers! Your health!
wohnen *v. reg.* live, reside *wohnt*; *hat gewohnt*
der **Wohnort** *nm.* place of residence *–orte*
wollen *v. modal irreg.* intend, want will
womit *interrog.* with what? what with?
wunderbar *adj./adv.* wonderful, marvellous
wunderschön *adj./adv.* beautiful, wonderful
wünschen *v. reg.* wish *wünscht*; *hat gewünscht*

z.B. *see zum Beispiel*
zahlen *v. reg.* pay *zahlt*; *hat gezahlt*
zehn *num.* ten
die **Zeit** *nf.* time *Zeiten*
der **Zentimeter** *nm.* centimetre *Zentimeter*
das **Zentrum** *nn.* centre *Zentren*
ziehen *v. irreg.* move, change residence *zieht*; *ist gezogen*
das **Zimmer** *nn.* room *Zimmer*
der **Zimmerschlüssel** *nm.* room key *–schlüssel*
die **Zitrone** *nf.* lemon *Zitronen*
der **Zoo** *nm.* zoo *Zoos*
zu *adv./prep. + dat.* too/to, on, at *zu früh*: too early *zu Fuß*: on foot *zu zwei Mark*: @ 2 Marks
der **Zucker** *nm.* sugar
zuerst *adv.* first, first of all
der **Zug** *nm.* train *Züge*
die **Zugfahrt** *nf.* train journey *–fahrten*
die **Zukunft** *nf.* future
der **Zukunftsplan** *see Plan, Zukunft*
zum = *zu dem*
zumachen *v. reg. sep.* close, shut *macht zu*; *hat zugemacht*
zum Beispiel for example
zur = *zu der*
zurück *adv.* back, in return
zurückgegangen *see zurückgehen*
zurückgehen *v. irreg. sep.* go back, return *geht zurück*; *ist zurückgegangen*
zurückrufen *v. irreg. sep.* call back (on phone) *ruft zurück*; *hat zurückgerufen*
zusammen *adv.* together, altogether
die **Zusammenfassung** *nf.* summary *–fassungen*
zwanzig *num.* twenty
zwei *num.* two
die **Zwiebelsuppe** *nf.* onion soup *–suppen*
der **Zwilling** *nm.* twin *Zwillinge*
zwischen *prep. + acc./dat.* between

Grammar index

The numbers below refer to **Lektionen**. Where more than one number is given, the first relates to the first explicit reference to that item, and subsequent numbers to further substantial references and/or exercises incorporating the item concerned. In practice, some items, of course, occur in many, most or even all twenty lessons, so the index is selective in order to be useful.